THE TRUE HORROR OF ISLAM AND SHARIA LAW

Sharia lessons for pupils aged six: BBC uncovers 'weekend schools' that teach pupils how to hack off thieves' hands

- Pupils asked to list the 'reprehensible' qualities of Jews
- Around 5,000 children attend a network of 40 schools
- Diagrams show children how to hack off hands and feet

Children in Britain are being taught brutal Sharia law punishments, including how to hack off a criminal's hand or foot.

So-called 'weekend schools' for Muslim pupils as young as six also teach that the penalty for gay sex is execution and that 'Zionists' are plotting to take over the world for the Jews.

One set textbook challenges youngsters to list the 'reprehensible' qualities of Jews.

Investigation: A BBC Panorama programme has found that around 40 weekend schools are teaching Sharia law to British children as young as six (file picture)

Another for six-year-olds asks them to answer what happens to someone who dies who is not a believer in Islam. The answer being looked for is 'hellfire'.

A BBC Panorama investigation, to be screened tonight, identified a network of more than 40 weekend schools teaching around 5,000 children, from age six to 18.

The schools – which offer the hardline Saudi National Curriculum – are run under the umbrella of 'Saudi Students Clubs and Schools in the UK and Ireland'.

They are not state-funded, and do not use Government buildings. They are able to exploit a loophole which means weekend schools are not inspected by Ofsted.

Last night, experts at the Policy Exchange think-tank warned that similar extremists could seek to exploit the Government's policy of giving greater freedoms from state control to free schools and academies.

Clear message: Education Secretary Michael Gove has said he would not tolerate anti-Semitism and homophobia in English schools

They call for the establishment of a due diligence unit to check whether those applying to open the schools have an extremist background.

Current checks are largely limited to fraud, criminal convictions and funding.

Education Secretary Michael Gove, who is believed to be supportive of the idea, said he would not tolerate anti-Semitism and homophobia in English schools.

The Panorama investigation identified a book for 15-year-olds being used in the classes which teaches about Sharia law and its punishments.

It says: 'For thieves their hands will be cut off for a first offence, and their foot for a subsequent offence.'

There are diagrams showing children where cuts must be made. One passage says: 'The specified punishment of the thief is cutting off his right hand at the wrist. Then it is cauterised to prevent him from bleeding to death.'

DESTROY THE QURAN OR BE DESTROYED BY IT

(READ THE BOOK MAJOR PUBLISHERS WILL NEVER PUBLISH AND MEDIA WILL NEVER DISCUSS. WORRY DON'T BE HAPPY)

JIHAD IS TREASON

By Denying The Existence of Evil You Become An Accomplice To Evil. You Give Evil Legitimacy and Respectability. The Blood of The Next 9/11 Will Be On The Hands of Congress.

"Hold to the Truth. Speak Without Fear" (Glenn Beck)
"The time will come when anyone who kills you will think that by doing this he is serving God." (John 16:2)

GOD IS NOT A CRIMINAL
GOD IS NOT A MALE CHAUVINIST PIG. ONLY A GOD OF MORAL PERFECTION™ IS GOD

IF GOD KILLED OR ORDERED THE KILLING OF JUST ONE HUMAN BEING OR ANY OTHER CREATURE THROUGHOUT THE ENTIRE UNIVERSE OR MULTIPLE UNIVERSES OR COMMITTED ANY CRIMINAL ACT THEN GOD WOULD NO LONGER BE MORAL PERFECTION AND THEREFORE NO LONGER GOD. GOD WOULD NOT EXIST

WHY THE IGNORING BY AMERICAN POLITICAL AND MILITARY LEADERSHIP OF THE TEACHINGS OF THE QURAN/HADITH/ SHARIA LAW THAT LED TO THE MASSACRE OF 9/11 AND ARE BEING USED TO MURDER AND PLOT THE MURDER OF TENS OF THOUSANDS OF US SOLDIERS AND TENS OF MILLIONS OF US CITZENS IS CRIMINAL?

WHY UNITED STATES, ISRAEL AND EUROPE ARE FIGHTING THE QURAN FOR THEIR NATIONAL SURVIVAL?

WHY MOSQUES ADVOCATING SHARIA LAW/QURAN/ HADITH TEACHINGS OF JIHAD/VIOLENCE/TERROR TO MURDER US SOLDIERS/CIVILIANS ARE GUILITY OF ACTS OF SEDITION/TREASON AND MUST BE SHUT DOWN? VERSE 9.111 IS 9/11 AND FT. HOOD MASSACRES.

SHAME ON US
WHERE IS THE OUTRAGE
WHAT KIND OF SOCIETY HAVE WE DEGENERATED INTO

BANALITY OF EVIL: BANALITY OF SILENCE

Before I begin the formal part of this book, I draw your attention to a very great crime that has been committed against an American citizen exercising her First Amendment Right of Freedom of Speech.

Where is the outrage for Seattle-based cartoonist <u>Molly Norris</u>, who this April called for an "Everybody Draw Muhammad Day" on her blog? Norris, who left her job at the **Seattle Weekly** after heated threats and protests came flooding from the Muslim world, has now reportedly been urged into hiding by the FBI. Think about this. An American citizen has been forced to give up her rights as an American and go into hiding. Where is the President, Congress, media elites expressing their immediate outrage over this travesty? What kind of country have we become when a fellow citizen has to hide like a criminal for exercising her First Amendment rights. **Shame on us.**

NO DEFENSEOF MOLLY NORRIS OR OUTRAGE BY PRESIDENT
NO DEFENSE OF MOLLY NORRIS OR OUTRAGE BY CONGRESS
NO DEFENSE OF MOLLY NORRIS OR OUTRAGE BY MEDIA ELITES
NO DEFENSE OF MOLLY OR OUTRAGE BY ANYONE RUNNING FOR CONGRESS

The American constitution is being systemically destroyed. Again, where is the outrage from the media elites who should be absolutely mortified that Molly has to flee for her life?

All these media elites are protected by the First Amendment.

We hold these truths to be self-evident, that all men are created equal, that they are endowed by their Creator with certain unalienable Rights, that among these are Life, Liberty and the pursuit of Happiness. These are powerful, timeless words. They stand as a beacon for all humanity.

Then you tell me:

Where are the unalienable Rights, to life, liberty and the pursuit of happiness for Molly Norris?

Molly Norris has been sentenced to death in America by Sharia Law. Following is the sentence of death mandated by Sharia and imposed on Molly: **Mocking anything in the Qur'an or the Sunnah of the prophet Muhammad is apostasy and therefore punishable by death. Criticizing Islam, shari'ah law or the Sunnah of the prophet Muhammad is apostasy and therefore punishable by death.**

SHAME ON US: SHAME ON ALL OF US COWARDS

For acts of 'sodomy', children are told that the penalty is death and it states a difference of opinion whether this should be done by stoning, or burning with fire, or throwing over a cliff.

Panorama alleges that a building used for one of the schools, in Ealing, West London, is owned by the Saudi government .
Mr Gove told the programme: 'I have no desire or wish to intervene in the decisions that the Saudi government makes in its own education system.

'But I'm clear that we cannot have anti-Semitic material of any kind being used in English schools. Ofsted are doing some work in this area.

'They'll be reporting to me shortly about how we can ensure that part-time provision is better registered and better inspected in the future.'

The text books for 15-year-olds revive the so-called 'Protocols of the Elders of Zion', which teach that Zionists want to establish world domination for Jews.

The Saudi text books instruct pupils: 'The Jews have tried to deny them (the Protocols) but there are many proofs of their veracity and their origin among the elders of Zion.'

The text books say the 'main goal' of the 'Zionist movement' is 'for the Jews to have control over the world and its resources' which, the book allege, Zionists seek to achieve partly by 'inciting rancour and rivalry among the great powers so that they fight one another.'

Mr Gove said anyone who cites the Protocols of Zion is 'indulging in one of the oldest and foulest anti Semitic smears that, that we know of'.

16,642 Islamic Jihad Attacks Since 9/11
Quoting Prophet Muhammad From The UnHoly Books of Islam:

> Bukhari: V4852N220 "Allah's Apostle said, "I have been made victorious with terror" NEVER HAS THERE BEEN A TRUER STATEMENT.

This book will demonstrate that THERE IS NO RADICALIZATION OF MUSLIM MEN. They are following EXACTLY the divine Quranic teachings of God as transmitted by Angel Gabriel to Prophet Muhammad to exterminate, murder, torture, terrorize, rape, enslave kafirs in the name of and to the greater glory of God and the Sunna of Muhammad recorded in Hadith and Sira. In Islam, these are not crimes but divine, holy acts guaranteeing accession to Paradise. (We will prove that Muhammad never met Angel Gabriel.)

It should be noted that the figures listed below for America would be much higher if these foiled attacks had succeeded. Since 9/11, more than 170 American Muslim men have been arrested on various jihad-related charges, ranging from bomb plots to providing material support to terrorists. More than half of those arrested are U.S.-born, and roughly one third are converts to Islam. The will to kill is there. What is presently lacking is proper application of existing technology and our luck which is running out.

Jihad by Year: (www.thereligionofpeace.com)

	ATTACKS	KILLED	INJURED	ATTACKS EXCLUDING IRAQ/AFGH	KILLED EXCLUDING IRAQ/AFGH	INJURED EXCLUDING IRAQ/AFGH
2002	549	2,723	6,039	542	2,686	5,877
2003	835	3,372	6,905	627	2,554	5,358
2004	994	7,210	14,632	578	4,265	8,348
2005	1,539	7,662	12,850	914	2,648	5,709
2006	2,286	15,251	19,540	1,105	3,733	6,108
2007	2,649	20,172	16,013	1,387	4,758	7,422
2008	2,204	10,779	18,213	1,284	5,061	8,905
2009	1,932	9,157	18,591	1,263	4,714	9,223
2010	1,867	9,008	17,032	1,000	4,796	8,147

Jihad in the U.S.:

	ATTACKS	KILLED	INJURED
2002	12	16	1
2003	2	2	-
2004	3	2	10
2005	-	-	-
2006	4	6	20
2007	2	5	5
2008	2	3	0
2009	5	17	33
2010	1	5	2

COMING TO AMERICA SOONER RATHER THEN LATER

(This is Sharia Law in action. If you don't think what is happening in London, the destruction of democracy and freedom by Islam/Sharia Law will not happen here then read on – it is ALREADY happening here.

UK: "London Taliban" threatens to murder women who don't wear headscarf

Several years ago we saw Islamic supremacist thugs target women who weren't wearing hijab in Iraq. Now this Sharia intimidation has come to London. "'Wear a headscarf or we will kill you': How the 'London Taliban' is targeting women and gays in bid to impose sharia law," from the Daily Mail, April 17 2011 :Women who do not wear headscarves are being threatened with violence and even death by Islamic extremists intent on imposing sharia law on parts of Britain, it was claimed today. Other targets of the 'Talibanesque thugs', being investigated by police in the Tower Hamlets area of London, include homosexuals. Stickers have been plastered on public walls stating: 'Gay free zone. Verily Allah is severe in punishment'.Posters for H&M which feature women in bikinis and a racy poster for a Bollywood film have been defaced.

It is believed Muslim extremists are behind a spate of attacks being investigated by police, according to the Sunday Times. An Asian woman who works in a pharmacy in east London was told to dress more modestly and wear a veil or the shop would be boycotted. When she went to the media to talk about the abuse she suffered, a man later entered the pharmacy and told her: 'If you keep doing these things, we are going to kill you'. The 31-year-old, who is not a practising Muslim, said she has since been told to take holiday by the pharmacy owners and now fears she may lose her job. She said: 'Why should I wear a hijab (headscarf) or burqa? I haven't done anything wrong.'... **To understand the brutality and barbarism of Islam go to**
http://www.memritv.org/clip/en/0/0/0/0/0/0/2722.htm

IT IS NOT ISLAMAPHOBIC

Anyone who opposes Islam is branded an evil, racist, bigoted, Islamaphobic.
(For 10 translations of these Quranic verses go to
http://qb.gomen.org/QuranBrowser/)

It is NOT ISLAMAPHOBIC to have a rational fear of Jihad – there are 164 Quranic teachings of Jihad. JIHAD IS TREASON (Quran 29.6, 29.53, 22.52)

It is NOT ISLAMAPHOBIC to have a rational fear of Pre-Pubescent Child Rape (65:4)

It is NOT ISLAMAPHOBIC to have a rational fear of Rape (4.3)

It is NOT ISLAMAPHOBIC to have a rational fear of Gang Rape (24:13)

It is NOT ISLAMAPHOBIC to have a rational fear of Sex Slavery (4:24)

It is NOT ISLAMAPHOBIC to have a rational fear of Torture (22.19-22)

It is NOT ISLAMAPHOBIC to have a rational fear of Whipping (24.2)

It is NOT ISLAMAPHOBIC to have a rational fear of Amputation and Crucifixion (5:33)

It is NOT ISLAMAPHOBIC to have a rational fear of Beheading (8:12, 47:4)

It is NOT ISLAMAPHOBIC to have a rational fear of Wife Beating (4:34)

It is NOT ISLAMAPHOBIC to have a rational fear of Inferiority of Women (2.228, 4.11, 4.176)

It is NOT ISLAMAPHOBIC to have a rational fear of Women as Sex Objects (2.223)

It is NOT ISLAMAPHOBIC to have a rational fear of Murder (2:191, 9:5,)

It is NOT ISLAMAPHOBIC to have a rational fear of Killing kafirs (47.4)

It is NOT ISLAMAPHOBIC to have a rational fear of Terrorizing kafirs (8.60, 3.151)

It is NOT ISLAMAPHOBIC to have a rational fear of Immoral Paradise guaranteeing accession to Paradise for Muslim men who kill kafirs or who die in the process of trying to kill kafirs (9.111)

It is NOT ISLAMAPHOBIC to have a rational fear of Massacre (8.67)

It is NOT ISLAMAPHOBIC to have a rational fear of Genocide (8.17)

It is NOT ISLAMAPHOBIC to have a rational fear of Theft and Robbery (Entire Chapter 8 called Booty)

It is NOT ISLAMAPHOBIC to have a rational fear of All other religions must submit to Islam (2.103, 2.286, 3.19, 48.16)

It is NOT ISLAMAPHOBIC to have a rational fear of Your children are your enemies (9.23, 64.15)

It is NOT ISLAMAPHOBIC to have a rational fear of Revenge (5.45)

It is NOT ISLAMAPHOBIC to have a rational fear of Hate (5.60, 2.61)

It is NOT ISLAMAPHOBIC to have a rational fear of Slavery (2.178)

It is NOT ISLAMAPHOBIC to have a rational fear of Extortion (9:29)

It is NOT ISLAMAPHOBIC to have a rational fear of Lying (3:28, 5:51)

Mohamed Atta's Final Instructions to His Muslim Compatriots: (From The FBI)

In order to educate the reader about the truth of Islam and the very grave danger Islam poses to democratic civilization, I have placed the letter written by Mohamed Atta to his Muslim Compatriots and released by the FBI at start of book. Once you read this horrifying letter you will be prepared to read the rest of the book.

Bill O'Reilly stated on the View (which caused an uproar nationwide) that it was Muslims who attacked us on 9/11 and that by stating this fact he was not denigrating the religion of Islam. Bill O'Reilly is wrong. As this letter from Mohamed Atta will demonstrate, it was the ideology of Islam as recorded in the Quran/Hadith/Sira that motivated Mohamed Atta and his other 18 killers that attacked us on 9/11. This letter is from a well educated man who wrote an exhaustive, intelligent, well reasoned, religious edict quoting extensively from the Quran sanctifying the 9/11 massacre. – sanctifying mass murder. Atta came not from a poverty stricken background but was raised in a well off middle class family being the son of a lawyer.

As will be shown in this book - Mohamed Atta was a good, moral, moderate, holy, Muslim man following EXACTLY the teachings of Islam as recorded in the Quran – the divine, holy, unchangeable word of God and the divine example of prophet Muhammad as recorded in Hadith and Sira. He was obeying the divine orders of God to kill kafirs and strike terror into kafir societies. Atta was a true man of God. Atta was not a radical, Islamist Muslim man. He was a normal Muslim man obeying the commandments of God. Mohamed Atta understood exactly the teachings of Islam. There was no misunderstanding or misinterpretation of these teachings whatsoever. He was a good, moral Muslim man fulfilling his good, moral Muslim man duty to God. Atta was not an aberration of Islam – he is Islam.

In Myth of the Moderate Muslim, the writer explains that a radical Muslim man is a Muslim man who declares that the Quran is not the word/teachings of God but the word/teachings of Muhammad and that Muhammad was no prophet of God. Indeed such a Muslim man is so radical that by making these declarations, he has become an apostate of Islam and must be murdered as per Sharia Law and Quran. **Islam attacked us on 9/11.** The Quran was the military instruction manual and Atta and his 18 killers were the instrument fulfilling God's justice. The message from this book is very direct **DESTROY THE QURAN OR BE DESTROYED BY IT.**

FOLLOWING ARE MOHAMED ATTA'S FINAL INSTRUCTIONS

One of the few - and certainly the most remarkable and troubling - glimpses into the minds and motives of the men who wrought the slaughter of 11 September is a four-page document, written in Arabic, found in the baggage of the suspected ringleader behind the carnage, Mohamed Atta.

THE LAST NIGHT

1) Making an oath to die and renew your intentions.

Shave excess hair from the body and wear cologne.

Shower

2) Make sure you know all aspects of the plan well, and expect the response, or a reaction, from the enemy.

3) Read al-Tawba and Anfal [Surahs 8 and 9 -- traditional war chapters from the Qur'an] and reflect on their meanings and remember all of the things God has promised for the martyrs.

4) Remind your soul to listen and obey [all divine orders] and remember that you will face decisive situations that might prevent you from 100 per cent obedience, so tame your soul, purify it, convince it, make it understand, and incite it. God said: 'Obey God and His Messenger, and do not fight amongst yourselves or else you will fail. And be patient, for God is with the patient.' (Surah 8:46)

5) Pray during the night and be persistent in asking God to give you victory, control and conquest, and that He may make your task easier and not expose us.

6) Remember God frequently, and the best way to do it is to read the Holy Qur'an, according to all scholars, as far as I know. It is enough for us that it [the Qur'an] are the words of the Creator of the Earth and the plants, the One that you will meet [on the Day of Judgment].

7) Purify your soul from all unclean things. Completely forget something called 'this world' [or 'this life']. The time for play is over and the serious time is upon us. How much time have we wasted in our lives? Shouldn't we take advantage of these last hours to offer good deeds and obedience?

8) You should feel complete tranquility, because the time between you and your marriage [in heaven] is very short. Afterwards begins the happy life, where God is satisfied with you, and eternal bliss 'in the company of the prophets, the companions, the martyrs and the good people, who are all good company' (Surah 4:69). Ask God for his mercy and be optimistic, because [the Prophet], peace be upon him, used to prefer optimism in all his affairs.

9) Keep in mind that, if you fall into hardship, how will you act and how will you remain steadfast and remember that you will return to God and remember that anything that happens to you could never be avoided, and what did not happen to you could never have happened to you. This test from Almighty God is to raise your level [levels of heaven] and erase your sins. And be sure that it is a matter of moments, which will then pass, God willing, so blessed are those who win the great reward of God. Almighty God said: 'Did you think you could go to heaven before God knows whom amongst you have fought for Him and are patient?' (Surah 3:142)

10) Remember the words of Almighty God: 'You were looking to the battle before you engaged in it, and now you see it with your own two eyes.' (Surah 3:143) Remember: 'How many small groups beat big groups by the will of God.' (Surah 2:249) And His words: 'If God gives you victory, no one can beat you. And if He betrays you, who can give you victory without Him? So the faithful put their trust in God.' (Surah 3:160)

11) Remind yourself of the supplications and of your brethren and ponder their meanings. (The morning and evening supplications, and the supplications of [entering] a town, and the [unclear] supplications, and the supplications said before meeting the enemy.

12) Bless your body with some verses of the Qur'an [done by reading verses into one's hands and then rubbing the hands over whatever is to be blessed], the luggage, clothes, the knife, your personal effects, your ID, passport, and all your papers.

13) Check your weapon before you leave and long before you leave. (You must make your knife sharp and must not discomfort your animal during the slaughter).

14) Tighten your clothes [a reference to making sure his clothes will cover his private parts at all times], since this is the way of the pious generations after the Prophet. They would tighten their clothes before battle. Tighten your shoes well, wear socks so that your feet will be solidly in your shoes. All of these are worldly things [that humans can do to control their fate, although God decrees what will work and what won't] and the rest is left to God, the best One to depend on.

15) Pray the morning prayer in a group and ponder the great rewards of that prayer. Make supplications afterwards, and do not leave your apartment unless you have performed ablution before leaving, because the angels will ask for your forgiveness as long as you are in a state of ablution, and will pray for you. This saying of the Prophet was mentioned by An-Nawawi in his book, The Best of Supplications. Read the words of God: 'Did you think that We created you for no reason...' from the Al-Mu'minun Chapter (Surah 23:115).

THE SECOND STEP

When the taxi takes you to (M) [this initial could stand for matar, airport in Arabic] remember God constantly while in the car. (Remember the supplication for entering a car, for entering a town, the supplication of place and other supplications).

When you have reached (M) and have left the taxi, say a supplication of place ['Oh Lord, I ask you for the best of this place, and ask you to protect me from its evils'], and everywhere you go say that prayer and smile and be calm, for God is with the believers. And the angels protect you without you feeling anything. Say this supplication: 'God is more dear than all of His creation.' And say: 'Oh Lord, protect me from them as You wish.' And say: 'Oh Lord, take your anger out on [the enemy] and we ask You to protect us from their evils.' And say: 'Oh Lord, block their vision from in front of them, so that they may not see.' And say: 'God is all we need, He is the best to rely upon.' Remember God's words: 'Those to whom the people said, "The people have gathered to get you, so fear them," but that only increased their faith and they said, God is all we need, He is the best to rely upon.' (Surah 3:173) After you say that, you will find [unclear] as God promised this to his servants who say this supplication: (Supplications –du'a– are prayers of submission, many taken from Abu Dawud hadiths.)

1) They will come back [from battle] with God's blessings

2) They were not harmed

3) And God was satisfied with them.

God says: 'They came back with God's blessings, were not harmed, and God was satisfied with them, and God is ever-blessing.' (Surah 3:174)

All of their equipment and gates and technology will not prevent, nor harm, except by God's will. The believers do not fear such things. The only ones that fear it are the allies of Satan, who are the brothers of the devil. They have become their allies, God save us, for fear is a great form of worship, and the only one worthy of it is God. He is the only one who deserves it. He said in the verses: 'This is only the Devil scaring his allies' who are fascinated with Western civilization, and have drank the love [of the West] like they drink water [unclear] and have become afraid of their weak equipment, 'so fear them not, and fear Me, if you are believers.' (Surah 3:175)

Fear is a great worship. The allies of God do not offer such worship except for the one God, who controls everything. [unclear] with total certainty that God will weaken the schemes of non-believers. God said: 'God will weaken the schemes of the non-believers.' (Surah 8:18)

You must remember your brothers with all respect. No one should notice that you are making the supplication, 'There is no God but God,' (Surah 37:35) because if you say it 1,000 times no one will be able to tell whether you are quiet or remember God. And among its miracles is what the Prophet, peace be upon him, said: 'Whoever says, "There is no God but God," with all his heart, goes to heaven.' The prophet, peace be upon him, said: 'If you put all the worlds and universes on one side of the balance, and "No God but God" on the other, "No God but God" will weigh more heavily.' (Sunan al-Tirmidhi hadith number 731) You can repeat these words confidently, and this is just one of the strengths of these words. Whoever thinks deeply about these words will find that they have no dots [in the Arabic letter] and this is just one of its greatnesses, for words that have dots in them carry less weight than those that do not. And it is enough that these are the words of monotheism, which will make you steadfast in battle [unclear] as the prophet, peace be upon him, and his companions, and those who came after them, God willing, until the Day of Judgment.

Do not seem confused or show signs of nervous tension. Be happy, optimistic, calm because you are heading for a deed that God loves and will accept. It will be the day, God willing, you spend with the women of paradise.

[poetry] Smile in the face of hardship young man/For you are heading toward eternal paradise

You must remember to make supplications wherever you go, and anytime you do anything, and God is with his faithful servants, He will protect them and make their tasks easier, and give them success and control, and victory, and everything...

THE THIRD PHASE

When you ride the (T) [probably for tayyara, aeroplane in Arabic], before your foot steps in it, and before you enter it, you make a prayer and supplications. Remember that this is a battle for the sake of God. As the prophet, peace be upon him, said, 'An action for the sake of God is better than all of what is in this world.' (Bukhari hadith Vol. 4, Book 52, Number 53) When you step inside the (T), and sit in your seat, begin with the known supplications that we have mentioned before. Be busy with the constant remembrance of God. God said: 'Oh ye faithful, when you find the enemy be steadfast, and remember God constantly so that you may be successful.' (Surah 8:45) When the (T) moves, even slightly, toward (Q) [unknown reference], say the supplication of travel. Because you are traveling to Almighty God, so be attentive on this trip.

Then [unclear] it takes off. This is the moment that both groups come together. So remember God, as He said in His book: 'Oh Lord, pour your patience upon us and make our feet steadfast and give us victory over the infidels.' (Surah 2:250) And His words: 'And the only thing they said Lord, forgive our sins and excesses and make our feet steadfast and give us victory over the infidels.' (Surah 3:147) And His prophet said: 'Oh Lord, You have revealed the book, You move the clouds, You gave us victory over the enemy, conquer them and give us victory over them.' (Source not found.) Give us victory and make the ground shake under their feet. Pray for yourself and all your brothers that they may be victorious and hit their targets and ask God to grant you martyrdom facing the enemy, not running away from it, and for Him to grant you patience and the feeling that anything that happens to you is for Him.

Then every one of you should prepare to carry out his role in a way that would satisfy God. You should clench your teeth, as the pious early generations did.

When the confrontation begins, strike like champions who do not want to go back to this world. Shout, 'Allahu Akbar,' because this strikes fear in the hearts of the non-believers. God said: 'Strike above the neck, and strike at all of their extremities.' (Surah 8:12) Know that the gardens of paradise are waiting for you in all their beauty, and the women of paradise are waiting, calling out, 'Come hither, friend of God.' (Source not found.) They have dressed in their most beautiful clothing.

If God decrees that any of you are to slaughter, dedicate the slaughter to your fathers and [unclear], because you have obligations toward them. Do not disagree, and obey. If you slaughter, do not cause the discomfort of those you are killing, because this is one of the practices of the prophet, peace be upon him. On one condition: that you do not become distracted by [unclear] and neglect what is greater, paying attention to the enemy. That would be treason, and would do more damage than good. If this happens, the deed at hand is more important than doing that, because the deed is an obligation, and [the other thing] is optional. And an obligation has priority over an option.

Do not seek revenge for yourself. Strike for God's sake. One time Ali bin Abi Talib [a companion and close relative of the prophet Muhammad], fought with a non-believer. The non-believer spit on Ali, may God bless him. Ali [unclear] his sword, but did not strike him. When the battle was over, the companions of the prophet asked him why he had not smitten the non-believer. He said, 'After he spat at me, I was afraid I would be striking at him in revenge for myself, so I lifted my sword.' After he renewed his intentions, he went back and killed the man. This means that before you do anything, make sure your soul is prepared to do everything for God only. (This story found in the biography of Imam Ali bin Abu Talib.)

Then implement the way of the prophet in taking prisoners. Take prisoners and kill them. As Almighty God said: 'No prophet should have prisoners until he has soaked the land with blood. You want the bounties of this world [in exchange for prisoners] and God wants the other world [for you], and God is all-powerful, all-wise.' (Surah 8:67)

If everything goes well, every one of you should pat the other on the shoulder in confidence that (M) and (T) number (K). Remind your brothers that this act is for Almighty God. Do not confuse your brothers or distract them. He should give them glad tidings and make them calm, and remind them [of God] and encourage them. How beautiful it is for one to read God's words, such as: 'And those who prefer the afterlife over this world should fight for the sake of God.' (Surah 9:38?) And His words: 'Do not suppose that those who are killed for the sake of God are dead; they are alive... ' (Surah 3:169) And others. Or they should sing songs to boost their morale, as the pious first generations did in the throes of battle, to bring calm, tranquility and joy to the hearts of his brothers.

Do not forget to take a bounty, even if it is a glass of water to quench your thirst or that of your brothers, if possible. When the hour of reality approaches, the zero hour, [unclear] and wholeheartedly welcome death for the sake of God. Always be remembering God. Either end your life while praying, seconds before the target, or make your last words: 'There is no God but God, Muhammad is His messenger'. (Surah 37:35 and Surah 48:29)

Afterwards, we will all meet in the highest heaven, God willing.

If you see the enemy as strong, remember the groups [that had formed a coalition to fight the prophet Muhammad]. They were 10,000. Remember how God gave victory to his faithful servants. He said: 'When the faithful saw the groups, they said, this is what God and the prophet promised, they said the truth. It only increased their faith.' (Surah 3:173)

And may the peace of God be upon the prophet.

• The document was released by the F.B.I. and translated for The New York Times by Capital Communications Group, a Washington-based international consulting firm and by Imad Musa, a translator for the firm.

DANGER OF MUSLIM STUDENT ASSOCIATION (aka) THE MUSLIM BROTHERHOOD

The Muslim Student Association has 600 chapters and 150 associated organizations throughout The United States and Canada. The MSA joins together University students for Jihad. To understand the very grave danger of this Muslim Brotherhood front group visit the following websites. Many of the front organizations for the Muslim Brotherhood obtain government funding.

http://www.investigativeproject.org/documents/misc/31.pdf

http://www.newsrealblog.com/2010/05/11/for-it-msa-student-confesses-she-wants-a-second-holocaust/

http://bigpeace.com/teamb/2010/10/31/mapping-the-muslim-brotherhood-in-america/

What the Imams Told Students at the Muslim Student Association Conference

MSA PLEDGE OF ALLEGIENCE

Here is the word for word "pledge of allegiance" from the speech given at the Muslim Student Assoc conference key note address. This is the Muslim Brotherhood pledge of allegiance.

Allah is my lord.
Islam is my life.
The Koran is my guide.
The Sunna is my practice.
Jihad is my spirit.
Righteousness is my character.
Paradise is my goal.
I enjoin what is right.
I forbid what is wrong.
I will fight against oppression.
And I will die to establish Islam.

Read the other 9 pages of the MSA at http://www.islamreform.net/new-page-124.htm

DON'T BURN THE QURAN READ IT DECLARE READ THE QURAN, HADITH, SIRA, SHARIA LAW DAY

On May 10 1933 Nazis gathered 25,000 un German books and set them on fire. 40,000 attended the burning. While the Quran is a book of pure evil far more evil then Mein Kampf, it is a crime to ban, burn, tear up, or flush down the toilet any book. Burning books is an act of barbarism. Intellectually you destroy, burn, tear up and flush down the toilet bowl of history - the Quran. In this struggle at no time can violence be directed at Muslims. At no time should headscarfs/burqas (except for security concerns) be banned.

To truly understand the beauty of Islam, the wondrous words and teachings of God as recorded in the Quran, the miraculous life of prophet Muhammad – the most merciful man of mercy who ever lived SIT DOWN AND READ FROM THESE HOLIER THEN THOU BOOKS. The Quran will bring tears of joy to your eyes so great is the word of God. The love story between the prophet and a 6 year old child (Baby Aisha) will bring ecstasy to your heart. Indeed you don't even have to bother reading these books as I have quoted thousands of these teachings in this book.

As you will quickly discover, it cannot be stated strongly enough that the Quran is no holy book. 64% of the Quran is nothing more then hatred, extermination, slaughter, torture, terror, violence, rape, sex slaves, slavery, subjugation of kafirs (non-believers). As will be detailed in this book: All Muslims must believe that every word of the Quran is the word of God: written by God himself. To challenge just one word of this very evil book is to commit a capital offense against Islam for which you must be murdered. The Quran is nothing more then words on paper bound into a book. As will be clearly shown throughout this work, these words are the teachings of prophet Muhammad. God NEVER spoke or wrote one word of the Quran. Every word is from the mouth of Muhammad who was no prophet. It is Muslim men following the divine example of the prophet who turn these murderous teachings into evil.

9/11 WAS GREATEST VICTORY IN HISTORY FOR ISLAM THEY FLEW. THEY CRASHED. THEY CONQUERED.

General Osma bin Laden (the greatest general in history), Mohammed Atta and the other 18 Muslim men have succeeded beyond their wildest dreams. By their successful attack on 9/11, (costing $200,000.00 US) they have started the Islamization and conquest of the United States and Europe. If this Islamization is not halted then sooner rather then later, a mosque will be built at the World Trade Center to these 19 martyrs of Islam. Millions of Muslims will travel yearly to New York to celebrate their great victory. History will record that the beginning of the end of Western Civilization was 9/11, 2001. Make no mistake about this. Indeed why wait. Let us build the greatest mosque the world has ever seen, with minarets soaring into the stratosphere taller then the demolished Trade Center to show our good will and beg forgiveness for all the wrongs we have ever committed against the AntiGod Allah.

GUTS AND COURAGE TIME

IT WILL TAKE REAL GUTS AND COURAGE TO READ THIS BOOK

You are living in Germany when Hitler seizes power. Your next door neighbour Jewish family is banging on your door begging you to grant him and his family refuge hiding them in the attic or cellar from the SS who are coming to arrest them. Would you let them in knowing that if they are discovered your family will be arrested and sent to a concentration camp?

This is a true test of courage. What would you do? This is the kind of courage you will need to stand against Islam. Most people would not admit the family. They would cower in their living rooms hoping that the family just goes away. Germans failed the greatest moral dilemma of their lives. 99.9% of our political. media, intellectual elites would refuse sanctuary so great is their moral cowardice. Some of them would even call the SS to come and pick the family up. By doing so, by refusing to fight Islam these elites are granting Islam respectability and legitimacy. They are doing a reverse Ronald Reagan who condemned the evil Soviet Union refusing to grant it respectability.

Tonight Molly Norris is banging on the doors of Congress begging for her Constitutional Rights to life, liberty and happiness. Tonight Jews are banging on the doors of European legislatures begging for protection from Muslim attacks and are being refused. They are being forced out of Europe in the 3rd mass exile. Gays are banging the corridors of justice for legal protection from Muslim attacks and are being refused. Muslim women are being beaten. Muslim girls are being honor killed. They are all banging on the doors of European parliaments and are being refused. Kafir women are being raped throughout Europe in Rape Jihad and are being refused protection. Christians throughout the Middle East/Pakistan/Indonesia are being persecuted/murdered enmass – they are banging on the doors of Congress crying for help and are being denied any assistance.

The ghosts of the thousands of Christians/Jews killed during the 60 massacres Muhammad committed in Saudi Arabia are banging on the doors of Western Civilization demanding justice. The 120,000,000 blacks and all the other 150,000,000 kafirs murdered by Islam are marching towards the Congress crying for justice. Rayhana bint Amr, (Massacre of Banu Qurayza), Saiya (Massacre of Khaybar) Juwairiya (Massacre of Bani Mustaliq) whose husbands, families were murdered and then personally raped by Muhammad to celebrate these victorious massacre victories and the millions of other kafir women raped throughout history by Muslim men in the name of the AntiGod Allah are crying out for justice. But all these tormented souls will never obtain justice. Their memory has been erased from history.

Today, we are faced with a stark choice between good and evil. By denying the existence of evil that is Islam, you become an accomplice to evil, coated by the evil of Sharia Law, Quran, Hadith, Sira and prophet Muhammad. And in many respects just as evil if not more evil then those who follow Allah and his messenger. The reason is very simple. By standing against evil you become a shining beacon of guts and courage and others stand with you and others and others until you number millions and millions of good people – an unstoppable force that cannot be cowed nor defeated. Quoting a famous saying "Evil Triumphs When Good People Do Nothing." This is true courage. This is the kind of courage it will take to read this book. You will never read a book like it. This book is a take no prisoners, no political correctness examination of a very great, evil, political, military ideology – Islam **masquerading as a re**ligion.

The front and back covers are grotesque but reality. The picture of the Iranian woman hanging from a construction boom on the front cover is dedicated to the millions of women murdered, raped, enslaved by Islam. (Read further for a summary of young women murdered by Islam in Iran.) It is dedicated to Sakineh Mohammadi Ashtiani who was recently condemned to death by stoning in Iran for adultery and 99 lashes for a picture showing her full face. (Google her name for her picture and story.) Only after a massive outpouring of outrage from the West did the Iranian government halt the stoning. It is important to understand that if there was no West, no America this poor woman would have been stoned to death. To truly understand the horrible suffering by boulders smashing your head read further about the stoning of a woman in front of her baby by prophet Muhammad. Stoning is Sunna in Islam – following the divine example of Muhammad. It is not an aberration. Lashing is an order from AntiGod Allah Quranic verse 24.2. It is not an aberration. Stoning and lashing are not an Iranian or Saudi version of Islam. Stoning and lashing are Islam. (Sakineh may have been given 99 lashes. There are conflicting reports.) Note Sakineh may still be hanged and if so the picture on the front cover will be how she will be strung up. Pray for Sakineh. The 3 men hanging on the back cover are gays – the reason why as President Ahmadinejad stated there are no gays in Iran. This is Sharia Law in action. The pictures of these murdered/tortured Muslim women on pages xxv to xxx are real pictures of real women murdered/tortured by Islam. They will be your daughters, wives, mothers if you don't fight Islam.

Hanging is a very gruesome way to die. The humane method to hang someone (of course there is no humanity in hanging) is to break their neck by opening a trap door. This ensures instant death with little or no suffering. This Iranian woman is strangled to death by a rope attached around her neck. Can you imagine choking to death hanging in midair at the end of a rope – a process that would take 15 to 30 minutes? Can you imagine your daughter being dragged to the city center, her hands tied behind her back, a rope lowered over her head, and then swinging in midair strangling to death. Can you imagine your daughter being buried in a hole then stoned to death? Can you imagine your daughter being whipped 100 lashes (basically a death sentence)? Can you imagine your daughter being beheaded?

You will read why the Quran is the greatest book of evil ever written. Why Islam is a total renunciation of and a great crime and sin against God. The total moral depravity of prophet Muhammad will be exposed in all its sickening detail. The questions that will be asked - how can 1.2 billion people believe in this evil? How can 57 nations be supporters of the AntiGod Allah? How can the President and Western political, intellectual, religious, media elites support such diabolical evil? The cold, hard reality is that Osama Bin Laden and Major Hasan are true, good, holy, moral, moderate Muslims following exactly the teachings of Islam. It will be demonstrated throughout this book that the Quran is not a holy book of the divine, timeless words/teachings of God but again - an evil book containing the words/teachings of prophet Muhammad.

A BURQA TOO FAR

Western Civilization is in the death grip of the Islamic python and is being devoured alive. Our elites are busy heaping praise on Islam even as the digestive juices are dissolving freedom and democracy. In fighting Islam, we need to behead the ideology by destroying the Quran, Muhammad and Sharia Law.

This book utilizes Islam's own teachings, words, and writings directly from Islam's mouth so to speak. All the hateful, murderous teachings quoted by the thousands are directly from the Quran/ Hadith/Sira. They are Islam. It cannot be stated strongly enough - in this struggle at no time can violence be directed at Muslims. Again, at no time should headscarfs/burqas (except for security concerns) be banned.

To expose this evil, the author pits the teachings of the God of Moral Perfection against those of Allah (the AntiGod) of the Muslims. The author also details a series of laws to be passed by the Congress such as:

DEFENSE OF AMERCIA: DEMOCRACY AND FREEDOM ACT
CONSTITUTIONAL AMENDMENT TO FIRST AMENDMENT

CONSTITUTIONAL AMENDMENT: UNIVERSAL DECLARATION OF TOTAL EQUALITY OF WOMEN TO BE ADOPTED BY ALL NATIONS OR FACE EXPULSION FROM THE UN

HISTORCIAL DECLARATION OF A GOD OF MORAL PERFECTION
JIHAD IS TREASON
BAN SHARIA LAW NATIONWIDE
BAN STEALTH CENSURESHIP
BAN STEALTH JIHAD

NO TAX EXMPT STATUS FOR ISLAM
TOTAL PROTECTION FOR APOSTATES OF ISLAM

UNIVERSAL DECLARATION OF TOTAL EQUALITY OF GAYS TO BE ADOPTED BY ALL NATIONS OR FACE EXPULSION FROM THE UN

PROPOSAL FOR CONGRESS TO PASS A SPECIAL ACT HONORING THE IRANIAN WOMEN MURDERED BY THE ISLAMIC REVOLUTION AND BUILD A MEMORIAL IN THEIR MEMORY

IT'S RONALD REAGAN TIME: SHOW ISLAM NO RESPECT
YOU ARE NOT US
WHO WILL BE THE NEW REAGAN

President Roosevelt said in his 1932 inaugural address "Only Thing We Have To Fear Is Fear Itself".
WELL–IT'S TIME TO FEAR, FEAR

IF YOU ARE NOT WILLING TO FIGHT FOR YOUR FREEDOM THEN YOU DON'T DESERVE TO BE A FREE PEOPLE. FREEDOM IS NOT ONLY A RIGHT- IT IS A RESPONSIBILITY THAT MUST BE DEFENDED FOR FUTURE GENERATIONS.

DEDICATED TO THE 270,000,000 KAFIRS MURDERED BY ISLAM – THE GREATEST HOLOCAUST IN HISTORY

80,000,000 Hindus
120,000,000 Blacks
60,000,000 Christians, Jews, Zoroastrians, others
10,000,000 Buddhists. And the tens of millions of Hindu, Negro, European, Asian women raped, brutalized and enslaved by most evil ideology ever created by man. A special dedication to the victims of the Iranian Revolution. No words can describe their bravery and courage. If Islam conquers the world, extermination of kafirs, castration of black male slaves, castration of white male slaves, stoning and whipping women to death, hanging them in city centers from construction booms, chopping off hands, burning out eyes, cutting out tongues will be you and your children's future.

WHY I WROTE THE BOOK

My mother – in – law's best friend's son (25 years) who worked at the Twin Towers had a day off from work scheduled for 9/11. Late at night 9/10, he received a call from an associate who had taken ill and asked if he wouldn't mind covering the next day and in return he would trade his day off the following week. He left for work at 6:00 am on September 11 and was dead by 9:30 am. There must be dozens of stories just like this.

I'm the only non Jewish person in my Jewish family. Once Hitler came to power my wife's grandfather changed the entire lineage of the family going back and altering birth records and names from the family history. Their entire Jewish history was wiped out and replaced with a different history. When Hitler conquered Vienna many Jews fled to Prague. My wife's mother fell in love with a young, Jewish, Austrian man who went into hiding from the SS and my wife was conceived. Within months of her conception, the SS arrested her father and he was taken away and executed. 86% or 155,000 Czech Jews were murdered.

As you read farther in this book, you will read about the massacre of Banu Qurayza where prophet Muhammad sat all day long beside his 12-year-old wife Baby Aisha while they watched as 600/900 Jews heads were removed by sword after he had personally beheaded 2 of the Jewish leader's heads and to distinguish young Jewish boys from young Jewish men had the pants of 13/14 year old Jewish boys pulled down and their groin inspected for pubic hairs and those boys with the slightest growth of hair were dragged away and beheaded and their mothers/sisters raped and gang raped and those not sold into slavery taken as sex slave booty. Their heads were cut off because they had said that Muhammad was not the prophet of Allah. Muslims view these deaths as necessary because denying Muhammad's prophet-hood was an offense against Islam and beheading is the accepted method of punishment, sanctioned by Allah.

This massacre will be mentioned throughout this work. You tell me the difference between the murdered Jews of Czech Republic/Europe and Banu Qurayza? You tell me how anyone can believe that this killer Muhammad is a prophet of God? You tell me why President Obama/Bloomberg and all the other political/media/intellectuals are supporting this killer? **YOU TELL ME WHAT KIND OF SOCIETY WE HAVE DEGENERATED INTO WHEN WE REJECT MOLLY NORRIS BUT ACCEPT SUCH A KILLER INTO OUR MIDST AND EMBRACE HIM. WHERE IS THE MORAL OUTRAGE**

I had 2 uncles who fought against Hitler. It was a horrid experience that scarred them both mentally and physically for life. How can we make a farce out of the great sacrifice of millions of soldiers who saved democracy and freedom by surrendering to Islam? (When I wrote my book, I predicted that sooner rather then later a mosque would be built at the World Trade Center. I never in my worst nightmare believed it would happen within months abet 2 blocks away :(http://www.911familiesforamerica.org/?p=4010). (See page xlii) The proposed building of this mosque near the sacred ground of the World Trade Center not only makes a farce out of the blood, sweat and tears of these patriots not to mention the betrayal of hundreds of thousands of brave soldiers of a new generation following in their footsteps fighting and dying in Iraq and Afghanistan but a mockery of the murder of all those brave New Yorkers on that horrendous day of 9/11. The spear of Islam has been plunged into the hearts of their loved ones. It's just a matter of time before women are hanged or stoned or whipped or beheaded in the name of Allah at the World Trade Center (or at another mosque if this one is not built.) It's just a matter of time before a true, good, holy, moral Muslim man obeying Quran 9:5, 9:111 and thousands of other evil Quranic teachings smuggles a nuclear weapon into a major US or Indian city murdering tens of millions. This will be the end of civilization.

You tell me how it is possible that President Obama/Mayor Bloomberg and the political elites of New York can approve the building of a mosque to this murderer who (as will be documented) had a pregnant woman stoned to death after giving birth, stoned adulators, married, raped, and molested a child, raped his sex slaves, raped his wives, forced sex during their menstruation, owned slaves, burnt Muslims and their families alive in their homes for missing prayer, raped a retarded woman, again, had 600 to 900 Jewish men and young Jewish boys with pubic hair beheaded in front of a 12 year old child wife. (If you are not sickened by this then you have lost your immortal soul.) Not to mention the torture, terror, murder, rape, slavery, that prophet Muhammad inflicted on Jews, Christians, and Arabs of Saudi Arabia who refused to believe in his prophethood and after his death Muslim men following in his footsteps inflicted on the world murdering 270,000,000 culminating in the Massacre of the World Trade Center 1400 years later. Again, the massacre of 9/11 was done by good, holy, divine, moderate Muslim men obeying Sharia Law and the teachings of the Quran. This book is 980 pages of sheer horror – that is Islam. Today, Muhammad would be charged for child molestation under Jessica's Law and for Crimes against Humanity.

LEARNING TO LIVE WITH AND ACCEPT A LIFE BASED ON FEAR: WE ARE ALL EXPENDABLE

In Chapter 31, Dr Peter Hammond demonstrates that as the percentage of the Muslim population increases, the violence perpetuated on kafir society increases exponentially. The more kafirs try to appease Islam and Muslims, the more violence they are subjected to. Rather then attack the source – the Quran and Islam - the poor, pathetic kafir lacking guts and courage refuses to face the truth that they are engaged in a life and death struggle with Islam and the Quran and that terms such as radical Islam/political Islam /Islamism/Islamic terrorism do not exist. If kafirs do not break this self denial of the reality of Islam then they will lose this struggle. The issues raised by the recent revivalism of Islam are of life and death to the democratic world. Islam is one of the most serious threats freedom loving people have ever faced. It is the greatest threat that Western women have faced to their hard won freedoms and legal protection of their basic rights. Again - Islam is one of the most diabolical ideologies ever created. You must understand what Islam truly represents and participate in the fight against this very evil ideology. Ignorance is not an option. **WHO REMEMBERS THE FT HOOD MASSACRE?**

WHERE IS THE OUTRAGE
MURDERED BY ISLAM
THE FIRST NEDAS

Mona Mahmoudnejad 16 year old.
Hanged for being a Baha'i

**Neda Aghasoltan. 26 year old.
Murdered for wanting freedom.**

Neda Aghasoltan was brutality murdered in Tehran in front of TV cameras during the unrest following the rigged election of Ahmadinejad. For Neda Aghasoltan's story go to:
(http://www.cnn.com/2009/WORLD/meast/06/23/iran.neda.profile/index.html)

The first Neda's were the 10 Bahá' religious women hanged in Shiraz Iran in 1983 after they refused to renounce their religion and become Muslims - Mona Mahmudnizhad, who was just 17 years old, 23 year old Roya Ishraqi, a promising veterinary student, was executed with her 50 year old mother, Izzad Janami Ishraqi, 20 year old Akhtar Sabit, a graduate nurse, 28 year old Mahshid Nirumand a physics graduate from the University of Shiraz, Shirin Dalvand 25 years old, Tahirih Siyavushi a 32 year old nurse, 20 year old Simin Sabiri, Zarrin Muqimi and the oldest 54 year old Mrs Nosrat Yalda'I.

Another Neda was Dina Parnabi an Iranian high school student, accused of smuggling forbidden literature and criticising the regime in her talks with her classmates. She was hanged on the 10th of July 1984 in a Teheran prison. The hanging was done in private and after the execution was over; her body was stripped, washed and delivered for dissection at medical school.

ATEFEH RAJABI

16 year old Atefeh Rajabi was hanged in public in the town of NekaAtefeh. Atefeh was executed for "engaging in acts incompatible with chastity." At the place of execution in the town's square, the judge personally put the rope around the girl's neck and gave the signal to the crane operator to begin her hanging. Witnesses reported that she begged for mercy and had to be dragged kicking and screaming to the execution truck. Judge Haji Rezaie said he was pleased to hang her and is quoted as saying, "Society has to be kept safe from acts against public morality." Her body was left dangling from the crane for some time so people could see what happened to teenagers who committed acts incompatible with chastity.

187 of these first Neda's were under the age of 18, with 9 girls under the age of 13. The youngest girl executed was just 10 years old. Thirty two of these women were reported to have been pregnant at the time of their execution. Many of those executed were high school and college students. Hanging is the most common method of execution for women, although some are shot. Men and women were hanged in large groups in Tehran prisons from cranes and forklift trucks. Each crane jib or forklift had a wooden or steel beam to which the noose was attached and when the preparations were complete, the prisoners were simply hoisted into the air.

Under Revolutionary law, young girls who were sentenced to death could not be executed if they were still virgins. Thus, they were "married off" to Revolutionary Guards and prison officials in temporary marriages and then raped before their execution, to prevent them going to heaven. The Mullahs believed that these women were ungodly and did not deserve paradise in the next life and that if they were deprived of their virginity, it would ensure that they went to hell. Therefore, on the night prior to execution, the condemned girl was injected with a tranquilliser and then raped by her guard(s). After the execution, the religious judge at the prison would write out a marriage certificate and send it to the victim's family along with a box of sweets.

Again, the back cover is of 3 gays murdered by Iranian justice according to the holy teachings of Islam. This book exposes the evil of Islam and the very grave danger Islamic ideology poses to all freedom loving peoples everywhere.

THE SECOND NEDAS

Taraneh Mousavi

    Many young Iranian women have been raped and brutalized in dungeons by the Islamic thugs of Ahmadinejad. Hospitals in Tehran are filled with these women suffering from gang rapings and sodimization that have left their sexual organs seriously damaged. They are all the Second Nedas.
    Unlike Neda who was shot in the street in front of TV cameras that recorded her horrifying dying moments for the entire world to witness these second Nedas have suffered out of sight, out of sound.
    Very beautiful Taraneh Mousavi, a young Iranian woman, was literally scooped off the streets without any provocation on her part and with no arrest warrant. This young woman was taken to one of the Islamists torture chambers where she was repeatedly brutalized, raped, and sodomized by Ahmadinejad's agents and with the consent of the "supreme leader" Ali Khamenei.
    Near death from repeated beating, raping and sodomizing, the fragile young woman, bleeding profusely from her rectum and womb, was transferred to a hospital in Karaj near Tehran. Eventually, an anonymous person notified Taraneh's family that she had had an "accident" and had to be taken to the hospital.
    The devastated family rushed to the hospital only to find no trace of their beloved daughter because, the gang of Islamic thugs, the foot-soldiers of Allah's "divine representative" Ali Khamenei, decided to eliminate all traces of their savagery. These beasts of Allah removed the dying woman from the hospital before the family's arrival, burned it beyond recognition and dumped her charred remains on the side of the road.

Taraneh means melody in Persian. According to her bereaved family and friends, true to her name, she used to sing with a beautiful warm voice and played the piano with skill. It is beyond imaginable cruelty to have her precious young life extinguished after an extended period of torture and rape. Worse, because of her beauty, she was singled out for the special treatment of gang-raping by her torturers. Let us hope that the Iranian revolution of 2009 will not fail. That the Islamic Republic built on the corpses of hundreds of thousands does not survive. Otherwise, the murders of the first and second Nedas will soon be forgotten just as the 2,976 murdered on 9/11 are now a distant memory.

REALITY OF ISLAM

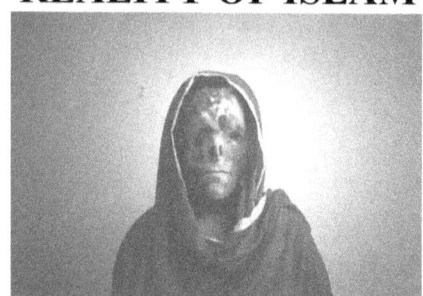

Najaf Sultana, 16, poses for a photograph at her home in Lahore, Pakistan on Wednesday, July 9, 2008. At the age of five Najaf was burned by her father while she was sleeping, apparently because he didn't want to have another girl in the family. As a result of the burning Najaf became blind and after being abandoned by both her parents she now lives with relatives. She has undergone plastic surgery around 15 times to try to recover from her scars. It's just a matter of time before these attacks are launched in Europe and the United States. For more pictures of Muslim women horribly disfigured by acid go to: thttp://pajamasmedia.com/phyllischesler/2009/11/23/under-the-islamic-veil-faces-disfigured-by-acid/

COMING TO A MOSQUE MEAR YOU
THE PUNISHMENT FOR VERY BAD WOMEN

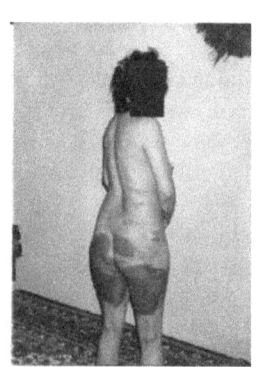

Torture of women under the Islamic Republic regime

This picture was sent to Dr. Homa Darabi from a woman in Iran. This picture was taken 20 days after she was lashed fifty times for being present at a family gathering where men other than her father and brother were present. Her crime? She is a single woman. It is forbidden for women to be present under the same roof with men other than their close relatives (father, brother and son) without proper hijab. This is sharia Law in action. This is Islam in action..

74 lashes for women who are "un-Islamically" dressed as per Sharia and Quran verse 24.2

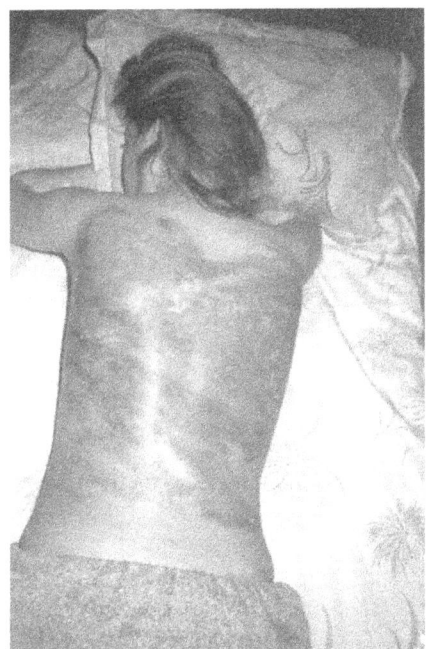

Gholam-Hossein Mohseni-Ejehei, Iran's public prosecutor announced: "Proper veiling and Islamic dress code that upholds women's chastity and modesty is a public issue. Indubitably this is an absolute legal and Sharia matter that is a religious imperative. Being un-Islamically dressed is a crime."

(For color pictures of these savage beatings go to: http://www.islamreform.net/new-page-99.htm)

Citing legal cases related to crimes against public morals and ethics in the Islamic punishments that are handed down, he specified: "Article 638 of this law clarifies that if any woman acts indecently and against this religious regulation in public places, other than the punishment of 10 days to two months detention, they will also receive 74 lashes. Also according to the punitive laws that we set in place in the year 1365 (1986) any shop keeper, importer or distributor of clothes injurious to morality, will first receive a warning by the Ministry of Islamic Guidance; if it happens a second time they will be severely reprimanded, a third time they will be threatened and finally, the forth time, their shops and business will be fined, their shops and businesses shut down for a period of anywhere between 3 to 6 months and they will receive 10 to 20 lashes."

International fury over Saudi Arabia's plans to behead woman accused of being a witch.

Being beheaded for the love of AntiGod Allah who loves us so much that we must lose our heads or be stoned, lashed, tortured, hanged.

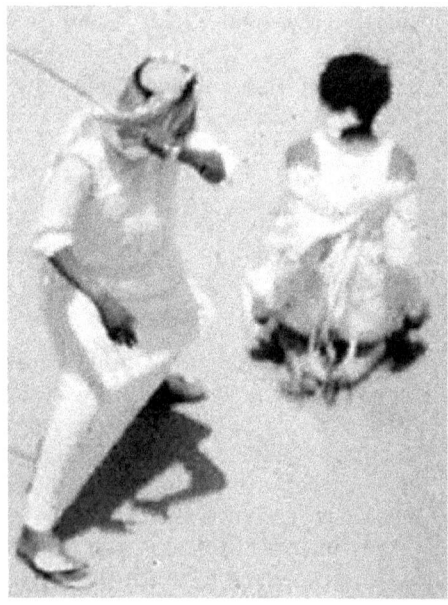

Brutal: Saudi law punishes 'witches' by beheading them.

Saudi Arabia's religious police plan to behead a woman accused of being a witch, a human rights group said yesterday. Human Rights Watch has asked the country's king to intervene over "absurd charges that have no basis in law". Fawza Falih was arrested and interrogated in the northern town of Quraiyat two years ago and was sentenced to death. The judges who convicted her relied on her forced confession and the statements of witnesses who said she had "bewitched" them.

One man claimed that he became impotent after Falih cast a spell on him.

Witchcraft is considered an offence against Islam in the conservative kingdom.

Falih retracted her confession in court, saying it was extracted under duress and that she could not understand the document because she is illiterate.

The death sentence was lifted on appeal, but reimposed in the name of "public interest" shortly afterwards.

The most frequent victims are women, who already suffer severe restrictions in their daily life. Last year, a woman was sentenced to a public lashing after being gang-raped by five men who found her in a car with a man who was not related to her - a crime in itself. The sentence was lifted after an international outcry.

But once we are all Muslims there will be no international outcry to stop these murderers.

BOOK REVIEWS
THIS IS THE BOOK ON ISLAM THAT AMERICA HAS BEEN WAITING FOR!

By: J. McCain (Washington, DC

"God of Moral Perfection" is a rip-away-the-facade, stunningly BOLD book of FACTS on the Koran. From cover to cover it holds back absolutely nothing concerning the violence, perversion and abject immorality of the Koran. "God of Moral Perfection" opens up the Koran, verse by verse like a recipe book to show how Muslims can validate murder, torture, sexual slavery and the subjugation of entire societies. The fact of the matter is best summarized by the author's words on page 30: "The Koran is the most evil, vilest book ever written in human history." and "Islam is a total and complete rejection of God..."

The author wisely withholds his name on the book itself for safety reasons no doubt. Another book that preceded this triumph by 2 years, "Bleeding for Allah. Why Islam will Conquer the Free World. What Americans Need to Know" similarly and directly addressed the horrors of Muhammad's lifestyle and the subsequent evil directives of his Koran. That author went missing in the spring of 2008 and authorities believe that it was his body strapped to a chair in a madrass in Pakistan. However, it is precisely this violence that substantiates the penetrating messages of both of these authors: that orthodox Islam IS violent, it IS wholly intolerant of freedom of thought and expression as well as any freedom to choose...whether it is your religion, political inclination or sexual orientation.

"God of Moral Perfection" shows clearly in Chapter 32 how Muslim demographics work globally. At very low percentages, they remain dormant within their greater accepting societies like the United States and Canada. But then as the Muslim population grows, "God Moral Perfection" shows how disproportional a control that Muslims begin to exert on the political systems. Then when their population grows large enough (not even a majority) Muslims then apply extreme violence to achieve their ultimate goal of absolute control. By then, it is too late for the "host" society. If you doubt this equation just check the names of the countries with large or near-majority Muslim populations: Ethiopia, Bosnia, Lebanon, Sudan, the break-away Russian "republics". Countries that are primarily Muslim like Pakistan, Iran, Iraq and Afghanistan already permanently chained to Islam. France has only an 8% Muslim population (p 248) and has been experiencing chronic street violence.

Ironically, it is America's liberal politicians, led by our ultra-liberal President Barak Hussein Obama, who play directly into the Muslims' hands. We are like lambs being literally sent to slaughter. Yet President Obama is a brilliant man. And the facts contained in this book have been written about for at least 4 centuries and are clearly understood by Homeland Security. So what could Barak

Hussein Obama's true intentions be if the truth is ignored and the Muslim countries embraced?

Read this masterpiece of truth and take note: America is next.

NONIE DARWISH: Author Cruel and Unusual Punishment

Dear Jake,

It is a shame that your book is not in the front of every bookstore. America and the West is ignoring the threat of Islam and it is scary for those who understand the danger, like you and me..
God Bless you,
Nonie

An Analytical Documentary of the Real Islam
By Desert Fox (Alpine, TX)

"God of Moral Perfection" This analytical analysis of Islam, past/present/future! It is a chilling analysis of the Qu-ran (Koran)--and "tells it like it is!" I read the Koran over 48 years ago, and nothing in Islam has changed. Past/present/future-- the choices in Islam, are that "infidels" have three choices: (1) Convert to Islam (2) Pay tribute (3) DIE! PERIOD!

YOUR MORAL OBLIGATION AS A KAFIR

In fighting this very great evil as an editor, political commentator, politician, a free citizen living in a democratic society under a democratic constitution with a democratically elected government you have a responsibility to understand Islam. If you refuse to fight this evil, then you become part of the evil – encased in the evil and in many respects just as evil if not more evil then the followers of Allah (the AntiGod) and his messenger Muhammad. Ignorance is not an option and definitely no excuse. **Join with me and let us explore together the immoral depravity that is the Quran, fictional Allah (AntiGod) of the Muslims and Islam**. The future of democracy and freedom, Western Civilization, indeed even the species Homo sapiens is at stake. Read the Tragedy of Germany Will Be America's Tragedy, The Defence of America: Democracy and Freedom Act, Declaration of a God of Moral Perfection, Letter to President Obama, Plan of Action, and The Crimes of Muhammad etc. **Sitting on your bum is not an option.**

THE DESTRUCTION OF ISLAM WITH JUST ONE WORD

GOD OF MORAL PERFECTION™ VERSUS ALLAH (the ANTIGOD) OF THE MUSLIMS

By

The Last Prophet of God

An Unknown Kafir But Not Yet A Dhimmi of Islam

Felibri publications are distributed by Ingram Book Group
© 2011   All rights reserved. No part of this publication may be reproduced, stored in a retrieval system, or transmitted in any form or by any means, electronic, mechanical, photocopying, recording, or otherwise, without the prior written permission of the Author. godofmoralperfection@yahoo.com
"God of Moral Perfection" and "Evil In The Name of God" are trademarked by author. There can be no use without written permission of author.
ISBN 13: 9780980994872
ISBN 10:   0980994872
Printed in USA

In order for you to understand the true reality of Islam I have quoted from the main chapters of this book, the most important concepts of Islam and recorded them at the front under title: EXCERPTS. You will read some of these pages again in the main text. This repetition will give you a good introduction to the concepts of Quran, Hadith, Sira, prophet Muhammad, Sharia Law, ideology of Islam. The 9/11 tragedy will be repeated again and again to reinforce the reality that 9/11 was Quranic teaching 9:111 and Sharia Law. The Crimes of Muhammad will be repeated to truly understand the prophet's evilness. The reality that Muhammad was Allah (the AntiGod) and ALL teachings of Quran were from Muhammad and Islam is fraudulent will be repeated. The total book including the website set up to accompany this work is 980 pages.

WHERE IS THE OUTRAGE EXCERPTS

THE CRIMES OF PROPHET MUHAMMAD

Jesus Christ was a true Prophet of peace and love, goodness and mercy. Prophet Muhammad was a true prophet of extermination, murder, slaughter, rape, terror, torture, hate, slavery. These are crimes against humanity. These are crimes against God. As will be shown in the following chapters, the Quran is a unique book and cannot be compared to the Old Testament or Torah. There is no moral equivalence between Christians/Jews and Muslims. Christians/Jews worship God – Muslims worship the AntiGod Allah – a fictitious creation of Muhammad. As we will explain further, it is a central tenet of Islam that Muhammad met Angel Gabriel and received from God through Gabriel the Quranic verses. We will show that Muhammad never met Angel Gabriel, never talked to Gabriel, and never received any teachings from either Gabriel or God. Muhammad made up the Allah of the Quran (the AntiGod) and all the Quranic teachings to create a perfect **totalitarian** system. How could the word of God be challenged? Muhammad was Allah and Allah was Muhammad. Crimes committed by Christians in the name of God such as slavery were crimes against God - whereas in Islam the crimes committed by prophet Muhammad and his followers are the divine, holy acts of AntiGod Allah – the eternal laws of the AntiGod, deserving of Paradise. Again, the Quran is the teachings of Muhammad and must be compared to the teachings of Jesus.

The greatest crime against God is any act of violence: suicide bombings, extermination, and murder, war, terror, torture, brutality against humans in the name of and to the greater glory of God. The second greatest crime is any act of violence against humans including the crimes of rape and slavery. The greatest gift Homo sapiens received from God is his brain that directs the hands to create. The human body is a miracle – a holy vessel from God. To take this supreme creation, and with the brain directing the hands build vests filled with bombs and strap them to the body and then blow up this miracle or take a weapon and kill in the name of and to the greater glory of God is such an abomination against God as to be unprintable. No words can describe such hideous evil.

Throughout history, God has never committed a criminal act. Not one. We hold the following truth to be self evident – ONLY A GOD OF MORAL PERFECTION IS GOD. As we will demonstrate in Chapter 1, if God committed just one criminal act, killed or ordered the killing of just one human being or any other creature in the entire universe then God would no longer be Moral Perfection and therefore no longer God. If Jesus had committed any of these crimes listed below He would no longer be the Son of God. Just as Adolf Hitler and Comrade Stalin were not prophets of God so to Muhammad was no prophet of God.

There are many men who have lived horrid lives. They have raped, murdered, and burned cities to the ground. Horrible acts. Then one day, they come into the light of God and totally change. Begging forgiveness, they spend the rest of their lives atoning for their great crimes as holy men of God. In the case of Muhammad, we have a criminal who created the AntiGod Allah to sanction his criminality: A child molester. Wife abuser. Rapist. Murderer. Torturer. Terrorist just a small sample of the criminality of Muhammad listed below. If God picked such a prophet to represent him anywhere in the universe and gave divine sanction and support/encouragement to His prophet's criminal acts then God would no longer be Moral Perfection and therefore no longer God but just an accomplice to his evil prophet. God would be equally guilty in all the criminal acts perpetrated by Muhammad. God would be just a wanton criminal.

In order to have received Quranic verses transmitted by Angel Gabriel from God then every word of the Quran must be Moral Perfection. As we shall see, given that the Quran is filled with thousands of immoral words/teachings then Muhammad never met Gabriel. Not one word was ever spoken to Muhammad by Gabriel.

Muhammad was a hands on Fuhrer Prophet. He not only ordered mass murder, torture, raping of sex slaves but he personally beheaded his enemies, raped their women, plundered their property, and sold the women - he and his men did not want as sex slaves and their children into slavery to raise funds to finance his jihadi armies. The prophet owned 40 slaves.

Following is a listing of prophet Muhammad's crimes against God – crimes against humanity, none of which Jesus ever committed or allowed his disciples to commit. Again, if Jesus had committed just one of these criminal acts He would no longer be the Son of God. Christians are sanctified by receiving the blood of Christ at Holy Communion. Muslims are sanctified by the blood of murdered kafirs.

A child is the very essence of Moral Perfection. To take a child and sexually molest the child is evil. To molest a child while proclaiming to be a prophet is a despicable evil act. To involve a child in a massacre is a depraved horrid act of pure diabolical evil.

Molested his wife - six year old Baby Aisha. One of Baby Aisha's wifely duties was to clean semen stains from the prophet's clothes. The prophet would take a bath with Baby Aisha and thigh with Baby Aisha taking his penis and rubbing it up and down her thighs. Being a man of mercy he did not penetrate Baby Aisha until she was nine.

Raped Baby Aisha when she was nine. Advocated sex with baby girls. Raped a retarded woman. Murdered a woman. Had sex with his dead aunt.

Captured women and raped them. Kept women as sex slaves. Muhammad had sex with 61 women: many he raped. There is no consensual sex between a child girl and a man. There is no consensual sex between a master and his sex slave. There is no consensual sex between a woman conquered in war and her husband conqueror. All such sexual acts are rape. RAPE IS RAPE.

Had eleven wives at one time. Sexually abused his wives. Raped his wives. Forced sex during their menstruation including Baby Aisha. Mentally abused his wives. Can you imagine taking a child (or any aged woman) and molesting with your hand/fist her menstruating vagina?

Beheaded his enemies. 600/900 Jewish men at one massacre. Had Jewish boys as young as 13 years old beheaded after pulling down their pants and inspecting groin for pubic hair.

Ordered the murder, torture, terrorization of Christians and Jews if they did not convert to Islam. Forced Christians and Jews from Saudi Arabia (the mass exile).

Assassinated people for insulting him or Islam. Established totalitarian rule. Had followers and their families burnt alive in their homes for missing prayer. Ordered the extermination, torture and terrorization of kafirs. Instigated 60 massacres and personally participated in 27 of them.

Owned and sold slaves. Enslaved women and children.
No befriending Christians and Jews.
Called his black slaves pug noses and compared them to Satan.
Treated his black slaves as beasts of burden.

Subjugated and oppressed Muslim women. Required them to cover their faces.
Married his daughter – in – law.
Approved prostitution.
Encouraged the rape of women in front of their husbands.
Recommended wife beating. Hit his own wife – Baby Aisha.

Murdered prisoners of war. Committed acts of terror.
Advocated suicide attacks.
Executed apostates and homosexuals.

Beat children who didn't pray. Abolished adoption.
Honor killings of Muslim women and children.
Beat alcoholics. Lied.
Stoned adulators to death. Stoned a woman to death after she had given birth.

Ordered thief's hands/feet chopped off.
Tortured a man out of greed.
Looted and plundered.
Preached hate for people of other religions.

Extorted money from other religions.
Forced conversions to Islam
Allowed his companions to execute, behead, rape and enslave.

ISLAM IS FRAUDULENT

ISLAM IS A TOTAL RENUNCIATION OF GOD. THE GREATEST CRIME AND SIN EVER COMMITTED BY MAN AGAINST GOD

PROPHET MUHAMMAD WAS ALLAH

THE ALLAH (OF THE QURAN) NEVER EXISTED EXCEPT IN THE MIND OF MUHAMMAD

As already stated - Allah (of the Quran) was the fictional creation of Muhammad who slaughtered, murdered, tortured, terrorized, raped, and enslaved kafirs (non-Muslims). Again, at the Massacre of Banu Quraiza, (Chapter 5) prophet Muhammad personally assisted in the beheading of 600 to 900 Jewish men and in order to distinguish young Jewish boys from young Jewish men ordered their pants pulled down and groin area inspected for pubic hairs by his SS known as – the Companions. Those boys with the slightest growth of hair were dragged away naked and beheaded. The Jewish women were raped and those not made sex slaves sold along with their children into slavery.

THE TEACHINGS OF THE QURAN ARE THE TEACHINGS OF A PSYCHOTIC AND THAT PSYCHOTIC WAS PROPHET MUHAMMAD.

HOW CAN THE PRESIDENT CELEBRATE SUCH A CRIMINAL PROPHET WITH A WHITE HOUSE RAMADAN DINNER? WHY NOT HONOR THE BIRTHDAY OF ADOLF HITLER? (Indeed, since both Hitler and Muhammad were born on April 20th - Hitler born on April 20, 1889 and Muhammad born April 20th 570 - 1319 years apart, we should declare April 20th a national holiday and celebrate a dual birthday party. Kill two birthdays with one party.)

ISLAM IS ISLAM
THERE IS NO ISLAMISM

IT'S ALL ABOUT ISLAM STUPID - HEAR NO EVIL, SEE NO EVIL, DO NOTHING ABOUT EVIL KAFIR

Islam is not a wonderful religion of peace and love that has been hi - jacked and perverted by a few bad apples of evil Islamo - Fascists, Islamic militants, Islamic Fundamentalists, jihadists, Wahhabists, radical Islamists, political Islamists etc. There has been no hijacking. There has been no perversion. There is no moderate Islam. There is no radical Islam. There is no political Islam. There is no Islamism. Islam is Islam. These demented souls are following EXACTLY the teachings of the Quran and in the divine footsteps of the prophet Muhammad as described in the Hadith. **IT'S ALL ABOUT ISLAM STUPID KAFIR.**

We don't care what Muslims eat/drink, how they dress, how many times a day they pray. What we must care about is the ideology of Islam contained in the Quran, Hadith/Sira and Sharia Law that order Muslim men to conquer all nations for Allah (the AntiGod) thru jihad, exterminate all kafirs, destroy their constitutions and replace with the totalitarianism of Sharia Law. Praying is a religious activity. Conquering and imposition of Islam is political. Islam is a direct threat to democracy and freedom.

What you must fully understand in order to protect your family and country against this very great evil living and flourishing among us is that the Quran defines the kafir (non-believer) as a vile sub-human with zero humanity who can be murdered, raped, robbed, terrorized, and tortured. For Allah, these are holy, divine acts deserving of a Paradise filled with lustrous eyed, full breasted virgins who regenerate as virgins after each sex act with Muslim men sporting external erections. A Muslim man has the full right granted to him by God to murder kafir men, take their wives and child girls as sex slaves or sell them into slavery to be bred like cattle, seize the kafir's property and keep 80% of the proceeds from the looted property and sale of kafir slaves sharing 20% with God. All these Quranic teachings of extermination, murder, rape, slavery, looting, terror, sex with little girls, the non-humanity of kafirs, sexual Paradise for Muslim killers etc are the divine, timeless word of God. **THEY ARE ISLAM. IT'S ALL ABOUT THE QURAN STUPID KAFIR.**

MOST EVIL, DIABOTICAL TEACHING IN HISTORY

Osama Bin Laden, Major Hasan, Khalid Shaikh Mohammed, Umar Farouk Abdlmutallab, Faisal Shazad, Mohamed Osman Mohamud Are Good, Moral, Holy, Moderate Muslims

9/11/Ft. Hood Massacre, Attempted Christmas Tree Celebration Portland Oregon bombing, Last Years Attempted Detroit Airliner Christmas Day Massacre, Failed Times Square Car Bombing Massacre, Mumbai Massacre, And All Other Acts Of Terror/Murder By Muslim Men Are Quran Teaching 9.111

Quran 9:111 "Lo! Allah hath bought from the believers their lives and their wealth because the Garden will be theirs: they shall fight in the way of Allah and shall slay and be slain. It is a promise which is binding on Him in the Torah and the Gospel and the Qur'an. Who fulfilleth His covenant better than Allah? Rejoice then in your bargain that ye have made, for that is the supreme triumph."

9/11 and the Ft. Hood massacre are Quran Teaching 9:111. The murder of 2,976 human beings on 9/11 masterminded by Osama bin Laden, Khalid Shaikh Mohammed and Mohamed Atta, 13 soldiers by Major Hasan at Ft. Hood and attempted blowing up of US airliner over Detroit that would have murdered 250 on Christmas Day by Umar Farouk, the attempted blowing up by Mohamed Osman Mohamud of the Potland Oregon Christmas tree celebration that would have spread death and carnage are not crimes in Islam but holy, divine, religious acts guaranteeing accession to a Paradise filled with lustrous eyed, full breasted virgins. Again, kafirs are sub-humans to Muslims possessing absolutely no humanity. The killing of 2,976 meant no more to Muslims then stepping on 2,976 ants. The 13 murdered at Ft. Hood meant no more to Major Hasan then killing 13 flies. The attempted mass murder of 250 would have been no more then killing 250 cockroaches. The attempted Times Square car bombing that would have murdered hundreds would have meant no more then killing hundreds of grasshoppers. These massacres are like driving your car late at night in the summer on a highway passing farmers fields and thousands of insects plaster your windshield with the juices of their dead bodies. In Islam, kafirs are no more then insects.

My mother – in – law's best friend's son and the 2,975 other 9/11 victims were murdered on 9/11 so their 19 holy, Muslim killers who "fight in the way of

Allah and shall slay and be slain" (Quran 9:111) could ascend to Paradise. Indeed, the only way Muslim men can be guaranteed accession to Paradise is to slay or be slain in the service of God. Osama bin Laden, Khalid Shaikh Mohammed, Mohamed Atta and Major Hasan have guaranteed their accession to Paradise. As already stated in the Introduction to Mohammed Atta's letter - they are all true, good, moral, moderate Muslims following EXACTLY the teachings of the Quran and the divine example set by prophet Muhammad as recorded in the other holy book of Islam – the Hadith. Umar Farouk by failing in his attempt to blow up the airliner, Faisal Shahzad by bungling the van explosives and the foiling of Mohamed Osman Mohamud by the FBI have not guaranteed their accession to Paradise. God only rewards Muslim murderers who succeed in murdering kafirs or are killed in the attempt. God does not reward failure.

Umar Farouk is not a radical Muslim who travelled to Yemen and was radicalized. He is a good, holy Muslim who travelled to Yemen to be trained in demolition so he could blow up an airliner in accordance with Quran verse 9.5 and ascend to Paradise. For a cost of US 7,000, Faisal Shahzad nearly succeeded in murdering hundreds of New Yorkers enjoying a beautiful night out in Times Square. The carnage that would have covered the streets in blood and blown off body parts was a well planned act including having Shahzad obtain US citizenship. The politically correct dribble being put out by the media and political elites that Shahzad had emigrated to the US from Pakistan, failed to realize the American dream, lost his home to bank foreclosure and therefore became a radicalized jihadist or like Mayor Bloomberg initially blaming the attack on the health care debate i.e. tea partiers is morally reprehensible.

Shahzad was in Times Square to DESTROY the American dream. Like Farouk, Bin Laden, Hasan, Atta, he is a good, holy, moral, Muslim man obeying exactly Quranic teachings and following the divine example of prophet Muhammad striking fear and terror into kafirs.

Mohamed Osman Mohamud 19, a US citzen didn't want anyone to escape his planned carnage. Quoting from the Portland News "During this meeting, Mohamud explained how he had been thinking of committing some form of violent jihad since the age of 15," the affidavit says. "Mohamud then told (the FBI operatives) that he had identified a potential target for a bomb: the Christmas tree-lighting ceremony in Portland's Pioneer Courthouse Square on Nov. 26, 2010." The FBI operatives cautioned Mohamud several times about the seriousness of his plan, noting that there would be many people, including children, at the event, and that Mohamud could abandon his plans at any time with no shame.

"You know there's going to be a lot of children there?" an FBI operative asked Mohamud. "You know there are gonna be a lot of children there?"

Mohamud allegedly responded he was looking for a "huge mass that will ... be attacked in their own element with their families celebrating the holidays."

On the drive back to Corvalis, FBI operatives quizzed Mohamud about whether he was capable of looking at the bodies of those who would be killed in his planned Portland attack.

"I want whoever is attending that event to leave, to leave either dead or injured," Mohamud reportedly told the FBI operatives, the affidavit says. END QUOTE

Failure to recognize these killers for the monsters they are and Islam for the barbaric ideology it represents will lead to our destruction. These media and political elites by supporting Islam will be accomplices to mass murder. By giving aid and comfort to Islam - they will be covered in the blood of more Twin Towers.

Again, Farouk, Hasan, Atta, Shahzad, Mohamed Osman and all the other Muslim murderers are not murderers but holy men of Allah (the AntiGod) fulfilling the will of the AntiGod. Forget Yemen, Pakistan. All Mosques in the United States are teaching the Quran. Imams are teaching verses 9.5, 9:111 and. the other 4,000 immoral, teachings calling for the extermination of kafirs and conquering the world for Allah. They are teaching Islam. Think about this.

MUSLIM MEN ARE GUARANTEED ACCESSION TO PARADISE FOR MURDERING KAFIRS.

MURDERING HUMAN BEINGS.

How can any normal, rational, moral person believe in such evil?

AND WHAT A PARADISE

The Islamic paradise is filled with full-breasted, lustrous-eyed virgins who regenerate as virgins after each sex act. Muslim men, who gain access into Allah's paradise, can sexually enjoy these virgins for all eternity. About the sensual attractions of Islamic paradise, aka Allah's whorehouse, says the Quran:

Quran: (44:51-55): "As for the righteous (Muslims)...We (Allah) shall wed them to beautiful virgins with lustrous eyes"

Quran: (78:31-33) The righteous (Muslims) they shall triumph... Theirs shall be voluptuous women"

Muslim men are promised 72 young virgins for perpetual enjoyment. For the sake of propriety, I will not include the quotes, but this all is right there in the Quran, in verses 37:40-48, 44:51-55, 52:17-20, 55:56-58, 70-77, 56:7-40, and 78:31. Prophet Muhammad and Islamic martyrs, such as the suicide bombers, who occupy the high rung in Islam's paradise, may be rewarded with higher number of virgins. To maximize Muslim men's enjoyment of these numerous virgins, they will be endowed with superb sexual power in the heaven:

The Holy Prophet (Muhammad) said: "The believer will be given tremendous strength in Paradise for sexual intercourse." It was questioned: "O prophet of Allah! can he do that?" He said: "He will be given the strength of one hundred persons.'" (Mishkat al-Masabih 4:42:24; Sunan al-Tirmidhi 2536).

When asked, "Do we have sex in Paradise?" Ibn Kathir, the renowned Islamic scholar explained: 'Yes, by him who holds my soul in his hand, and it will be done... and when the sex is finished she will return pure and virgin again.' [Tafsir Ibn Kathir]

Al-Suyuti (15th century) another famous Islamic theologian and Quranic commentator adds: "Each time we sleep with a houri (heavenly virgins) we find her virgin. Besides, the penis of the Elected (Muslims in heaven) never softens. The erection is eternal; the sensation that you feel each time you make love is utterly delicious and out of this world ...Each chosen Muslim will marry seventy houris, besides the women he married on earth, and all will have appetizing vaginas."

Think About This

A Paradise filled with virgin whores who regenerate as virgins after each copulation with Muslim men

EXTERNAL SEX FOR THE 9/11 - 19 MUSLIM MARTYRS.

A REAL MAN'S, MAN'S GOD. ISN'T GOD WONDERFUL?

How can President Obama support such an evil ideology?

BELIEF IN RELIGION/GOD IS SUPPOSED TO AID MANKIND IN HIS DAILY STRUGGLE AGAINST EXTINCTION AS A SPECIES NOT TO BE USED AS THE MAIN INSTRUMENT IN HIS EXTINCTION.

MYTH OF MODERATE MUSLIMS

The greatest myth that's ever been perpetuated on kafir societies is the myth of the moderate Muslim. We are told that most Muslim men are peaceful, peace loving, people who want to raise their families in the peaceful, peace of Islam. The terrorist acts are being committed by a handful of evil Muslim men who are misinterpreting the teachings of the Quran – the Great Misunderstanders.

THE TRAGEDY OF GERMANY WILL BE AMERICA'S TRAGEDY

The tragedy of Germany was that very few people were true Nazis, but many enjoyed the return of German pride, and many more were too busy to care. Many Germans thought that the Nazis were a bunch of fools. So, the majority just sat back and let it all happen. Then, before they knew it, the Nazis owned the country and ordinary Germans had lost control, and the end of the world had come. The destruction of Germany and the death of 9 million Germans had been set in motion. Do you know how many thousands of wonderful, nice Germans were killed in the fire bombing of Dresden?

We are told again and again by 'experts' and 'talking heads' that Islam is a religion of peace, and that the vast majority of Muslims just want to live in peace. Although this unqualified assertion may be true, it is entirely irrelevant. It is meaningless fluff, meant to make us feel better, and meant to somehow diminish the specter of fanatics rampaging across the globe in the name of Islam. The fact is that the fanatics rule Islam at this moment in history. It is the fanatics who march. It is the fanatics who wage any one of 50 shooting wars worldwide. It is the fanatics who systematically slaughter Christian or tribal groups throughout Africa and are gradually taking over the entire continent in an Islamic wave. It is the fanatics who are murdering Christians in Iraq, Egypt, Pakistan, Philippines, and Buddhists in Thailand. It is the fanatics who bomb, behead, murder or honor-kill. It is the fanatics who zealously spread the stoning and hanging of rape victims and homosexuals. It is the fanatics who teach their young to kill and to become suicide bombers.

The hard quantifiable fact is that the peaceful majority, the 'silent majority', is cowed and extraneous. Communist Russia was comprised of Russians who just wanted to live in peace, yet the Russian Communists were responsible for the murder of about 20 million people. The peaceful majority were irrelevant. If there had been a nuclear war between the Soviet Union and the United States hundreds of millions of wonderful good Russians would have died. China's huge population was peaceful as well, but Chinese Communists managed to kill a staggering 70 million people.

The average Japanese individual prior to World War II was not a war mongering sadist. Yet, Japan murdered and slaughtered its way across South East

Asia in an orgy of killing that included the systematic murder of 12 million Chinese civilians, most killed by sword, shovel, and bayonet.
And who can forget Rwanda, which collapsed into butchery. Could it not be said that the majority of Rwandans were 'peace loving'?

History lessons are often incredibly simple and blunt, yet for all our powers of reason we often miss the most basic and uncomplicated of points: Peace-loving Muslims have been made irrelevant by their silence. The Banality of Silence (Read Chapter 40, page 256.) Peace-loving Muslims will become our enemy if they don't speak up, because like Germans, they will awaken one day and find that the fanatics own them, and the end of their world will have begun. Peace-loving Germans, Japanese, Chinese, Russians, Rwandans, Serbs, Afghans, Iraqis, Palestinians, Somalis, Nigerians, Algerians and many others have died because the peaceful majority did not speak up until it was too late.
As for us who watch it all unfold, we must pay attention to the only group that counts: the fanatics who threaten our way of life. The first thing the fanatics will do to the silent majority is to disarm them and then murder them.

If you told me that you believe Jesus Christ was the Son of God, and oh by the way Christ was a real man's man who conquered cities and beheaded those men who refused to convert to him, tortured and murdered his prisoners, raped and enslaved their wives and child girls, looted their property and shared 20% of the booty with his father – God, thighed with and then raped his child wife, stoned a pregnant women to death after giving birth, beheaded young Jewish boys with pubic hair and God - his father sent to his son Christ teachings that ordered and sanctified His son's rampaging then I would state without any equivocation that you are an evil person.

As already shown and will be demonstrated throughout this book, Muhammad personally beheaded, tortured, raped sex slaves, owned slaves, terrorized, and massacred entire populations on orders of God. The most merciful prophet had Muslims tortured, children beaten and families burnt alive in their homes for not fulfilling prayer duties, homosexuals and apostates murdered, alcoholics beaten, thieves hands chopped off, adulators stoned to death, and fornicators lashed. When murdering adulterous women, the merciful prophet used to have them buried in a hole covering up to the breasts, then mercifully stoned until their life extinguished.

Repeating from "Why I Wrote The Book" and "Islam is Fraudulent" – "at the Massacre of Banu Quraiza, Muhammad personally assisted in the beheading of 600 to 900 Jewish men and in order to distinguish young Jewish boys from young Jewish men ordered their pants pulled down and groin area inspected for pubic hairs by his SS known as – the Companions. Those boys with the slightest growth of hair were dragged away naked and beheaded."

Do you understand what I just wrote? A prophet of God had the heads chopped off 600 to 900 Jewish men and the pants of 13/14 year old Jewish boys pulled down to inspect their groin for pubic hairs – the slightest trace of hair and these poor boys were taken away naked and beheaded. Re-mentioning that these acts of murder were committed in front of a 12 year old child. Dear Reader – Are you not outraged? Where is the outrage? Where is humanities, humanity?

Where is Muslim's humanity? What kind of people have we become that we can no longer comprehend evil? We have lost our souls – the very essence of our being. We have evolved into living, dead people.

Quoting from Chapter 35 page 273: "How could Colin Powell give aid and comfort to an ideology whose God and prophet had the pants of Jewish boys pulled down and genital area inspected for pubic hair? Can you imagine the terror in these boys? To be beheaded at the age of 13/14. Can Powell not hear the wailing of the women and the children as the prophet of God orders the Jewish men dragged out completely shackled, forced to bend down in front of a trench Muhammad had assisted in constructing to control the blood flow as the beheaded heads fell into the trenches by the hundreds: a stagnant river of blood flowing nowhere. Does Powell not picture the prophet's sword being raised - the bright Arabian sun flashing off the sharp blade and then the prophet smashing downward with all his might – the skin and tissues binding the Jewish head to the Jewish body violently severed spurting blood in all directions covering the prophet's face and clothing. The head of the still living Jew would slump over not yet fully chopped off requiring the prophet covered in blood to bring down his bloody sword a second time smashing through the remaining skin and tissue and the head finally falling to the ground then stacked in a pile like bloody cordwood with eyes.

What a fearsome sight Muhammad was that day.

What of these poor 13/14 year old Jewish boys dragged away naked and beheaded.

Employing your minds eye, go back to the market place all those many years ago; having been found to possess pubic hair and therefore knowing that beheading will be their fate, the Jewish boys will be frantically begging for mercy. It will take two Muslim men to control this frightened young child man and drag his naked bum across the hot desert ground. The poor Jew will be yelling and screaming frantically, his arms moving wildly in all directions. Upon arrival at the killing station, another Muslim man will grab the boy's head as he tries to avoid the downward thrust of the sword. Stretched out like a human airplane, with the eyes and bloody severed heads of his father, older brothers, uncles, friend's fathers, older brothers, uncles, staring up into the wild eyes of this helpless man child, the sword will make a clean thrust right thru the skin and neck bones severing the head in one great flourish. Blood will spurt all over these holy Muslims sanctifying their heroic deeds. Blood will pour from the empty cavity. The head will be tossed into the street joining the head pile. Laughter will ensue as these holy of holies congratulate each other on a job well done.

Is there no humanity for these poor, murdered, murdered?

What of Hitler who's SS had Jews (young and old, men, women and children, healthy and infirm) stand naked in front of mass graves as in Baby Yar, Ukraine and then shot in the head, so they would fall forward into the ditches. Blood would spurt from the blown off head onto the SS executioners. For this massacre go to; http://www.deathcamps.org/occupation/byalbum/list44.html

At the massacre of Banu Qurayzah, Muhammad obeyed Allah's teaching Quran 8:6 to the letter:

"It is not fitting for an Apostle that he should have prisoners of war until He thoroughly subdued the land…." (Allah insisting Prophet to kill all the prisoners, and should not keep any surrendered prisoners alive until He (Prophet) occupied entire Arabia."

EXTERMINATION OF JEWS ORDERED BY MUHAMMAD

Quoting From Islam

Bukhari:V4B52N177 "Allah's Apostle said, 'The Hour will not be established until you fight with the Jews, and the stone behind which a Jew will be hiding will say. "O Muslim! There is a Jew hiding behind me, so kill him."'"

Repeating from 16,642 Islamic Attacks article **Bukhari: V4852N220 "Allah's Apostle said, 'I have been made victorious with terror"**
        If you believe that Muhammad was the prophet of God, that God wrote the Quran and the 4,000 evil teachings contained within giving divine sanction to the crimes of Muhammad, that Islam is the true religion of God then I state without equivocation that you are an evil person. I state that any person who prays with the Quran to such a God and believes in such a prophet and acts on the evil teachings recorded in this book is an evil person.
        You cannot be a good, moral human being and believe in Allah and his messenger. In order to be a good, moral, human being, a Muslim must declare that the Quran is not the word of God; Muhammad was no prophet of any God and demand that these 4,000 teachings be renounced, denounced and removed from the Quran. But in order to be a good, moderate, moral Muslim, you must believe that the Quran is the word of God and that Muhammad was His prophet. If a Muslim tries to change just one word of the Quran then he is no longer a Muslim but an apostate of Islam and will be murdered. As a good, moral, moderate Muslim, you can murder kafirs or you can be an accomplice to murder by not condemning these verses and declaring that the Quran is not the word of God. Again, a good, moral, moderate Muslim follows the divine example of Muhammad and the teachings of the Quran. If he dares to question just one word of the Quran he is no longer a Muslim but a kafir. If he declares that a kafir is a human being deserving of respect who cannot be murdered, tortured, terrorized, raped, enslaved then he is no longer a Muslim. Repeating: the reality of Islam is that Osama bin Laden and Major Hasan are good, holy, moderate, moral Muslims.
        Sharia Law is the constitution of God and can never be changed in any way. Sharia law is the basis for the religious, political and cultural life of all

Muslims. As with the Quran, a good, holy, moderate, moral Muslim must believe ALL Sharia Law. He cannot challenge any teaching of Sharia otherwise he can be killed. Following are just a few of the teachings of Sharia Law: **Mocking anything in the Qur'an or the Sunnah of the prophet Muhammad is apostasy and therefore punishable by death. Criticizing Islam, shari'ah law or the Sunnah of the prophet Muhammad is apostasy and therefore punishable by death. Any Muslim who states a preference for democracy rather than shari'ah law or questions anything in the Qur'an or Sunnah is a kafir (disbeliever), considered an apostate, and therefore sentenced to death.** The attack on the World Trade Center was done in adherence to the rules of war, jihad, found in Sharia law. You cannot be a good moral human being and believe in the legal barbarism that is Sharia Law. But again, as a good, moral, holy Muslim man you MUST believe in Sharia. (For a beginners guide to Sharia go to http://www.islamreform.net/new-page-63.htm)

Therefore you cannot be a good, moral human being and be a good, moral, Muslim. It would be like being a member of Hitler's SS and declaring that you are a good, moral person. You could not be a member of the SS, or believe in Adolf Hitler and be a good, moral person.

A radical Muslim – a radicalized Muslim is a Muslim who declares that the Quran is not the word of God, but the word/teachings of Muhammad - that Allah is not God but the imaginary creation of Muhammad - that Sharia Law is not the divine law of God and therefore Islam is totally and completely bogus – a fraud perpetrated by Muhammad. The only good, moral, Muslim is an apostate of Islam. But an apostate of Islam is no longer a Muslim. In order to be a moderate Muslim, you cannot believe in the Quranic verses calling for the murdering and torturing of kafirs. But as a good, moral Muslim you must believe every word of the Quran otherwise you are no longer a Muslim. Therefore there are no moderate Muslims. They are a cruel myth designed to deceive the kafir into believing that Islam is a true religion of peace hijacked by evil men. These Muslims presenting themselves as moderates are a fifth column preparing kafir society for the implementation of Sharia Law and eventual conquest. They are the allies of the killer jihadists. They are accomplices to murder and just as evil as those good, moral Muslim men doing the killing. They are one and the same.

Just as Nazism or Communism cannot be reformed so to Islam cannot be reformed. Muslims must abandon Islam. Just as Muhammad created monstrous teachings of evil and coated them with religious practices to give them divine legitimacy – the 4 pillars of Islam, so to Muslims who are good people must do a reverse Muhammad throwing the Quran and the AntiGod Allah into the historical garbage can joining Nazism and Communism, take the 4 pillars namely: establishment of the daily prayers; concern for and almsgiving to the needy; self-purification through fasting one month per year (Ramadan), pilgrimage to Mecca once in a lifetime (Hajj) for those who are able and adopt the Declaration and Teachings of a God of Moral Perfection (see chapter 1) - that Only a God of Moral Perfection is God. In this way, Islam will become a religion of Moral Perfection worshipping a God of Moral Perfection.

The message to Muslims must be very clear. We reject Allah and his messenger. We reject the Quran. We reject Islam. In a free and democratic society, you have the right to religious freedom to worship and follow the teachings of a God of Moral Perfection. You do not have the right to practice the AntiGod teachings of the Quran. You are not allowed to use religion as a Trojan horse to undermine democracy and freedom and replace democratic constitutions with religious totalitarianism.

Again, prove that you are a good, moral person of peace by declaring that the Quran is not the word of God, that Muhammad was no prophet of God, remove the 4,000 teachings of extermination, hate, murder, terror, torture, rape, slavery etc that are not Moral Perfection (see chapter 33 for 15 different classifications of these Quranic teachings) and abandon Islam. (Remember if only one word of the Quran is altered/changed in any way let alone 4,000 teachings then Islam ceases to exist.)

WHO IS A GOOD, MORAL, AMERICAN

A good, moral American believes in the following:

Democracy and Freedom
Constitution of the United States
Rule of Law
Equality Before The Law
Equality of Men and Women
Equality of All Races
Dignity of All Human Beings
No Right To Own Slaves
No Right To Sex Slaves
No Right to Rape Any Woman Including Their Wife
No Right to Have Sex With Children
Freedom of Speech
Freedom of Press
Freedom of Legitimate Religion
Freedom of Assembly
Equality of Believers and Non Believers in Any Faith
Right not to believe in God
The Right to Leave Any Religion
The Right Not To Be Stoned, Lashed or Beheaded For Any Reason
The Right To Sexual Freedom
Women are Not The Property of Men
Children Cannot Be Killed By Their Parents For Any Reason
Dogs are Wonderful Creatures

CAN YOU BE A GOOD MUSLIM AND BE A GOOD, LOYAL AMERICAN: THE ANSWER IS A RESOUNDING NO

Theologically - no. . . . Because his allegiance is to Allah (of the Quran)
Humanity – no ... **Because** to be a good, moral, moderate, Muslim you cannot be a good, moral human being.
Constitutionally – no ... Because all manmade constitutions are an obscenity against Allah and must be destroyed and replaced with Sharia Law.
Democratically - no ... Because democracy means equally of kafirs with Muslims. A kafir can never be the equal of a Muslim.
Morally – no ... Because he can own and rape kafir women, murder their husbands and sell her children and herself into slavery if he does not want her as his sex slave.
Legally – no ... Because kafirs can never be equal before the law.
Freedomly – no ... Because he is the slave of Allah and must obey Allah without question. There can be no freedom of thought, conscience, speech, press,
Equality – no ... Because he is superior to all other races,
Religiously - no. . . Because no other religion is accepted by his Allah except Islam (Quran, 2:256)(Koran)
Scripturally - no. . . Because his allegiance is to the five Pillars of Islam and the Quran.
Geographically - no .. Because his allegiance is to Mecca , to which he turns in prayer five times a day.
Socially - no. . . Because his allegiance to Islam forbids him to make friends with Christians or Jews .
Politically - no. . . Because he must submit to the mullahs (spiritual leaders), who teach annihilation of Israel and destruction of America , the great Satan.
Domestically - no. .. . Because he is instructed to marry four Women and Beat and scourge his wife when she disobeys him (Quran 4:34) He can rape his wive(s). His wives are his property.
Criminally – no ... Because he has a right to murder non believers, gays, apostates, chop off thieves hands, stone/lash adulators.
Intellectually - no. . Because he cannot accept the American Constitution since it is based on Biblical principles and he believes the Bible to be corrupt. Again, a good Muslim must replace the Constitution with Sharia Law. If he swears allegiance to the Constitution and is not lying then he is no longer a Muslim but an apostate of Islam and must be killed.
Philosophically - no. . . . Because Islam, Muhammad, and the Quran does not allow freedom of religion and expression. Democracy and Islam cannot co-exist. Every Muslim government is either dictatorial or autocratic.
Spiritually - no. . . Because when we declare 'one nation under God,' The Christian's God is loving and kind, while Allah is NEVER referred to as Heavenly father, nor is he ever called love in the Quran's 99 excellent names.

MYTH OF REFORMING ISLAM: PUTTING A HAPPY FACE ON EVIL IT'S RONALD REAGAN TIME: SHOW ISLAM NO RESPECT YOU ARE NOT US

We can never prove or disprove that God exists. When it comes to questions of God/religion we must ask the question: Is it a rational, reasonable normal, moral human thought of a rational, reasonable, normal, moral human being that God exists? And the answer is yes. It is rational, reasonable and normal to believe in God's existence. However, it is not rational, reasonable, normal, and moral to believe in a criminal God. Such a God does not exist. If God exists then - Only a God of Moral Perfection is God.

Does anyone truly believe that God would have as His prophet for His one and only true religion a criminal – Muhammad and teachings of slavery, rape, murder, terror, torture, etc? Is this a rational, reasonable, normal, moral human thought that God chose such a criminal to represent Him on earth and not only represent Him but God Himself, a criminal actively involved in these evil, criminal acts perpetrated by His prophet? You cannot be a rational, reasonable, normal, moral human being and believe in Islam, Quran, Allah and the prophet Muhammad. (As already stated - a God with such a prophet would no longer be Moral Perfection and therefore no longer God.)

One of our greatest freedoms guaranteed by the constitution is freedom of religion. However this great freedom of religious belief does not allow the establishment of a state religion, human sacrifice, honor killing, murdering apostates, dhimmitude for Christians and Jews, raping and then enslaving kafir women and children, subjugation and repression of women, extermination of unbelievers, killing those who condemn Islamic teachings, destroying the constitution and with it freedom and democracy by implementing Sharia Law. The Quran is nothing more then a book of ritualistic human sacrifice to worship Allah and guarantee accession to Paradise. Beheading of unbelievers, flying planes into their buildings, bombing subways, gunning them down is ritualized murder - human sacrifice to the greater glory of God. Again, Osama, Atta and Hasan are good, moral, moderate Muslims following EXACTLY the teachings of the Quran and the divine example of Muhammad

It was Hitler who said when you lie tell a big lie - a lie so monstrous and people will believe it. The two biggest lies ever told are: Islam is a religion of peace and Muhammad - a prophet of peace. To this famous saying, we can add that when you create evil make it so monstrously, diabolically evil that people will refuse to believe that such evil can exist. Both Hitler/Muhammad created such diabolical evil that is incomprehensible to normal people. Hitler industrialized mass murder with concentration camps that Churchill and Roosevelt could never imagine Jews being gassed by the millions. This is why they never ordered the bombing of the trains and rail lines leading to these camps of horror. Muhammad cloaked his diabolical evil in religious practices that sanctified mass murder and is so incomprehensibly evil that most people dismiss it as harmless, foolishness and do not see the very grave danger Islam represents until it will be too late when they will be offered the choice of becoming Muslims and losing their souls or fighting a civil war in the streets for democracy and freedom.

You cannot reform evil. You cannot co-exist with evil. You cannot reform Islam. The test of true goodness is when you confront evil head on and expunge it from your heart and soul. This sounds easy but it is not. It means reaching into the very core of your being and pulling out all your mental insides, everything you have ever been taught from childhood, washing it out with the soap of truth. This requires expunging from the Muslim mind - the Quran with its 4,000 teachings of evil, terror, murder, torture and subrogation of women. Once these teachings are removed you no longer have Islam.

As will be stipulated further in article Plan of Action: It's Ronald Reagan time. When he refused to give the Soviets respect by declaring that the Soviet Union was an evil empire and YOU ARE NOT US, Reagan was vilified by the left but he destroyed the Soviet Union. He realized that you cannot make an accommodation with evil. Evil accepts only total subjugation and enslavement. If you try to co-exist with evil – sooner rather then later evil will grow and over power good. We need to follow Reagan's example and refuse to show Islam RESPECT. We must declare to Muslims that YOU ARE NOT US. That Islam is not Christianity/Judaism. Again, there is no moral equivalence. We must demand that Muslims declare that the Quran is not the word of God, that Allah is not God and Muhammad is no prophet of any God. As detailed in Chapter 33, we need to make 17 demands on Islam and discussed in chapter 45, the Congress needs to legislate the Defense of America: Democracy and Freedom Act, the Declaration of A God of Moral Perfection (Chapter 1), Constitutional Amendment to the First Amendment, Constitutional Amendment: Equality of Women, declare Jihad is treason and BAN SHARIA LAW.

Wafa Sultan (a Syrian apostate) (Google her name) stated that when she was a young girl going to school in Syria (hardly a fundamentalist country); she was taught the Massacre of Banu Qurayza. The teacher would teach with pride the beheading of 600/900 Jewish men, the enslaving and raping of the women, pillaging the Jew's property, pulling down of the pants of young frightened Jewish boys to check their genital area for pubic hair – the slightest trace of which they were taken away and beheaded and Muhammad's enslaving of one of the Jewish women as his sex slave. This Massacre was taught not out of hate or a radical presentation of Islam but as normal teachings because they are normal in Islam. There is nothing morally wrong. The Jews of Banu Qurayza were kafirs whose killing Allah has ordained as a holy divine act. No more important than stepping on a bunch of ants.

President Obama knows this Massacre very well. He studied it at Muslim schools in Indonesia. The President could make a similar Reaganesic act of courage and bravery by giving an address stating that his father and step father were Muslims, that he - Obama studied the Quran and when he came of age rejected Islam and embraced Christianity.

Obama is no Reagan. He lacks the courage, moral fortitude and foundation that made Ronald Reagan, Ronald Reagan. Unfortunately, Obama will be the Neville Chamberlain of his time. The great appeaser. Instead of demanding Muslims leave Islam, he will speak instead of the fantasyland of peace and love and brotherhood of Islam, Christianity, and Judaism, that Islam is a true religion of peace and love that has been hijacked by Islamists, jihadists who are not true Muslims. That he will usher in a new era of American, Muslim relations. To ensure his own historical legacy, Obama will do everything possible to strong arm Israel and force them to withdraw from the Golan Heights, West Bank, and acceptance of a nuclear armed Iran – not land for peace but land for war – not a peace settlement but a phony piece of paper that will allow the jihadists to surround Israel on all sides and armed with tens of thousands of rockets start a guerrilla missile war attacking all Israeli cities, shutting down the economy and forcing many to flee the country.

In his speech approving the 30,000 troop surge into Afghanistan, and his trip to India - Obama talked as he had in Cairo about Islam – the religion of Peace being hi-jacked by extremists. Rather then expose the cold, brutal reality that is Islam, he has made this evil mainstream and RESPECTED.

Iran Ayatollahs Issue Fatwa's Against All Those Who Insult Quran and Quran-Burners

As we have already seen with Molly Norris, being the Last Prophet of God aka Jake Neuman aka me is a very dangerous profession. Former Muslim and author Wafa Sultan, former Muslim and Dutch MP Ayaan Hirsi Ali, scholar Robert Spencer, former Muslim Ibn Warraq, former Muslim/ Nonie Darwish, Father Botros, cartoonist Lars Vilks, cartoonist Kurt Westergaard, Danish newspaper publisher Flemming Rose, South Park producers Trey Parker and Matt Stone, Salman Rushdie and countless others have all been threatened with death.

I live in a very dangerous part of the world where my head can be chopped off and stuffed inside my bloody cut open stomach – to say the least. (English is not my first language so please excuse spelling errors and improper wording.) This is how these men of the AntiGod Allah operate through fear and murder. These Ayatollahs are following EXACTLY the teachings of the Quran and the divine example of Muhammad as recorded in the Hadith. They are good, holy, moderate Muslim men. It is the duty of all freedom loving peoples to reject and stand against these thugs. Unfortunately, this book has been banned from many websites and also media outlets have refused to acknowledge its existence. No major publisher will ever publish this book. This is Stealth Censorship.

Sept. 13 (Bloomberg) – "Two Iranian grand ayatollahs issued fatwa's calling for the killing of those who insult the Quran, including anyone who burns the Islamic holy book, the state-run Fars news agency reported. No one was specified in the decrees, which were issued by Nasser Makarem-Shirazi and Hossein Nouri-Hamedani in response to questions asked by student groups from universities in Tehran, Fars said. Such an action against any individual could only be carried out with the authorization of an Islamic religious judge, they said. "Undoubtedly, the blood of a person who burns the Quran should be shed."

BAN SHARIA LAW UNEQUIVOCALLY NATIONWIDE OTHERWISE THE CONSTITUTION, DEMOCRACY AND FREEDOM, RULE OF LAW WILL BE DESTROYED. SHARIA LAW WILL BECOME THE RULE OF LAW

BANNING SHARIA AND PASSING A CONSTITUTIONAL AMENDMENT ON EQUALITY OF WOMEN WILL SHOCK THE WORLD AND CRIPPLE ISLAM AND STAND AS A BEACON OF HOPE FOR EUROPE. WE ARE NOT ONLY FIGHTING FOR OUR FREEDOM BUT ALSO FOR THE FREEDOM OF EUROPE

Sharia Law: The Divine, Unchangeable Law of AntiGod Allah:

9/11 MASSACRE AT WORLD TRADE CENTER WAS DONE IN ACCORDANCE WITH SHARIA LAW

For Muslim men, all democratic constitutions are evil and must be destroyed and replaced by Sharia Law: the constitution of Allah (the AntiGod). It is the prime, religious duty of all Muslim men to conquer the nations of the world for Allah, murder all kafirs who refuse to convert to Islam and establish Sharia Law over all mankind. This is the insane, irrational, evil reality that is Islam.

Islamic law does not prescribe retaliation against a parent for killing his or her child. For example: "not subject to retaliation" is "a father or mother (or their fathers or mothers) for killing their offspring, or offspring's offspring." ('Umdat al-Salik o1.1-2)." Most religions have a softer feminine aspect (e.g. Virgin Mary) but all trace of the feminine has been eradicated from Islam to give something which is consequently only half human.

Predatory and domineering, Islam is a brutal, hypermasculine, barbarian, tribal warrior cult that glories in murder, mutilation, rape, genocide, terrorism, destruction and anarchy. Women, girls and all the feminine aspects human nature are chattelised and subjugated. Weakness is despised and seen as ripe for predation.

A Muslim woman or girl is not treated as an equal but is the owned property of her father or husband. A Muslim man has the full right granted to him by the AntiGod Allah to beat his wife and even behead her. This is NOT A CRIME. There is no concept of spousal rape in Islam. In Islamic Sharia, rape of a Muslim woman is adultery by force. So long as the woman is his wife, it cannot be termed as rape.

But for those who naively—and smugly—proclaim such phenomena are absent within the Muslim communities of North America, consider AMJA, the **Assembly of Muslim Jurists of America**. AMJA's mission statement claims the organization was, "…founded to provide guidance for Muslims living in North America…AMJA is a religious organization that does not exploit religion to achieve any political ends, but instead provides practical solutions within the guidelines of Islam and the nation's laws to the various challenges experienced by Muslim communities."

In response to the specific query, "Is there a such thing as Marital Rape?," the AMJA issued fatwa #2982: "In the name of Allah, all praise is for Allah, and may peace and blessing be upon the Messenger of Allah and his family. To proceed: For a wife to abandon the bed of her husband without excuse is haram [forbidden]. It is one of the major sins and the angels curse her until the morning as we have been informed by the Prophet (may Allah bless him and grant him peace). She is considered nashiz (rebellious) under these circumstances. As for the issue of forcing a wife to have sex, if she refuses, this would not be called rape, even though it goes against natural instincts and destroys love and mercy, and there is a great sin upon the wife who refuses; and Allah Almighty is more exalted and more knowledgeable."

The Muslim wife must be ready for sex at any and all times even on the saddle of a camel. A Muslim woman who is raped must have 4 Muslim men who witnessed the raping testify on her behalf. If she fails to produce 4 male witnesses, the Muslim woman will be sentenced for the very grave crime of adultery and lashed 100 times or stoned to death. If a Muslim wife punctures the ego of her husband, then she must be killed to restore the man's 'honor' among his peers. A Muslim child who dishonors her father must be killed. Honor killing is rampant in Europe and the United States. Kafir women and children are war booty.

Wearing of a headscarf by Muslim women and covering up of their flesh is not an expression of religious chasteness but her total submission to the AntiGod and her husband owner. The subjugation, oppression and enslavement of Muslim women and children are enforced by Sharia Law: the divine, unchangeable constitution of the AntiGod. Please note what I just wrote. THIS IS VERY IMPORTANT. Just as the Quran is the divine, unchangeable word of the

AntiGod Allah so to Sharia Law is the divine, unchangeable constitution of the AntiGod.

It is absolutely imperative to ban Sharia Law. Banning Sharia will be like defanging Dracula. A toothless Dracula will still be a dangerous creature who could use a sword to slit your throat and drink your blood. Islam without Sharia will still be a danger to humanity. By banning Sharia, we are declaring that the only source of law in a democratic society is the democratic constitution. Banning Sharia will not destroy Islam but it will definitely cripple it. (You must implore your Congressman to ban Sharia and enact at the same time a Constitutional Amendment proclaiming the equality of Women. This Amendment is detailed on page cvi. The banning of Sharia will be an historical moment. Again, the banning of Sharia Law will stand as a beacon of hope for the freedom fighters of Europe who are fighting a losing battle to save democracy from Islamic totalitarianism If Europe falls, America will truly stand alone)

Further in this article, read a small sample of the barbarism that is Sharia Law. There is no place in a democratic society for sanctifying murder and oppression. Kafirs are not subhumans but human beings. Women are not men's property. They are the complete equal of men in every way. Support of women is absolutely essential to obtaining victory over Islam. There is a saying that a fish rots from the head downward. But this is wrong. A fish rots equally from the head down and the tail upwards. Failure to ban Sharia Law will leave Western societies a rotten, smelly, corpse not fit for burial. Being not Moral Perfection, Sharia Law is not the divine Constitution of God.

Following is a brutal story of Islamic depravity suffered by millions of Muslim women. For more stories of Islamic immoral depravity http://www.islamreform.net/new-page-50.htm
http://www.islamreform.net/new-page-52.htm
http://www.islamreform.net/new-page-54.htm
http://www.islamreform.net/new-page-51.htm
http://www.islamreform.net/new-page-55.htm
http://www.islamreform.net/new-page-67.htm

101 LASHES FOR BEING RAPED

When a rape victim in a particular country receives 101 lashes and the rapist gets off scott-free, one can only assume that rape is condoned, and that message only encourages men to continue raping, knowing full well there will be no consequences for that violation. That's the way it is in Bangladesh, and many other countries that re-victimize the victim by punishing them and not the rapists.

A 16-year-old Bangladeshi girl just received 101 lashes after it was revealed that she had become impregnated after being raped by 20-year-old Emamul Mia last April. At first she was reluctant to report the rape, because of the shame and stigma involved, although I'm sure much also had to do with the fact that rape victims are punishable by Sharia law. But it wasn't until she had been married off, after the attack, to a man in a neighbouring village, that it was discovered she was pregnant. Divorced after one month of marriage, the rape revealed, and forced to abort the child, the family of the rapist (and village elders) decided the girl and her family needed to be punished. So not only was a fatwa issued for the lashing, the father has also been fined 1,000. The rapist? Nothing.

Eight months after being raped, a 16-year-old at Khargor of Kasba upazila in Brahmanbaria had to receive 101 lashes as "punishment".

A village arbitration found her guilty and issued the 101 lashes fatwa (religious edict) but amazingly left alleged rapist Enamul Mia, 20, untouched.

The arbitration also fined the victim's father Tk 1,000 and issued another fatwa that her family would be forced into isolation if he failed to pay up

On January 17, the influential group arranged the arbitration at the yard of the victim. At one stage of the inhuman torture, the girl collapsed and fainted. She regained her sense after two hours.

Ullashi presided over the arbitration while Wahid Mia, Basu Mia, Manik Mia, Shahjahan Mia, Dulal Mia, Maulana Md Kawser Mia, Imam of Gupinathpur Baro Mosque, Maulana Md Ishaque Mia, Imam of Khargor Jame Mosque, and a few others played key roles.

"Enamul has spoiled my life. I want justice," said the girl as tears rolled down from her eyes,

There is much talk in the media about Islam's stated goal of implementing Sharia Law in democratic Western countries. Often, the demand for Sharia Law is painted in the guise of a desire by Muslims to rule themselves in accordance with their culture and customs. Most efforts to institute Sharia Law focus primarily on civil law matters, giving it the kinder, gentler appeal of applying principally to settlement of family issues and disputes such as marriage, divorce and wills, areas that would have little bearing or impact on the rest of the Western population. Proponents of Sharia Law argue that it's only "fair" to allow Muslims to govern themselves rather than "force" them to comply with prevailing laws that may conflict with their religion or ideology.

However, this is misleading. What these proponents of Sharia Law are saying, in essence, is that Muslims refuse to assimilate into the Western culture of their host countries and instead expect Western legislative and judiciary systems to bend to accommodate them, even to the point of having separate Sharia courts of law as Britain allows.

Historically, Western civilizations have welcomed diverse ethnic groups on the premise that unique views and culture focused on the cause of achieving common goals would make our nations stronger, smarter and more adaptable to change. In reality, focusing on diversity for diversity's sake has weakened us. While the 1800's and 1900's saw an influx of foreigners to Western societies who made tremendous contributions to our nations, these foreigners viewed democracy in the West as something valuable, precious, and made dedicated efforts to assimilate. Foreigners fought in our wars, pledged allegiance to our flags, and raised their children to hold Western principles dear. They learned the language, they adopted the customs, and they lived their lives under the same rules and ordinances as every other person in their nation. Today, Islam teaches its people not to assimilate, to live separately and hold to Islamic customs and law.

All this begs the question: can a house divided still stand?

Many ask whether Sharia Law and democracy can co-exist. However, the larger question is whether shari'ah law and human rights can co-exist. The answer to this question is a resounding "NO".

So what is Sharia Law? Sharia translates as "the path." Sharia is a comprehensive framework designed to govern all aspects of life. Though it has spiritual elements, it would be a mistake to think of it as a "religious" code in the Western sense because it seeks to regulate all manner of behavior in the secular sphere - economic, social, military, legal and political. It is the fusing of religion, government and private life into one codified body of law based on Islam's religious ideology that governs everything from politics to economics, from banking to business, and from family issues to sexuality, even going so far as to legislate private matters such as hygiene. Separation of church and state, a principle on which democracy in America was founded, is non-existent in Islamic countries ruled by Sharia Law. Sharia regulation is oppressive, discriminatory, utterly inimical to our core constitutional liberties and destructive of equal protection under the law, especially for women.

Sharia law is so all-encompassing that it leaves no room for independent thought, freedom of speech or freedom of religion. Wonder how to pray or when to pray? Sharia law will dictate that. Wonder how to divide your possessions to your heirs upon your death? Sharia law will tell you how. Wonder whether you should bathe after being intimate with your wife? Yes, Sharia Law will even legislate this matter, for obedience to the law requires obedience to Allah and His Messenger and the jurisprudence they implemented in 7th century Arabia.

Let's look at some specific Sharia Laws to see whether they are compatible with Western principles. Since Islamic countries currently implement Sharia Law to varying degrees, we'll focus on fundamental jurisprudence as dictated by Saudi Arabia, the home of Mecca and the keeper of the "purest" form of Islam and Islamic law. All laws listed below are directly from Alifta.com, a website for official "fatwas" (legal opinions) issued by the General Presidency of Scholarly Research and Ifta (issuing fatwas) of the Kingdom of Saudi Arabia.

In order to be the divine constitution of God – ALL of the following teachings of Sharia Law must be Moral Perfection. If only one teaching is not Moral Perfection then Sharia Law is not the divine constitution of God and all Islam is fraudulent. Needless to say all Sharia is an immoral obscenity.

If you have not already done so please view the brutal whipping video that will become our daily reality if we do not ban Sharia.
http://www.memritv.org/clip/en/0/0/0/0/0/0/2722.htm
For article: 228,000 US Women circumcision mutilation
http://www.islamreform.net/new-page-59.htm

LEGAL BARBARIC BARBARISM

Sharia Law & Freedom of Speech:

- The punishment for apostasy (changing or discarding one's Islamic relgion) is death. *Fatwa 4400, Part No. 1, Page 334 & 335*

- Mocking anything in the Qur'an or the Sunnah of the prophet Muhammad is apostasy and therefore punishable by death. *Fatwa 2196, Part No. 2, Page 42*

- Criticizing Islam, shari'ah law or the Sunnah of the prophet Muhammad is apostasy and therefore punishable by death. *Fatwa 21021, Part No. 1, Page 414*

- Any Muslim who states a preference for democracy rather than shari'ah law or questions anything in the Qur'an or Sunnah is a kafir (disbeliever), considered an apostate, and therefore sentenced to death. *Fatwa 19351, Part No. 22, Page 239-248*

Sharia Law & Human Rights:

- The punishment for theft is amputation of the right hand up to the elbow. *Fatwa 3339, Part No. 22, Page 218 & 219*

- The penalty for premarital sexual intercourse is 100 lashes with a whip and one year of exile. *Volume 3, Part No. 3, Page 359*

- The penalty for adultery between a married man and a married woman is 100 lashes with a whip and death by stoning. *Volume 3, Part No. 3, Page 359*

- The penalty for homosexuality is death. *Fatwa 4324, Part No. 22, Page 53 & 54*

- Non-Muslims living in lands ruled by Islamic law (shari'ah) must pay a poll tax (jizyah) in order to be subdued and feel subjugated to Muslims. Refusal to pay the tax grants Muslims the right to wage war against the non-muslims. *Fatwa 4461, Part No. 1, Page 215 Volume 3, Part No. 3, Page 183-190*

- Waging war against non-Muslims (jihad), even those who are peaceful, is encouraged so that other religions and atheism will be purged from the earth. *Volume 2, Part No. 2, Page 437-440*

- If a Muslim kills a Jew or Christian dhimmi (one who pays the poll tax), he must pay only half the amount of "blood money" he would have to pay for killing a Muslim. *Fatwa 5414, Part No. 21, Page 245*

Sharia Law & Women's Rights:

- Women are permitted an education in Islamic issues (religious education) and family duties, but academic study is not encouraged. *Fatwa 9019*

- Women are not permitted to attend universities where both men and women are taught or all-female schools with male teachers. *Fatwa 13814, Part No. 12, Page 150*

- Women over the age of puberty are not permitted to leave the house without covering the body (except face and hands). *Fatwa 667, Part No. 17, Page 142-150*

- Women are not permitted to visit the graves of loved ones. *Fatwa 2501, Part No. 1, Page 429*

- Women are not permitted to obtain passports (since their photographs in them may tempt men), unless for the purpose of making Hajj (pilgrimage to Mecca). *Fatwa 2595, Part No. 1, Page 719*

- Women are not permitted to travel without a spouse or male relative. *Fatwa 12139, Part No. 11, Page 38*

- Women are not permitted to be alone with men who are not relatives or spouses, and the punishment for such "indecency" is whipping or stoning. *Fatwa 9693, Part No. 12, Page 381 & 382*

- Women are not permitted to speak softly to a man or otherwise provoke his desire with letters, phone calls or glances, the punishment of which is whipping or stoning. *Fatwa 9693, Part No. 12, Page 381 & 382*

Sharia Law & Civil Matters:

- A man may divorce his wife by simply giving her a triple talaq (saying "I divorce you" three times simultaneously). *Fatwa 6542, 2nd question*

- A woman whose husband divorces her three times by simply saying "I divorce you", even if divorced against her will, cannot seek alimony unless she is pregnant. *Fatwa 20918, Part No. 20, Page 227*

- A man may not adopt any children, even if they are his stepchildren born to his wife from a prior marriage. *Fatwa 5124, Part No. 9, Page 10*

- Men are entitled to twice the amount of inheritance a woman receives, regardless of what a person's wishes are as detailed in a will. *Fatwa 8778, Part No. 21, Page 234*

Sharia Law & Business Matters:

- Since usury (charging or paying interest) is a sin, working at banks with interest-bearing deposits, keeping money in interest-bearing deposits, or accepting loans that charge interest is prohibited. *Fatwa 4011, Part No. 12, Page 80*

- It is illegal to work in certain industries, such as retailers selling musical instruments, wine, tobacco, or music CDs; a photography studio; or any company that requires its employees to be photographed *Fatwa 5436, Part No. 13, Page 42*

- Muslims are encouraged not to enter into business partnerships with non-Muslims. *Fatwa 5855, Part No. 2, Page 98 & 99*

Sharia Law & Personal Hygience:

- Women are required to pluck, depilate or otherwise remove all facial and body hair, with the exception of shaving the eyebrows or head. *Fatwa 5007*

- Men must let their beards grow without cutting but keep their mustache trimmed so as to appear different from non-Muslims. *Fatwa 2196, Part No. 2, Page 41 & 42*

- Failure to take a ritual bath for the purpose of purifying oneself after sexual intercourse is a sin that must be repented from and will invalidate one's prayers to Allah. Fatwa 11188, Part No. 6, Page 19

Death Compensation

As already stated in · *Fatwa 5414, Part No. 21, Page 245* **If a Muslim kills a Jew or Christian dhimmi (one who pays the poll tax), he must pay only half the amount of "blood money" he would have to pay for killing a Muslim.** Following is a listing of the required death compensation.

From the website of the Consulate General of India, Jeddah, who is recording these matters because they come up in connection with his people who are working in Saudi Arabia :

Mode of Payment:

All Death Compensation cases (except industrial accidents) in Saudi Arabia are settled through concerned Sharia Courts in accordance with the Sharia Law.

Maximum Amount admissible :

The maximum amount of Death Compensation (Diyya) generally admissible in Saudi Arabia, in respect of road/traffic/fire accident, murder, etc. is as under: Death Compensation in respect of a male person:
i. Muslim - SR. 100,000/-
ii. Christian/Jew - SR.50,000/-
iii. Other religions : such as Hindu, Buddhist, Jain, etc. - SR 6666.66

In the case of death of a female, death compensation allowed is equal to half the amount as admissible to males professing the same religion. Further the amount of compensation admissible, is based on the percentage of responsibility fixed on the causer e.g. if the causer is held 50% responsible for the accident resulting in the death of a Muslim, the amount of Death Compensation admissible will be SR 50,000 only.
100,000 Saudi riyals = $26,665.25
50,000 Saudi riyals = $13,332.62
6,666.66 Saudi riyals = $1,777.69

To truly understand the evil we face read the following quotation from the Secretary General of the Islamic Sharia Council Suhaib Hasan, describing his plans for Sharia in Britain. There are 89 Sharia Law courts presently operating legally in Britain. There is rapidly evolving two different systems of law which will eventually merge into only one legal system – Sharia. Quoting "If Sharia law is implemented, then you can turn this country [Great Britain] into a haven of peace because once a thief's hand is cut off nobody is going to steal." Furthermore, "once[,] just only once, if an adulterer is stoned[,] nobody is going to commit this crime at all," and finally, "[w]e want to offer it to the British society. If they accept it, it is for their good and if they don't accept it they'll need more and more prisons."

Recently the good people of Oklahoma voted by 70% to ban Sharia Law forbidding their courts from considering Sharia in any of its rulings. It is important to understand that Sharia has invaded the legal system of the United States. Under the guise of religious freedom, Sharia rulings are been made by judges everywhere. Incredibility an Oklahoma judge just ruled that such a ban is unconstitutional because it infringes on the religious rights of Muslims. The horror of Sharia has been given legal protection.

In their defense of Sharia, Muslims hid under the cloak of religious practice stating that the ballot measure would infringe on the constitutional rights of ordinary Oklahomans — including the right to wear religious head scarves in driver's license photographs, choose Islamic marriage contracts, implement Islamic wills, or to be buried according to one's religious beliefs.

This is a bunch of nonsense. The Oklahoma law forbids lawmakers from legislating for Oklahomans as a whole using Sharia rather than American law. It does not forbid private individuals from getting married or writing wills in any way they wish. The idea of the Oklahoma Sharia ban is to prevent judges from making decisions based on a legal system that contradicts the principles of American law in numerous particulars.

Again it is imperative that Sharia be banned throughout the USA. Do not allow yourself to be fooled or tricked by the elites into any false sense of security. Islam is a direct threat to our way of life. Do not sit on the sidelines of life like the Germans did allowing Hitler to come to power. Demand from your congressmen the banning of Sharia, criminalization of Jihad and then the passage of the Democracy and Freedom Act, Constitutional Amendment: Equality of Women, banning Stealth Jihad and the other recommendations listed in the forth coming section - Plan of Action.

This book is written from the nonbeliever point of view. Everything in this book views Islam from how it affects non-Muslims. This also means that the religion is of little importance. A Muslim cares about the religion of Islam, but all nonbelievers are affected by Islam's political views. This book discusses Islam as a political system. There is no need to talk about Muslims or religion. Muslims are people and vary from one to another. Religion is what one does to go to Paradise and avoid Hell. It is not useful nor necessary to discuss Islam as a religion. But we have to talk about Islam in the political realm, because it is a powerful political system. To further understand Sharia Law read: Sharia Law For Non-Muslims: http://www.islamreform.net/new-page-63.htm and Sharia Law and Women:

Sharia in Europe Today

When you study Islam in Europe today, you are seeing America in 20 years. Why? The actions by Muslims in Europe are based on Sharia law, the same Sharia law that is beginning to be implemented in America today. For truly frightening video of the reality of Islam in France go to : http://islamreform.net/new-page-100.htm

· Traffic cannot move in London streets as Muslims commandeer the streets to pray-a political result based on Sharia law.

· Entire areas of Europe are no-go zones for non-Muslims, this includes the police. These are Islamic enclaves where only Muslims live. The Muslim-only policy is based on Sharia.

· In England an Anglican bishop calls for the rule of Islamic law for Muslims. The bishop is obeying Sharia law.

· In the schools only Islamic approved texts can be used. This is based on Sharia law.

· Christians may not speak to Muslims about Christianity nor may they hand out literature. This is a political result based on Sharia law enforced by British courts.

· Rape by Muslims is so prevalent that Sweden has forbidden the police to collect any data in the investigation that would point to Islam. Rape is part of Islamic doctrine as applied to non-Muslim women.

· In London mass demonstrations by Muslims call for the end of British law and Sharia law to rule all people. This political action is based on Sharia.

· In some English hospitals, during Ramadan fast (an Islamic religious event) non-Muslims cannot eat where a Muslim can see them. The submission of non-Muslims is based on Sharia law.

· At British hospitals, Muslim women are treated only as Sharia law demands.

· If a Dane says that he is proud to be Danish near a Muslim, it can be seen as hate speech and racism. This is in accordance to Sharia law.

Police are being murdered so their Muslim killers can ascend to Paradise as per Quran verse 9.111.

Sharia Law In New Jersey

Sharia Law is rapidly replacing US law in governing relations between Muslims. Sharia is also starting to be applied throughout the US against kafir Americans. Read this recent ruling by a judge in New Jersey. This is why it is absolutely critical to ban Sharia Law and enshrine in the Constitution – The Declaration of The Equality of Women that will protect ALL women including Muslim women from suffering at the hands of Islam and these outrageous judges. (Page lvii) **ONLY THE CONSTITUTION OF THE UNITED STATES CAN BE APPLIED IN ANY AMERICAN COURT.**

Muslim husband rapes wife, judge sees no sexual assault because Islam forbids wives to deny sex to their husbands.
Muhammad said: "If a husband calls his wife to his bed [i.e. to have sexual relation] and she refuses and causes him to sleep in anger, the angels will curse her till morning" (Bukhari 4.54.460).

He also said: "By him in Whose Hand lies my life, a woman can not carry out the right of her Lord, till she carries out the right of her husband. And if he asks her to surrender herself [to him for sexual intercourse] she should not refuse him even if she is on a camel's saddle" (Ibn Majah 1854).

And now a New Jersey judge sees no evidence that a Muslim committed sexual assault of his wife -- not because he didn't do it, but because he was acting on his Islamic beliefs: "This court does not feel that, under the circumstances, that this defendant had a criminal desire to or intent to sexually assault or to sexually contact the plaintiff when he did. The court believes that he was operating under his belief that it is, as the husband, his desire to have sex when and whether he wanted to, was something that was consistent with his practices and it was something that was not prohibited."
Luckily, the appellate court overturned this decision, and a Sharia ruling by an American court has not been allowed to stand. This time.

"Cultural Defense Accepted as to Nonconsensual Sex in New Jersey Trial Court, Rejected on Appeal," by Eugene Volokh in The Volokh Conspiracy, July 23 (thanks to CameoRed):

From today's opinion in *S.D. v. M.J.R.* (N.J. Super. Ct. App. Div.), a domestic restraining order case: The record reflects that plaintiff, S.D., and defendant, M.J.R., are citizens of Morocco and adherents to the Muslim faith. They were wed in Morocco in an arranged marriage on July 31, 2008, when plaintiff was seventeen years old. [FN1] The parties did not know each other prior to the marriage. On August 29, 2008, they came to New Jersey as the result of defendant's employment in this country as an accountant....
[Long discussion of the wife's allegations of abuse, which included several instances of nonconsensual sex as well as other abuse, omitted for space reasons. - EV]

Upon their return to the apartment, defendant forced plaintiff to have sex with him while she cried. Plaintiff testified that defendant always told her this is according to our religion. You are my wife, I c[an] do anything to you. The woman, she should submit and do anything I ask her to do.

After having sex, defendant took plaintiff to a travel agency to buy a ticket for her return to Morocco. However the ticket was not purchased, and the couple returned to the apartment. Once there, defendant threatened divorce, but nonetheless again engaged in nonconsensual sex while plaintiff cried. Later that day, defendant and his mother took plaintiff to the home of the Imam and, in the presence of the Imam, his wife, and defendant's mother, defendant verbally divorced plaintiff....[...]

While recognizing that defendant had engaged in sexual relations with plaintiff against her expressed wishes in November 2008 and on the night of January 15 to 16, 2009, the judge did not find sexual assault or criminal sexual conduct to have been proven. He stated:

This court does not feel that, under the circumstances, that this defendant had a criminal desire to or intent to sexually assault or to sexually contact the plaintiff when he did. The court believes that he was operating under his belief that it is, as the husband, his desire to have sex when and whether he wanted to, was something that was consistent with his practices and it was something that was not prohibited.

After acknowledging that this was a case in which religious custom clashed with the law, and that under the law, plaintiff had a right to refuse defendant's advances, the judge found that defendant did not act with a criminal intent when he repeatedly insisted upon intercourse, despite plaintiff's contrary wishes.

Having found acts of domestic violence consisting of assault and harassment to have occurred, the judge turned to the issue of whether a final restraining order should be entered. He found such an order unnecessary, vacated the temporary restraints previously entered in the matter and dismissed plaintiff's domestic violence action....

The appellate court reversed this absurd decision, saying:
As the judge recognized, the case thus presents a conflict between the criminal law and religious precepts. In resolving this conflict, the judge determined to except defendant from the operation of the State's statutes as the result of his religious beliefs. In doing so, the judge was mistaken. A close call. But no doubt more of this is to come. Following is a short listing of how sharia is invading the daily life of Americans.

Sharia in America Today

Here are current and historical events in America that are driven by Sharia law:

· On September 11, 2001 jihadists attacked and destroyed the World Trade Center. This was in compliance to the laws of jihad found in the Sharia law. The attack was a political action based upon a religious motivation.

· All textbooks in America must be approved by Islamic councils that are controlled by the Muslim Brotherhood. This is in accordance with Sharia law.

· American employers and schools are met with demands for time and space to do Islamic prayer. These demands are based on Sharia law.

· The American banking system is becoming Islamicized with Sharia financing. Our banking system indulges in Sharia financial law and does not know the rest of Sharia law.

· Universities are asked to close swimming pools and other athletic facilities to be used for Muslim women.

· Hospitals are being sued for not having Sharia compliant treatment.

· No course at the college level uses critical thinking in the history and doctrine of Islam. Under Sharia no aspect of Islam may be criticized.

· Muslim charities give money to jihadists, as per Sharia law.

· Muslim foot-baths are being installed in airport facilities, using tax money. This is in accordance with Sharia law.

· American prisons are a stronghold of proselytizing for Islam.

· Workplaces are being made Islamic worship sites through special rooms and time off to pray. This is in accordance to Sharia law.

· Islamic refugees bring all of their wives for welfare and medical treatment to America. Authorities will not act even when presented with evidence. Polygamy is pure Sharia.

· We are fighting wars in Iraq and Afghanistan to implement constitutions that have the supremacy of Sharia law as their first article.

Why Do We Need to Know Sharia?

ISLAMIC SCHOLARS CLAIM: Islamic law is perfect, universal and eternal. The laws of the United States are temporary, limited and will pass. It is the duty of every Muslim to obey the laws of Allah, the Sharia.

SHARIA: Sharia is based on the principles found in the Koran and other Islamic religious/political texts. There are no common principles between American law and Sharia.

Under Sharia law:

- There is no freedom of religion
- There is no freedom of speech
- There is no freedom of thought
- There is no freedom of artistic expression
- There is no freedom of the press
- There is no equality of peoples-a non-Muslim, a Kafir, is never equal to a Muslim
- There are no equal rights for women
- Women can be beaten
- A non-Muslim cannot bear arms
- There is no equal protection under Sharia for different classes of people. Justice is dualistic, with one set of laws for Muslim males and different laws for women and non-Muslims.
- Our Constitution is a man-made document of ignorance, jahiliyah, that must submit to Sharia
- There is no democracy, since that means that a non-Muslim is equal to a Muslim
- Non-Muslims are dhimmis, third-class citizens
- There is no Golden Rule
- There is no critical thought
- All governments must be ruled by Sharia law

Unlike common law, Sharia is not interpretive, nor can it be changed

THE SOLUTION

This book uses a fact-based approach to knowledge that uses analytic or critical thought. When you finish reading, you will know what Sharia law is. More importantly you will know why Sharia is what it is. You will understand how Sharia "works" and why it cannot change. For the first time, you will understand Islam. It will all make sense.

HOW SHARIA LAW WILL DESTROY THE CONSTITUTION

This is the barbarism that Imam Feisal Abdel Rauf (The Iman who wants to build the 9/11 mosque and all his supporters) want to impose on the United States and Europe. As you can clearly see, democracy and freedom ceases to exist, women are destroyed, slavery, sex slaves and Islamic totalitarism are imposed. Imam Feisal Abdel Rauf claims that the U.S. constitution is Sharia compliant. Now let us examine below a few laws of Sharia to see how truthful Imam Rauf is:

1- Jihad, defined as "to war against non-Muslims to establish the religion," is the duty of every Muslim and Muslim head of state (Caliph). Muslim Caliphs who refuse jihad are in violation of Sharia and unfit to rule.
2- A Caliph can hold office through seizure of power meaning through force.
3- A Caliph is exempt from being charged with serious crimes such as murder, adultery, robbery, theft, drinking and in some cases of rape.
4- A percentage of Zakat (charity money) must go towards jihad.
5- It is obligatory to obey the commands of the Caliph, even if he is unjust.
6- A caliph must be a Muslim, a non-slave and a male.
7- The Muslim public must remove the Caliph if he rejects Islam.
8- A Muslim who leaves Islam must be killed immediately.
9- A Muslim will be forgiven for murder of: 1) an apostate 2) an adulterer 3) a highway robber. Vigilante street justice and honor killing is acceptable.
10- A Muslim will not get the death penalty if he kills a non-Muslim, but will get it for killing a Muslim.
11- Sharia never abolished slavery, sexual slavery and highly regulates it. A master will not be punished for killing his slave.
12- Sharia dictates death by stoning, beheading, amputation of limbs, flogging even for crimes of sin such as adultery.
13- Non-Muslims are not equal to Muslims under the law. They must comply to Islamic law if they are to remain safe. They are forbidden to marry Muslim women, publicly display wine or pork, recite their scriptures or openly celebrate their religious holidays or funerals. They are forbidden from building new churches or building them higher than mosques. They may not enter a mosque without permission. A non-Muslim is no longer protected if he leads a Muslim away from Islam.
14- It is a crime for a non-Muslim to sell weapons to someone who will use them against Muslims. Non-Muslims cannot curse a Muslim, say anything derogatory about Allah, the Prophet, or Islam, or expose the weak points of Muslims. But Muslims can curse non-Muslims.
15- A non-Muslim cannot inherit from a Muslim.
16- Banks must be Sharia compliant and interest is not allowed.
17- No testimony in court is acceptable from people of low-level jobs, such as street sweepers or bathhouse attendants. Women in low level jobs such as

professional funeral mourners cannot keep custody of their children in case of divorce.

18- A non-Muslim cannot rule — even over a non-Muslim minority.

19- Homosexuality is punishable by death.

20- There is no age limit for marriage of girls. The marriage contract can take place anytime after birth and can be consummated at age 8 or 9.

21- Rebelliousness on the part of the wife nullifies the husband's obligation to support her, gives him permission to beat her and keep her from leaving the home.

22- Divorce is only in the hands of the husband and is as easy as saying: "I divorce you" and becomes effective even if the husband did not intend it.

23- There is no community property between husband and wife and the husband's property does not automatically go to the wife after his death.

24- A woman inherits half what a man inherits.

25- A man has the right to have up to 4 wives and none of them have a right to divorce him — even if he is polygamous.

26- The dowry is given in exchange for the woman's sexual organs.

27- A man is allowed to have sex with slave women and women captured in battle, and if the enslaved woman is married her marriage is annulled.

28- The testimony of a woman in court is half the value of a man.

29- A woman loses custody if she remarries.

30- To prove rape, a woman must have 4 male witnesses.

31- A rapist may only be required to pay the bride-money (dowry) without marrying the rape victim.

32- A Muslim woman must cover every inch of her body, which is considered "Awrah," a sexual organ. Not all Sharia schools allow the face of a woman exposed.

33- A Muslim man is forgiven if he kills his wife at the time he caught her in the act of adultery. However, the opposite is not true for women, since the man "could be married to the woman he was caught with."

34- It is obligatory for a Muslim to lie if the purpose is obligatory. That means that for the sake of abiding with Islam's commandments, such as jihad, a Muslim is obliged to lie and should not have any feelings of guilt or shame associated with this kind of lying.

      This is why we are fighting Islam. Do you want some Iman and his religious police to order how you and your family must live your lives and if you refuse murder you and your family?

      ISLAMIC SCHOLARS CLAIM: The perfect Islamic family law is sacred law since it is based upon the words of Allah in the glorious Quran and the Sunna of Muhammad. All other laws are man-made and must submit to the will of Allah; therefore, only Sharia law is suitable for Muslims. For Muslims to be ruled by Kafir laws is an abomination. If we do not stop Islam, this is how you and your family will be living your lives. Again, this is why it is absolutely critical to ban Sharia Law and Stealth Jihad (see further). It will not be the end of Islam but it definitely will be the beginning of the end.

Key Tenets of Sharia

I believe that the most vulnerable aspect of the Islamist ideology is Sharia Law. Any rational person would conclude that Sharia Law is racist, sexist, and discriminates on the basis of religion. These are no-no's in the 21st Century. If Sharia Law can be condemned on rational grounds, it throws in to question the entire Islamic ideology. You can't have one without the other. Notice how apologists for Islam always try to parce words when it comes to Sharia Law. They say, "Well, there are different interpretations of Sharia Law, and we don't agree with what you just quoted." No, there is one standard and it is reflected in "'Umdat al-Salik" ("The Reliance of the Traveller") by al-Misri (died 1368) which has been around since the Middle Ages. The English translation has been approved by Al-Ahzar University in Cairo. It doesn't get any more authentic than that.

Key Tenets of Sharia

The following are some of the most important—and, particularly for Western non-Muslims, deeply problematic—tenets of sharia, arranged in alphabetical order. The citations for these findings are drawn from the Koran, schools of Islam and other recognized sources are offered as illustrative examples of the basis for such practices under sharia.

1. Abrogation ('Al-mansukh wa al-nasikh' in Arabic—the abrogated and the abrogating): Verses that come later in the Koran, chronologically, supersede, or abrogate, the earlier ones. In effect, this results in the more moderate verses of the Meccan period being abrogated by the later, violent, Medinan period.

2. Adultery ('Zina' in Arabic): Unlawful intercourse is a capital crime under sharia, punishable by lashing and stoning to death.

3. Apostasy ('Irtidad' or 'Ridda' in Arabic): The established ruling of sharia is that apostates are to be killed wherever they may be found.

4. Democracy & Islam: Any system of man-made law is considered illicit under Islamic law, for whose adherents Allah already has provided the only law permitted, sharia. Islam and democracy can never co-exist in harmony.

5. Female Genital Mutilation.

6. Gender Inequality: Sharia explicitly relegates women to a status inferior to men.

• Testimony of a woman before a judge is worth half that of a man.

• Women are to receive just one half the inheritance of a male.

- Muslim men are given permission by Allah in the Koran to beat their wives.

- Muslim men are given permission by Allah to commit marital rape, as they please.

- Muslim men are permitted to marry up to four wives and to keep concubines in any number.

- Muslim women may marry only one Muslim man and are forbidden from marrying a non-Muslim.

- A woman may not travel outside the home without the permission of her male guardian and must be accompanied by a male family member if she does so.

- Under sharia, to bring a claim of rape, a Muslim woman must present four male Muslim witnesses in good standing. Islam thus places the burden of avoiding illicit sexual encounters entirely on the woman. In effect, under sharia, women who bring a claim of rape without being able to produce the requisite four male Muslim witnesses are admitting to having had illicit sex. If she or the man is married, this amounts to an admission of adultery.

Rape is a felony under U.S. law, but under Sharia Law it is not. It is akin to damaging something (the woman's virginity), so the penalty is the usual cost of what was damaged – typically, $400 and up. There would be no jail time for rape, unless the man didn't pay for the damages.

- A Muslim woman who divorces and remarries loses custody of children from a prior marriage.

7. 'Honor' Killing (a.k.a. Muslim family executions): A Muslim parent faces no legal penalty under Islamic law for killing his child or grandchild.

8. Hudud Punishments: The plural of hadd, is "a fixed penalty prescribed as a right of Allah. Because hudud penalties belong to Allah, Islamic law does not permit them to be waived or commuted."

- "Sharia stipulates these punishments and methods of execution such as amputation, crucifixion, flogging, and stoning, for offenses such as adultery, homosexuality, killing without right, theft, and 'spreading mischief in the land' because these punishments were mandated by the Qur'an or Sunnah." (Islamic Hudood Laws in Pakistan, Edn 1996, 5.)

9. Islamic Supremacism: belief that Islam is superior to every other culture, faith, government, and society and that it is ordained by Allah to conquer and dominate them.

10. Jew Hatred: Anti-Semitism is intrinsic to sharia and is based on the genocidal behavior of Mohammed himself in wiping out the entire Jewish population of the Arabian Peninsula.

11. Jihad: Jihad is warfare to spread Islam.

12. Lying/Taqiyya: It is permissible for a Muslim to lie, especially to non-Muslims, to safeguard himself personally or to protect Islam.

13. Slander/Blasphemy: In sharia, slander means anything that might offend a Muslim.

14. Underage Marriage: Islamic doctrine permits the marriage of pre-pubescent girls. There is no minimum age for a marriage contract and consummation may take place when the girl is age eight or nine.

15. Zakat: the obligation for Muslims to pay zakat arises out of Koran Verse 9:60 and is one of the Five Pillars of Islam. Zakat may be given only to Muslims, never to non-Muslims. What amounts to a mandatory tax is required to be given to those engaged in jihad which is among the authorized recipients.

• According to sharia, there are eight categories of recipients for Zakat: The poor; Those short of money; Zakat workers (those whose job it is to collect the zakat); Those whose hearts are to be reconciled; Those purchasing their freedom; Those in debt; Those fighting for Allah (Jihad); Travelers needing money ('Umdat al-Salik, h8.7-h8.18)

• "It is not permissible to give Zakat to a non-Muslim." ('Umdat al-Salik, h8.24)

    Following is a very small sample of Sharia Law teachings dictating "how Muslim men deal with their spouses"?
    "Good women are obedient....As for those from whom you fear disobedience, admonish them and send them to beds apart and beat them." -- Qur'an 4:34"
    Circumcision is obligatory "The Reliance of the Traveller, a respected manual of Shafi'i jurisprudence, states "Circumcision is obligatory (for every male and female) by cutting off the piece of skin on the glans of the penis of the male, but circumcision of the female is by cutting out the clitoris" - 'Umdat al-Salik e4.3
    "If a husband calls his wife to his bed [i.e. to have sexual relation] and she refuses and causes him to sleep in anger, the angels will curse her till morning." -- Sahih Bukhari 4.54.46
    "By him in Whose Hand lies my life, a woman can not carry out the right of her Lord, till she carries out the right of her husband. And if he asks her to surrender herself [to him for sexual intercourse] she should not refuse him even if she is on a camel's saddle." -- Ibn Majah 1854

BENEFITS OF BEING A MUSLIM MAN

All Muslim men are the exalted of the AntiGod Allah - the holy blood of the AntiGod flows thru their veins. Women exist solely at the will and for the pleasure of Muslim men both in this world and for all eternity. He can rape and murder them. Islam is the most sexually depraved ideology ever created.

Repeating again this harsh Islamic reality - It is the holy, divine duty of all Muslims to conquer all nations of the world, murder all male kafirs who refuse to convert to Islam, enslave their women and children, destroy ALL other religions and replace them with Islam. Freedom of religion in Islam is only the freedom to practice Islam. It is the holy, divine duty of all Muslim men to destroy all man made constitutions and replace them with Sharia Law. By supporting the 9/11 mosque, Obama/Bloomberg are aiding Muslims in their goal of destroying the US Constitution and its replacement with Sharia. Democracy is abhorrent to the AntiGod Allah and totally against Sharia since both Muslims and non-Muslims are equal. Muslims are the exalted of the AntiGod and ALL kafirs are subhumans.

Following are the benefits of being a Muslim man. If the 9/11 mosque is built then this will be the barbarism that will come to the World Trade Center. If any mosque is built anywhere then this is the barbarism along with Sharia Law, the 4,000 evil Quranic teachings and the Hadith/Sira describing in detail the despicable crimes of prophet Muhammad that will be celebrated. According to New York Mayor Bloomberg, American soldiers are dying so Muslim men in the United States can enjoy their freedom to practice their religion and reap the fruits of Islam. Bloomberg wants us to support the religious freedom of Muslim men and the AntiGod Allah who only wants his Muslim men to be happy. The price you must be willing to pay as a Muslim man is the forfeiture of your immoral soul for as Jesus taught: "What benefits a man if he conquers the entire world but forfeits his immortal soul." Indeed, we all want to keep Muslim men happy so they won't get mad and blow up a subway system or shoot up airport terminals or blow us to smithereens with a nuclear weapon etc.

UNLIMITED SEX SLAVES

Kafir women have zero humanity. They are subhumans but very important subhumans because they possess a vagina. A Muslim man can own unlimited sex slaves and enjoy unlimited sexual raping and molestation of his sex slaves – no matter the age of the kafir woman. He can torture them while enjoying sex or do to them whatever his Muslim man's heart desires.

UNLIMITED RAPE OF KAFIR WOMEN: RAPE IS SUNNA

If the Muslim man does not wish to take a kafir woman as his sex slave then he can unlimitedly rape any kafir woman. Rape is Sunna in Islam.

MARRY UP TO 4 WIVES: MUSLIM WIFE/WIVES ARE HIS CHATTEL

The AntiGod allows each of his holy ones the right to own 4 wives any time. Muslim wife/wives are the chattel property of her husband. He can beat, confine, deprive her of food and water and behead her if she displeases him. The AntiGOD hates all Muslim women. The most important thing that a Muslim woman brings to the marriage is her vagina for enjoyment of the holy ones and produce jihadists to conquer the world for the AntiGod. *[Bukhari 7,62,81] Mohammed said, "The marriage vow most rightly expected to be obeyed is the husband's right to enjoy the wife's vagina."*

From the Sira, we have some more about a husband's rights: *Ishaq 957 Mohammed sent Muadh to Yemen to proselytize. While he was there he was asked what rights a husband has over the wife. He replied to the woman who asked, "If you went home and found your husband's nose running with pus and blood and you sucked it until it was cleaned, you still would not have fulfilled your husband's rights."*

UNLIMITED SEX AND RAPING OF MUSLIM WIVES

There is no concept of raping your wife in Islam. As his domestic animal, the Muslim wife must grant sex to her husband any time he desires even on the back of a camel. It is obligatory for a woman to let her husband have sex with her immediately when: he asks her or at home and she can physically endure it. Allah curses the woman who resists sex. *[Bukhari 7,62,121] Mohammed: "If a woman refuses her husband's request for sex, the angels will curse her through the night."* Ghazali: "A wife should not refuse her husband if he wants to enjoy her body. If the wife of a man dies while he is pleased with her she will enter paradise. If a man wants sex his wife must comply with him even she is on the back of a camel". -(volume 2, p.43)

DIVORCE YOUR WIVES

If you want to get rid of your wife/wives and replace them with another set, you need only state I divorce you three times. There are no nasty court fights and no alimony to pay unless a wife is pregnant.

MARRIAGE OF CHILD BRIDES IS SUNNA

The AntiGod in his infinite wisdom and mercy in seeking to enhance the sexual pleasures of his exalted encourages the rape, sexual molestation of young Muslim Child Girls.

MURDER KAFIR MEN GUARANTEES ACCESSION TO PARADISE

Kafir men are not only a danger to the AntiGod but also potential sexual competitors to Muslim men. The kafir men who are kept as beasts of burden cannot enter the harem of the Muslim man without being castrated.

UNLIMITED TORTURE

If torture is what a Muslim man desires for his enjoyment and pleasure then the AntiGod allows the fulfillment of his desire to inflict pain.

ALL PROPERTY OF KAFIRS BELONGS TO MUSLIM MEN

The property of the kafirs belongs to the Muslims. They have only to take it giving the AntiGod a 20% cut of the booty/plunder.

UNLIMITED SEX WITH VIRGINS FOR ALL ETERNITY

For those Muslim men who kill kafirs or are killed in the attempt, their reward from the AntiGod is immediate accession to a Virgin Delight Paradise filled with virgins whom they can sexually molest for all eternity and who regenerate as virgins after each sex act.

UNLIMITED OWNERSHIP OF SLAVES

Muslim men can own and trade in kafir slaves to work the lands he has conquered from the kafirs.

MURDER YOUR CHILDREN

The honor of the Muslim man is defined by his wife/children. If they dishonor him, do not obey his will etc then he can kill them anyway he wishes including burying them alive.

MURDER HOMOSEXUALS

Muslim men can terrorize torture and murder homosexuals in the worst ways imaginable.

MUSLIM MAN INHERITS TWICE AS MUCH AS MUSLIM WOMAN.

No matter what a will declares - the Muslim man receives twice what a Muslim woman receives.

MUSLIM WOMEN MUST HAVE 4 WITNESSES IF RAPED

If A Muslim man is not happy with sexually molesting all his wives, raping his sex slaves, raping kafir women then he can rape Muslim women provided he ensures that there are not 4 Muslim men standing around to witness the rape. If a Muslim woman cannot provide 4 witnesses she will be stoned to death for adultery

A MOSQUE TOO FAR

SURRENDER IN OUR TIME

"In God We Trust" will Become "In Allah We Trust"

BANALITY OF EVIL

WHY 9/11 AND ALL MOSQUES MUST BE STOPPED

ALL MOSQUES ARE TROJAN HORSES

Sun Tzu (Ancient Chinese Philosopher) "For to win one hundred victories in one hundred battles is not the acme of skill. To subdue the enemy without fighting is the acme of skill."

Author: "For to have your enemies army and soldiers fighting and dying on your behalf in your cause and building monuments to your God who preaches their destruction and conquest, pay you tribute that you use to purchase weapons to give to your enemy to attack your tribute paying enemy while your army and soldiers are relaxing in the shade or sun tanning on a beach is the true, superior acme of skill."

THE 9/11 MASSACRE WAS COMMITTED BY GOOD, HOLY MUSLIM MEN OBEYING SHARIA LAW and QURAN TEACHING 9:111

(REMEMBER EVEN IF DUE TO TREMONDOUS POLITICAL PRESSURE THE 9/11 MOSQUE IS MOVED (AS NOW APPEARS LIKELY) NOTHING CHANGES. ALL MOSQUES (100%) TEACH THE QURAN, HADITH, SIRA, SHARIA LAW - THEY TEACH ISLAM. PRESIDENT OBAMA, BLOOMBERG ARE GIVING ISLAM RESPECTABILITY. THE MOVING OF THE MOSQUE WILL NOT BE A VICTORY AT ALL. IN FACT MOVING THE MOSQUE WILL BE A GREAT VICTORY FOR ISLAM. OUR ELITES WILL BE FALLING ALL OVER THEMSELVES TO PROCLAIM MODERATE ISLAM AND ISLAMIC TOLERANCE AND THIS WILL CLEAR THE WAY FOR MEGA MOSQUES TO BE BUILT EVERYWHERE. ALL MOSQUES ARE

THE HOUSES OF SHARIA LAW AND STAND AGAINST EVERYTHING AMERICA STANDS FOR

On September 30 1938, Neville Chamberlain signed the Munich Agreement with Adolf Hitler, flew back to London, and waved a piece of paper in the air and proclaimed: "Peace in our time."

President Obama and Mayor Bloomberg have taken to the airwaves, standing in front of microphones and proclaiming by their support of the 9/11 Mosque; " SURRENDER IN OUR TIME."

God created man in his own image. Prophet Muhammad created a God in his image - the AntiGod Allah. All mosques stand as monuments to the AntiGod Allah and his messenger. A mosque is a country within a country. The ground upon which the mosque has been built is now the conquered territory of Islam. A mosque is where Sharia Law is enforced on Muslim women and children depriving them of their Constitutional rights as Americans.

By building the 9/11mosque, Muslims have in effect made it into a gigantic minaret – a symbol of Islamic power. From atop this minaret mosque as far as the Muslim eye can see all lands within his view are the conquered territory of Islam. Unless this mosque is stopped, the World Trade Center has now been conquered by Islam. It's just a matter of time before Muslims demand the same right of churches in New York to issue their call to prayer – which in Islam is a warning to all kafirs convert to Islam or die.

The struggle against Islam is an intellectual struggle in which symbolism means everything. Muslims cannot conquer with armies the United States or any European country. The West is being conquered from within. By not confronting Islam and destroying its ideology, the US and the West are surrendering to the process of Islamization. Our elites in their hatred of Western/American civilization have formed an unholy alliance with Muslims using democracy and freedom to destroy democracy and freedom.

To truly understand what ALL mosques represent, we re-state the reality of Islam that is taught in ALL mosques: it is the holy, divine duty of all Muslims to conquer all nations of the world, exterminate all Jews and Christians who refuse to convert or pay Jizya tax and accept dimmi status, murder all other male kafirs who refuse to convert to Islam, enslave their women and children, destroy ALL other religions and replace them with Islam. Again, **freedom of religion in Islam is only the freedom to practice Islam. The above ideology is Islam and it is taught in every mosque.**

Following is just a sample of Quranic verses that are taught in every mosque calling for destruction of all other religions. Don't forget every word was written by God.

The only religion is the religion of Allah, Islam...16:52
Muslims (Islam) are the best of righteous people...3:110

Allah has perfected Islam and it is the only religion for mankind (last verse revealed, and so, the final word of Allah disclosed to Muhammad)...5:3

Islam is the perfect religion; it will dominate all other religions...9:33

Can't worship anything other than Allah; Islam is the only right religion (the purpose of an Islamic state)...12:40

There is only one God (Allah) and all should bow to Islam...21:108
Allah proclaims Islam (the religion of truth) over all other religions…48:28

Allah has sent Muhammad to proclaim the 'Religion of Truth' (Islam) over all religions...61:9

As already stated in "Myth of Moderate Muslim" but because of its importance repeated here – "Sharia Law is the divine constitution of God and can never be changed in any way. Sharia law is the basis for the religious, political and cultural life of all Muslims. As with the Quran, a good, holy, moderate, moral Muslim must believe ALL Sharia Law. He cannot challenge any teaching of Sharia otherwise he will be killed. Following are just a few of the teachings of Sharia Law: **"Mocking anything in the Qur'an or the Sunnah of the prophet Muhammad is apostasy and therefore punishable by death. Criticizing Islam, shari'ah law or the Sunnah of the prophet Muhammad is apostasy and therefore punishable by death. Any Muslim who states a preference for democracy rather than shari'ah law or questions anything in the Qur'an or Sunnah is a kafir (disbeliever), considered an apostate, and therefore sentenced to death."** The 9/11 attack on the World Trade Center was done in adherence to the rules of war, jihad, found in Sharia law. You cannot be a good moral human being and believe in the legal barbarism that is Sharia Law. But again as we have already shown, as a good, moral, holy Muslim man you MUST believe in Sharia." In the United States and all western democracies Muslims are not living in freedom and democracy but under the dictatorship and oppression of the kafir. Only when the Muslim is living under Sharia Law and the kafir constitution has been destroyed and replaced with Sharia will the Muslim finally be free.

Again, in this mosque (and ALL mosques) the 4,000 evil teachings of the Quran will be taught. As we have already demonstrated, 9/11 was teaching 9:111 of the Quran. Can you imagine building a monument to the 19 9/11 killers and Muslims celebrating in their community center/swimming pool - the greatest victory in Islam's history? Can you imagine Mayor Bloomberg stating that young Americans are fighting in Afghanistan/Iraq so Muslims can build a mosque to celebrate an ideology that has as its major teachings their mass murder, extermination of Jews and Christians, rape, slavery, sex slaves, oppression of women and the destruction of democracy and freedom. Again, in Islam, these teachings are not crimes but holy, divine sacraments guaranteeing accession to Paradise for those Muslims who slay or are slain in the service of God.(9:111)

Young Americans are being murdered in Afghanistan/Iraq by Muslims following the teachings of the Quran that are taught in ALL mosques. There are not 2 Qurans. There is only one. There are not two Islams. There is only one Islam.

The 9/11 families are an embarrassment to President Obama/Bloomberg. By their defiant, heroic stand against the 9/11 mosque, they don't fit the Obama/Bloomberg narrative of tolerance. President/Mayor don't dare try to cow them by branding these 9/11 loved ones racist bigots. Both wish these families and their supporters would just fade away. President Obama and Mayor Bloomberg have formed an alliance with prophet Muhammad who as we have already seen (and we cannot repeat often enough to drive home how evil this man was) had a woman stoned to death in front of her child, stoned adulterers, married, raped and molested a child, raped and sexually molested his other wives, forced sex during menstruation, raped a retarded woman, raped his sex slaves, owned and traded in slaves, had the pants of 13 and 14 year old Jewish boys pulled down and those boys with the slightest growth of pubic hair were beheaded along with 600 to 900 of their fathers, brothers, uncles, neighbors, had followers and their families burnt alive in their homes for missing prayer – the on ending horror of prophet Muhammad. This is what President/Bloomberg is bringing to New York – on ending barbarism. This is the on ending barbarism in every mosque no matter their location. It will be just a matter of time before Jewish mothers can no longer send their children to school wearing kippahs. It will be just a matter of time before Jewish men will not be able to walk the streets of New York without fear of being attacked. Just as in Europe where Jews are being driven from their cities and country in the third mass exile, Jews in New York will be forced to flee for their lives. Just as in Europe where rape jihad is in full force so to New York kafir women will be raped by Muslim men. Just as in Europe the legal system will turn a blind eye to these rapings.

All Americans who oppose the teachings of Islam, the Quran, the building of this mosque or any mosque have committed capital crimes against Islam and the AntiGod Allah and must be murdered. President Obama/Bloomberg and all supporters of this mosque are using the freedoms granted by the Constitution to destroy the Constitution. They are using Freedom of Religion to destroy Freedom of Religion. The Second World War was a titanic struggle between THE GOOD and THE EVIL. There was no in-between. Tonight mankind faces another titanic struggle between THE GOOD and THE EVIL that is Islam. All the supporters of this Mosque have chosen to stand with THE EVIL. They have joined the forces of the AntiGod Allah. This mosque is a travesty and stands against everything America stands for. **ALL mosques are a travesty and stand against everything America stands for.**

FREEDOM OF RELIGION IN ISLAM IS FREEDOM TO PRACTISE ISLAM ONLY

Muslims throughout the USA are demanding their religious rights to practice their religion guaranteed by the constitution. Our elites are demanding that we respect the religious freedom of Muslims. They are calling all those who oppose Islam racist bigots and comparing opposition to the 9/11 mosque as Islamophobia and hatred against Muslims. Why are so many including this author opposing Islam? We are not fighting Muslims. We are fighting Islam.

Muslims are immigrating not to live in freedom and democracy but to conquer, destroy the constitution, impose Sharia Law and make Islam the only religion. Following are the holy, divine sacraments of Islam. This is what freedom of religion means to Muslim men. Repeating this central tenat in Islam - Freedom of Religion is Freedom To Practice Islam Only. Again, Muslims are blessed by kafir blood.

HOLY, DIVINE SACRAMENTS OF ISLAM

1. Exterminate kafirs. Christians/Jews must pay Jizya tax to Muslims, accept dimmi status as per Quran 9.29 or die. In Denmark, Christian churches are paying Jizya. Murder of kafirs is a divine, holy act.
2. Declare Jihad to conquer the kafirs. War against kafirs is a divine act.
3. Rape kafir women (no matter their age.) Rape is a divine, holy act.
4. Own and rape sex slaves.
5. Own and breed slaves. Slavery is a divine institution of the AntiGod.
6. Loot/plunder kafir property. Robbery is sunna.
7. Destroy all other religions.
8. Impose Sharia Law.
9. Stone adulterers.
10. Assassinate Islam's enemies.
11. Murder all those who challenge Islam.
12. Impose Islamic supremacy.
13. Terrorize kafirs.
14. Torture kafirs.
15. Murder homosexuals.
16. Murder apostates of Islam.
17. Preach hate of Jews/Christians/ all other kafirs.

These are the sacraments of the AntiGod Allah sanctifying the divine actions of Muslim men. This is the religious freedom President Obama/Bloomberg and all the other political/media/intellectual elites supporting Islam are fighting for under the guise of religious freedom. The AntiGod Allah is no God and Islam is no religion. All those supporting Islam are supporting not democracy and freedom but totalitarianism. Islam stands against everything the Constitution stands for. We are on the verge of entering a black hole from which we can never emerge.

COMPARISON OF BIBLE AND QURAN

One of the most frequently used arguments heard in the defense of Islam is that the Bible is just as violent as the Koran. The logic goes like this. If the Koran is no more violent than the Bible, then why should we worry about Islam? This argument is that Islam is the same as Christianity and Judaism. This is false, but this analogy is very popular, since it allows someone who knows nothing about the actual doctrine of Islam to talk about it. "See, Islam is like Christianity, Christians are just as violent as Muslims." If this is true, then you don't have to learn anything about the actual Islamic doctrine.

However, this is not a theological argument. It is a political one. This argument is not about what goes on in a house of worship, but what goes on the in the marketplace of ideas. Now, is the doctrine of Islam more violent than the Bible? There is only one way to prove or disprove the comparison and that is to measure the differences in violence in the Koran and the Bible.

The first item is to define violence. The only violence that matters to someone outside of either Islam or Christianity or Judaism is what they do to the "other", political violence. Cain killing Able is not political violence. Political violence is not killing a lamb for a meal or making an animal sacrifice. Note, however, a vegan or a PETA member considers both of these actions to be violent, but it is not violence against them.

The next item is to compare the doctrines both quantitatively and qualitatively. The political violence of the Koran is called "fighting in Allah's cause", or jihad. We must do more than measure the jihad in the Koran. Islam has three sacred texts: Koran, Sira and Hadith, the Islamic Trilogy. The Sira is Mohammed's biography. The Hadith are his traditions—what he did and said. Sira and Hadith form the Sunna, the perfect pattern of all Islamic behavior.

The Koran is the smallest of the three books, the Trilogy. It is only 16% of the Trilogy text . This means that the Sunna is 84% of the word content of Islam's sacred texts. This statistic alone has large implications. Most of the Islamic doctrine is about Mohammed, not Allah. The Koran says 91 different times that Mohammed is the perfect pattern of life. It is much more important to know Mohammed than the Koran. This is very good news. It is easy to understand a biography about a man. To know Islam, know Mohammed.

It turns out that jihad occurs in large proportion in all three texts. Here is a chart about the results:

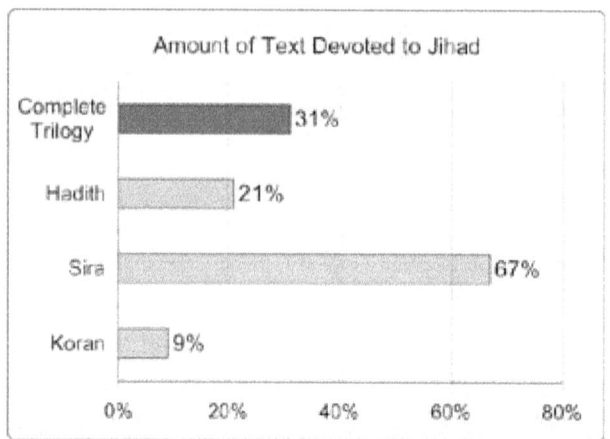

It is very significant that the Sira devotes 67% of its text to jihad. Mohammed averaged an event of violence every 6 weeks for the last 9 years of his life. Jihad was what made Mohammed successful. Here is a chart of the growth of Islam.

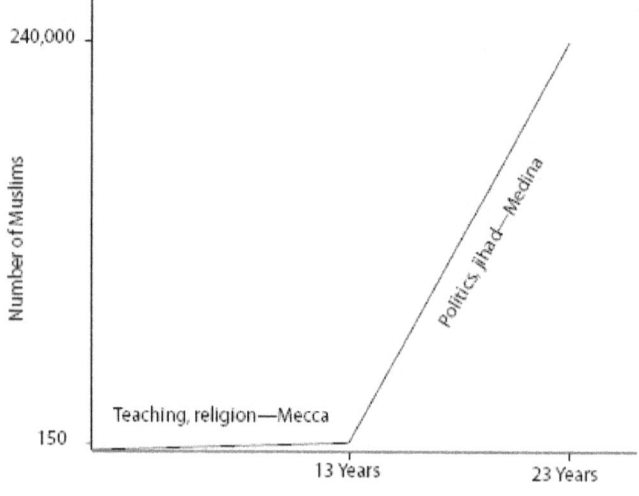

Growth of Islam

Basically, when Mohammed was a preacher of religion, Islam grew at the rate of 10 new Muslims per year. But when he turned to jihad, Islam grew at an average rate of 10,000 per year. All of the details of how to wage jihad are recorded in great detail. The Koran gives the great vision of jihad—world conquest by the political process. The Sira is a strategic manual and the Hadith is a tactical manual of jihad. Now let's go to the Hebrew Bible. When we count all of the political violence, we find that 5.6% of the text is devoted to it. There is no admonition towards political violence in the New Testament. When we count the magnitude of words devoted to political violence, we have 327,547 words in the

Trilogy and 34,039 words in the Hebrew Bible. The Trilogy has 9.6 times as much wordage devoted to political violence as the Hebrew Bible.

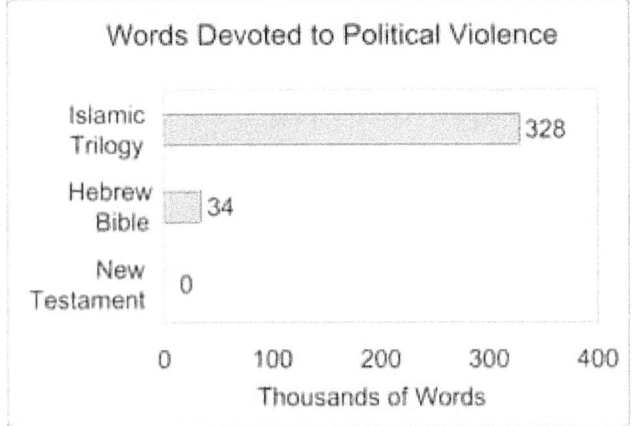

The real problem goes far beyond the quantitative measurement of ten times as much violent material; there is the qualitative measurement. The political violence of the Koran is eternal and universal. The political violence of the Bible was for that particular historical time and place. This is the vast difference between Islam and other ideologies. The violence remains a constant threat to all non-Islamic cultures, now and into the future. Islam is not analogous to Christianity and Judaism in any practical way. Beyond the one-god doctrine, Islam is unique unto itself. Another measurement of the difference between the violence found in the Judeo/Christian texts as opposed to that of Islam is found in the use of fear of violence against artists, critics and intellectuals. What artist, critic or intellectual ever feels a twinge of fear if condemning anything Christian or Jewish? However, look at the examples of the violent political threats and murders of Salman Rushdie, Theo van Gogh, Pim Fortune, Kurt Westergaard of the Danish Mohammed cartoons, and many others. What artist, critic or intellectual has not had a twinge of fear about Islam when it comes to free expression? The political difference in the response to the two different doctrines is enormous. The political fruit from the two trees is as different as night and day. It is time for so-called intellectuals to get down to the basics of judging Islam by its actual doctrine, not making lame analogies that are sophomoric assertions. Fact-based reasoning should replace fantasies that are based upon political correctness and multiculturalism. The crimes that were committed by Christians were crimes against the teachings of Jesus/God whereas in Islam crimes against God are holy, divine, external sacraments –the laws of the AntiGod Allah. They are Islam. All teachings in all religious texts of violence, hate are not Moral Perfection and therefore not the word of God but of man. In Christianity this invalidates only the teaching but in Islam if only one word of the Quran is immoral imperfection then the entire Quran is not the word of God but of man and therefore Islam is fraudulent.

STATISTICAL ISLAM

As stated previously, we will demonstrate throughout this book, throughout history God has never committed a criminal act. Not one. Before we begin examining the Quran word by word, teaching by teaching for one word of immoral imperfection, we will first study a statistical analysis of the Quran and Islam. Let us restate the three major requirements for Islam to be from God: every word of Quran must be Moral Perfection. Every teaching of Sharia Law must be Moral Perfection. Muhammad cannot be a criminal. Repeating from "Crimes of Muhammad" "We hold the following truth to be self evident – ONLY A GOD OF MORAL PERFECTION IS GOD. If God committed just one criminal act, killed or ordered the killing of just one human being or any other creature in the entire universe then God would no longer be Moral Perfection and therefore no longer God. If God created teachings of extermination, murder, war, fighting, violence, terror, torture, slaughter, looting, stealing, slavery, sex slaves, rape, hate, revenge, oppression and inequality of women, races, Muslims and non Muslims, then God would no longer be Moral Perfection and therefore no longer God.

In order for the Quran to be the divine, timeless, unchangeable word of God, every word of the Quran must be Moral Perfection. If only one word is immoral imperfection – just ONE WORD then not only is the Quran not from God but ALL Islam is fraudulent.

In order for Sharia Law to be the divine constitution of God every teaching of Sharia must be Moral Perfection. If just ONE teaching is immoral imperfection then Sharia Law is not from God and ALL Islam is fraudulent.

In order to be a prophet of God and receive divine teachings from God via Angel Gabriel, Muhammad could not be a criminal. There are many men who have lived horrid lives. They have raped, murdered, and burned cities to the ground. Horrible acts. Then one day, they come into the light of God and totally change. Begging forgiveness, they spend the rest of their lives atoning for their great crimes as holy men of God. In the case of Muhammad, we have a criminal who created the AntiGod Allah to sanction his criminality: A child molester. Wife abuser. Rapist. Murderer. Torturer. Terrorist just a small sample of the criminality of Muhammad listed below. If God picked such a prophet to represent him anywhere in the universe and gave divine sanction and support/encouragement to His prophet's criminal acts then God would no longer be Moral Perfection and therefore no longer God but just an accomplice to his evil prophet. God would be equally guilty in all the criminal acts perpetrated by Muhammad. God would be just a wanton criminal. " End quote

Again, in order to have received Quranic verses transmitted by Angel Gabriel from God then every word of the Quran must be Moral Perfection. As we shall prove next with Statistical Analysis and later with a detailed examination of thousands of teachings - given that the Quran is filled with thousands of immoral words/teachings then Muhammad never met Gabriel. Not one word was ever spoken to Muhammad by Gabriel.

We will destroy Islam not with one word of immoral imperfection but with thousands of words/teachings. Now lets examine Islam employing Statistical Analysis complied by Bill Warner – www.politicalislam.com for a detailed analysis of the evil, immoral, depravity of Islam. Bill has statistically examined EVERY word/teaching of the Quran/Hadith/Sira. As stated, there are 327,547 words of violence in the trilogy. This is about 800/900 pages.

As Bill will prove there is not one teaching of the Quran that is Moral Perfection. **Not One**. Quoting from later in his statistical analysis:

" **The Good in the Koran**

In the face of these negative statistics, everyone knows of good verses in the Koran. Exactly how much material in the Koran is positive for Kafirs? There are 245 verses, 4,018 words, in the Koran that say something positive about Kafirs. This is about 2.6% of the total Koranic text . **However, in every case, the verse is followed by another verse that contradicts the "good" verses. Also, except for 7 verses (58 words), the "good" verse is abrogated later in the same chapter. The other 7 verses are contradicted in later Suras.**"

Bill Warner is one of the great unsung heroes in the struggle against Islam.

STATISTICAL ISLAM

Statistical Islam, Part 1

One of the great questions of the 21st century is: What is the true nature of Islam? There are two distinct answers to this question from the media and leaders. The popular message is that Islam is one of the great world religions, a peaceful religion, a foundation of world civilization, its Golden Age was the highpoint of history, and it preserved Western thought while we were in the Dark Ages. The alternative message is that Islam is a brutal, backward, woman abusing, violent, intellectually narrow ideology that is out to annihilate civilization.

Which side is right? How do we resolve this issue? Can it even be resolved? If we turn to the "experts" of any of the opinions, they will tell you that their view is correct. What then is the ultimate authority that will give us a firm foundation for reasoning and judgment about Islam? Is it possible to use critical thought or must we just accept the authority of experts?

There is way to achieve consensus about ideas that goes beyond expert opinion. The use of facts along with logic is the basis of critical thought. The ultimate form of critical thought uses measurements and numbers to resolve questions. This paper will use the foundational texts of Islam and measure the importance of ideas by how many words are given to concepts. The assumption is that the more content that is devoted to a subject, the greater the importance of the subject is. As an example: the Koran devotes 64% of its text to the subject of the unbeliever. This is assumed to imply that the unbeliever is important in Islamic doctrine.

The use of critical thought may seem counter-intuitive since many people view Islam as a religion that does not have a rational basis. Actually, Islam is not only rational; it is hyper-rational, but it uses another form of logic than the one we take for granted.

If we are to use critical thought, we must have a firm foundation.

All Muslims agree that: "There is no god, but Allah and Mohammed is His messenger."

When this is repeated as a public testimony, you become a Muslim. However, this statement is not only the beginning of Islam, it is also the foundation and totality of Islam. It is not enough to worship Allah; you must worship as Mohammed worshipped.

Who is Allah and where do we learn about Him? This question points directly to the Koran.

Then the Koran, in turn, points directly to Mohammed. It says 91 times that Mohammed is the perfect Muslim. He is the divine human prototype, the only pattern acceptable to Allah. The actions and words of Mohammed are so important that they have a special name—Sunna. We find the Sunna in two texts. The Sira is the biography of Mohammed and the Hadith is the collection of hadiths (small stories, traditions) about Mohammed.

Islam is based on Koran and Sunna. Since the Sunna is found in the Sira and the Hadith, this means that three books contain all the doctrine of Islam—the Trilogy. If it is in the Trilogy (Koran, Sira, Hadith), then it is Islam. If something is not in the Trilogy, then it is not Islam. All of the Islamic doctrine is found in the Trilogy. Now, we have the complete information with no missing pieces.

We have established our first criteria of knowledge. All authoritative statements about Islam must include a reference to the Trilogy to be authenticated. It does not matter what a scholar, imam, media guru, or anyone else says, if what they say cannot be supported by the doctrine in the Trilogy, then it is not Islam. If it is supported by the Trilogy, then it is Islam.

We have been taught that the Koran is the source of Islamic doctrine. However, the Koran is only 14% of the total sacred texts . Actually, the Sira and the Hadith are 86% of the total textual doctrine: Hadith is 60% and Sira is 26%. Islam is 14% Allah and 86% Mohammed. This is very good news. The Koran is obscure, but anyone can understand the life and sayings of Mohammed. These statistics point to the easy way to know Islam—know Mohammed. Anyone, absolutely anyone, can understand Mohammed and hence, Islam.

Islam is a text-based doctrine, so the nature of these texts must be made clear. A Muslim believes that the Koran is perfect, complete, universal and eternal. It does not contain the slightest error and it is the exact words of the only god of the universe. Mohammed is the perfect example of how to live the sacred life. This idea of complete, final, universal, and perfect textual truth is very hard for non-Muslims to comprehend. Most people read the Koran with the attitude of: "Oh, they don't really believe this." When Muslims read the Koran, their attitude is: "These are the perfect words of Allah." Muslims call themselves the "believers" and by that they mean that they believe the Koran is perfect and Mohammed is the perfect pattern of life.

Remember, we started with the question: Can we evaluate what the media commentators, politicians, imams and other "experts" say about the true nature of Islam? Yes, we can know the true nature of Islam—it is found in the Trilogy. If what the expert has to say can be supported by the doctrine found in the Trilogy, then it is valid, since the Trilogy is the final arbiter of all opinions and statements about Islam.

Critical thought provides a powerful first step. Now, let us measure the doctrine of Islam. The following cases show how the technique of counting the number of words that are devoted to a topic can be used to discover the dominant themes of Islamic texts and, hence, Islamic doctrine.

Statistical Islam, Part 2

Case 1: The Koran of Mohammed

Mohammed can be clearly understood, but the Koran must be the most famous book that has been read so little and understood even less. Contrast this with Mohammed's day. In the Sira (the biography of Mohammed), we find accounts of illiterate Muslims debating the meaning of the Koran. The Muslims of Mohammed's day understood the Koran for a simple reason. The Koran of 632 AD (Mohammed's death) is not the one of today. Every verse had the immediate context of Mohammed's life. A new verse had the context of what he needed at that time. To all those near Mohammed, each new verse made sense; it had a context and therefore meaning. The voice of Allah resolved Mohammed's problems. It is Mohammed's life that gives the Koran its context and meaning.

The Koran of the bookstore is not the historical Koran of Mohammed, because Uthman, a caliph (supreme ruler) had it arranged starting with the longest chapter and ending at the shortest chapter. After he created the Koran we know today, he burned the originals. The time and story have been annihilated by the rearrangement. From a statistical point of view, the text was randomized and, hence, very difficult to understand.

It is an easy task to reconstruct the Koran of Mohammed's day, the historical Koran. Take the Koran and rearrange the pages of the chapters in the proper chronological order in a line on a table, since the time order of the chapters is well known. Then take the pages of the Sira (Mohammed's biography) and lay them out in a line beneath the Koran. It will be seen that the Sira and the Koran fit together like a key in a lock. The Koran is the warp and the Sira is the woof that forms a single fabric, the historical Koran. If these two are integrated into one text, the historical Koran is reconstructed.

When this reconstruction is done, the Koran becomes the epic story of the rise and triumph of Islam over all of the native Arab culture. The historical Koran is straightforward and not confusing at all. Just as in Mohammed's day, anyone can understand it.

The historical Koran reveals the primary division of the text. The early Koran written in Mecca is very different from the later Koran written in Medina. The early Koran is more religious and poetic. The later Koran is more historical and political. There is a radical change in its tone, subject and language in the two texts. The difference is even clear to a first-time reader. There is a Meccan Koran and a Medinan Koran. The relative sizes of the two Korans are: Meccan Koran is about 64% of the total Koran; the Medinan Koran is 36% of the total .

Statistical Islam, Part 3

Case 2: The Kafir

There is a second division that overwhelms the reader of the historical Koran. A majority of the text concerns the Kafir (unbeliever). It is not about being a Muslim, but about the Kafir. A note: most Koran translations use the word "unbeliever" instead of Kafir, but Kafir is the actual Arabic word.

This term is so important and so unknown that the meaning of Kafir must be defined. The original meaning of the word is one who covers or conceals the known truth. A Kafir knows that the Koran is true, but denies it. The Koran says that the Kafir may be deceived, plotted against, hated, enslaved, mocked, tortured and worse. The word is usually translated as "unbeliever" but this translation is wrong. The word "unbeliever" is logically and emotionally neutral, whereas, Kafir is the most abusive, prejudiced and hateful word in any language.

There are many religious names for Kafirs: polytheists, idolaters, People of the Book (Christians and Jews), atheists, agnostics, and pagans. Kafir covers them all, because no matter what the religious name is, they can all be treated the same. What Mohammed said and did to polytheists can be done to any other category of Kafir.

Islam devotes a great amount of energy to the Kafir. Not only is the majority (64%) of the Koran devoted to the Kafir, but also nearly all of the Sira (81%) deals with Mohammed's struggle with them. The Hadith (Traditions) devotes 32% of the text to Kafirs. 60% of the entire Trilogy text is devoted to the kafir.

Statistical Islam, Part 4

Case 3: Political Islam

Religious Islam is defined as doctrine concerned with going to Paradise and avoiding Hell by following the Koran and the Sunna. The part of Islam that deals with the "outsider", the Kafir, is defined as political Islam. Since so much of the Trilogy is about the Kafir, the statistical conclusion is that Islam is primarily a political system, not a religious system.

Mohammed's success depended on politics, not religion. The Sira, Mohammed's biography, gives a highly detailed accounting of his rise to power. He preached the religion of Islam for 13 years in Mecca and garnered 150 followers. He was forced to move to Medina and became a politician and warrior. During the last 9 years of his life, he was involved in an event of violence every 6 weeks. When he died every Arab was a Muslim. Mohammed succeeded through politics, not religion.

An estimate can be made that there were 100,000 Muslims when Mohammed died.

There are two distinct growth processes-religion and politics. Teaching and religion grew at a rate of about 12 new Muslims per year. Politics and jihad grew at a rate of 10,000 new Muslims per year, an enormous increase. This is a process yield improvement of over 800%. Politics was almost a thousand times more effective than religion.

If Mohammed had continued with preaching religion we can extrapolate that there would have only been 265 Muslims when he died, instead of the 100,000 that resulted from his politics and jihad. This gives us an estimate of 265 conversions due to religion and 99,735 conversions to due the political jihad process. We can calculate the relative contributions of religion and politics in growth. Islam's success was 0.3% religion and 99.7% politics at the time of Mohammed's death, 632 AD.

This political importance is reflected in the text of the Sira. There are many more pages devoted to a year of jihad than there are devoted to preaching Islam. It is instructive to see the amount of the Sira text devoted to these stages of development.

AMOUNT OF SIRA DEVOTED TO TOPIC

Teaching Religion Mecca   4,300

Politics/Jihad Medina   22,000

The Sira devotes about 5 times as many words to politics than religion on a yearly basis. It gives politics 5 times the coverage because it is that much more important.

Islam's political nature is also found in the Hadith that devotes 37% of its text to the Kafir.

There would be no Islam today, if it were only a religion. Statistics show that Islamic politics is what brought Islam success, not religion. To say that Islam is the religion of peace misses the point, since the religion is not the core of Islam's power. It is politics that count, not religion.

The statistical conclusion: Islam is primarily a political ideology.

Statistical Islam, Part 5

Case 4: Abrogation and Dualism

Not only are there two Korans, Meccan and Medinan, that are different in tone and subject matter, but also the Koran has many verses that contradict each other.

Koran 2:219 says that Muslims should be tolerant and forgiving to People of the Book.

Koran 9:29 says to attack the People of the Book until they pay the jizyah, the dhimmi tax, submit to Sharia law and be humbled.
Which verse shows the true nature of Islam?

The Koran recognizes its contradictions and even gives a rule to resolve the contradictions. The later verse abrogates (supercedes) the earlier verse. This does not mean, however, that the earlier verse is wrong or in error. This would be impossible since the fundamental hypothesis is that Allah created the Koran and, hence, the earlier verse must be true or Allah would be wrong.

Abrogation has an impact on the arguments about the true nature of Islam. At endless interfaith dialogs, the early tolerant verse is quoted to show the nature of Islam as being peaceful. When both verses are quoted and then abrogation is applied, we see that the later verse trumps the earlier tolerant one. Jihad abrogates tolerance. In general, the Medinan Koran abrogates the Meccan Koran. In the two verses above, tolerance is abrogated by jihad against the Christians.

But, the earlier verse is true and still used. Abrogation does not negate the early verse. Indeed, the earlier "peaceful" verse that is abrogated is the one most apt to be used in public discourse.

This creates a logical problem, since if two things contradict each other, at least one of them must be false. This is a fundamental element of Western unitary logic. In Koranic logic, two statements can contradict each other and both are true. This is dualistic logic.

An alternative explanation is that the early verse is first stage in a process, like a seed, and the later verse is a second stage, like a plant. There is truth to this, but the process model does not take into account the fact that both truths are available at the same time. To go back to the analogy, you don't have the seed and the plant at the same time. The verses contradict each other and are both true at the same time. This is dualistic logic.

The contradictions are usually explained by abrogation, the classical doctrine, but the principle of abrogation is limited to the Koran. Duality includes the special case of abrogation and it explains how the entire doctrine of Koran and Sunna work. It is not just the Koran that is contradictory, but all of the Sunna.
Another dualistic aspect of Islam is its ethics. One of the chief features of Islam is the doctrine of the Kafir. It treats them dreadfully and horribly. No one would ever want to be treated as a Kafir is treated in the Trilogy. This leads us to the Golden Rule. There is no Golden Rule in Islam because of the division of humanity into believer and Kafir. The Golden Rule is to treat ALL people as you would be treated. Since no one wants be treated like a Kafir, and the Kafir is so central to Islamic doctrine, it proves that Islam has no Golden Rule. Islam has one set of rules for Muslims and another set of rules for Kafirs. This is dualistic ethics. An example of the dual ethics is the subject of friends. The Koran has 13 verses that say that a Muslim is not to be a friend of Kafirs.

Case 5: Jews

One of the biggest examples of ethical dualism in Islam is the Jews. The Meccan Koran is filled with stories about Moses, Noah, Adam, and other Jewish figures. The early Koran is very Jewish. The perception of the Jews completely changes in Medina. Every verse, story, and hadith is negative and anti-Jew. The Trilogy devotes a great deal of material to the Jews.

ANTI JEWISH TEXT IN TRILOGY

Meccan Quran   1%
Medinan Quran   17%

Sira   12%

Hadith   8.9%
_____
Total Trilogy   9.3%

Mein Kampf   7 %

The Trilogy of Medina is even more negative about the Jews than Hitler's *Mein Kampf*. What marks the biggest difference between *Mein Kampf* and the Trilogy is that Hitler did not write a first section in *Mein Kampf* detailing how much he admired the Jews. There is a contradiction about how the Koran treats Jews in Mecca and how they are treated in Medina. Due to dualistic reasoning, both attitudes about the Jews are true, at the same time.

Case 6: The Good in the Koran

In the face of these negative statistics, everyone knows of good verses in the Koran. Exactly how much material in the Koran is positive for Kafirs? There are 245 verses, 4,018 words, in the Koran that say something positive about Kafirs. This is about 2.6% of the total Koranic text . However, in every case, the verse is followed by another verse that contradicts the "good" verses. Also, except for 7 verses (58 words), the "good" verse is abrogated later in the same chapter. The other 7 verses are contradicted in later Suras.

The media emphasizes Islam's positive verses about the People of the Book, the Jews and Christians. Even this turns out to be illusive. Christians and Jews receive the goodness of Islam only if they agree that their sacred texts are corrupt, the Koran is true, and that Mohammed is a prophet of the Christian and Jewish religion.

In the end there is no unmitigated good for Kafirs in the Koran. What good can be found in the 2.6% of the text is denied later.

Case 7: Jihad

> Jihad must be one of the most famous Islamic concepts. It takes up a large portion of the Trilogy. Material for jihad is 24% of the Medinan Koran and 9% of the total of the entire Koran. Jihad takes up 21% of the Bukhari material and the Sira devotes 67% of its text to jihad.

Amount of Trilogy Text Devoted to Jihad

Meccan Quran   0%

Medinan Quran   24%

Sira   67%

Hadith   21%

Total Trilogy   31%

Percentage of Koran Text Devoted to Jihad

Statistics gives us a measure of the claim that the real jihad is inner struggle, the so-called "greater jihad", whereas the jihad of the sword is the "lesser jihad". The term "greater jihad" is not found in any of the canonical texts and Reuven Firestone[12] claims that it does not exist. However, we do find in the Hadith that some hadiths refer to some religious acts that are equal to jihad of the sword. These quasi-greater jihad hadiths total 2% of the Bukhari hadiths that relate to jihad. Of course, the other 98% of the hadiths devoted to jihad claim that jihad of the sword is the supreme act. The statistical answer to the true nature of jihad is that the "greater jihad" of inner struggle is 2% and the "lesser jihad" of the sword is 98%. In other words, jihad is overwhelmingly violent and a little inner struggle.

Statistics also give us a measure of the importance of the jihad of pen and mouth. The Sira devotes 23% of its text to war poetry that is propaganda. This poetry, which is not the only example of how Mohammed used propaganda for his jihad, furnishes us with an insight into its importance. The Sira devotes roughly a quarter of its jihad text to the jihad of the pen and mouth, and three quarters of the text to jihad of the sword. The Sira makes no mention of the "greater jihad", the inner struggle

Case 8: Women

Islam demonstrates duality in its treatment of women. There are separate sets of rules for women that come from the Koran and the Sunna.

The Islamic Trilogy has a large amount of material that forms the doctrine about women. Each verse can be judged on the position of the female in society. There are a number of verses that praise the mother above all men. There are many verses that say that women and men will be judged equally as to their actions on Judgment Day. In many cases there is no power relationship at all; it is a neutral reference.

The process for generating the tables below selects all of the text that contains a reference to the female. Then the female data is sorted into four categories: High status, equal status, low status and neutral. Obviously, there are judgments to be made, but in general, if women are selected for special rules and treatment by men, then those rules make the woman subject to male power.

The first data is from the Koran:

Women's Status in the Koran

	Wrds	Fraction of total	Num Verses	Fraction of 151 Verses
High Status	693	5.7%	11	0.73%
Equal Status	2831	23%	38	25%
Low Status	8592	71%	102	67%
Total (Non-neutral)	12066		151	

Women's Status in the Hadith

	Wrds	Num Hadiths	As a Fraction of Hadith(331)	Fraction of Total(49151)
High Status	62	2	0.60%	0.13%
Equal Status	3509	33	10%	7.1%
Low Status	45580	296	89 %	93%
Total	49151	331		

(Non-neutral)

Notice the broad trend here. In both the Koran and the Hadith the profiles are similar. There is very little high status and a small amount of equality. The great majority of the Koran and Hadith text places the woman in an inferior or low status to men. This is not unexpected. The Koran and the Sunna are the warp and woof, a single fabric, of Islam.

The Importance of Numbers

We have always had an interest in numbers as they relate to life. There are two numbers that come up repeatedly in Islam. The number "1" comes up with the constant proclamation of there is only one god. What is noticeable is how often the number "2" arises. There are two Korans, the division of humanity into two groups, believer and kafir, two manifestations of Mohammed, the preacher and the politician. Even the Shahada [the testimony to become a Muslim] is made of two parts, one is about god and the other is about Mohammed. The ultimate statement is both divine and human, dualism. Islam's ethics are dualistic and based on the division of humanity

into two classes, believer and kafir. The Koran advances a dualistic logic. Islam uses the practice of political duality to try to attain the goal of spiritual unity.

Statistics

Statistics give us a very different vision of any text, but in the case of Islamic texts, it is a revelation. Statistics show us an entirely different view of Islam. The statistical vision is holistic and includes the entire text as a reference. It is a common criticism that any negative comment about Islam is taken out of context. Statistics gives us a complete context.

A question was posed at the beginning of this article: How do we decide which is the true view of Islam? Based upon unitary logic, we expect that one side or the other is true, but in a dualistic truth system both sides of the question can be valid. Therefore, the proper answer is that both sides are true.

In fact, the question is poorly posed. You can never resolve the question by looking for the one true answer. It does not exist in a dualistic system. Instead statistics must be used to measure the answer. We saw, in the case of the lesser jihad/greater jihad that jihad is 2% inner struggle and 98% lethal force. Only statistical answers can be used in a dualistic system. The well-posed question is how much doctrine is on one side of the question and how much doctrine is on the other side?

Statistical models give us a systemic look at Islamic doctrine and show broad trends. The usual verse-quoting method not only ignores Mohammed, but also examines a single point, a verse. Statistics gives us a macro-view, not a micro-view. We can see the entire pattern and can identify the general principles at work.

Summary

Critical thought brings new insights to the study of Islam. Islam is not a matter of opinion, but has a solid rational basis in its foundational texts. Simple statistics reveal the systemic nature of Islamic doctrine.

What do these cases demonstrate? Here are some of the principles that a simple statistical analysis shows:

Islamic doctrine is found in the Koran, the Sira and the Hadith—the Trilogy. Any explanation of Islam that does not include the doctrine found in the Trilogy is wrong or incomplete.

The Koran is a small part of Islamic doctrine. The Sunna of Mohammed is textually more important than the Koran.

The Koran can be understood by reconstructing the Koran of Mohammed, the historical Koran.

The kafir is the major doctrinal focus of Islam. The kafir has the lowest status of all animal life. The doctrine of the kafir is defined as political Islam.

Islam's success was not based on the religion alone, but also on politics and jihad. The Sira devotes most of its attention to jihad and politics, not religion.

Islamic doctrine is dualistic in its reasoning and ethics.

Jew hatred is an integral part of the Trilogy.

There is no unmitigated good in the Koran for kafirs.

Jihad was integral to Islam's success and forms a large part of the Trilogy.

The Islamic doctrine subjugates women.

The Foundationalist School

It is clear by now that there is an intellectual underpinning to this paper. The actions and words of Muslims have their foundation in the doctrine of Islam found in the Koran and the Sunna, the Trilogy. This doctrine must be analyzed and understood on a rational basis and on its own merits. Know the foundational doctrine and apply it to every action by Muslims, but first know the doctrine. If an opinion or comment about Islam does not have a reference, or a possible reference, to the foundation of the Trilogy, then the opinion has no merit.

PLAN OF ACTION

Following is a Plan of Action to combat this very great evil that has invaded our country. This proposed Plan of Action will be described in detail in subsequent chapters: Also read the letters to President Obama, President Netanyahu (Israel) and Geert Wilders (leader of PVV Party in the Netherlands.) (Although all proposals stated here are worded in terms of America/US Congress just mentally change them to your country and parliament/legislature.)

RONALD REAGAN TIME

Do a Ronald Reagan: Show Islam no respect. Declare YOU ARE NOT US. WE ARE NOT YOU. (Reagan's philosophy in fighting evil is so critical that it will be repeated numerous times.) No more inviting Imams to political, social or religious events. The US Army just banned Rev. Franklin Graham from the Prayer Day ceremony for saying that Islam was wicked. Meantime, Imans will be attending this event praying from the Quran – a book that has murdered and wounded countless thousands of US soldiers. Could you imagine General Eisenhower inviting Gobbels and have him pray from Mein Kampf. These soldiers are risking their lives to protect our freedom while our military and political leaders are betraying and making a farce of their sacrifice. This is simply outrageous. This borders on treason.

Quoting from newsmax.com "The entire National Day of Prayer task force, including the Rev. Franklin Graham, has been "disinvited" to the National Day of Prayer observance to be held at the Pentagon, sources tell Newsmax. And evangelist Franklin Graham believes the military's effort to ban him and other Christian leaders is nothing short of an effort to stamp out Christianity from the military. The Pentagon's decision to disinvite not only Graham, but also the National Day of Prayer task force led by author Shirley Dobson, the wife of influential Focus on the Family founder Dr. James C. Dobson, suggests the Pentagon's rejection of Christian leaders is much broader than previously recognized." END QUOTE There is a German Muslim government minster that seeks to ban all crucifixes from schools. Jews are being driven from Europe in the third mass exile: the first mass exile and extermination being from Saudi Arabia ordered by prophet Muhammad and the second extermination/mass exile by Adolf Hitler.

Both Reagan and Churchill understood that you can never accommodate evil. Any appeasement of evil and you become part of the evil – you give evil RESPECTABILITY. The Quran and Islam must be ostracized from society. Appeasement only leads to more appeasement and more appeasement and finally a life and death struggle. Once Islam is denied respectability and firmly rejected that will be the beginning of the beginning of destroying this very great evil and liberation of Muslims from the clutches of the AntiGod. Surrender or fight for freedom that is the choice. **WHERE IS THE NEW RONALD REAGAN?**

DEFENSE OF AMERCIA: DEMOCRACY AND FREEDOM ACT

We must declare WHO WE ARE AND WHAT WE STAND FOR AS A PEOPLE. Restoring pride in America. Revitalize the Constitution making it relevant to young Americans. A statement that America and the West have created the greatest civilization in history. The rights of women to be paramount in this declaration (see next) with complete protection of the law for Muslim women and children who seek refuge from martial abuse. This declaration to be taught to every student in every school, every year. (Read Chapter 44.)

We hold these truths to be self-evident, that all men are created equal, that they are endowed by their Creator with certain unalienable Rights, that among these are Life, Liberty and the pursuit of Happiness. These are powerful, timeless words. They stand as a beacon for all humanity. Islam not only seeks the destruction of these words but the destruction of all non-Muslims. As we have already demonstrated, all non-Muslims are subhumans and are not endowed by God with unalienable Rights, life, liberty but must murdered as ordered by God. All Muslim women are the property of their husbands. All kafir women are subhumans who can be raped and enslaved. All Christians/Jews that refuse to convert/pay jizya tax/accept dimmi status are to be exterminated on God's orders. Rape, slavery, sex slaves, terror, torture - these are the unalienable brutality delivered by God against ALL who dare oppose Islam. **Where are the** unalienable Rights, to life, liberty, pursuit of happiness for all the women stoned, raped, whipped, hanged, enslaved by Islam. **Where are the** unalienable Rights, to life, liberty, pursuit of happiness for all the murdered Iranian women? **Where are the** unalienable Rights, to life, liberty, pursuit of happiness for women denied their humanity and equality by Islam? **Where are the** unalienable Rights, to life, liberty, pursuit of happiness for Christians, Jews, gays, being murdered by Muslims across the Middle East? **Where are the** unalienable Rights, to life, liberty, pursuit of happiness for apostates of Islam? **Where are the** unalienable Rights, to life, liberty, and pursuit of happiness for the 2,976 murdered on 9/11 and their families or the 13 massacred at Ft. Hood? **Where are the** unalienable Rights, to life, liberty, pursuit of happiness for the 270,000,000 kafirs murdered by Islam?

Where are the unalienable Rights, to life, liberty, pursuit of happiness for Molly Norris?

Where are the unalienable Rights, to life, liberty, pursuit of happiness for Rivera Bary?

The Democracy and Freedom Declaration must state that we stand for the equality of all human beings; the total equality of women, the humanity of all races, and against slavery. Read on page xliii "Who Is A Good Moral American" All this morality would be stated in this Act. Everything that Islam stands for this Declaration will state that America stands against.

CONSTITUTIONAL AMENDMENT TO FIRST AMENDMENT

As we will discuss extensively - it is absolutely imperative to ban Sharia Law, Stealth Jihad, and Stealth Censorship. This will cripple Islam. In order to destroy Islam you must **DESTROY THE QURAN**.

Again, the hideous reality we face is that the Quran is a book of extermination, genocide, mass murder masquerading as a religious text. The key to Islam's destruction is not only that this book is not the word of God since only a God of Moral Perfection is God and therefore every word of the Quran must be Moral Perfection to be from God and therefore the Quran filled with immoral words/teachings is not from God and therefore Islam is fraudulent but also by an amendment to the First Amendment making incitement to violence either verbal or written illegal and punishable by 5 years in jail.

AMENDMENT

"Every person residing in the United States has the Constitutional Right to the protection of their physical person. There can be no incitement to violence either written or verbal directed at any person or group of persons calling for bodily harm or death. Such incitement shall be punishable by a 5 year jail term."

It is a criminal act to threaten the President. We are no less then the President. The legal protection afforded the President must be applied equally to all citizens. The thousands of teachings of Islam calling for the death and destruction of kafirs in the name of and to the greater glory of God are incitement to violence to inflict bodily harm and death. These teachings are criminal acts against humanity and must now be made criminal in law. Imams teaching this evil would be arrested and their mosques shut down. Since the Quran is nothing more then a terrorist manual, I guarantee that within one/two years 80% of all mosques would be shut down for inciting acts of violence: jihad, terror, murder etc.

JIHAD IS TREASON

In a democratic society I have the full right to think whatever I want to think. I have the full right to dream whatever I want to dream no matter how monstrously evil my dreams may be. I have a right to speak whatever I want to speak. I have the right to write whatever I want to write. I have the full right to denigrate any ideology, religion, race, and creed no matter how despicable. In fact I have the democratic right to be a despicable outrageous bastard. Nothing is off limits. However my rights to freedom of speech cannot be used to destroy your right to freedom of speech. The fastest way to terminate someone's freedom of speech is to kill him. By murdering, you not only end that person's freedom of speech but you instill a terminating fear into the heart of freedom. You send a powerful message to all free people's that they are next to be killed if they dare defy you. I have absolutely no democratic right to speak violence, write to encourage or instigate acts of violence, threaten violence or commit acts of violence. Period.

This is the death knell of freedom. Jihad is treason. Jihad seeks to conquer the world for antiGod Allah and murder all those who refuse to convert to Islam. (For Islamic teachings of Jihad go to (http://islamreform.net/new-page-130.htm). To have a well organized group of men willing to use violence to overthrow democracy and destroy its constitution and rule of law is treason. Teaching violent jihad is to incite violence that will destroy freedom of speech and with it the freedom of others to practice their religion is an act of treason.

UNIVERSAL CONSTITUTIONAL DECLARATION OF TOTAL EQUALITY OF WOMEN TO BE ADOPTED BY ALL NATIONS OR FACE EXPULSION FROM THE UN:

The total and complete equality of women to be recorded in an Amendment to the Constitution titled: Universal Declaration of Total Equality of Women that would form an integral part of the Defense of America: Democracy and Freedom Act. All states would present this proclamation to amend the Constitution to their legislatures. All nations asked by the President to enact this historical Declaration and those nations that refuse would no longer have any UN voting rights or better still deny US visas to all their government officials. For a copy of this Woman's Declaration of Freedom go to: page l

UNIVERSAL HISTORCIAL DECLARATION OF A GOD OF MORAL PERFECTION: GOD IS NOT A CRIMINAL

If we do not declare that only a God of Moral Perfection is God, Islam will conquer the world. Allah is not Moral Perfection and therefore is the AntiGod of the Muslims. Sharia Law is not Moral Perfection and therefore not the constitution of God. The Quran being not a book of Moral Perfection was never written by God; not one word and therefore Islam is fraudulent. The Declaration of A God of Moral Perfection will destroy Allah (the AntiGod) and Islam. The Declaration of A God of Moral Perfection to be attached to the Defense of America Act. This Declaration is not telling anyone which religion they should follow. It is only stating the moral conception of God – that only a God of Moral Perfection is God. This Declaration will not have the force of law but the moral force of the American people. It will change history for all history. (Chapters 1, 3, 4)

BAN SHARIA LAW UNEQUIVOCALLY.

The Congress would pass the Defense of America Act, Constitutional Amendment Universal Declaration of Women's Equality and Declaration of a God of Moral Perfection. The Congress then passes an Act of Congress banning Sharia Law - this means banning totally and completely Sharia Law without any exceptions. This will send a tsunami tidal wave earth quake cascading across the world and I believe other nations will follow suit. In banning Sharia Law, Congress documents all the teachings of slavery, oppression of women, and totalitarianism that are central to Sharia. Congress must state unequivocally that we - the people of the United States stand for the equality and freedom of every human being, every race, and every woman. By these actions, the United States will be declaring to the world that we stand against slavery, against degradation of women and for human rights.

SHARIA LAW MUST BE BANNED.

Our constitutional republic is built upon the foundation of separation of church and state, with a representative form of government that derives all of its power from the will of the people, framed by a Constitution that is the supreme law of the land. Islam is built on a foundation of church and state being one, an inseparable autocratic form of government that derives all of its power solely from the will of Allah, framed exclusively by Islamic law-which Islam holds to be divine, supreme, and immutable. So the danger that Islam poses to America is that Islam, at its core, is ideologically at war with our Constitution. It is a declared war against everything our Constitution stands for. This is a war of polarized ideologies, and they are irreconcilable

BAN STEALTH CENSURESHIP

Freedom to intellectually destroy Islam and the prophet Muhammad. (chapter44)

BAN STEALTH JIHAD

Total Separation of Business and Religion. (Chapter 44)

NO TAX EXMPT STATUS FOR ISLAM

Italy has refused to grant religious status to Islam on the basis of its treatment of women. America must cancel the tax exempt status for Islam
To be tax-exempt under section 501(c)(3) of the Internal Revenue Code, an organization must be organized and operated exclusively for exempt purposes set forth in section 501(c)(3). I t may not be an action organization, **i.e.,** it may not attempt to influence legislation as a substantial part of its activities and

it may not participate in any campaign activity for or against political candidates. The exempt purposes set forth in section 501(c) (3) are charitable, religious.... eliminating prejudice and discrimination; defending human and civil rights secured by law; ....

Religious practices are done by those who follow that religion and are motivated for achieving paradise and avoiding hell. Outsiders are not involved in those religious acts. If it is about going to heaven and avoiding hell, then it is religious. However, if the religion makes a demand on those outside of its own group, then that demand is political.

Islam is a political organization bent on conquest of kafirs, destruction of all other religions, enslavement of women. Conquest is a political activity not religious.

Most people think that the Koran is a religious text. Instead, 64% of the text (by word count) is about non-Muslims, who are called Kafirs. The Koran is fixated on Kafirs and makes many demands on them. Not the least is that Kafirs submit to the rule of Islamic Sharia law. Ultimately Sharia law is the pure expression of Islamic politics and it completely contradicts our Constitution and the Bill of Rights. Under Sharia there is no freedom of speech, wives may be beaten and apostates murdered. Sharia law and the Quran are in direct conflict with our Bill of Rights and Constitution. Mosques and Islam are in direct opposition to our national heritage, our legal system and all other religions. Islam seeks the destruction of our constitution. It promotes prejudice and discrimination against kafirs and Muslim women and seeks the destruction not the defending of human and civil rights secured by law; .... **THEREFORE ISLAM MUST BE DENIED TAX EXEMPT STATUS.**

BAN QURAN FROM PRISONS:
How can this criminal book be taught to criminals. Under no circumstances should Quran be banned from society.

DO NOT BAN HEADSCARFS/BURQAS:
As we have already stated in the Constitutional Amendment: Equality of Women – women have the right to dress in any manner they wish to. The burqua can only be banned as a security concern and for no other reason.

BAN SAUDI MONEY

The enemy of my enemy is my enemy. Saudi Arabia is the mortal enemy of America. Oil money is being used by the Saudis to finance Al-Qaeda and other Jihadi groups and fund the spread of Islamic studies in universities and build Mosques throughout the West. Saudi Arabia is funding the rapid expansion and moderation of the Pakistani nuclear arsenal. Pakistan is no friend of the US. It is a Sharia Law state where Christians are being oppressed and murdered daily. To truly understand the danger posed by Pakistan read "Pakistani Third Reich" http://frontpagemag.com/2010/04/28/the-pakistani-third-reich/?utm_source=FrontPage+Magazine&utm_campaign=1402be8da8-

RSS_EMAIL_CAMPAIGN&utm_medium=email Quoting from this article "The motto of the Pakistani army is "faith, piety and jihad in the path of Allah." In the 1980s Brigadier S.K. Malik of the Pakistani army produced an authoritative military manual on jihad called **The Quranic Concept of War**. It is a required reading of Pakistan's military officers.

Malik writes: "the Holy Prophet's operations …are an integral and inseparable part of the divine message revealed to us in the Holy Quran… The war he planned and carried out was total to the infinite degree. It was waged on all fronts: internal and external, political and diplomatic, spiritual and psychological, economic and military… The Quranic military strategy thus enjoins us to prepare ourselves for war to the utmost in order to strike terror into the heart of the enemy, known or hidden… Terror struck into the hearts of the enemy is not only a means; it is the end in itself." End Quote

TEACHING ISLAM TO CHILDREN IS CHILD ABUSE

As a free person living in a free society I do not have the religious right to raise my children to hate non-believers in my religion, and teach them that these non-believers are subhumans who must be killed. (In order to comprehend the psychological damage done to Muslim children read Chapter 21 – "Teaching Children Islam Is Child Abuse") If my religion demands the yearly sacrifice of a virgin I do not have the religious freedom to take a virgin no matter how willing and slit her throat to celebrate the glory of God.

I do not have the religious right to teach my child that blacks are subhumans who can be tortured and murdered. I do not have the right to name my child Adolf Hitler. I can be arrested for these abusive acts and my children taken from me. I do not have the religious right to deny my children medical treatment because my religion declares that such treatment is against God. If my child dies or is seriously injured because I refused to give proper medical care I will be charged with murder/man slaughter. I do not have the religious right to teach my child that Jews are pigs and apes, nonbelievers are subhumans and my daughter is an inferior, shameful creature. Teaching Islam to children is child abuse and must be banned.

SEIZE MOSQUES FROM RADICAL FUNDAMENTALISTS (NOT TRUE MUSLEMS) AND GIVE TO MODERATE, GOOD, MORAL MUSLIMS (THE TRUE MUSLIMS)

After banning Sharia Law, Congress commences a debate on the Quran by calling on all Muslims to declare that the Quran is not the word of God and asks them to prove that Islam is a true religion of peace and they are good, true, peaceful Muslims by renouncing, denouncing and removing from the Quran the 4,000 verses of extermination, murder, hate, terror, torture, rape, slavery etc that are not Moral Perfection. If however Muslims refuse to make this declaration that the Quran is not from God and reject these evil teachings then the authorities will inform them that they must obey the laws of the United States and if they preach violence and hate in their mosques, or if they incite violence to cause bodily harm or death they will be arrested, sent to prison for 5 years and their mosques will be shut down. Let us be very clear - advocating the destruction of the Constitution and its replacement with Sharia, advocating jihad, violence against kafirs are acts of sedition are acts of treason and those Mosques teaching this evil do not have the right to freedom of religion and will be shut down.

Lets us play the politically correct game. We must form an alliance with the true, moderate Muslims who worship the good, moral Islam of peace. We must ban Sharia Law since the radical Muslims are using it as justification to undermine freedom and democracy and no good, moral, moderate, Muslim man could ever support the evil barbarism of Sharia Law and be a good, moral, moderate human being. We must shut down any mosque where these radical, fundamentalist Muslim men are misinterpreting the Quran and are preaching the teachings 9.5, 9.29. 9.111 etc and acting on these teachings by encouraging Muslims to terrorize and murder kafirs in the name of the AntiGod Allah and hand these mosques over to the good, moral Muslims. We will march in with the good, moral Muslims and drive out the radical Islamists. We will replace the Quran containing 4,000 teachings of immoral imperfection that these Islamists were preaching with a brand new Quran containing the true teachings of the true Islam of peace. Since no good, moral, moderate Muslim man can ever believe in these evil Quranic teachings of the subhumanness of kafirs who can be murdered, raped, tortured, robbed, enslaved, etc. as divine, holy acts guaranteeing accession to Paradise and remain a good, moral, moderate human being then these true Muslims will gather in the streets by the millions supporting our actions. But wait a moment – as soon as a Muslim man rejects just one teaching of Sharia Law let alone the entire Sharia and just one word of the Quran let alone 4,000 evil teachings he is no longer a good, moral, moderate Muslim man but only a good, moral, moderate human being who has rejected Islam becoming an apostate and must be murdered by the good, moral, holy, moderate Muslim men who are the true Muslims believing unequivocally in Sharia Law and the Quran.

As stated previously, the message to Muslims must be clearly stated:. We don't care if you pray 5 times a day or 24 times a day. We don't care about Ramadan or the Hajj. We value our democracy and freedom and will fight against Sharia Law and the Quran. You are not us and we will no later tolerate Islam but will treat it with the distain it deserves and will legally move against it to protect our democracy and freedom. Let the message go out to President Obama/ Bloomberg and all the supporters of the AntiGod Allah that we will defend our democracy: **TO THE DEATH: TO THE DEATH: TO THE DEATH.**

As will be demonstrated in this book - by not standing against Islam, our political, media, intellectual, religious elites (not all but all too many) are in effect giving respectability and legitimacy to this very great evil. They are saying that it is normal to believe in a God that teaches that kafirs (non-believers) are subhumans who can be murdered, raped, tortured, terrorized as holy, divine acts of God guaranteeing accession to Paradise filled with virgins. They are saying it is normal to wage war to conquer the nations of the world for God and murder all male kafirs who refuse to convert to Islam and rape and enslave their women. They are saying it is normal that Muslim women are the property of their husbands/fathers and can be beaten and killed. All these horrors are just normal.

TOTAL PROTECTION FOR APOSTATES OF ISLAM Total and complete protection of the law for Muslims who want to abandon Islam.

UNIVERSAL DECLARATION OF TOTAL EQUALITY FOR GAYS AND RIGHT OF CHRISTIANS/JEWS TO PRACTISE THEIR RELIGION IN ANY COUNTRY TO BE ADOPTED BY ALL NATIONS OR FACE EXPULSION FROM THE UN

PROPOSAL FOR CONGRESS TO PASS A SPECIAL ACT HONORING THE IRANIAN WOMEN MURDERED BY THE ISLAMIC REVOLUTION AND BUILD A MEMORIAL IN THEIR MEMORY 2000 Iranian women have been murdered by the government in Iran in the worst ways imaginable. Congress needs to pass a special act immortalizing for all time the courage of these brave women and possibly built a memorial in their honor otherwise their great sacrifice and suffering will have been for nothing.

BAN IMMIGRATION OF MUSLIM MEN

Ban immigration of Muslim men. We have the right to decide who can immigrate. We cannot bring into our country those who seek our destruction. Muslims are here to colonize not integrate: not to live in democracy and freedom but in total submission to the antiGod Allah under Sharia Law.

DRACION MEASURE ONLY AS A LAST, LAST RESORT

Ban Islam: Islam is a totalitarian ideology far worse then Communism or Nazism. Question that must be asked – Can a well organized group that seeks to over throw the democratic state, abolish its constitution and employs violence as a political tool of intimidation and fear to impose a totalitarian dictatorship be allowed to freely function as the Brown and Black shirts were allowed to function in Germany leading to the disaster of Hitler and total destruction of World War 2?

EMANCIPATION OF WOMEN IS THE CIVIL RIGHTS ISSUE OF OUR TIME

HITLER/NAZISM AND COMMUNISM WERE THE LIFE AND DEATH DEFINING ISSUES OF THE GREATEST GENERATION. ISLAM IS THE LIFE AND DEATH DEFINING ISSUE FOR THE SECOND GREATEST GENERATION AND THEIR CHILDREN.

Islam is a life and death issue for Western women. All human rights and freedoms women have won in the Western World are now endanger from Islam. It is shocking that feminists are not rising up against Islam but are instead going meekly to their eternal fate as the chattel of their husband/father. As already shown, kafir women are being raped enmass in Europe and probably the US as Rape Jihad grips the European continent.

To prevent the enslavement of women, Sharia Law must be banned. All ANTI WOMAN teachings of the Quran and Hadith condemned and rejected as well as a total rejection of Islam. The rights of women must be enforced and protected through the Rule of Law and a Constitutional Amendment: Universal Declaration Of The Total Equality of Women. This Constitutional Amendment to be submitted to all states and 100% would be expected to ratify this amendment. In this Proclamation, each ANTIWOMAN teaching of the Quran and Sharia Law are condemned and made legal. By doing this and making these rights denied by Islam - Constitutional we are reinforcing our rejection of Sharia Law and the Quran making it impossible for Muslims to undermine the democratic rights of women. Again, this Amendment to be taught to every student in every school, every year.

This Constitutional Amendment would be in addition to the already existing Constitutional rights enjoyed by women otherwise this will be your daily reality. *[Bukhari 3, 38,508]* Mohammed said, "Unais, confront this man's wife and if she admits committing adultery have her stoned to death." *[Bukhari 8, 82,803] Ali had a woman stoned to death on a Friday and said, "I have punished her as Mohammed would have."*

Women are the key to defeating Islam. All Islamic nations must enact the following Constitutional Amendment granting their women total humanity and equality. Those nations that refuse will not be granted visas to travel to New York leaving their UN seats EMPTY.

We (who oppose Islam) must become the champion of the worldwide total and complete equality of ALL women. We must become the champion of defending Muslim women and children. We are not in conflict with Muslim women. They are the property of their men and enslaved by Islam. We must fight for their equal human rights and dignity.

THIS WILL BE A MOMENT OF TRUE HISTORCAL GREATNESS

CONSTITUTIONAL AMENDMENT DECLARATION OF THE EQUALITY OF WOMEN

We hold these truths to be self-evident, that all WOMEN and MEN are created equal, that they are endowed by their Creator with certain unalienable Rights, that among these are Life, Liberty and the pursuit of Happiness.

Women being the total equal of men therefore: women have the complete right to equality before the law. Women are legally equal to men in all aspects of life and the rule of law. There can be no law that does not treat women as equals of men.

Women being the total equal of men therefore: women have the full right to dress (or not dress) however they see fit. Women have the full legal right to display their heads, faces, hands, arms, legs, midsection, neck, wear headscarfs or not wear headscarfs, display their hair in whatever style they desire, put on lipstick and make up in whatever design they wish. Women are not required to pluck, depilate or otherwise remove facial and body hair.

Women being the total equal of men therefore: women are not deficient in intelligence to men. They are not worth 50% of men. Women are the intellectual equals of men.

Women being the total equal of men therefore: women have the full legal right to sexual equality with men. A woman has the full right to marry the man of her free will choice regardless of the wishes of her parents.

Women being the total equal of men therefore: women are not the property of their husbands. Women - single or married are independent human beings and cannot be forced to commit any act against their will. A married woman has the full right not to have sex with her husband any time she chooses. A married man has absolutely no right to force sex upon his wife and any such attempt is felony rape.

Women being the total equal of men therefore: women are not the property of her father or brothers.

Women being the total equal of men therefore: women have the full right to be treated with respect and dignity by men. A husband has no right to beat his wife. A father has no right to beat his daughter. Brothers have no right to beat their sister(s).

Women being the total equal of men therefore: women cannot be sexually abused by any man. All marriages under the age of 18 are illegal. Sex with a minor under the age of 16 is illegal and will be charged as rape.

Women being the total equal of men therefore: fathers or any other man cannot sexually mutilate their daughters or any other woman.

Women being the total equal of men therefore: women cannot be forced to have sex by any man or kept as a sex slave by any man or sold into slavery by any man.

Women being the total equal of men therefore: women cannot be segregated in society from men. It is totally and completely illegal for any public, governmental institution, organization or other entity to allow the segregation of women from men. There can be no segregation of women in public, school swimming pools etc. Women have the right to belong to any public, governmental, institution, organization etc.

Women being the total equal of men therefore: women have the full right to medical treatment by male medical personnel including male doctors and no women can ask for treatment by only female medical personnel or doctors what – so – ever.

Women being the total equal of men therefore: women have the full right to an education including being taught by male teachers.

Employers have the full right to set their dress and appearance policies for their employees and in demanding adherence to these codes of conduct cannot be sued for discrimination by any employee. If an employee does not wish to conform to the dress/appearance code then that employee has the full right to quit. Schools can also dictate the dress code for students.

Women being the total equal of men therefore: women over the age of puberty are permitted to leave the house without fully covering the body. Women have the right to wear full body covering unless the wearing of such covering possess a security threat to be determined solely by Congress.

Women being the total equal of men therefore: women are permitted to travel without a spouse or male relative.

Women being the total equal of men therefore: women are permitted to be alone with men who are not relatives or spouses, and cannot be punished by whipping or stoning or any other punishment for being alone with man/men who are not relatives or spouses.

Women being the total equal of men therefore: women do not require their husband's permission to be employed.

Women being the total equal of men therefore: women do not require a male guardian.

Women being the total equal of men therefore: women can marry by herself whether single or widowed.

Women being the total equal of men therefore: men can have only one wife at any one time.

Women being the total equal of men therefore: women are permitted to obtain passports and cannot be punished by whipping or stoning or any other form of punishment for doing so.

Women being the total equal of men therefore: women are permitted to speak softly to a man and can communicate with a man by letters, phone calls or glances, and there can be no punishment such as whipping or stoning or any other form of punishment for doing so.

Women being the total equal of men therefore: women are permitted to visit the graves of loved ones.

Women being the total equal of men therefore: men are not entitled to twice the amount of inheritance a woman receives, regardless of what a person's wishes

Women being the total equal of men therefore: a man cannot divorce his wife by simply giving her a triple talaq (saying "I divorce you" three times simultaneously).

Women being the total equal of men therefore: a woman whose husband divorces her must be granted alimony and child support as decided by the courts.

Women being the total equal of men therefore: they cannot be confined to their rooms and deprived of food and water.

Women being the total equal of men therefore: they have total freedom of sexual expression.

THESE RIGHTS OF WOMEN ARE INVIOLATE FOR ALL ETERNITY AND CAN NEVER BE ALTERED NOR DIMINISHED BY MAN OR GOD.

THE BANNING OF ISLAM: MAKING THE PRACTISE OF ISLAM ILLEGAL: A POSSIBLE LAST, LAST, LAST RESORT

It was Winston Churchill who said that the Second World War was the unnecessary war. At any time Hitler could have been stopped. By giving Hitler free rein, the Germans allowed him to use democracy to destroy democracy. They allowed a well organized, violent ideology to function in their society dedicated to the destruction of the Constitution, overthrow of the government and imposition of a brutal dictatorship. Germany paid a horrific price. The world barely averted a major disaster.

Again, democracies in the United States and Europe are in a life and death struggle with a very evil, violent ideology seeking the destruction of their Constitutions and replacement with Sharia Law, the destruction of their democracy and the imposition of a barbaric, totalitarian dictatorship. Unlike Nazism which never pretended to be divinely inspired, Islam cloaks its evil in religious trappings. As already discussed and will be elaborated further, in fighting Islam we need to start by copying Ronald Reagan's destruction of Communism strategy - showing no respect, declaring you are not us, and like Reagan who refused to co-exist with evil and ostracized Communism from society so to we must refuse to co-exist but ostracize Islam and the Quran, to be followed by the Defense of America Act, Declaration of Rights and Freedoms of a God of Mora d l Perfection: Only A God of Moral Perfection is God, banning Sharia Law and demanding Muslims declare that the Quran is not the word of God, abandoning the evil Quranic teachings, and incorporating the 4 pillars of Islam with the teachings of a God of Moral Perfection.

If Muslims refuse to declare that the Quran is not the divine, timeless word of God, renounce, denounce the 4,000 evil Quranic teachings, and the evilness of Muhammad, then the next to final step would be to inform all Muslims that those mosques and Imams, that do not abide by the law and the Constitution, will be shut down and the Imams arrested, jailed or deported. The last, last, last, last resort will be to declare Islam illegal and ban this ideology. If nothing is done to combat Islam, we will end up like the Germans, with a violent ideology imposing its version of a barbaric civilization, starting with the destruction of women's rights, then children, then gays, then Jews, then Christians, then blacks, then democracy and freedom, then you and your family.

Following is the intellectual and legal basis for this draconian act. This is not an action that I endorse. I support the intellectual destruction of Islam, not it's banning:

Banning Islam is more difficult in the United States than in Europe, because of the First Amendment. Congress shall make no law respecting an establishment of religion, or prohibiting the free exercise thereof; or abridging the freedom of speech, or of the press; or the right of the people peaceably to assemble, and to petition the Government for a redress of grievances. On the surface of it this is a fairly straightforward formulation barring the legislative branch from taking any action to create a state religion or barring the practice of any religion. The founders were English citizens and well aware of the way in which religion could stoke political violence. In the late 18th century, Cromwell was not ancient history, neither were the Covenanters or the Gunpowder Plot. While they did not anticipate like the rise of an Islamic insurgency in America, they understood quite well that religion and violence ccould and would intersect.

That of course was one of the reasons for barring a State Church, to avoid giving the government control over religion, a situation that had resulted in much of the religious violence in England. By giving religion independence, but not political power, the First Amendment sought to avoid a repeat of the same ugliness that had marked centuries of wars in Europe. That of course is a key point. The separation of church and state was meant to protect the integrity of both, and avoid power struggles between religious groups. There was to be no state religion, the government could not leverage religious authority and religious factions could not begin civil wars in a struggle to gain power or autonomy. For the most part it worked.

Until now the only real acid test for this approach involved the Mormon Church, an ugly history on both sides that has mostly been buried under the weight of time. More recently Scientology flared up as a cult turned church that demanded its own autonomy and did its best to make war on the government and its critics.

And then there is Islam. The first problem with using the First Amendment in defense of Islam-- is that its goal is to violate the First Amendment. Islam's widely stated goal is to become a State Religion, around the world and in America as well. Sharia has been making steady advances in Africa and parts of Asia. Majorities of Muslims in the UK have said that they want Sharia law, and leading British figures such as the Archbishop of Canterbury have supported the introduction of Islamic law into the British legal system. Domestic advocates for Sharia, such as Noah Feldman, are pushing for the normalization of Sharia law in the United States as well.

This would in effect turn Islam into an Established Religion in the United States, itself a violation of the First Amendment. Furthermore Islam abridges the remaining portions of the First Amendment, which protect Freedom of Speech and the Press. Islam rejects both of these. To protect Islamic rights therefore means depriving non-Muslims of freedom of religion--- and both Muslims and non-Muslims of freedom of speech and the press.

These are not hypothetical scenarios, the Mohammed cartoon controversy has demonstrated exactly how this will work. So did the persecution of Salman Rushdie. To accept Islam is to reject freedom of speech and religion... in the same way that accepting Communism meant rejecting freedom of speech and religion. Islam and the Constitution of the United States are incompatible in the same way that Communism and the Constitution are incompatible.

The Founders sought to protect religious freedoms, at no point in time did they seek to protect religious terrorism. And Supreme Courts throughout

American history have found that the First Amendment does not provide license for significant lawbreaking. That is why polygamy is not legal in the United States.

Having to choose between religious freedom and the rights and dignity of women and children-- America correctly chose the latter.

In 1785, James Madison, Father of the Constitution, wrote, "We hold it for a fundamental and undeniable truth that religion or the duty which we owe our Creator and the manner of discharging it can be directed only by reason and conviction, not by force or violence."

Yet Islamic history and recent events in Eurabia demonstrate that Islam does indeed spread by force and violence. Upholding the right of Islam to force its statues and views on Americans, violates Madison's fundamental and undeniable truth.

In 1802, Jefferson wrote his explanation for the First Amendment to the Danbury Baptist Association;

"Believing with you that religion is a matter which lies solely between man and his God, and that he owes account to none other for his faith or his worship, that the legitimate powers of government reach actions only, and not opinions, I contemplate with sovereign reverence that act of the whole American people which declared that the legislature should "make no law respecting an establishment of religion, or prohibiting the free exercise thereof," thus building a wall of separation between Church and State."

There is a key phrase in this statement, which is that the legitimate powers of government reach actions only, and not opinions. This statement was used as a legal principle by the Supreme Court in 1878 in the case of Reynolds vs the United States. Reynolds had been charged with bigamy and claimed that his faith required him to engage in polygamy.

The Court found that while Reynolds had the right to believe that polygamy was his duty, he did not have the right to practice it-- thus upholding Jefferson's distinction between action and belief.

As the court put it;

In our opinion, the statute immediately under consideration is within the legislative power of Congress. It is constitutional and valid as prescribing a rule of action for all those residing in the Territories, and in places over which the United States have exclusive control. This being so, the only question which remains is, whether those who make polygamy a part of their religion are excepted from the operation of the statute. If they are, then those who do not make polygamy a part of their religious belief may be found guilty and punished, while those who do, must be acquitted and go free. This would be introducing a new element into criminal law

Laws are made for the government of actions, and while they cannot interfere with mere religious belief and opinions, they may with practices. Suppose one believed that human sacrifices were a necessary part of religious worship, would it be seriously contended that the civil government under which he lived could not interfere to prevent a sacrifice? Or if a wife religiously believed it was her duty to burn herself upon the funeral pile of her dead husband, would it be beyond the power of the civil government to prevent her carrying her belief into practice?

So here, as a law of the organization of society under the exclusive dominion of the United States, it is provided that plural marriages shall not be allowed. Can a man excuse his practices to the contrary because of his religious belief? [98 U.S. 145, 167] To permit this would be to make the professed doctrines of religious belief superior to the law of the land, and in effect to permit every citizen to become a law unto himself. Government could exist only in name under such circumstances.

The outcome then was that we could not have a situation in which crimes could be committed in the name of religion and protected by the First Amendment. Belief could not be criminalized, but practice could be.

But what does that actually mean and how exactly do we distinguish between action and practice? Does it merely mean that it is legal to believe in seizing America in the name of Islam, but not to practice it.

We can begin by pointing out that any number of Islamic practices which violate American law or promote an unhealthy social consequence can be banned, for much the same reason that polygamy was. In Reynolds vs the United States, the Court upheld the right of the Utah legislature to brand the spread of polygamy as a threat to innocent women and children, that had to be arrested through strong measures. The spread of Islam's practices can be seen in the same way.

France has treated the Hijab in a similar way. The United States can too, if it finds any abuse or violence associated with its enforcement or use. Honor killings over the Hijab demonstrate that this is the case. State Legislatures can then move to ban the Hijab.

Thus while we cannot charge someone with believing in Islam, we can stamp out many Islamic practices that are dangerous or abusive. The First Amendment does not protect religious practices that are illegal or made illegal, it protects only the beliefs themselves.

And we can go much further at an organizational level, based on the Sedition Act of 1918 and the 1954 Communist Control Act, which give us some guidelines for cracking down on Islam.

Sec. 2. The Congress hereby finds and declares that the Communist Party of the United States, although purportedly a political party, is in fact an instrumentality of a conspiracy to overthrow the Government of the United States. It constitutes an authoritarian dictatorship within a republic, demanding for itself the rights and privileges accorded to political parties, but denying to all others the liberties guaranteed by the Constitution. Unlike political parties, which evolve their policies and programs through public means, by the reconciliation of a wide variety of individual views, and submit those policies and programs to the electorate at large for approval or disapproval, the policies and programs of the Communist Party are secretly prescribed for it by the foreign leaders of the world Communist movement. Its members have no part in determining its goals, and are not permitted to voice dissent to party objectives

This applies to Islam just as much as it applies to Communism. And this preamble was part of a passage demonstrating the fundamental distinction between Communism and legitimate political parties.

The assumption of the Communist Control Act was that the First Amendment did not apply to the Communist party or to Communist controlled parties... because they did not fit the democratic template of the First Amendment. As such the Communist party was not a legitimate party, but an overseas directed conspiracy to overthrow the United States and replace it with a Communist system. Not only can this same argument also apply to Islamic organizations such as CAIR, but Islam can be distinguished from other religions on similar grounds. The following phrase from the original document represents the key point here; It constitutes an authoritarian dictatorship within a republic, demanding for itself the rights and privileges accorded to political parties, but denying to all others the liberties guaranteed by the Constitution. And that is the core of the problem. While we cannot criminalize individual beliefs alone, we can criminalize organizations dedicated to overthrowing the United States and replacing it with a totalitarian system. An organization is not merely "belief", it also represents an attempt to put those beliefs into practice.

The Internal Security Act of 1950, along with the 1954 Communist Control Act provides extensive legal grounds for criminalizing organizations dedicated to the overthrow of the United States, as well as membership in such organizations-- and even provides for the removal of citizenship from members of such organizations.

While succeeding courts have thrown out many portions of these laws, had the United States truly gotten serious about the War on Terror, it could have passed a real Patriot Act that would have clamped down on Islamist organizations in a similar way.The bill could have easily retrofitted some of the language of the Communist Control Act as follows;

Sec. 3. Islamic organizations, regardless of their assumed name, whose object or purpose is to overthrow the Government of the United States, or the government of any State, Territory, District, or possession thereof, or the government of any political subdivision therein by force and violence, are not entitled to any of the rights, privileges, and immunities attendant upon legal bodies created under the jurisdiction of the laws of the United States or any political subdivision thereof; and whatever rights, privileges, and immunities which have heretofore been granted to said party or any subsidiary organization by reason of the laws of the United States or any political subdivision thereof, are hereby terminated:

Sec. 4. Whoever knowingly and willfully becomes or remains a member of such organizations, or (2) any other organization having for one of its purposes or objectives the establishment, control conduct, seizure, or overthrow of the Government of the United States, or the government of any State or political subdivision thereof, by the use of force or violence, with knowledge of the purpose or objective of such organization shall be subject to all the provisions and penalties of the Internal Security Act of 1950.

The question then becomes one of defining what exactly an Islamist organization is. If we define Islamist under the same guidelines as Communist, but specifically modified as representing a belief in the overthrow or takeover of the United States or any part of it, thereby placing the United States under Islamic law... we already have a very broad net to work with. Or to simply quote the Internal Security Act again.

Sec. 4. (a) It shall be unlawful for any person knowingly to combine, conspire, or agree, with any other person to perform any act which would substantially contribute to the establishment within the United States of a totalitarian dictatorship

Since Islam represents a totalitarian dictatorship, any organization or individual seeking to establish Islamic Law or Sharia within the United States, can be held liable and charged over its violation. This would apply to both Muslims and non-Muslims. And the Koran or Quran itself represents a volume whose contents implicitly call for the violent overthrow of the United States. Consider **Chapter 9 of the Koran,** which governs the interaction between Muslims and non-Muslims. Particularly Sura 9:29 "Fight those who do not believe in Allah, nor in the latter day, nor do they prohibit what Allah and His Apostle have prohibited, nor follow the religion of truth, out of those who have been given the Book, until they pay the tax in acknowledgment of superiority and they are in a state of subjection."

There are numerous other verses in the Koran which similarly call for Muslims to subjugate non-Muslims and take power. This parallels the charge against the Communist party and places Muslims who believe in the Koran on the same level as Communists who believed in the overthrow of the United States.

Participation in any Muslim organization therefore becomes the equivalent of participating in a Communist organization-- and can be banned. So back to the original question, can we ban Islam? While we cannot ban an individual from personally believing in Islam, we can ban Islamic practices and organizations-- which would effectively ban any practice of Islam in an organized way. While the First Amendment does not permit a ban on any specific religion, this is limited to religious belief, not religious practice. And the laws enacted against Communism in the 1950's demonstrate that organizations aimed at the overthrow of the United States can be banned and membership in them can even be criminalized.

Thus we can be Islam from the public sphere, ban Muslim organizations as criminal organizations, criminalize Muslim practices and even denaturalize and deport Muslims who are United States citizens. The legal infrastructure is there. Despite the fact that the United States is far more protective of political and religious rights, within a decade every single Muslim organization, from the national to the mosque level, can be shut down... and the majority of professing Muslims can be deported from the United States regardless of whether they are citizens or not. We can do it. Whether we could or will do it is another matter. It would require rolling back a number of Supreme Court decisions that are a legacy of the corrupted Warren Court. But it was possible post 9/11. It may yet become possible again.

GOD IS NOT A CRIMINAL
GOD IS NOT A MALE CHAUVINIST PIG
ONLY A GOD OF MORAL PERFECTION IS GOD

Just as with the Second World War, (and mentioned earlier) tonight mankind is faced with a titanic struggle between THE GOOD and THE EVIL. On the side of THE GOOD stands God of Moral Perfection and all those who believe in democracy and freedom and the equality of all human beings. On the side of THE EVIL stands Allah (the AntiGod) of the Muslims and all believers in Allah and his messenger prophet Muhammad and their political, religious, media. intellectual Western supporters. There is no in-between middle ground. God of Moral Perfection will not intervene to ensure the victory of THE GOOD. THE GOOD must ensure their own victory. The fate of civilization and mankind hangs in the balance.

As already atated, it is absolutely central to Islam that Allah is God, that the Quran is the divine word of God delivered from God by Angel Gabriel to Muhammad who was the last prophet of God and that Sharia Law is the divine constitution of God. In order for these truths to be true - for Allah to be God and the Quran to be the holy book of God every word of the Quran must be Moral Perfection. For Muhammad to be a prophet of God, he could not be a criminal and lastly every teaching of Sharia must be Moral Perfection,

We have already proven that the teachings of Sharia Law are barbaric and not Moral Perfection - that God of Moral Perfection would never impose the totalitarianism of Sharia. We have already shown and will show throughout this book that Muhammad was an horrendous criminal that a God of Moral Perfection would never appoint as His prophet. We will prove that the Quran is filled not with one immoral word but with thousands of words/teachings of immoral depravity. If anyone of these 4 tenets is not true, then Islam is bogus – a sham and a fraud. We will demonstrate that ALL 4 are not true.

Again, to be from God - all teachings of God must be Moral Perfection. Any writings in any religious text that are not Moral Perfection are not the teachings of God but the teachings of man. Any religious text that pertains to be the divine, timeless word of God that contains just one word of immoral imperfection, then the entire religious text is not the word of God but the word of man and therefore, the entire religion is fraudulent.

All Muslims, regard the Quran as a holy, divine law book - the ETERNAL word/teachings of God that are unchangeable (forever). Muslims cannot question or doubt the allegedly uncreated words of God contained in their Quran - that God authored the Quran and a copy of the Quran is in heaven. Quranic teachings, the words of God, are immutable and stand valid for all times. Its ideas are absolutely true and beyond all criticism. To question it is to question the very word of God, and hence blasphemous. A Muslim's duty is to believe it and obey its divine commands without question.

We will demonstrate that all teachings recorded in the Quran and all other Islamic texts, revelations, writings, sayings, fatwa's - of extermination, war, murder, mass murder, killing, death and destruction, violence, terror, rape, unlimited sex with sex slaves, hate, violent jihad, terrorism, torture, brutality, savagery, maiming, beheading, inferiority of women, honor killings, stoning, cutting off limbs, child sex, women as instruments of sexual pleasure in paradise, Sharia law, bigotry, intolerance, extortion, slavery, mutilations, looting, pillaging, sexual depravity, child molestation, oppression and subordination of women, wife beating, inferiority of kafirs, that kafirs can be murdered and their property stolen as a holy duty, that Muslims who renounce Islam can be killed, that Muslims (or anyone) who challenge the teachings of Islam can be murdered, that believers who slay and are slain in the service of God will ascend to a sexual Paradise of lustrous eyed, voluptuous breasted virgins who they can sexually molest for all eternity are immoral, evil and irrational and not the perfect moral teachings of God – a God of Moral Perfection – a God of all pure love, peace and mercy – but again – the teachings of Allah (the AntiGod) – the teachings of Muhammad. Repeating, the Quran being not the teachings of a God of Moral Perfection is totally false - not a holy book but a book of evil. Being not a God of Moral Perfection, Allah is the fictional AntiGod of the Muslims and Islam is fraudulent.

Virtually every teaching of the Quran will be examined against the highest Moral Standard in the Universe – The Moral Perfection of A God of Moral Perfection. Again, if just one word of the Quran is not Moral Perfection then Allah is not God and therefore the entire Quran is not from God and Islam is totally fraudulent. Although the author only needs to find just one word of immoral imperfection in the Quran, he does not nit pick the Quran - he examines thousands of teachings and exposes thousands of words and teachings that are immoral to say the least for the fraud they represent - that these are not the words of God but of Muhammad. Over and over, again and again - the whole point of book will be repeated and repeated to make crystal clear that **ONLY A GOD OF MORAL PERFECTION IS GOD - THAT ALLAH IS NOT MORAL PERFECTION AND THEREFORE NOT GOD, THAT THE QURAN CONTAINS THOUSANDS OF WORDS/TEACHINGS OF IMMORAL IMPERFECTION AND THEREFORE IS NOT THE WORD OF GOD , MUHAMMAD WAS A CRIMINAL AND THEREFORE NO PROPHET OF GOD, SHARIA LAW IS IMMORAL BARBARIC DEPRAVITY AND THEREFORE NO DIVINE CONSTITUTION OF GOD AND THEREFORE ISLAM IS TOTALLY FRAUDELENT.**

At the end of each teaching the author will express his outrage in what can best be described as a tirade of disgust that such ridiculous evil that makes such a farce out of God could be embraced by our elites granting this barbarism intellectual legitimacy. He will ask repeatedly WHERE IS THE OUTRAGE? How can such diabolical evil be tolerated in our society let alone granted respect? By the end of this book, you will feel like a lunatic trapped in an insane asylum.

The author will describe again and again- the evilness of Muhammad and ask - how can any normal, rational, good, moral person be 'proud' to follow a heartless monster – a man who was a child molester, endorser of clitoridectomy, slave trader, rapist, owned slaves and raped his sex slaves, polygamist, endorsed whipping/beating women and ploughing them like fields, stoned women to death, flogged his slave women for fornication while he raped his slaves, propositioned women and passed them round to friends, denied women equal inheritance or equality under the law forever and abused and denigrated them in every way--not to mention his general sadism to others, mass murder, beheading captives, massacres, terror, torture, looting and pillaging, amputations, flogging, thievery, lying, hate, megalomania, had followers burned alive in their homes, the eyes burnt out of people's heads - unending horror. As already stated, any one of these crimes let alone all of them disqualifies Muhammad as a prophet.

Answering the above and following questions - how can, a rational, good, moral person believe that God would choose a demented, psychotic criminal as His prophet and then allow this evil person to declare that obeying the messenger was obeying God and vice versa? The answer is that you cannot be a good, moral person and believe in such a prophet, worship such an antiGod - Allah or pray with such an evil book- the Quran, or believe in such an evil ideology – Islam.

ISLAMIZATION OF KAFIR SOCIETY

Given that Islam cannot conquer Kafir nations with military force any longer, Muslims have embarked on a process of Islamization of Western democratic societies conquering them from within. This Islamization process employs violence to instill fear in the kafir and utilize the goodwill of kafir societies employing their own legal system of rule of law, equality and non discrimination as a sword to impose tyranny and supremacy of Muslims over kafirs. This process starts innocently enough with Muslims demanding their religious rights (read Stealth Jihad by Robert Spencer) then demanding that Sharia Law courts be established to handle only divorce and estate issues between Muslims. Once established, these courts impose Sharia on immigrant Muslim communities and embark on imposing it on kafir society through Stealth Jihad. The next step is to force kafirs living in Muslim areas of cities to move out creating a separate state within the country. Violence is employed against kafirs to force them out. Kafirs are harassed and physically attacked. Women are raped. Muslim areas are declared no go zones where police can no longer enter and the constitution of the state no longer is recognized nor enforced.

Violence is directed against the state to force a change in foreign policy toward Muslim terrorist groups. We saw this after the Madrid train bombings with the Spanish government withdrawing forces from Iraq. This Islamization process is explained in the book as well as Western political, intellectual, media, religious elites joining forces with Muslims to destroy Western civilization. For a truly frightening video of what is coming to America sooner then later go to http://www.islamreform.net/new-page-100.htm Islamization of Paris: A Warning To TheWest.

MUHAMMAD: MOST MERIFUL MAN OF MERCY EVER BORN HAD FOLLOWERS AND THEIR FAMILIES BURNT ALIVE IN THEIR HOMES FOR MISSING PRAYERS

What you will be reading next is the sheer horror that is Islam. Again – these teachings from Quran and Hadith are completely unique. You will not find anything like them in Old/New Testament or the Torah. As already stated, the Quran is the word/teachings of Allah (AntiGod of the Muslims - fictional creation of Muhammad) instructing us to commit horrendous criminal acts and in return for blind obedience, we will be guaranteed accession to a virgin delight Paradise. The Hadith is the teachings of Muhammad setting a timeless, divine example of how to live our lives in accordance with the AntiGod's Quranic teachings. There are no laws of God in the Old/New Testaments/Torah instructing Jews/Christians to commit crimes. NOT ONE.

Go through the Appendix teachings at www.islamreform.net and the chapters of this book containing other teachings of divine wisdom. Don't kid yourself. These teachings may be laughable but Islam is no laughing matter. These are the words that are destroying our country and way of life. This is a life and death situation. Failure to understand Islam and act against this very great evil will destroy civilization as we know it. A New Dark Age will descent over humanity. This time the darkness will be eternal.

Burnt Alive For Missing Prayers

Muhammad was so merciful that he instructed his followers to burn people alive who missed prayers according to Sahih Bukhari hadith.

Bukhari:V1B11N626 "The Prophet said, 'No prayer is harder for the hypocrites than the Fajr. If they knew the reward they would come to (the mosque) even if they had to crawl. I decided to order a man to lead the prayer and then take a flame to burn all those who had not left their houses for the prayer, burning them alive inside their homes.'"

Pregnant Woman Brutality Stoned To Death After Birth of Child

Muslim (17:4206) - A woman who became pregnant confesses to Muhammad that she is guilty of adultery. Muhammad allows her to have the child, then has her stoned (the description is graphic). For complete Hadith go to http://www.islamreform.net/new-page-26.htm and read from Muslim (17:4206)

"....She said: Allah's Apostle, here is he (baby) as I have weaned him and he eats food. He (the Holy Prophet) entrusted the child to one of the Muslims and then pronounced punishment. And she was put in a ditch up to her chest and he commanded people and they stoned her. Khalid b Walid came forward with a stone which he flung at her head and there spurted blood on the face of Khalid and so he abused her. Allah's Apostle (may peace be upon him) heard his (Khalid's) curse that he had huried upon her. Thereupon he (the Holy Prophet) said: Khalid, be gentle. By Him in Whose Hand is my life, she has made such a repentance that even if a wrongful tax-collector were to repent, he would have been forgiven. Then giving command regarding her, he prayed over her and she was buried."

Can you imagine stoning a woman to death after giving birth to a baby? Bringing the baby to the stoning, giving the child to the prophet, then being buried up to her breasts and stoned to death. Picture in your mind's eye, the dug out hole with the earth piled to one side. The boulders neatly assembled beside the hole. The woman is taken into the hole and the loose earth is thrown back until she is buried up to her breasts. Can you imagine the sheer horror of this poor mother, hearing her baby crying as she is being sent to her death? Can you imagine burying a woman up to her breasts and then hurling boulders at her head? Do you not see the blood gushing from her head like a blood fountain and running down the side of her head, matting her hair? Quoting "Khalid b Walid came forward with a stone which he flung at her head and there spurted blood on the face of Khalid and so he abused her." Do you not hear the yelling and screaming of this poor woman begging for mercy, the blood gurgling in her mouth? How could any moral person brutality murder a mother and deny the baby his mother to raise and care for the child? This poor woman begged for her life. She begged and she begged and she begged. Quoting Muhammad: "she has made such repentance that even if a wrongful tax-collector were to repent, he would have been forgiven." But Muhammad – the prophet of mercy, the protype of all humanity would not let the mere wailing of a woman and her crying baby move him for he was obeying Quranic verse 24.2 "...Let not compassion move you in their case, in a matter prescribed by God, if ye believe in God and the Last Day.." Muhammad was the first, last and only prophet of the AntiGod Allah. He was a true prophet with a heartless heart and soul as cold and lifeless as the bloody boulders that would soon be the executioners of the Antigod's will. Being most merciful Muhammad commands Khalid b Walid "Khaild be gentle." The boulders are now smashing gently into her defenseless head and face. Blood is pouring out from her hideous head and face wounds. The ground is soaked in blood – the boulders caked in blood. As her brain is smashed to bits, she will experience horrendous pain and suffering and mercifully go into a coma. Then her life breath will be finally extinguished and she will slump over a bloody pulverized mess of torn flesh. What was once a beautiful young mother will now be a piece of mauled bloody garbage. Even though Muhammad stated that he would have forgiven a wrongful tax-collector so great was her repentance he did not stop the stoning. Instead, she is murdered by Muhammad and then he mercifully prays over her torn bloody body. What hypocrisy. You tell me what kind of heartless beast could do such an immoral act of depravity? Muhammad was this heartless monster. He had the power of life and death over his subjects. He was the final arbiter of life or death. Muhammad was God. (There is a clandestine film that was taken during the Nazi occupation of Belorussia showing SS locking families inside a barn and setting it on fire. The film shows an SS soldier dragging a young woman with her baby in her arms from the farm house. The SS takes the baby from its mother and smashes the poor child - head first into the ground. You tell me the difference between this SS killer and the prophet of God – Muhammad?)

Wait a moment. How unfair of me. Oh Allah please forgive me for maligning your great prophet by comparing him to the SS baby killer. Of course there is a difference between this SS killer and Muhammad.

Muhammad never buried the baby in the hole and stoned the child to death for being born the product of an adulterous relationship. Oh no - being a man of mercy, the protype of all mankind, the divine example for all Muslim men to emulate for all time, he murdered the mother in cold blood.

To truly understand the danger of Islam to our society and way of life read Brutal Stoning Hadiths http://www.islamreform.net/new-page-26.htm

Men Horribly Tortured by Prophet Muhammad

BukhariV882N795; Narrated Anas:"The Prophet cut off the hands and feet of the men belonging to the tribe of Uraina and did not cauterise (their bleeding limbs) till they died."

Muhammad Orders An Alcoholic Beaten

Book 38, Number 4474: Narrated AbdurRahman ibn Azhar: "I saw the Apostle of Allah (peace_be_upon_him) …. a man who had drunk wine was brought (before him) and he ordered them (to beat him). So they beat him with what they had in their hands. Some struck him with whips, some with sticks and some with sandals. The Apostle of Allah (peace_be_upon_him) threw some dust on his face."

Muhammad Beats His Sex Slave Girl

Sunan Abu-Dawud, Book 38, Number 4458: Narrated Ali ibn AbuTalib: "A slave-girl belonging to the house of the Apostle of Allah (peace_be_upon_him) committed fornication. He (the Prophet) said: Rush up, Ali, and inflict the prescribed punishment on her. I then hurried up, and saw that blood was flowing from her, and did not stop. So I came to him and he said: Have you finished inflicting (punishment on her)? I said: I went to her while her blood was flowing. He said: Leave her alone till her bleeding stops; then inflict the prescribed punishment on her. And inflict the prescribed punishment on those whom your right hands possess (i.e. slaves)".

Martyred For The AntiGod Allah

Bukhari:V4B52N63 "A man whose face was covered with an iron mask came to the Prophet and said, 'Allah's Apostle! Shall I fight or embrace Islam first?' The Prophet said, 'Embrace Islam first and then fight.' So he embraced Islam, and was martyred. Allah's Apostle said, 'A Little work, but a great reward.'"

Poet Ordered Murdered By Muhammad To Shut Her Up

Ishaq: 676 "'You obey a stranger who encourages you to murder for booty. You are greedy men. Is there no honor among you?' Upon hearing those lines Muhammad said, 'Will no one rid me of this woman?' Umayr, a zealous Muslim, decided to execute the Prophet's wishes. That very night he crept into the writer's home while she lay sleeping surrounded by her young children. There was one at her breast. Umayr removed the suckling babe and then plunged his sword into the poet. The next morning in the mosque, Muhammad, who was aware of the assassination, said, 'You have helped Allah and His Apostle.' Umayr said. 'She had five sons; should I feel guilty?' 'No,' the Prophet answered. 'Killing her was as meaningless as two goats butting heads.'"

These are just a small sample from the thousands of Hadith of Muhammad inflicting heinous punishment. Ask yourself how any prophet of God could commit such evil acts? Again, if God had selected such a criminal to be His criminal prophet then God would be a criminal God but since God cannot be a criminal and be Moral Perfection – a criminal God cannot exist. Muhammad was no prophet. Can you imagine the sheer terror of 13/14 year old Jewish boys having their pants pulled down and groin inspected for pubic hairs and then their heads chopped off at the slightest trace? Can you imagine burning families alive? Can you imagine stoning a mother leaving a poor baby child motherless? You tell me what is the difference between prophet Muhammad and Fuhrer Adolf Hitler? There is none. Where is humanities outrage? For more Hadiths displaying the pure mercy of Muhammad go to http://www.islamreform.net/new-page-8.htm

SAMPLE OF 4,000 DIVINE, EVIL, FASCIST QURANIC TEACHINGS FROM ALLAH (THE ANTIGOD) OF BEHEADING, EXTERMINATION, GENOCIDE, MASS MURDER, TERROR, TORTURE, HATE SLAVERY THAT ARE NOT MORAL PERFECTION

These Quranic teachings will be examined in Chapters 4, 16, 17, 20.

OF SLAVERY

Quran 2.178: "O you who believe! retaliation is prescribed for you in the matter of the slain, the free for the free, and the slave for the slave, and the female for the female, but if any remission is made to any one by his (aggrieved) brother, then prosecution (for the bloodwit) should be made according to usage, and payment should be made to him in a good manner; this is an alleviation from your Lord and a mercy; so whoever exceeds the limit after this he shall have a painful chastisement."

You kill one of my slaves, females or free man and I'll kill one of your slaves, females or free man.

OF BARBARIC CRUELTY

Quran 5.33 "The only reward of those who make war upon Allah and His messenger and strive after corruption in the land will be that they will be killed or crucified, or have their hands and feet on alternate sides cut off, or will be expelled out of the land. Such will be their degradation in the world, and in the Hereafter theirs will be an awful doom;"

5:38 "Cut off the hands of thieves, whether they are male or female, as punishment for what they have done-a deterrent from God: God is almighty and wise." 39 "But if anyone repents after his wrongdoing and makes amends, God will accept his repentance: God is most forgiving and merciful. (Haleem)"

AN EYE FOR AN EYE
Quran 5:45 "And We prescribed for them therein: The life for the life, and the eye for the eye, and the nose for the nose, and the ear for the ear, and the tooth for the

tooth, and for wounds retaliation. But whoso forgoeth it (in the way of charity) it shall be expiation for him. Whoso judgeth not by that which Allah hath revealed such as wrong–doers."

In Islam, an eye for an eye means an eye for an eye.

OF BEHEADING

Quran 8.12 "Remember thy Lord inspired the angels (with the message): "I am with you: give firmness to the Believers: I will instill terror into the hearts of the Unbelievers: smite ye above their necks and smite all their finger-tips off them." There are 75 teachings of beheading in Quran.

SLAUGHTER IN THE LAND

Quran-8:67 "It is not for any prophet to have captives until he hath made slaughter in the land. Ye desire the lure of this world and Allah desireth (for you) the Hereafter, and Allah is Mighty, Wise." (Allah insisting Prophet to kill all the prisoners, and should not keep any surrendered prisoners alive until He (Prophet) occupied entire Arabia.)

MASS MURDER: THE INFAMOUS VERSE OF THE SWORD

Quran 9.5 "Then, when the sacred months have passed, slay the idolaters wherever ye find them, and take them (captive), and besiege them, and prepare for them each ambush. But if they repent and establish worship and pay the poor-due, then leave their way free. Lo! Allah is Forgiving, Merciful."

TORTURE

Quran 22:19-22 "fight and slay the Pagans, seize them, beleaguer them, and lie in wait for them in every stratagem" "for them (the unbelievers) garments of fire shall be cut and there shall be poured over their heads boiling water whereby whatever is in their bowels and skin shall be dissolved and they will be punished with hooked iron rods"

BARBARIC BARBARISM

24:2 "The woman and the man guilty of adultery or fornication, - flog each of them with a hundred stripes: Let not compassion move you in their case, in a matter prescribed by God, if ye believe in God and the Last Day: and let a party of the Believers witness their punishment.

STRETCHING FROM OSLO, NORWAY IN THE NORTH TO LONDON, ENGLAND IN THE SOUTH AN ISLAMIC CURTAIN IS RAPIDLY DESCENDING UPON EUROPE

THE CONCENTRATION CAMPS ARE COMING TO THE UNITED STATES AND AGAIN TO EUROPE

THE FINAL, "FINAL SOLUTION" OF THE JEWISH AND CHRISTIAN QUESTION

Why Europe is completing the work of Muhammad and Hitler – the final "Final Solution" of the Jewish and Christian question that has plagued the West ever since the West was the West.

THE COMPANIONS OF MUHAMMAD – THE FIRST NAZI SS MEN

Why the prophet Muhammad's beheadings, massacres and mass exile of Jews and Christians from Arabia was the first "Final Solution" of the Jewish and Christian question.

"the Apostle of Allah said, 'Kill any Jew that falls into your power." Ibn Ishaq, Siratul Rasul, v. 553

Quran: 5.60 "God has cursed the Jews, transforming them into apes and swine and those who serve the devil.

CONTENTS

CHAPTER 1: A God of Moral Perfection   1
    If God Exists Then God Is Great. It Is the
    So-called Men of God Who Are Not Great
    A Revolutionary Revolution in the Conception of God: Declaration of Universal Religious Rights and Freedoms of A God of Moral Perfection

CHAPTER 2: It's All About Islam, Stupid Kafir   13
    Your Democratic Obligation as a Kafir
    Organization of Islam
    The Truth of Islam
    Dar al-Islam and Dar al-Harb: The House of Islam and The House of War
    Sharia Law

CHAPTER 3: God of Moral Perfection versus Allah (the AntiGod) of the Muslims   29
    Requirements Necessary for the Quran to be the Eternal Divine Word of God
    Why the Quran Is Not the Word/Teachings of a God of Moral Perfection. Broad Overview of the Immoral Quran

CHAPTER 4: Examination of the Immoral Teachings of the Quran   33
    Verse 9:5 The Infamous Verse of the Sword
    Verse 9:29 People of the Book
    Verse 4:89 Of Apostasy
    Verse 5.32 Of Extermination
    Verse 5:33 Of Barbaric Cruelty
    Verse 8:12 Of Beheading
    Verse 47:4 Instructions of War
    Verses 4:74 & 2:207 Of Suicide Attacks
    Verses 8:60 & 3:151 Of Terrorism
    Verses 9:39, 3:169/70 & 8:16 Of Hell
    Evil Demented Depraved Islamic Paradise as Laws of God
    Verse 9:111 Muslims Passport to Paradise

CHAPTER 5: Allah's Teachings Celebrating the Massacre of the Jews 59
  At Banu Qurayza
  Banu Quraiza; Brief Description of the Massacre in Islam's Own Writings
  Muhammad Besieges Banu Quraiza for 25 Days. After the Jews Unconditionally Surrender All Men Are Beheaded, Women and Young Girls Raped and Sold Into Slavery. Their Property Is Looted.
  Merciful Muhammad Orders Trenches To Be Dug for the Beheaded Heads to Fall Into and Control the Blood Flow
  Big Problem: How Did the SS Jihadist Executioners Decide on Which Jewish Boys to Slaughter or Leave Alive to be Sold into Slavery
  Aisha Describes the Only Woman Murdered At Banu Qurayzah: She Was Delirious Because Her Husband Had Just Been Beheaded. She Was Taken by the SS Jihadist and Beheaded, Putting Her Out of Her Joyful Misery
  Muhammad Took One of the Jewish Women as His Sex Slave.
  The Looted Property and the Jewish Women and Children Were Divided Among the Muslims
  Allah Allows Muhammad and His Jihadists to Have Sex with Their Sex Slaves
  Muhammad Shows No Mercy
  Muhammad Enriches Himself
  Allah Shares In the Looting and Pillaging of Murdered Jews Property
  Why Does Muhammad Not Show Mercy?
  Allah (the AntiGod) Celebrates the Massacre at Banu Qurayza
  Enjoy the Booty

CHAPTER 6: God's Incitement to War 71
  Jihad: Holy War: War In the Name of and to the Greater Glory of God
  164 Jihad: Unholy War Verses in the Quran

CHAPTER 7: Where Is The Outrage: Horror of Rape: A Holy Act 91
Ordained by God as a Weapon of War
  Following are some of the immoral evil laws of Allah (the AntiGod) of raping sex slaves. These laws are eternal.
  Men can marry up to four women if they treat them equally; unlimited forcible concubines permitted

  Muhammad can go beyond the four-wife restriction, can treat his

own wives and sex slaves unequally.
This verse is for Muhammad. God allows Muhammad to own and rape his slave girls.

CHAPTER 8: The Massacre at Khaybar: Assassination of Muhammad — 97
Muhammad Attacks the Rich Jewish Settlement of Khaybar Without Warning.
Muhammad Takes Safiya As His Sex Slave After Murdering
Her Father, Brothers, and Torturing and Murdering Her Husband
Distribution of War Booty In Khaybar.
Muhammad Has Safiya's Husband Horribly Tortured to Try And Force Him to Reveal Where He Hid the Gold Treasure of the People of Khaybar. He Was Beheaded After He Refused to Give Up the Treasure.
The Looted Property and Women and Children Were Distributed among the Jihadists
Enjoying Special Booty (Gani-maater-maal): Muhammad Takes Safiya as Booty to Be His Sex Slave.
Muhammad Attacks and Rapes Seventeen-Year-Old Safiya: Muhammad Was Sixty.

CHAPTER 9: The Massacre at Banu Mustaliq — 103
Muhammad Attacks The Jewish Settlement of Bani Mustaliq: He Captures and Rapes a Twenty-Year-Old Jewish Girl, Juwairiya.

CHAPTER 10: Sex Slaves: Muhammad and Those His Right Hand Possess — 105

CHAPTER 11: Women Are Equal of Men: God Is Not A Sexist; God Is Not a Male Chauvinist Pig — 107
In Islam's Own Writings: Allah and His Messenger's Extreme Hatred of Women
Muslim Women are Dirty Polluting Creatures
Women are inferior, slave to men
Muslim women are sex object for men's enjoyment
Muslim Men can Capture Infidel Women as Sex-slave Booty
A Woman's Testimony is Worth Only Half of a Man's
Brutal Punishment for Women
Fewer seats for women in Allah's Paradise
The Tyranny of Men over Women
Polygamy
Wife Swapping
Wives as slaves
Wife Beating

Muslim Women: Islam's Domestic Animals

CHAPTER 12: Sexual Perversions of Prophet Muhammad 123
Necrophilia With His Dead Aunt
Sucking The Tongue of His Daughter and Cousin's Sons
Muhammad Transvestite Tendencies
Breast Feeding Grown Men by Muslim Women and The Billy Goa
From Islam's Unholy Book

CHAPTER 13: Allah Is a Pedophile Monster 127
Baby Tilths

CHAPTER 14: Muhammad: A Human Being of Perfection 129
Muhammad: The Perfect Husband and Family Man
Baby Aisha and Muhammad: A Love Story For The Ages Between a 6-Year-Old Child and a 53-Year-Old Sexual Pervert. It will bring Tears of Joy to Your Eyes and Heart: From The Holy Book Of Islam
Muhammad and Molestation of Baby Aisha (From the Writings of Islam)
Muhammad Would Sexually Abuse His Wives
The Prophet Would Do All His Wives In One Night
This Sickness of Islam and Raping Baby Girls Is An Evil Approved By Allah (the AntiGod) for All Time
Why Quran 65:4 Is Not The Word/Teaching of God and Therefore the Entire Quran Is Not the Words/Teachings Of God

CHAPTER 15: Where Is The Outrage: Cruelty, Torture 137
In Islam's Own Writings: Muhammad, the Most Merciful Prophet
Torture: Hands must be cut off for theft
Muhammad Ordered Feet and Hands Cut Off and Eyes Burnt Out, and Left To Suffer a Horrendous Death
Beat the children if they do not pray
Burnt alive for missing prayers
Homosexuals are to be killed
Apostates must be murdered
Alcoholics beaten
Stoning in Islam: Diabolical brutality

CHAPTER 16: Allah Is A Barbaric Barbarian 145
Why Quran 24:2 Is Not The Word/Teaching Of God And Therefore The Entire Quran Is Not The Word/Teachings Of God And Therefore Islam Is Fraudulent

CHAPTER 17: Owning Slaves is an Eternal Law of God   **147**

CHAPTER 18: The Quran Is a Book Filled with Hate   **153**
    Hitler: The Final Solution of the Jewish Question and Muhammad: The First, "Final Solution" of the Jewish Question of Saudi Arabia
    Mein Kampf versus the Quran
    Hitler and the Final Solution of the Jewish Question
    Hitler's Hatred of the Jews
    Muhammad and the First, "Final Solution" of the Jewish Question of Arabia
    Muhammad's Teachings of Pure Hate From the Hadiths. Kill All The Jews: The First, "Final Solution"
    Muhammad's Teachings of Hate from the Quran
    The Quran Celebrated the Massacre of the Jews of Banu Qurayza
    Anti-Jewish Hate Teachings in the Quran
    Following, from the Quran Are Teachings Not of Pure Love But of Pure Hate. Verses that show intolerance of and incite violence against non - Muslims and other religions.

CHAPTER 19: Islam Devours It's Young   **167**

CHAPTER 20: Honor Thy Father Or Be Murdered   **171**
    What is honor killing?
    Honor killing is different from other killings
    Some sample cases of horrific honor killing
    Honor killing is an ETERNAL Law of Allah (the AntiGod) in Islam. Dictums Of Quran and Hadiths Which Dictate/Incite Honor Killing

CHAPTER 21: Teaching Islam to Children Is Child Abuse   **179**
    (Recapitulation of Quranic Teachings Quoted In This Book: Why Teaching Them Is Child Abuse)
    How Can Any School Teach An Ideology That Owning Slaves Is An Eternal Law Of God?
    How Can Any School Teach An Ideology That Raping Slaves Is An Eternal Law Of God?
    How Can Any School Teach An Ideology That As Muslims They Can Loot and Pillage the Property Of Kafirs?
    How Can Any School Teach An Ideology That Teaches Children That Kafirs Must Convert to Islam or Pay A Jizya (Submission) Tax or Be Murdered As Eternal Laws Of God?
    How Can Any School Teach An Ideology That All Other Religions Must Submit To Islam?
    How Can Any School Teach An Ideology With An Evil Demented

Depraved Sexual Islamic Paradise?
How Can Any Western School System Allow the Teaching of An Ideology Created By An Evil Incarnate Child Abuser, Wife Abuser, Rapist and Murderer – Muhammad?
How Can Any School Teach An Ideology That Preaches the Oppression and Submission of Women to Men?
How Can Any School Proclaim An Ideology That Teaches Brutality as Eternal Laws of God?
How Can Any School Teach An Ideology That Teaches Rape with Young Female Muslim Children?
How Can Any School Teach An Ideology That Teaches Children Hate and Intolerance Toward Jews, Christians and All Other Kafirs?
Any School System That Allows Teaching Islam Is Guilty of Child Abuse and Charges Should Be Brought

CHAPTER 22: Islam Is To Be Superior Over All   191
    Quoting From The Quran

CHAPTER 23: Obeying The Messenger Is Obeying Allah   195
    The Criminality of Muhammad
    27 bogus, fraudulent teachings of obeying Allah and his messenger

CHAPTER 24: Very Important Statistics Concerning Quran   201
    Love versus Fear in the Quran: A Statistical Analysis
    Muhammad Versus Allah: Statistical Analysis
    Jihad: Statistical Analysis
    Women In Islam: Statistical Analysis

CHAPTER 25: Absurd Teaching of the Quran – Verses That Allowed   205
    Muhammad to Cancel the Adoption of His Adopted Son and
    Marry His Adopted Son's Wife

CHAPTER 26: Teachings Regarding Muhammad's Wives   209
    As Eternal Laws Of God: A Soap Opera
    Muhammad's Sheer Hatred of Dogs

CHAPTER 27: Murdering Musicians, Singers In Islam   215
CHAPTER 28: The Ten Commandments Are Not the   217
    Teaching of a God of Moral Perfection
CHAPTER 29: Jesus versus Muhammad   219
CHAPTER 30: Western Civilization: The Greatest
    Civilization in World History   225
CHAPTER 31: What Islam Isn't   229

CHAPTER 32: Is It a Rational – Is It a Reasonable Human Thought   233

CHAPTER 33: Turkey: The 36th Chapter   235
CHAPTER 34: Europe's Final, "Final Solution" of the Jewish and Christian Question: Finishing the Mission of Muhammad and Hitler
Let's Give A Red Card to the City of Cologne, Germany
How Stealth Censorship is Destroying Freedom of Speech   239

CHAPTER 35: The Boys from Mumbai: The Muslim Killers of the Mumbai Massacre: Soon To Be Followed By the Boys from New York City and the Boys from London   247

CHAPTER 36: Islam, the Religion of Peace   249

CHAPTER 37: Blacks Calling Themselves Muslims Should Be Ashamed   257

CHAPTER 38: Why a Muslim Can Never Be President of The United States, Ever   263

CHAPTER 39: Banality of Evil: Banality of Silence   271

CHAPTER 40: America and Europe's Future: Dhimmihood   275

CHAPTER 41: Sharia Law Will Be the Rule Of Law   279

CHAPTER 42: 11 Reasons Abomination of Sharia Law Must Be Banned   285

CHAPTER 43: Sharia: Islam's Warden Brutal Barbarism of The True Islam   296

CHAPTER 44: Defense of America   287
CHAPTER 45: Of Minarets and Freedom of Speech   293

CHAPTER ONE

A GOD OF MORAL PERFECTION

We do not know if God exists or not. The fact that the entire universe 14 billion years ago or more was a pulsating entity no larger than the dot at the end of a pencil then exploded giving birth to the universe and eventually earth/mankind is such a fantastic notation. Did this dot explode in the big bang as an act of nature or the will of God?

If a being created the entire universe - a being we will call the Creator - and this being who has the power to set the entire universe on fire with just a single thought, is filled with hate, enjoys torturing his creations and striking terror into their hearts, is the great destroyer of cities and worlds, utilizes war to smash his creations, condones their rape, approves of their slaughter, then this Creator is not God but an evil creature with an IQ to the order of zillions and zillions. If we took the entire length of the universe and then filled this distance starting with the number 9 followed by nines – this infinitesimal number would be this Creator's IQ. However, intelligence does not make you a God. Such an evil Creator who clearly has the power to command our obedience but not our respect would not be God.

The reality is that 80% of mankind believes in God. This belief in God whether it is part of the evolutionary process of Homo sapiens, or because God actually exists is natural.

Those intellectuals who claim that God Is Not Great - like Christopher Hitchens in his recent book " God Is Not Great," their dispute is not with God but with the men of God who have - through the millenniums - for power, domination, and control of society turned God into a murderous, psychopathical, evil, maniacal, beast.

IF GOD EXISTS THEN GOD IS GREAT: IT IS THE MEN OF GOD WHO ARE NOT GREAT

God gave mankind the greatest gifts in the entire universe – the human brain and an earth crawling with the bounty of life – a paradise in the vast, hostile, mostly lifeless, universe. The fact that throughout mankind's history, man has utilized his brain to murder a minimum of 350 million people - slaughtered in the worst ways imaginable in the name of and to the greater glory of God - is an abomination. The men of God responsible for this carnage deserve to be in Hell.

It is not irrational for some to state that the belief in a God who created the universe is totally and completely irrational. That there is no God. That God does not exist. That the universe was created 14 billion years ago from an accidental explosion – an act of nature. That the whole point and purpose of the universe is that there is no point or purpose. That the universe is just a collection of a bunch of dirt and rocks that just happened to coalesce into stars and planets. That mankind's creation was solely by chance with the aid of two comets blasting into the earth annihilating the dominant life forms and allowing man's ancestors to descend from the trees and evolve through natural selection into present day Homo sapiens. That the existence of mankind is no more important than the existence of a boulder lying on the ground.

It is not irrational for some of the species Homo sapiens to believe in a God of the universe - the Omniscient, Omnipotent, and Glorious Exalted Creator of the Universe, a God of peace, love, goodness and mercy – **A GOD OF MORAL PERFECTION.**

However, what is totally and completely irrational is the belief in a God that demands the murder of non-believers, their enslavement, torture, breeding and selling, rape and brutalization, the looting of their property – an evil, hateful, murderous, God of war, terror, violence, death and destruction. This conception of God borders on insanity.

How do we know that an evil God of hate, violence, war, death and destruction cannot exist in the universe?

Every day the human family wakes up, mankind is engaged in a struggle for survival as a species in a very hostile universe. The greatest threat to the survival of Homo sapiens is Homo sapiens. Many of us believe that the teachings of God: peace and love, mercy and goodness, that the meek shall inherit the earth, love thy enemy, turn the other cheek etc. are the teachings that will create relationships governing mankind's behavior guaranteeing that mankind will not go to extinction by his own hand. As will be shown later in this book, Muslims worship Allah (the AntiGod) a fictional being who delivers mankind a message of pure hate, kill your enemies, rape and molest them, torture and terrorize, enslave and breed them, that the strong and merciless shall inherit the earth, smash in your opponents cheek and behead him – teachings that given weapons of mass destruction (and worse weapons yet to be invented) guarantee not man's survival but his total destruction – suicide as a species through mass murder.

The entire purpose of life is life.

If God created the universe, then He created all the elements that made the existence of life possible. The whole essence of God's existence is life, love, mercy – otherwise what's the sense. It doesn't take a God to create death. Allah is the AntiGod of death. Allah does not exist.

We no longer have to worry about Muslim men on horse back riding into cities, beheading the male population with swords, then carting off the screaming and wailing females to be raped/enslaved. The greatest danger mankind faces is the smuggling of a nuclear weapon by a Muslim into a major Western or Indian city killing millions in the name of and to the greater glory of God. Can you imagine a city lying in ruins, millions crying out in unimaginable pain and agony? Troops moving through the streets, shooting hundreds of thousands of wounded in the head to terminate their suffering. This will be the end of civilization as we know it. This is the nightmare scenario that will happen in our lifetime if we do not adopt the teachings of a God of Moral Perfection.

If God exists then only a GOD OF MORAL PERFECTION is God.

A REVOLUTIONARY REVOLUTION IN THE CONCEPTION OF GOD

DECLARATION OF UNIVERSAL RIGHTS AND FREEDOMS OF A GOD OF MORAL PERFECTION

Following are self-evident truths of a GOD OF MORAL PERFECTION:

GOD AS THE CREATOR OF THE UNIVERSE - THE CREATOR OF ALL LIVING THINGS IS PERFECTION - MORAL PERFECTION

ALL TEACHINGS OF GOD - A PERFECT GOD – MUST BE MORAL PERFECTION

ANY WRITINGS IN ANY RELIGIOUS TEXT THAT ARE NOT MORAL PERFECTION ARE NOT THE TEACHINGS OF GOD BUT THE TEACHINGS OF MAN. IF A BOOK FROM A RELIGION PERTAINS TO BE THE DIVINE, TIMELESS, WORD OF GOD THEN EVERY WORD IN THAT BOOK MUST BE MORAL PERFECTION. IF ONLY ONE WORD IS NOT MORAL PERFECTION THEN THE ENTIRE BOOK IS NOT THE WORD OF GOD AND THE ENTIRE RELIGION IS TOTALLY FRAUDULENT

AS MORAL PERFECTION - GOD IS PURE PEACE AND LOVE, MERCY AND GOODNESS

BEING A GOD OF MORAL PERFECTION - GOD IS ANTI-WAR: THE EMBODIMENT OF PURE NON-VIOLENCE

ALL MANKIND IS CREATED EQUAL AND THEIR LIVES ARE SACRED TO GOD

GOD IS NOT AN IRRATIONAL, IMMORAL, EVIL BEING. IF GOD IS IRRATIONAL, IMMORAL, EVIL THEN GOD IS NOT MORAL PERFECTION AND THEREFORE SINCE GOD CANNOT BE MORALLY IMPERFECT, AN IRRATIONAL, IMMORAL, EVIL ENTITY IS NOT GOD.

God being a God of Moral Perfection therefore:
God is pure peace and love, mercy and goodness, a God for all mankind. All human beings are created in the image of God. All mankind is created equal and their lives are precious and sacred to God. As the glorious, exalted, creator of the universe and all living things God is the embodiment of Moral Perfection.

God being a God of Moral Perfection therefore:
God is the essence of pure peace. If God spoke just one word of violence - had just one violent thought - God would no longer be Moral Perfection and therefore, no longer God. God is not a violent being. If God committed just one act of violence or ordered an act of violence then God would no longer be Moral Perfection and therefore, no longer God. All words/teachings in any religious book that contain violence are not the word/teachings of God but the word/teachings of man.

God being a God of Moral Perfection therefore:
God is anti-war. All war is abhorrent to God - an affront to the intelligence He bestowed on mankind. God did not endow Homo sapiens with intelligence to war against fellow Homo sapiens like beasts in the jungle. War is an abomination and obscenity against God. It is the second greatest crime that man can commit against God. The greatest crime is war, violence, killing and murder in the name of and to the greater glory of God. God never intervened in any battle, never led an army into battle, changed the weather allowing (His) side to be victorious or any other form of divine intervention. There is no - His side. War is anti-God. War is anti-creation. War is the extinction of humanity from the face of the earth. All teachings that pertain to be from God preaching, ordering, encouraging or engaging in war or any other acts of violence are not from God but are the teachings of evil men. If God thought just one word of war, ordered the killing or actually killed with His own hand just one human being or any other creature throughout the entire universe then God would be an immoral murderer. If God believes in violence, believes in war, believes in killing, terror, torture, and maiming then God is no longer Moral Perfection and therefore, no longer God but the incarnation of evil.

God being a God of Moral Perfection therefore:

As stated, all violence, killing, maiming and torturing others in the name of and to the greater glory of God is the greatest evil anyone can commit. Suicide bombers killing themselves and others in the name of God – this is the supreme evil act. As Moral Perfection, God can never instruct anyone to commit acts of violence against any other human being. As anti-war, God is the pure embodiment of non-violence. Humanity must totally and completely renounce all violence in religion – without equivocation. Humanity must totally and completely renounce all teachings of war in religion. Humanity must totally and completely renounce all teachings of killing, murder, terror, torture and maiming in religion. Humanity must totally and completely renounce all killing and murdering in the name of God. There is no heaven for these murderers. Just the black hole of eternal damnation. You cannot climb to heaven on the corpses of the murdered. All such teachings are not the teachings of a God of Moral Perfection but the teachings of man.

God being a God of Moral Perfection therefore:
All hate is abhorrent to God. As Moral Perfection, God has never spoken a word of hate. As the essence of pure love, as a being whose very existence is pure love God is totally incapable of hate. If God had just one hateful thought, spoke just one hateful word, committed/ordered just one hateful act, then God would no longer be Moral Perfection. Since God cannot be imperfect and still be God a hateful God is no longer God. Again, ALL teachings of violence, hate, war, extermination, genocide, retaliation, terror, torture, maiming, rape, slavery, revenge, inequality, intolerance, in any holy book are not the word/teachings of God but the word/teachings of man.

God being a God of Moral Perfection therefore:
God is a non-religious being. For God, there exists no concept of believers or non- believers, no chosen people, no chosen holy land for any chosen people. God is God for all mankind. There is no chosen species of God. God is God for all creatures throughout the entire universe and possible other universes. There is no one truth - no such thing as the one and only true religion. Belief in any religion does not make you a superior human being or give you any special privileges over any other human. It does not give you any God-given right to enslave, discriminate against, kill, terrorize, rape or loot non-believers (in your faith) in the name of God. All such teachings are not from God but are created by evil men to usurp God's divine power and utilize this power for evil, justifying it as the will of God.

God being a God of Moral Perfection therefore:
Repeating this self evident very important truth, one of the greatest evils that anyone can commit is violence against human beings in the name of and to the greater glory of God. Another great evil is to preach hate in the name of God inciting violence against human beings. The third greatest evil is to record in a holy book teachings of extermination, genocide, murder, hate, violence, terror,

brutality against non-believers of the book and claim that these evil teachings are the divine, timeless word of God. There are many ways to God. None of these ways includes murder, violence, hate, torture, terror. Even a total non-believer in the existence of God can ascend to Heaven provided he does not have an evil soul. Religion was invented by man as a vehicle to allow humanity to comprehend God. Because mankind is imperfect then religion is imperfect.

God being a God of Moral Perfection therefore:
Everyone has the total and complete right to find his/her own way to God or not. Religious freedom is the unimpeachable right of all mankind. The right to build places of worship to practice one's religious beliefs - (the religious teachings of a God of pure love, peace, mercy - A God of Moral Perfection) should be a cornerstone of all civilized societies. The right to change one's religion without fear of death. The right to freely preach and practice one's religion without coercion or intimidation but with liberty and tolerance in every country. The right to explore the truth of any religious question, including the truth as to the origins, sources, and teachings of any religion. The unqualified liberty to question and differ from any religion and its teachings. The right to condemn all religious practices that violate human rights. The total and complete rejection of teachings of violence, terror, torture, murder, revenge, intolerance and bigotry. The right not to believe in God. Only an evil being would order people put to death for not believing in a religion or deciding to change one's beliefs from one religion to another, or believing in a different religion. God is a God of peace and love for all mankind. Again, any teaching that claims to be from a God of hate, inequality, intolerance, bigotry, rape, revenge, war, terror, extermination, murder, slaughter, death and destruction - that orders people killed, terrorized, maimed or tortured is a teaching of man and not of God. Any religion that proclaims the above teachings as the timeless, eternal word of God is not a religion but an evil ideology.

God being a God of Moral Perfection therefore:
In a democracy, freedom of religion gives man the right to freely practice non-violently his religion in accordance with the teachings of a God of Moral Perfection. There is no democratic right to utilize religion to destroy democracy and impose religious totalitarianism. There is no democratic religious right to murder human beings. You cannot kill under the guise of religious freedom. You cannot commit acts of violence and claim the protection of freedom to practice your religion. You cannot preach hate. To employ the sanctity of God to promote evil, utilizing religion to give this evil an aura of divine respectability is a very great crime against God. Such an ideology is not a religion and therefore not protected by freedom of religion.

God being a God of Moral Perfection therefore:
God gave man a free will to do good or evil, to explore the truth of any question including His existence. Freedom of speech and expression are unimpeachable

human rights. We have the right to reason, to explore, to seek the truth of any question - total freedom of thought. To think and reason without fear of jail/death. No one has the right to threaten, coerce, intimidate anyone with torture, prison or death for freely expressing, views that they do not agree with no matter how abhorrent those views. We have the right to challenge any ideology, government, leaders of any state, heads of any organizations, the tenets and beliefs of any organization, including all religions. The right to write any thought, read any book, pursue any intellectual enterprise in the arts, literature, sciences, paint any picture, and draw any caricature no matter how offensive. Having given man intelligence, God believes that no man should be ruled by dictators. **It must be declared that not even God can deny you your constitutional rights because if God denied these rights, he would no longer be Moral Perfection and therefore no longer God.**

God being a God of Moral Perfection therefore:
God is not an egotist. God does not seek your adoration nor does He demand it. All teachings of God basking in his own glory are the teachings of man.

God being a God of Moral Perfection therefore:
God wants every human being to come into His pure love of their own free will. He would never use force or the force of terror but only pure love. If God wanted to use violence, He wouldn't need the assistance of any human. All He has to do is make an announcement that everyone must obey His teachings immediately, or He'll hang one person from every tree on the planet. Needless to say there would be immediate obedience but there would be no love - just fear of God's power.

God being a God of Moral Perfection therefore:
God created women as the equal of men. God is not a sexist. God is not a male chauvinist pig. Women and men are equal in the eyes of God. Women are the equal of men. Women are not valued by God as worth 50% of men. God did not create women to be the chattel or slaves of men. Females have full rights in society before the law, under the rule of law, can dress any way they freely desire without fear of death, walk the streets without a male relative escort, do any occupation, have the right to vote, the full right to participate in the governance of any society, be the leader or member of government of any country, receive all educational rights, drive planes, trains, automobiles, fly to the stars, choose their own husbands, refuse to accept arranged, forced or child marriages etc. No man, whether husband, father, brother, relative, boyfriend, government official or stranger has the right to beat or mistreat a woman. Men who beat women are the lowest of the low. No woman should be forced to endure female circumcision. The equal rights of women in society to complete educational, economic, legal, and political equality - are very important. There is absolutely no way the West would be enjoying its modern prosperity without the full and equal participation

of women. All teachings of the oppression, subjugation and inferiority of women in any holy book/text/teaching are not the word/teachings of God but the word/teachings of man. If God is a sexist, a male chauvinist pig then God is no longer Moral Perfection and therefore, no longer God.

God being a God of Moral Perfection therefore:
All mankind is created equal. God is not a racist. No man is the property of any other man - God is not a slaver. All human beings are created equal. All races are created equal. God does not wish that any human be a slave. No one person is the lesser of the other. Slavery is one of the vilest institutions ever created by man. Slavery is an obscenity against God. All human beings (no matter their race, color, creed, ethnic origins) have the full right to protection of their human rights and human dignity. To use religion to spread hate against other races and other religions - in places of worship, employing television or any other medium, teaching hatred to the young in schools - this is evil incarnate. To use religion as an instrument of persecution and violence stands as an affront to the very concept of a God of pure love and pure mercy. If a God is a racist, believes in persecution, slavery and violence then God is immoral and therefore, no longer God.

God being a God of Moral Perfection therefore:
God is the very essence of pure love. The very existence of God is pure love. If God is not the embodiment of pure love then God is not Moral Perfection and therefore, since God cannot be immoral imperfection and still be God – a God who is not the embodiment of pure love does not exist.

God being a God of Moral Perfection therefore:
God is all pure mercy. God is all pure compassion. God is all pure forgiveness. God is anti-death penalty. God does not permit the killing of any human being - for committing murder or mischief and corruption in the land or for any other reason. When the state executes criminals, the state is committing murder. In short, the state itself becomes a murderer. Mankind does not have the right to kill mankind. If God cannot kill us and still be God then we certainly cannot kill each other. God is all mercy and forgiveness, love and compassion. Even the worst criminal murderers and killers in history like Hitler or Stalin or Muhammad (who roamed the earth to promote and commit atrocities and bloodshed) can come into the mercy and feel the love of God if they repent and ask God for forgiveness.

God being a God of Moral Perfection therefore:
God is not a criminal. He is not a murderer. He is not a torturer. Again, God has never killed or ordered the killing of any human being. He has never tortured or ordered the torture of any human being. He has never sent a storm or other calamity of nature to destroy any human being or city or drown any army. God does not have the moral authority to kill any creature. Re-emphasizing, if

God killed just one human being (or any other alien life form throughout the universe) then God is a murderer and no longer Moral Perfection and therefore, God is no longer God.

God being a God of Moral Perfection therefore:
God is all pure non-revenge. Retaliation is abhorrent to God and an obscenity against the very nature of God – an immoral violation of the pure love, pure peace, pure mercy, pure non-violence, Moral Perfection of God.

We emphasize the God given essence of mankind by repeating three teachings of this Declaration;

God being a God of Moral Perfection therefore:
God blessed man with an intelligence to reason, to explore, to seek the truth of any question – total freedom of thought. To think and reason without fear of jail/death. It is against the will of God to threaten anyone with death, torture or prison for freely exercising his God-given brain. The human brain is the greatest gift God has ever bestowed on man. It was given to mankind to pursue the arts, literature, sciences, and intellectual pursuits. Its free exercise is the will of God.

God being a God of Moral Perfection therefore:
All mankind has the right to freedom and democracy, equality before the law, freedom of action, freedom of thought, right to elect their leaders. God does not want dictators and tyrants to rule over other men. Freedom of speech and expression are unimpeachable rights. If God does not believe in the right of mankind to freedom and democracy then God is no longer Moral Perfection and therefore, God is no longer God.

God Being a God of MORAL PERFECTION Therefore:
Repeating this self evident truth: All teachings of God – a God of Moral Perfection must be Moral Perfection. Any writings in any religious text that are not Moral Perfection are not the teachings of God but the teachings of man. Any religious text that pertains to be the divine, timeless word of God that contains just one word of immoral imperfection, then the entire religious text is not the word of God but the word of man and therefore, the entire religion is fraudulent.

Belief in God is supposed to aid the species Homo Sapiens in his daily struggle with extinction not to be the driving force that will lead to his extinction. If mankind does not adopt the teachings of a God of Moral Perfection and destroy GOD AS A CRIMINAL then Homo sapiens will go to extinction as a species.

With my signature I hereby swear before God these truths.

Pope Benedict the 16th

All major religious and political leaders including but not limited to:
President Barack Hussein Obama
President Sarkozy (President France)
Gordon Brown (Prime Minister Britain)
Angela Merkel (Chancellor Germany)
Rick Warren (Preacher)
Franklin Graham (Preacher)
Archbishop of Canterbury Rowan Williams
Royal Aal al-Bayt Institute for Islamic Thought in Amman, Jordan
Sheik Mohammed Nur Abdullah, the Fiqh Council of North America;
Sheikh Salem Falahat, director-general of the Muslim Brotherhood in Jordan;
Hasan Shariatmadari, head of the Iranian National Republicans party
Sheikh Ikrima Said Sabri, former Grand Mufti of Jerusalem
Grand Imam Sheikh Muhammad Tantawi, rector of Al-Azhar University in Cairo
Egypt Grand Mufi, Ali Gomaa
Saudi Arabi Grand Mufi, Abdul-Azeez ibn Abdullaah Aal ash-Shaikh,
Syria Grand Mufti, Ahmad Badr Al-Din Hassoun
Lebanon's Grand Mufti, Mohammed Rashid Qabbani
Republic of Albania's Grand Mufti, Hafiz Sabri Cocki
Grand Mufti of Bosnia. Mustafa Ceric,
Bulgaria's Grand Mufti, Dr. Mustafa Hadji
Grand Mufti of Marseille (France), Soheib Bencheikh
Islamic Republic of Pakistan's Grand Mufti,Muhammad Rafi Usmani
Russian Federation's Grand Mufti, Ravil Gainutdin
Syria's Grand Mufti is Ahmad Bader Hassoun
The US Congress, UN and all world governments.

   Whether there is a Creator, whether this Creator is Moral Perfection and therefore God or whether we are just 6.5 billion accidental freaks of nature, we will all discover sooner rather then later.
   The reality for the species Homo sapiens is that if there is no afterlife then our stay on this planet will be the first and last chapter of our existence. During our short earthly existence, we have a duty to live our lives morally and leave to our children a better world – a better future. Neither the Creator or God is going to make an appearance on earth and solve our problems.
   You will not wake up tomorrow morning and see on TV the Breaking News that God has just appeared at UN headquarters and has scheduled a meeting with all world leaders. God is not going to solve global warming. Children worldwide are not going to be running outside with empty bowls to have God miraculously fill them. Schools for every kid will not miraculously appear. The sick and dying will not be miraculously given medical attention or even cured. There will not be full employment. Nations are not going to be forced by God to disarm. People and nations are not going to stop killing and murdering each other.
   These miracles are not going to happen.

The problems of Homo sapiens are the problems of Homo sapiens. Only he can solve them. Each of us must be the workers of miracles. We must ban weapons. We must ban war. We must ban all violence/hate from religion. We must destroy the depiction of God as a criminal. We must stop killing each other and start loving and caring for each other. We must stop polluting, destroying forests bringing extinction to thousands of species, and end global warming. We must turn the resources of the planet from financing violence to feeding, clothing, medically caring for and educating every child. There is absolutely no reason for poverty to exist anywhere. The resources are there. What we need is a miracle of the heart. The Declaration of A God of Moral Perfection is this miracle of the heart.

CHAPTER TWO

IT'S ALL ABOUT ISLAM STUPID KAFIR

Before we begin our comparison of the teachings of Allah (the AntiGod) to those of a God of Moral Perfection following is a description of the ideology of Islam.

YOUR DEMOCRATIC OBLIGATION AS A KAFIR

All kafirs (non-Muslims) living in a democratic society have an obligation as free citizens to understand what Islam truly is and the very grave danger this evil ideology poses to all freedom loving peoples everywhere. In this book, the true reality of Islam is exposed devoid of all the political correctness behind which Muslims are seeking to criminalize all criticism of Islam employing labels such as Islamophobia, racism, bigotry, hate, intolerance, to destroy anyone who dares to expose by quoting directly from Islam's holy books - the Quran, the Sira and the Hadith in Islam's **OWN WORDS, OWN WRITINGS** the hateful, evil, teachings of Islam.

IT'S ALL ABOUT ISLAM STUPID KAFIR

Islam is not boring that I can promise.
If Islam was a true religion of peace in which Muslims prayed 5 times a day, fasted for one month yearly, abstained from alcohol, donated to charity, went on a pilgrimage once in a lifetime then nobody would care. Unfortunately, this is the fantasy not the reality of Islam.
Since 9/11, numerous Western leaders have insisted that Islam is a peaceful religion, and that violence committed in its name contradicts the teachings of the Quran and the example of the prophet Muhammad. This is absolutely not true. Islam is no religion of peace. Islam is, in fact, a violent and

expansionist ideology that seeks the destruction or subjugation of all other faiths, cultures, and systems of government. As will be stated further, violence against non-Muslims is and has always been an integral aspect of Islam.

The issues raised by the recent revivalism of Islam are of life and death to the democratic world. Islam is one of the most serious threats freedom loving people have ever faced. It is the greatest threat that western women have faced to their hard won freedoms and legal protection of their basic rights. Islam is one of the most diabolical ideologies ever created. You must understand what Islam truly represents and participate in the fight against this very evil ideology. Ignorance is not an option.

Islam has the potential to change mankind and a create a new type of human being - a creature totally devoid of humanity, free will and empathy- living in total submission to the brutal, hateful will of Allah (the AntiGod). Islam wants to create a new human species: Homo-Islamo. It has the potential to lead to extinction of the species, truly human.

In trying to understand Islam, you must suspend all rationally and reason. You must abandon everything you have ever been taught since childhood - your entire moral frame work - concerning the Ten Commandments, God, morality, ethics, democracy and freedom, reason, rationality, freedom of conscience, Golden Rule, equality of all human beings, concepts of good and evil, love and hate, right and wrong. When you enter the study of Islam, it's as if you have left our universe and entered a totally different alien world – a world devoid of all humanity - the evil, irrational, immoral world of Allah (the AntiGod) where murder, assassination, extermination, genocide, rape, slavery, looting and pillaging, massacres, terror, torture, brutality, hate, violence, child molestation, are no longer crimes against humanity, no longer sins against God, no longer crimes against the laws of God but are all holy, blessed duties halal (legal) acts as long as they are perpetrated on kafirs to be rewarded by Allah (the AntiGod) with guaranteed accession to a Paradise filled with voluptuous breasted, lustrous eyed, sensuous virgins that they can sexually molest for all eternity. Islam permits polygamy, pedophilia, owning slaves, wife beating, marriage with adopted son's wives and unlimited sex with sex slaves. Allah (the AntiGod) is a pedophile permitting Muslim men to rape Muslim baby girls.

Unlimited sex raping kafir women after murdering their husbands. Unlimited sex with young Muslim child girls sanctioned by God. Unlimited sex including anal sex with your Muslim wife(s) anywhere, anytime demanded by her Muslim husband even on the saddle of a camel. Unlimited eternal sex with virgins for Muslim men blessed with eternal erections who murder kafirs in the name of God.

Islam is all about sex stupid kafir.

In addition to unlimited sex, Islam offers Muslim men unlimited booty. Kill the kafirs and steal their property.

Islam is all about the booty stupid kafir.

Since Islam is so far outside the realm of all human intellectual rationality and reason, so diabolically evil that no normal person can comprehend such evil - there will be repetition throughout this book of very important concepts of Islamic thought/teachings purposely repeated over and over, to ensure that you fully understand completely the immoral, irrationality of this very great, evil and dangerous ideology.

We will prove that a careful study of the Quran and Muhammad's life will reveal to any objective minded person that Muhammad never talked to a supernatural deity (he called Allah) or received revelations from such an entity. Muhammad invented Allah and turned him into a criminal god - the AntiGod to give political power to himself and utilize his made-up teachings, allegedly received from his fictional Allah, as a religious and legal justification for his criminality. Allah existed only in Muhammad's imagination. Muhammad and Allah were the same - two in one. Sanctioned by Allah, Muhammad practiced all the evil acts listed above epically deceit, torture, murder, assassination, massacre, genocide, pillage, robbery, enslavement and rape and made them halal (legal) acts, deserving of paradise, as long as they were perpetrated on the kafirs. These evil, immoral teachings became the eternal laws of Allah (the AntiGod). These eternal laws of Allah (the AntiGod) are divine and can never be changed.

We will show that Islam is not a wonderful religion of peace and love that has been hi–jacked and perverted by a few bad apples of evil Islamo–Fascists, Islamic militants, Islamic Fundamentalists, jihadists, Wahhabists, radical Islamists, political Islamists etc. There is no radical Islam. There is no moderate Islam. Islam is Islam. There has been no hijacking. There has been no perversion. These demented souls are following exactly the teachings of the Quran and in the footsteps of their prophet – Muhammad.

ORGANIZATION OF ISLAM

All Muslims believe that there is no God but Allah and Muhammad is his last prophet. Islam demands that Muslims follow the Quran (the timeless, divine, eternal, word of God) and the perfect pattern of Muhammad's words and deeds (his Sunna). The Sunna is found in the Hadith (Traditions of Muhammad) and the Sira (Muhammad's biography). These three texts are the Islamic Trilogy.
The doctrine is political and religious. Islam is contained in these three books. It is very simple--three books--a Trilogy. To know Islam, read the Quran, Sira and Hadith. It should be noted that the Quran is only 16% of the sacred texts of Islam.

Islamic doctrine says that moderation consists of patterning your life after Muhammad's perfect example and living by the Quran. By this standard of moderation, Osama bin Laden and Major Hasan are good, true, moderate Muslims – holy men of the book – who are following exactly the teachings of Islam as recorded in the Quran and the example of Muhammad, the warrior jihadist. A jihadist is a moderate Muslim.

Islam is a process, not just a name. Both the Quran and the Sira, Muhammad's life, show a process of starting off with civility, then demanding and next moving to violence as Islam grows stronger. This process is the Islamification of society.

The Sunnah -- the "Way" of the Prophet Muhammad

In Islam, Muhammad is considered *al-insan al-kamil* (the "ideal man"). Muhammad is in no way considered divine, nor is he worshipped (no image of Muhammad is permitted lest it encourage idolatry), but he is the model par excellence for all Muslims in how they should conduct themselves. It is through Muhammad's personal teachings and actions -- which make up the "way of the prophet," the Sunnah -- that Muslims discern what is a good and holy life. Details about the prophet -- how he lived, what he did, his non-Quranic utterances, his personal habits -- are indispensable knowledge for any faithful Muslim.

Knowledge of the Sunnah comes primarily from the hadith ("reports") about Muhammad's life, which were passed down orally until codified in the eighth century AD, some hundred years after Muhammad's death. The hadith comprise the most important body of Islamic texts after the Quran; they are basically a collection of anecdotes about Muhammad's life believed to have originated with those who knew him personally. There are thousands upon thousands of hadith, some running to multiple pages, some barely a few lines in length. When the hadith were first compiled in the eighth century AD, it became obvious that many were inauthentic. The early Muslim scholars of hadith spent tremendous labor trying to determine which hadith were authoritative and which were suspect.

Most hadith here come exclusively from the most reliable and authoritative collection, Sahih Al-Bukhari, recognized as sound by all schools of Islamic scholarship, translated by a Muslim scholar and which may be found here. Different translations of hadith can vary in their breakdown of volume, book, and number, but the content is the same. For each hadith, the classifying information is listed first, then the name of the originator of the hadith (generally someone who knew Muhammad personally), and then the content itself. While the absolute authenticity of even a sound hadith is hardly assured, they are nonetheless accepted as authoritative within an Islamic context.

Because Muhammad is himself the measuring stick of morality, his actions are not judged according to an independent moral standard but rather establish what the standard for Muslims properly is.

Volume 7, Book 62, Number 88; Narrated Ursa: The Prophet wrote the (marriage contract) with Aisha while she was six years old and consummated his marriage with her while she was nine years old and she remained with him for nine years (i.e. till his death).

Volume 8, Book 82, Number 795; Narrated Anas: The Prophet cut off the hands and feet of the men belonging to the tribe of Uraina and did not cauterise (their bleeding limbs) till they died.

Volume 2, Book 23, Number 413; Narrated Abdullah bin Umar: The Jews {of Medina} brought to the Prophet a man and a woman from amongst them who have committed (adultery) illegal sexual intercourse. He ordered both of them to be stoned (to death), near the place of offering the funeral prayers beside the mosque.

Volume 9, Book 84, Number 57; Narrated Ikrima: Some Zanadiqa (atheists) were brought to Ali {the fourth Caliph} and he burnt them. The news of this event, reached Ibn 'Abbas who said, "If I had been in his place, I would not have burnt them, as Allah's Apostle forbade it, saying, "Do not punish anybody with Allah's punishment (fire)." I would have killed them according to the statement of Allah's Apostle, "Whoever changes his Islamic religion, then kill him."

Volume 1, Book 2, Number 25; Narrated Abu Huraira: Allah's Apostle was asked, "What is the best deed?" He replied, "To believe in Allah and His Apostle (Muhammad). The questioner then asked, "What is the next (in goodness)?" He replied, "To participate in Jihad (religious fighting) in Allah's Cause."

In Islam, there is no "natural" sense of morality or justice that transcends the specific examples and injunctions outlined in the Quran and the Sunnah. Because Muhammad is considered Allah's final prophet and the Quran the eternal, unalterable words of Allah himself, there is also no evolving morality that permits the modification or integration of Islamic morality with that from other sources. The entire Islamic moral universe devolves solely from the life and teachings of Muhammad.

Along with the reliable hadith, a further source of accepted knowledge about Muhammad comes from the Sira (life) of the prophet, composed by one of Islam's great scholars, Muhammad bin Ishaq, in the eighth century AD.

Muhammad's prophetic career is meaningfully divided into two segments: the first in Mecca, where he labored for thirteen years to make converts to Islam; and later in the city of Medina (The City of the Apostle of God), where he became a powerful political and military leader.

MECCA STAGE

While living in Mecca, Muhammad taught that he had received revelations from Allah relayed to him by the Angel Gabriel. Allah had revealed himself through Gabriel as the same God that the Christians and Jews worshipped and that Muhammad was the Last prophet of God sent to establish Islam as the one and only true religion. For thirteen years, Muhammad labored to convince the Christians, Jews, pagan Arabs that he was a prophet sent by God with messages for all mankind. During this stage of Islam when Muhammad was weak, he showed respect for the monotheism of the Christian and Jewish inhabitants. The teachings of Islam were benign and for the most part, respectful, tolerant and peaceful. Of course, the Christians/Jews rejected him as a FALSE PROPHET and after thirteen years with about 150 followers he was forced to flee Mecca for his life to Medina. END OF STAGE ONE OF ISLAM

LATER POST MEDINA

It was in Medina that Muhammad gained power and transformed Islam from a relatively benign form of monotheism into an expansionary, military-political ideology that persists to this day. Now we see a very different side of Muhammad and a very different concept of Islam and a very different Allah.

The reality was that if Muhammad had continued going down the same path as he had in Mecca, Islam would have died. He had nothing more to offer that Jesus hadn't already offered.

Muhammad changed Islam into a criminal Mafia enterprise to make war against kafirs, murder those kafirs who refused to convert to Islam or pay a devastating submission tax (jizya) (criminal extortion) enslave their women and children, rape and breed them like cattle, loot their property and share 80% of the looted proceeds with the criminal Muslim jihadists – the remaining 20% going to Allah and his messenger. If no fighting was involved then 100% of the proceeds went to Muhammad.

He re- invented Allah and turned him into a criminal God – the AntiGod to give political power to himself and utilize the teachings received from Allah as religious and legal justification for his evil criminality. There were never any revelations from Allah to Muhammad. Allah never existed. Muhammad made up all the teachings of the Quran.

In order to implement the NEW ISLAM – Muhammad faced a huge problem - how to get rid of the initial teachings of Islam of peace and tolerance. Allah (the AntiGod) came to his rescue with a teaching that basically said that God could change his mind. That God being God could abolish whatever He has taught before. Crazy but very smart. Muhammad was the incarnation of evil on an equal par with Hitler, Stalin and like all evil men – he was very clever and ruthless. For a detailed listing of the verses that were abrogated go to http://www.islamreform.net/new-page-27.htm

Quran 2:106. "Whatever a Verse (revelation) do We {Allah} abrogate or cause to be forgotten, We bring a better one or similar to it. Know you not that Allah is able to do all things?"

Quran 16:101 "And when We change (one) communication for (another) communication, and Allah knows best what He reveals."

It is in his reformed Medina Islam, that the pre-mentioned acts of evil: deceit, torture, murder, assassination, massacre, genocide, pillage, robbery, enslavement and rape were made halal (legal) acts, deserving of paradise, as long as they were perpetrated on kafirs. As already stated, these evil, immoral AntiGod teachings became the new eternal Laws of Allah (the AntiGod).

Islam changed from trying to be a religion into an evil ideology whose sole purpose is to conquer the world for Allah. The Quran is a declaration of war against the kafirs. This war is permanent until ALL kafirs have converted to Islam, or are in dhimmitude (institutionalized discrimination akin to second class slavery status) or have been murdered.

In Mecca, we see a quasi-Biblical figure, preaching repentance and charity, harassed and rejected by those around him; later, in Medina, we see an able commander and strategist who systematically conquered and killed those who opposed him. It is the later years of Muhammad's life, from 622 AD to his death in 632, (Muhammad was born in 570) that are rarely broached in polite company. In 622, when the prophet was better than fifty years old, he and his followers made the Hijra (emigration or flight), from Mecca to the oasis of Yathrib -- later renamed Medina -- some 200 miles to the north. Muhammad's new monotheism had angered the pagan leaders of Mecca, and the flight to Medina was precipitated by a probable attempt on Muhammad's life. Muhammad had sent emissaries to Medina to ensure his welcome. He was accepted by the Medinan tribes as the leader of the Muslims and as arbiter of inter-tribal disputes.

Shortly before Muhammad fled the hostility of Mecca, a new batch of Muslim converts pledged their loyalty to him on a hill outside Mecca called Aqaba. Ishaq here conveys in the Sira the significance of this event:

Sira, p208: "When God gave permission to his Apostle to fight, the second {oath of allegiance at} Aqaba contained conditions involving war which were not in the first act of fealty. Now they {Muhammad's followers} bound themselves to war against all and sundry for God and his Apostle, while he promised them for faithful service thus the reward of paradise."

That Muhammad's nascent religion underwent a significant change at this point is plain. The scholarly Ishaq clearly intends to impress on his (Muslim) readers that, while in its early years, Islam was a relatively tolerant creed that would "endure insult and forgive the ignorant," Allah soon required Muslims "to war against all and sundry for God and his Apostle." The Islamic calendar testifies to the paramouncy of the Hijra by setting year one from the date of its occurrence. The year of the Hijra, 622 AD, is considered more significant than the year of Muhammad's birth or death or that of the first Quranic revelation because Islam is first and foremost a political-military enterprise. It was only when Muhammad left Mecca with his paramilitary band that Islam achieved its proper political-military articulation. The years of the Islamic calendar (which employs lunar months) are designated in English "AH" or "After Hijra."

Muhammad - the prophet of peace, the apostle of God, ordered 60 massacres and personally participated in 27 of these acts of carnage. As the exemplary example and the perfection of humanity and the prototype of the most wonderful human conduct Muhammad massacred, beheaded, tortured, terrorized, raped, and looted in the name of God. He lived the teachings of the Quran.

Before there was a Hitler, Mein Kampf, the SS, concentration camps and final solution of the Jewish question, there was Muhammad, the Quran, the SS Jihadists (who were known as the Companions) and the first final solution: the mass murder and forced exile of Jews/Christians from Arabia.

Ibn Ishaq, Life of Muhammad (Karachi) p. 553:

...the Apostle of Allah said, "Kill any Jew that falls into your power."

Bukhari 4:52:176 Narrated 'Abdullah bin 'Umar: Allah's Apostle said, "You (i.e. Muslims) will fight with the Jews till some of them will hide behind stones. The stones will (betray them) saying, 'O 'Abdullah (i.e. slave of Allah)! There is a Jew hiding behind me; so kill him."

As will be demonstrated later in the chapter "The Massacre of Banu Quraiza," Muhammad personally beheaded Jewish men and ordered the beheading of 600 to 900. To distinguish young Jewish boys from young Jewish men, he ordered his SS jihadists – "the Companions" to pull down the pants of the terrified boys. Just the slightest traces of hair around the genital area and the young Jewish boy were taken away and beheaded. Muhammad took a Jewish woman as his sex slave and looted the property of the murdered Jews and sold their women and little girls that the jihadists did not want as sex slaves into slavery. Allah – the godfather and mafia chieftain of the Muhammad crime family rejoiced by creating as eternal laws of God – 5 teachings in the Quran (discussed later) celebrating the great slaughter of the Banu Quraiza Jews and enslavement of terrified women and children.

At the Massacre of Kaibyr, (which will also be examined) Muhammad brutally tortured a Jewish chieftain to reveal where he had hidden the cities golden treasure. When the chieftain refused to give Muhammad the treasure, he was taken away and beheaded. This chieftain was the husband of a most beautiful 17 year old Jewish woman - Safiyaah. After murdering her father, brothers, uncles, husband – Muhammad will attack and rape Safiyaah.

During the massacre of The Jewish Settlement of Bani Mustaliq - Muhammad will capture and rape a twenty year old Jewish girl – Juwairiya.

One of the most important revelations about Islam is the myth of moderate, peaceful Muslims. As already explained, there are no moderate Muslims. Those "moderate" Muslims represent the early stages of Islamification.

This "peaceful Muslims = peaceful Islam" statements are actually about Muslim-ology, not Islam. It is perfectly fine to study Muslims, but do not draw conclusions about Islam from them. There is a cause and effect relationship that is confused. Islam causes Muslims. Muslims do not cause Islam. Muslim-ology teaches little about Islam.

This means that you judge Muslims by Islam, not Islam by Muslims. If you want to know anything about Islam read the Trilogy. If you want to know if someone is a moderate Muslim, use Islam to measure them, not personal opinion.

Again, what you must understand is that Osma bin Laden and Major Hasan are moderate Muslims. They are Islamic holy men. All the jihadist killers and murderers are moderate Muslims performing holy, divine acts. This is the evil, insane but cold, hard reality of Islam. 1.2 billion people believe in this madness. In Islam, doctrine matters.

THE TRUTH OF ISLAM

Allah is not God but the AntiGod of the Muslims.
Muhammad is no Christ but the Anti Christ. The first Adolf Hitler.
Islam is not a religion but an evil ideology akin to Nazism.
The Quran is not the bible but the Islamic Mein Kampf.
Islam is Anti God. Islam is a total and complete renunciation of God.

Again, while Muslims believe that there is only one God of the universe, their conception of God - a being they call Allah is not God but the AntiGod. This Allah (the AntiGod) worshipped by Muslims has divided all human beings into believers (Muslims) and non-believers (kafirs i.e. YOU - Non-Muslim.) Allah (the AntiGod) hates all kafirs with an intense passion. Kafirs are vile sub-human beings. They have zero humanity. Iran's revolutionary leader Grand Ayatollah Ruhollah Khomeini once declared that "the following eleven are unclean: first urine, second feces, third semen, fourth corpses, fifth blood, sixth dogs, seventh pigs, eighth non-Muslims, ninth wine, tenth beer, and eleventh the sweat of a camel which has consumed impure food." Khomeini had gone on to add, "every aspect of a non-Muslim is unclean."

Islam means submission. Islam demands surrender of all human beings to Allah. Muslim men must blindly submit without question to the will of Allah (the AntiGod.) Muslim women must submit and be totally obedient to Muslim men. (Obedience is their only hope of ascending to Paradise – a very faint hope since in Islam the eternal fate for the overwhelming majority of Muslim women is descendent into hell and eternal damnation.) Kafirs must submit to and be the slaves of Muslims or be murdered. This is the eternal order of the universe as decreed by the AntiGod Allah.

Islam is all about Muslim men. It is an evil ideology created by Muhammad for his male followers granting them unlimited sex, riches, and political power. Allah (the AntiGod) hates all Muslim women with a deep seated loathing. Muslim women are vile, dirty, stupid creatures. Muslim men can have multiple wives, unlimited sex slaves, can marry and rape Muslim baby girls, beat his wives, and murder his daughters if they dare to impugn his honor. Whereas kafirs have zero humanity, Muslim women are only just slightly higher on the human evolutionary scale having reached the status of a dog. Muslim women must shut up and spread their legs. This is the divine order of the universe ordained by Allah (the AntiGod). This vision of the inequality of Muslim women to Muslim men, and the eternal sub-humanness and lack of humanity of kafirs are the divine teachings of Allah (the AntiGod) and therefore, eternal and can never be changed in any way.

Islam is a dangerous political-military ideology with religious trappings masquerading as a religion intended for conquering the world for imaginary Allah (the AntiGod). Only 10% of Islam has anything to do with religion, the other 90% is political.

It is the prime directive of Islam to conquer the nations of the world for Allah (the AntiGod) by whatever means necessary. Again, the Quran is a declaration of open-ended war against the kafirs. This war is permanent until all kafirs have converted to Islam, or been reduced to dhimmitude (institutionalized discrimination akin to slavery status), murdered or enslaved - a cold-hard reality for the hear-no-evil, see-no-evil, do-nothing-about-evil naive kafirs.

Allah (the AntiGod) seeks the extermination of all kafirs. By refusing to convert to Islam, kafirs have declared war against Islam, are a grave danger to Allah and must be destroyed. A most important concept that must be emphasized repeatedly is that Islam is a declaration of war against kafirs. What you must understand is that Islam is not anti Jewish – it is anti kafir. The Jews are the most reviled of kafirs followed by Christians, Hindus, etc. The Quran is not a holy book but a book of war. A book of genocide. Allah is the AntiGod of war. This war is permanent until all kafirs convert to Islam or if Christians/Jews agree to pay a devastating jizya (submission tax) and accept dhimmude status (see chapters 43 and 44) or be murdered.

For Muslims, it is a holy religious duty to murder kafirs. The Quran is written in the language of terrorism. It is filled with numerous verses urging the Muslims to terrorize the non-Muslims, kill them, and take possession of their lands and properties. The important points to remember are that whatever Muhammad did to terrorize the kafirs was actually the actions of God. Among the many verses which exhort Islamist terrorism, the following verses stand out as naked aggression of Allah/Muhammad on the unbelievers: 2:63, 3:151, 8:12, 8:60, 8:59, 9:5, 9:29, 9:55, 11:102, and 17:59 etc. These teachings are the eternal laws of Allah (the AntiGod) authorization of murder and extermination as a holy duty.

Again as a kafir, you are not a human being to a Muslim. You have absolutely no humanity. A Muslim has the full right granted to him by God, to murder you, take your wife and young daughter(s), rape and gang rape them (no matter what the age of your daughter), take them as sex slaves or sell into slavery to be bred like cattle for future sex slaves and profit. Your male children will be beheaded if they are young men. If there is any doubt as to whether your young son is a young man or a young boy, Muslims will pull down his pants and examine his genitals for the slightest growth of hair. Just the slightest hair growth is enough for him to be beheaded. All your property will be seized and whatever the Muslim does not want to keep as his property, will be sold.

As a kafir you have absolutely NO RIGHT TO OWN ANYTHING. It is a sacrilege against Allah (the AntiGod). All your property - your home, car, money, furniture, stocks and bonds, corporations, farms, is the property of the Muslims, who have holy blood flowing through their veins. Your wife and children are the Muslim's property to be tortured, brutalized, raped as the Muslim desires.

In Muhammad's words: *"I have been ordered to fight the people till they say: 'None has the right to be worshipped but Allah.' And if they say so, pray like our prayers, face our Qibla and slaughter as we slaughter, then their blood and property will be sacred to us and we will not interfere with them..."* (Bukhari 8:387)

We cannot emphasize enough that if a Muslim kills or is killed murdering, raping, pillaging non-Muslims then they are guaranteed accession by God to a Paradise of voluptuous breasted, lustrous eyed virgins who regenerate as virgins after each sex act that they can sexually molest with external erections for all eternity. **THIS IS THE EVIL INSANITY THAT IS ISLAM.**

Dar al-Islam and dar al-harb: the House of Islam and the House of War

Islam is based on an uncompromising division of the world between Believer and Unbeliever, or kafir - The house of Islam and the House of War. There must be a state of war between the two -- though not always a state of open warfare. For Muslims have a duty to spread Islam, and to constantly expand the boundaries of Dar al-Islam, the place where Islam dominates, and Muslims rule. This is a duty, not a suggestion.

All Muslims Must Make Jihad.

Jihad is an obligation from Allah on every Muslim and cannot be ignored nor evaded. Allah has ascribed great importance to jihad and has made the reward of the martyrs and the fighters in His way a splendid one. Only those who have acted similarly and who have modeled themselves upon the martyrs in their performance of jihad can join them in this reward. Furthermore, Allah has specifically honored the Mujahideen {those who wage jihad} with certain exceptional qualities, both spiritual and practical, to benefit them in this world and the next. Their pure blood is a symbol of victory in this world and the mark of success and felicity in the world to come.

Those who can only find excuses, however, have been warned of extremely dreadful punishments and Allah has described them with the most unfortunate of names. He has reprimanded them for their cowardice and lack of spirit, and castigated them for their weakness and truancy. In this world, they will be surrounded by dishonor and in the next they will be surrounded by the fire from which they shall not escape though they may possess much wealth. The weaknesses of abstention and evasion of jihad are regarded by Allah as one of the major sins, and one of the seven sins that guarantee failure.

Islam is concerned with the question of jihad and the drafting and the mobilization of the entire Umma {the global Muslim community} into one body to defend the right cause with all its strength than any other ancient or modern system of living, whether religious or civil. The verses of the Qur'an and the Sunnah of Muhammad are overflowing with all these noble ideals and they summon people in general (with the most eloquent expression and the clearest exposition) to jihad, to warfare, to the armed forces, and all means of land and sea fighting.

The violent injunctions of the Quran and the violent precedents set by Muhammad set the tone for the Islamic view of politics and of world history. Again, Islamic scholarship divides the world into two spheres of influence, the House of Islam (dar al-Islam) and the House of War (dar al-harb). Islam means submission, and so the House of Islam includes those nations that have submitted to Islamic rule, which is to say those nations ruled by Sharia law. The rest of the world, which has not accepted Sharia law and so is not in a state of submission, exists in a state of rebellion or war with the will of Allah. It is incumbent on dar al-Islam to make war upon dar al-harb until such time that all nations submit to the will of Allah and accept Sharia law. Islam's message to the non-Muslim world is the same now as it was in the time of Muhammad and throughout history: submit or be conquered. The only times since Muhammad when dar al-Islam was not actively at war with dar al-harb were when the Muslim world was too weak or divided to make war effectively.

But the lulls in the ongoing war that the House of Islam has declared against the House of War do not indicate a forsaking of jihad as a principle but reflect a change in strategic factors. It is acceptable for Muslim nations to declare hudna, or truce, at times when the kafir nations are too powerful for open warfare to make sense. Jihad is not a collective suicide pact even while "killing and being killed" (Sura 9:111) is encouraged on an individual level. For the past few hundred years, the Muslim world has been too politically fragmented and technologically inferior to pose a major threat to the West. But that is changing.

Sharia Law (THE LAW OF GOD)

Democracy and freedom are an affront to Allah. All constitutions are offense to Allah and must be destroyed and replaced with Sharia Law. For Muslims - Sharia Law is the Rule of Law. Muslims are being oppressed and subjugated by Kafirs. Only after the world has been made for Allah, Islam is the only religion and Sharia imposed on all mankind will Muslims be finally free of oppression and the humiliation of Kafir subjugation. This is the ideology of Muslim victimization.

Large parts of the Quran are legal code and form Islamic constitutional law. Since Muslims believe that these laws come from Allah and Muhammad they are of a higher order truth than any man-made laws. Therefore, Sharia law must replace all other forms of government.

Sharia is the legal code ordained by Allah for all mankind. To violate Sharia or not to accept its authority is to commit rebellion against Allah, which Allah's faithful are required to combat.

Under Sharia law, all kafirs are second class citizens. Women can be beaten and slavery is allowed. And just as in political Islam, Sharia law cannot be reformed. As the Law of God. Sharia law is divine and unchangeable. But in order to be the Law of God, every word/every teaching of Sharia Law must be Moral Perfection. To understand the abomination of Sharia Law and why it is not the divine word of God read on page 635 - 11 Reasons Why Abomination of Sharia Law Must Be Banned: Page 648 - Sharia: Islam's Warden Brutal Barbarism of True Islam: Page 659 - How Sharia Law Punishes RAPED Muslim Women. Page 611- Brutal Stoning Hadiths.

It is the long term goal of Islam to replace the US Constitution with the Sharia, since it contradicts Islam. For that matter, democracy violates Sharia law. Democracy assumes equality of all peoples. Islam teaches that a Muslim is a better person than kafirs and that the kafirs should submit to Islam. But in voting, a Muslim's vote is equal to a kafir's vote. This violates Islamic law, since a Muslim and a kafir are never equal.

There is no separation between the religious and the political in Islam; rather Islam and Sharia constitute a comprehensive means of ordering society at every level. While it is in theory possible for an Islamic society to have different outward forms -- an elective system of government, a hereditary monarchy, etc. -- whatever the outward structure of the government, Sharia is the prescribed content. It is this fact that puts Sharia into conflict with forms of government based on anything other than the Quran and the Sunnah.

The precepts of Sharia may be divided into two parts:

1. Acts of worship (al-ibadat), which includes:

- Ritual Purification (Wudu)
- Prayers (Salah)
- Fasts (Sawm and Ramadan)
- Charity (Zakat)
- Pilgrimage to Mecca (Hajj)

2. Human interaction (al-muamalat), which includes:

- Financial transactions
- Endowments
- Laws of inheritance
- Marriage, divorce, and child care
- Food and drink (including ritual slaughtering and hunting)
- Penal punishments
- War and peace
- Judicial matters (including witnesses and forms of evidence)

As one may see, there are few aspects of life that Sharia does not specifically govern. Everything from washing one's hands to child-rearing to taxation to military policy fall under its dictates. Because Sharia is derivate of the Quran and the Sunnah, it affords some room for interpretation. But upon examination of the Islamic sources, it is apparent that any meaningful application of Sharia is going to look very different from anything resembling a free or open society in the Western sense. The stoning of adulterers, execution of apostates and blasphemers, repression of other religions, and a mandatory hostility toward non-Islamic nations punctuated by regular warfare will be the norm. It seems fair then to classify Islam and its Sharia code as a form of totalitarianism.

In Islam there is no Golden Rule - treat others as you wish to be treated. The Ten Commandments does not apply to kafirs.

The Golden Rule is centered on ethics, not God, and is universal to all cultures, except Islam. Indeed, the whole Islamic Trilogy (Quran, Sira and Hadith) denies the truth of the Golden Rule.

If the Golden Rule was applied to Islam removing hate and violent teachings directed against the kafir - and the hate directed against Muslim women about 61% of the Quran would vanish, 75% of the Sira and 20% of the Hadith would also go away.

The Golden Rule even changes Hell. Islamic Hell is primarily political. Hell is mentioned 146 times in the Quran. Only 9 references are for moral failings - greed, lack of charity, love of worldly success. The other 137 references to Hell involve eternal torture for not agreeing that Muhammad is right. That is a political charge, not a morals failure. Thus 94% of the references to Hell are as a political prison for dissenters. The Golden Rule would empty Islam's political prison.

The Golden Rule annihilates the ethics of cruelty. Golden Rule Islam would be a reformed Islam that the kafirs would not fear and dread. We are tired of living in fear of political Islam. We have suffered enough and would welcome an Islam that did not argue, demand, pressure, dhimmize, threaten, deceive and destroy kafirs and their civilization.

As already stated and what you must fully understand in order to protect your family and country against this very great evil living and flourishing among us, is that the Quran defines the kafir as a sub-human who can be insulted, raped, robbed, killed, threatened or tortured. For Allah (the AntiGod), these are holy, divine acts. These Quranic teachings of murder, rape, terror, looting, slavery etc.

are not sins against God - are not crimes against the laws of God but are the eternal divine laws of Allah (the AntiGod). They are Islam.

For an excellent article Islam 101 by Robert Spencer on the Fundamentals of Islam go to:
http://islamreform.net/new-page-56.htm

For article: Organization of Quran go to: http://www.islamreform.net/new-page-70.htm

For article: Jihad; What is Jihad and Rape As Warfare In Islam go to http://islamreform.net/new-page-73.htm

For article: Political Islam go to http://islamreform.net/new-page-74.htm

For article: What Is Islam go to http://islamreform.net/new-page-75.htm

CHAPTER THREE

WHY ALLAH IS NOT GOD

GOD OF MORAL PERFECTION VERSUS ALLAH (THE ANTIGOD) OF THE MUSLIMS

AS we have already explained in the Excerpt section of this book titled God Is Not A Criminal/Crimes of Prophet Muhammad/Statistical Islam and will re-examine here in more depth - ALL Muslims, regard the Quran as a holy, divine law-book - the ETERNAL word/teachings of God that are unchangeable (forever). Muslims cannot question or doubt the allegedly uncreated words of God contained in their Quran, that God authored the Quran and a copy of the Quran is in heaven. Quranic teachings, the words of God, are immutable and stand valid for all times. Its ideas are absolutely true and beyond all criticism. To question it is to question the very word of God, and hence blasphemous. A Muslim's duty is to believe it and obey its divine commands without question. Therefore, all teachings and sanctions of the Quran must be followed by Muslims until the end of the world. Muslims who question just one word of the Quran are no longer Muslims but apostates of Islam and must be murdered.

Muslims can be killed (beheaded) for doing any of the following:
(1)Reviling Allah or his Messenger; (2) being sarcastic about Allah's name, His command, His interdiction, His promise, or His threat'; (3) denying any verse of the Quran or 'anything which by scholarly consensus belongs to it, or to add a verse that does not belong to it'; (4) holding that 'any of Allah's messengers or prophets are liars, or to deny their being sent'; (5) reviling the religion of Islam; (6) being sarcastic about any ruling of the Sacred Law; (7) denying that Allah intended 'the Prophet's message to be the religion followed by the entire world.'

This means exactly what it says. **ALL MUSLIMS MUST BELIEVE** that the Quran is the **ETERNAL** word/teachings of God to be followed without question. Again, if a Muslim challenges or questions the Quran, (even if just one word let alone an entire teaching) he is no longer a Muslim but an apostate of Islam and must be killed.

The Quran can never be changed not even one word. When you are reading teachings of the Quran, you are reading the word of God, written by God Himself and you must obey. There is no choice. There is no exercising free will, no employing logic, reason, rationality, morality. These teachings are for all time - FOREVER AND EVER AND EVER. This means that there can never be any evolution of morality in Islam. The barbaric teachings of 7th century Arabia are totally valid in the 21st century.

Our mission is to prove beyond all doubt that the Quran is not the word/teaching of God - that God never authored the Quran and no copy is in heaven. In order to disprove the teachings of the Quran, we will not utilize the many inconsistencies/contradictions that exist in Quranic teachings, we will not prove that the scientific teachings of the Quran are fraudulent; we will not hold God's word to the literary standard of a Shakespeare, Hemingway or Dostoevsky. (As a literary work, the Quran is a mess and will never win the Noble Prize for literature.)

In the pursuit of our holy mission to determine whether the Quran is the Eternal, Timeless, Divine Word of God, the only standard that we will employ is to examine each word, each teaching of the Quran to the highest, ethical standard of MORAL PERFECTION - Timeless Moral Perfection of A God of Moral Perfection.

This conception of Moral Perfection is only attainable by a God of Moral Perfection. If God is not a God of Perfection, a God of timeless, Moral Perfection then God is not God and therefore God does not exist.

Our mission is not only to prove that the Quran is not the word/teaching of God but to destroy the violent conception of God as the great slaughterer, destroyer, exterminator, avenger, hateful, evil being that pollutes most religions. The intellectual destruction of this evil depiction of God is absolutely essential to the survival of mankind.

In order to prove that the Quran is not the word/teaching of God, we only need show that one word - just one word of the Quran is not Moral Perfection - then the entire Quran is not the word of God and therefore, Islam is totally and completely fraudulent.

In our search for this one word, lets us begin our mission by describing requirements necessary for the Quran to be the divine word of a God of Moral Perfection.

REQUIREMENTS NECESSARY FOR THE QURAN TO BE THE ETERNAL DIVINE WORD OF GOD

In order for the Quran to be the divine word of God - every word, every teaching must be Moral Perfection. Since God is Moral Perfection, every word, every teaching of God must be Moral Perfection. If only one word/teaching of the Quran is not Moral Perfection - TRANSLATABLE Moral Perfection - Moral Perfection for all mankind for all time, then the entire Quran is not a work of Moral Perfection and therefore, not the word/teachings of God and therefore, Islam is totally and completely false. Every word - every teaching must be non-violent. There can be no word/teachings of war, terror, extermination, torture, brutality, rape, murder, revenge. There can be no words of hate - no hateful teachings. Again, every word - every teaching must be Moral Perfection. If only one word, one teaching is violent – one word/teaching of war - if, there is only one word of hate - if only one hateful teaching - if only one violent or hateful thought, if only one word - one teaching that is not Moral Perfection then the entire Quran is not a work of Moral Perfection and therefore, not the word/teaching of God. God cannot have some perfect teachings and other teachings that are imperfect. In order to be the divine word of God, the entire Quran must be a work of Moral Perfection - the perfect moral word/teachings of a perfect moral God of Moral Perfection. Again, any word/teachings in the Quran and all Islamic texts (written or verbal) that are not Moral Perfection are not the word/teachings of God - a God of Moral Perfection but the word/teachings of man - the word/teachings of Muhammad and his phony Allah (the AntiGod) and ALL Islam is fraudulent.

WHY THE QURAN IS NOT THE WORD/TEACHINGS OF A GOD OF MORAL PERFECTION

BROAD OVERVIEW OF THE IMMORAL QURAN

Before we begin our examination of the teachings of the Quran, searching for just one word that is immoral, one teaching that is not Moral Perfection, we can state as a broad overview of the Quran the following:

We will demonstrate that all teachings recorded in the Quran and all other Islamic texts, revelations, writings, sayings, fatwa's - of extermination, war, murder, mass murder, killing, death and destruction, violence, terror, rape, unlimited sex with sex slaves, hate, violent jihad, terrorism, torture, brutality, savagery, maiming, beheading, wife beating, inferiority of women, honor killings, stoning, cutting off limbs, child sex, women as instruments of sexual pleasure in paradise, Sharia law, bigotry, intolerance, extortion, slavery, mutilations, looting, pillaging, sexual depravity, child molestation, oppression and subordination of women, inequality of kafirs, inequality of any human being, that kafirs can be murdered and their property stolen as a holy duty, that Muslims who renounce

Islam can be killed, that Muslims (or anyone) who challenge the teachings of Islam can be murdered, that believers who slay and are slain in the service of God will ascend to a sexual Paradise of lustrous eyed, voluptuous breasted virgins who they can sexually molest for all eternity are immoral, evil and irrational and not the perfect, moral teachings of God – a God of Moral Perfection – a God of all pure love, peace and mercy – but again – the teachings of Allah (the AntiGod) – the teachings of Muhammad.

To record in a Holy Book - the Quran - teachings of extermination, war, rape, slavery, looting, pillaging, hate, terror, etc. is a very great evil. The Quran is the most evil, evilest book ever written in human history. Just declaring that such immoral, evil teachings in the Quran are the eternal, divine word of God is evil incarnate and an obscenity against everything God stands for - a blasphemy and a crime against God himself. Again, Islam is a total and complete rejection of God, a very great sin and crime against God.

Killing, murder, slaughter, rape, looting are all crimes to all normal, rational human beings. Murder is not a multicultural difference. Religion is supposed to represent the best of mankind not the worst.

As stated, since every word/teaching must be absolute Moral Perfection for the Quran to be from God therefore as will be proven further in this book not one word /teaching of the Quran is the word/teaching of God and therefore Islam is fraudulent.

CHAPTER FOUR

THE DESTRUCTION OF ISLAM WITH JUST ONE WORD

EXAMINATION OF THE IMMORAL TEACHINGS OF THE QURAN

Now let us begin our examination of the teachings of the Quran looking for just one immoral word, just one teaching of immoral depravity that is not the teaching of a God of MORAL PERFECTION.

QURAN 9:5 MASS MURDER: THE INFAMOUS VERSE OF THE SWORD

Following are the translations of verse 9.5 by the three foremost translators of Islam.

YUSUFALI: "But when the forbidden months are past, then fight and slay the Pagans wherever ye find them, an seize them, beleaguer them, and lie in wait for them in every stratagem (of war); but if they repent, and establish regular prayers and practice regular charity, then open the way for them: for Allah is Oft-forgiving, Most Merciful."

PICKTHAL: "Then, when the sacred months have passed, slay the idolaters wherever ye find them, and take them (captive), and besiege them, and prepare for them each ambush. But if they repent and establish worship and pay the poor-due, then leave their way free. Lo! Allah is Forgiving, Merciful."

SHAKIR: "So when the sacred months have passed away, then slay the idolaters wherever you find them, and take them captives and besiege them and lie in wait for them in every ambush, then if they repent and keep up prayer and pay the poor-rate, leave their way free to them; surely Allah is Forgiving, Merciful."

Brief History

Verse 9.5 is among the last teachings of Muhammad (not Allah). This teaching was created as rumors swept Arabia that a large army from the Byzantine Empire had massed in Northern Arabia. Being one of the last teachings, this verse abrogates or abolishes from the Quran 124 earlier teachings of peace including the famous verse 2:256 - Let there be no compulsion in religion.

Examination of Teaching

No God who is a God of Moral Perfection would ever teach the revelation of extermination, genocide, violence, war, terror, that is Verse 9:5. The title - "Verse of The Sword" says it all. Can you imagine the words – "Verse of The Sword" in a holy book titling a divine revelation from God?

You can hear Muhammad and Allah yelling at their followers – the Muslims "Slay the Idoltars" (unbelievers) if they don't convert to Islam and perform all Islamic obligations. Muhammad and his overlord, Allah, instruct Muslims to wage wars against the idolaters, giving instructions of war – "besiege them and lie in wait for them in every ambush" When they come within Muslims reach and power, "slay" them. Do you think a God of Moral Perfection, Creator of the universe would order murder and then micro manage these murders telling Muhammad how to kill his prey? Muhammad gave these instructions – "besiege them" and "lie in ambush."

God as Moral Perfection is the very essence of non-violence; "Slay the Idolators" is an instruction to commit murder - even mass murder. It calls for the extermination of ALL (non-Christian/Jewish) kafirs from the face of the earth, unless they convert to Islam. This means the potential slaughter of 2.5 billion humans.

This, claimed Muhammad, is the teaching of Allah, who should be all peace and love for his creatures—irrespective of Idolaters, Muslims, Christians or Jews. God of Moral Perfection, the all powerful and compassionate, would never use violence to bring a deviant creature of his own to the right path. How can God give such an opened-ended and unconditional order to Muslims for killing a section of humanity, whom God has created and nurtured with love? As Moral Perfection, an all-perfect, all-knowing God will not create his creatures in the first place, if he/she has to kill them in such barbaric manners. Obviously, such a teaching is not from God. Muhammad himself gave these instructions to his followers in the name of God in order to succeed his personal design.

Verse 9:5 is not the word or teaching of God. It is a violent, immoral teaching of mass murder. All kafirs must either convert to Islam, agree to keep up prayer and pay the poor-rate, or be murdered. All unbelievers must be killed throughout all the earth.

"Slay" is defined in the Webster dictionary as - "to put to death with a weapon, or by violence; hence, to kill violently; to put an end to; to destroy, to murder, annihilate, exterminate."

Slay is an evil, immoral word. A God of Moral Perfection could never speak the word - "slay" or the words "slay the idolaters." He could never write such a word, or even think such a thought. By giving such instructions, God is ordering the killing of human beings. If only one human was killed on God's instructions then God would be himself an accomplice to murder and therefore, no longer God. Again, in order for the Quran to be the word/teachings of God - every word, every teaching must be Moral Perfection. If only one word is not Moral Perfection then the entire Quran is not the word/teachings of God and therefore, Islam is totally and completely false – a sham and a fraud. "Slay" is an immoral word and Verse 9.5 is an immorally, depraved teaching.

All the Quranic verses are the teachings of Muhammad. He created Allah (the AntiGod) of the Quran and presented Allah as the same God worshipped by the Christians and Jews. Muhammad staged the revelations from Allah (the AntiGod) as revelations from God to give him authority over his followers and justification to war against the neighboring tribes of so called idolaters (pagan Arabs) and Jews and Christians - the first kafirs that faced the murderous onslaught of this killer and the murderous conquering ideology of Islam.

When Muhammad spoke, he was speaking the word of God – the laws of God - that had to be obeyed without question.

"Whoso obeyeth the messenger hath obeyed Allah, and whoso turneth away: We have not sent thee as a warder over them." Quran 4:80

How could the word of God be challenged? By morphing into Allah, Muhammad set up the perfect totalitarian system whereby his rule could not be challenged. Muhammad was Allah and Allah was Muhammad. Allah (the AntiGod) of the Quran never existed except in the mind of Muhammad.

Verse 9:5 is not the only teaching of the Quran that is immoral - there are close to 4,000 Quranic verses that are filled with murder, hate and evil. Although, we have succeeded in our mission proving that a God of Moral Perfection could never speak, write, or think, the Word " slay" - could never teach verse 9.5 and therefore, the Quran and Islam are totally fraudulent let us continue to examine the most important teachings of the Quran so we can truly understand the evil that Muhammad brought into the world - a very great evil that 1,400 years later is living and flourishing among us and possesses the very real possibility of conquering the entire world for his fictional Allah (the AntiGod). As documented in Chapter 2 - Verse 9:5 abrogates 124 peace teaching from the Quran. For a detailed listing of these verses go to http://www.islamreform.net/new-page-27.htm

VERSE 9:29 CRIMINAL EXTORTION

YUSUFALI: "Fight those who believe not in Allah nor the Last Day, nor hold that forbidden which hath been forbidden by Allah and His Messenger, nor acknowledge the religion of Truth, (even if they are) of the People of the Book, until they pay the Jizya with willing submission, and feel themselves subdued."

PICKTHAL: "Fight against such of those who have been given the Scripture as believe not in Allah nor the Last Day, and forbid not that which Allah hath forbidden by His messenger, and follow not the Religion of Truth, until they pay the tribute readily, being brought low."

SHAKIR: "Fight those who do not believe in Allah, nor in the latter day, nor do they prohibit what Allah and His Messenger have prohibited, nor follow the religion of truth, out of those who have been given the Book, until they pay the tax in acknowledgment of superiority and they are in a state of subjection."

Here, Allah (the AntiGod) orders Muslims to attack and kill the so-called 'people of the book' (i.e. Jews and Christians), until they are defeated and submitted to the supremacy of Islam and in willing humiliation, pay jizya (submission) tax to Muslims. Like 9:5, Verse 9:29 is a call to mass murder and extermination. Only Hitler instructed his followers to exterminate the Jews so completely in such an open instruction to slay them. These teachings are not historical niceties that kafirs can laugh off. The Quran is neither the Old Testament nor the Torah. (there is not one teaching of the Bible or Torah that exhorts Christians or Jews as Laws of God to commit murder, torture, etc. of non-believers or believers.) Again, Muslims believe these Quranic verses are from God. The People's of The Book have no choice. Convert to Islam or pay a submission tax or be murdered. In this modern age of weapons of mass destruction, mass murder ordered by God becomes a very real, frightening possibility.

Verses 9:29 and 9:5 are Allah (the AntiGod's) declaration of war against kafirs. These Laws of War are permanent and will not end until ALL kafirs are murdered or pay the jizya (submission) tax or convert to Islam. This is criminal. Again and again - this is not God's law - this is the law of Allah (the AntiGod). The true God gave mankind an intelligence to comprehend the universe and a free will to do good or to do evil. God wants all mankind to come to Him of their own free will. God would never use the force of violence or coercion of a tax (or any other means except love, goodness, mercy) to force anyone to believe in Him.

"Fight those who do not believe in Allah" was never spoken by God. "Fight" is a word of violence. A God of Moral Perfection could never order people to fight those who do not believe in Him. God could never write or speak the word "fight" - not even express a thought containing the word "fight". If God created such a teaching, He would be an immoral being and therefore, no longer Moral Perfection - therefore no longer God.

Verses 9:29 and 9:5 - revealed during the final days of Muhammad's life - are the two most important and finalized teachings of the Quran. They are Allah's declaration of permanent war against Jews and Christians until they are murdered, converted to Islam or pay the jizya tax in humiliation and all other kafirs either converted or exterminated. This barbarism is obviously not fitting of a perfect creator. As stated, the true God, having endowed humankind with intelligence, will let his/her creatures follow their own free will to do good or evil. If at all, God would want all human beings to come to his/her path of their own free will. The thought of extracting taxes that too, through such brutality from a section of his/her creatures would never cross God's mind.

Again, God orders Muslims to attack and kill the so-called 'people of the book' (i.e. Jews and Christians)', until they are defeated and submit to the supremacy of Islam and in willing humiliation, pay jizya tax to Muslims. Such is the punishment God renders to people for following, in His own admission, scriptures, which He Himself had sent to them through Christ a few hundred years earlier. Extraction of jizya from dhimmi Jews and Christians is obviously designed for Muslims to enjoy a good life on the labor and sweat of the dhimmis.

God declares that the Peoples of The Book must not only pay the jizya tax but the dhimmis must be "disgraced, humiliated and belittled. They must pay the tax in acknowledgment of superiority of Islam and in a state of subjugation- in a state of complete abasement. Muslims are not allowed to honor the people of Dhimmah or elevate them above Muslims, for they are miserable, disgraced and humiliated. The jizya should be collected with belittlement and humiliation.

In his own words, Allah (the AntiGod) is a barbaric exterminator of his own creatures, a tax-collecting overlord. As stated, extraction of jizya is obviously designed for the Muslims to enjoy a good life on the labor and sweat of the dhimmis. God would never order the killing of Christians and Jews. He would never order them to pay a submission tax. He would never teach that Muslims are superior to any other people - that they have a right to subjugate non-believers – disgrace, humiliate and debase them into submission. This is immoral and evil. If God used the word "Slay" - the word "fight" ordering people to be killed – an instruction to murder – engaged in criminal extortion – engaged in oppression and subjugation – established a system of humiliation and inferiority of kafirs that is dhimmihood then He would not be Moral Perfection and therefore, no longer God. These verses can come only from a vilest of human being, as worse as Hitler. Obviously such actions and attitudes are not befitting of an omnipotent God of Moral Perfection and pure love for all - regardless of race, religion or creed. As with teaching 9.5 since verse 9:29 is not a teaching of Moral Perfection - the entire Quran is not the word/teaching of God. Islam is false. (For a detailed listing of the 129 evil teachings of Surah 9 go to the University of Southern California website and read each of these teachings directly from the Quran in Islam's own words ;)

http://www.usc.edu/schools/college/crcc/engagement/resources/texts/muslim/quran/009.qmt.html

VERSE 4:89 OF APOSTASY

YUSUFALI: "They but wish that ye should reject Faith, as they do, and thus be on the same footing (as they): But take not friends from their ranks until they flee in the way of Allah (From what is forbidden). But if they turn renegades, seize them and slay them wherever ye find them; and (in any case) take no friends or helpers from their ranks;"

PICKTHAL: "They long that ye should disbelieve even as they disbelieve, that ye may be upon a level (with them). So choose not friends from them till they forsake their homes in the way of Allah; if they turn back (to enmity) then take them and kill them wherever ye find them, and choose no friend nor helper from among them,"

SHAKIR: "They desire that you should disbelieve as they have disbelieved, so that you might be (all) alike; therefore take not from among them friends until they fly (their homes) in Allah's way; but if they turn back, then seize them and kill them wherever you find them, and take not from among them a friend or a helper."

How could the Creator of the universe be so merciless, vengeful to his own creations? No father, at least in the civilized world, kills his sons/daughters for their failure to do or be what he wants them to do/be. A true God obviously cannot order the murder of any human being for whatsoever reason. He would instead try to salvage every life, he has created with love. He will try to guide, not order to kill, any person for whatsoever reason. God obviously has the supreme power and can guide the deviant ones among his creatures just by wishing so. This teaching can only be befitting of the vilest of human beings, who engage is honor-killings of their sons and daughters for deviating from their wishes.

The word "seize' is an immoral word of violence that God would never utter. "Kill them wherever you find them" is a command to murder that is abhorrent to God. The very essence of God is life not death. God as a murderer, a killer, a being filled with hate and vengeance" take not from among them a friend or a helper" - if such a creature exists that created the universe, then this being is no God. Therefore, Verse 4:89 is immoral and not the teaching of a God of Moral Perfection and therefore repeating since every word/teaching of the Quran must be Moral Perfection for the Quran to be from God - the entire Quran is not from God and therefore ALL Islam is totally fraudulent.

APOSTLEY HADITH

From the Hadith:

The reason why executing apostates has always been well-ensconced in Islamic law is that there is an indisputable record of Muhammad and his companions doing exactly that.

Bukhari (52:260) - "...The Prophet said, 'If somebody (a Muslim) discards his religion, kill him.' "

Bukhari (83:37) - "Allah's Apostle never killed anyone except in one of the following three situations: (1) A person who killed somebody unjustly, was killed (in Qisas,) (2) a married person who committed illegal sexual intercourse and (3) a man who fought against Allah and His Apostle and deserted Islam and became an apostate."

Bukhari (84:57) - "[In the words of] Allah's Apostle, 'Whoever changed his Islamic religion, then kill him.'"

Bukhari (89:271) - A man who embraces Islam, then reverts to Judaism is to be killed according to "the verdict of Allah and his apostle."

Bukhari (84:58) - "There was a fettered man beside Abu Muisa. Mu'adh asked, 'Who is this (man)?' Abu Muisa said, 'He was a Jew and became a Muslim and then reverted back to Judaism.' Then Abu Muisa requested Mu'adh to sit down but Mu'adh said, 'I will not sit down till he has been killed. This is the judgment of Allah and His Apostle (for such cases) and repeated it thrice.' Then Abu Musa ordered that the man be killed, and he was killed. Abu Musa added, 'Then we discussed the night prayers'"

Bukhari (84:64-65) - "Allah's Apostle: 'During the last days there will appear some young foolish people who will say the best words but their faith will not go beyond their throats (i.e. they will have no faith) and will go out from (leave) their religion as an arrow goes out of the game. So, wherever you find them, kill them, for whoever kills them shall have reward on the Day of Resurrection.'

VERSE 5:32 OF EXTERMINATION

YUSUFALI: "On that account: We ordained for the Children of Israel that if any one slew a person - unless it be for murder or for spreading mischief in the land - it would be as if he slew the whole people: and if any one saved a life, it would be as if he saved the life of the whole people. Then although there came to them Our apostles with clear signs, yet, even after that, many of them continued to commit excesses in the land."

PICKTHAL: "For that cause We decreed for the Children of Israel that whosoever killeth a human being for other than manslaughter or corruption in the earth, it shall be as if he had killed all mankind, and whoso saveth the life of one, it shall be as if he had saved the life of all mankind. Our messengers came unto them of old with clear proofs (of Allah's Sovereignty), but afterwards lo! many of them became prodigals in the earth."

SHAKIR: "For this reason did We prescribe to the children of Israel that whoever slays a soul, unless it be for manslaughter or for mischief in the land, it is as though he slew all men; and whoever keeps it alive, it is as though he kept alive all men; and certainly Our apostles came to them with clear arguments, but even after that many of them certainly act extravagantly in the land."

When President Barrack Obama gave his speech in Cairo, he quoted from Verse 5.32 "whosoever killeth a human being, it shall be as if he had killed all mankind, and whoso saveth the life of one, it shall be as if he had saved the life of all mankind."

Isn't this a wonderful teaching from a wonderful God worthy of quotation by the President? Wait a moment while I grab my handkerchief and clear the tears from my eyes. It is just such a beautiful teaching. "whosoever killeth a human being, it shall be as if he had killed all mankind, and whoso saveth the life of one, it shall be as if he had saved the life of all mankind." Only a true God could create such a teaching of love. Could provide such guidance for mankind. A divine, timeless teaching worthy of a divine, timeless God.

But wait a moment. The President did not quote Verse 5:32 correctly. He left out a most important part of the teaching. God has created in his infinite wisdom two exceptions to his teaching." whosoever killeth a human being for other than manslaughter or corruption in the earth, it shall be as if he had killed all mankind," We can killeth a human being for manslaughter and corruption in the earth and it will not be the killing of all mankind.

And what does the exception "corruption in the land" mean. All human beings who do not convert to Islam have declared war on Islam and Allah, are a danger to Allah, and therefore have created corruption in the land and must be murdered.

Verse 5:32 is a teaching of mass extermination and genocide. The President quoted a teaching that justifies the mass murder of 305,000,000 Americans who are non-Muslim.

This is a teaching of madness masquerading as a teaching of love. This is not a teaching of Moral Perfection from a God of Moral Perfection. It is a death warrant issued by the AntiGod Allah. This is the incarnation of evil. Again, not being of Moral Perfection, the Quran is a book of evil and all Islam is evil. As will be shown in Chapter 40 Barrack Obama was taught this teaching at the Muslim school in Indonesia. He understands Verse 5:32.

And how are the kafirs to be murdered for making "corruption in the land." Read the following Verse 5:33

VERSE 5:33 OF BARBARIC CRUELTY

YUSUFALI: "The punishment of those who wage war against Allah and His Messenger, and strive with might and main for mischief through the land is: execution, or crucifixion, or the cutting off of hands and feet from opposite sides, or exile from the land: that is their disgrace in this world, and a heavy punishment is theirs in the Hereafter;"

PICKTHAL: "The only reward of those who make war upon Allah and His messenger and strive after corruption in the land will be that they will be killed or crucified, or have their hands and feet on alternate sides cut off, or will be expelled out of the land. Such will be their degradation in the world, and in the Hereafter theirs will be an awful doom;"

SHAKIR: "The punishment of those who wage war against Allah and His messenger and strive to make mischief in the land is only this, that they should be murdered or crucified or their hands and their feet should be cut off on opposite sides or they should be imprisoned; this shall be as a disgrace for them in this world, and in the hereafter they shall have a grievous chastisement."

Can you comprehend God ordering people to be "murdered or crucified or their hands and their feet should be cut off on opposite sides" God ordering people to be horribly tortured. God ordering people to be crucified. Do you understand the sheer pain and suffering, the extreme torture of crucifying a human being? **GOD AS A MONSTER.**

Such horrifying tortures of barbaric nature are unacceptable in any manmade civilized society of our time. How could a God of compassion, love and mercy render such punishment to his/her own creatures? How could one accept such penal codes as the eternal laws of the human society? It is needless to emphasize that such laws cannot come down from the supreme creator of Moral Perfection.

Hitler had people tortured by the SS and then hung alive on meat hooks to be filmed screaming in horrible agony for his later enjoyment. God has humans chopped up for his enjoyment and pleasure. This is not a teaching of Moral Perfection but of moral depravity. Verse 5:33 makes a farce of God's name. Can one imagine a God killing, murdering and crucifying "those who fight god and his messenger and seek to corrupt the land?" In the first place, how can one fight the almighty creator, under whose control is everything on earth? If God simply wishes, everything in the universe falls in place. God would never order Muslims to kill other human beings, whom he has created with love.

There is nothing more nonsensical as ideas like this, which prophet Muhammad, the purported messenger of Allah, used to cause great human tragedies, such as to murder, torture or banish those who oppose his rule.

The hate and venom pours from verse 5:33 across the pages of the Quran soaking the book in blood. Take your sword and cut human beings into pieces like you would carve up a pig for slaughter. Crucify them. Execute them. Murder them. Again, these are not words of Moral Perfection - these are evil orders that could only be given by an evil incarnate - a Hitler, a Stalin, a Muhammad, not God. (For more teachings of torture: http://www.islamreform.net/new-page-8.htm teachings of murder: - http://www.islamreform.net/p7.htm
teachings of fighting: – http://www.islamreform.net/p1.htm teachings of violence: - http://www.islamreform.net/new-page-2.htm

There are many other verses in the Quran exhorting similar punishment of people for no crime at all or for negligible offences. For example,

VERSE 8:12 OF BEHEADING

YUSUFALI: "Remember thy Lord inspired the angels (with the message): "I am with you: give firmness to the Believers: I will instill terror into the hearts of the Unbelievers: smite ye above their necks and smite all their finger-tips off them."

PICKTHAL: "When thy Lord inspired the angels, (saying): I am with you. So make those who believe stand firm. I will throw fear into the hearts of those who disbelieve. Then smite the necks and smite of them each finger."

SHAKIR: "When your Lord revealed to the angels: I am with you, therefore make firm those who believe. I will cast terror into the hearts of those who disbelieve. Therefore strike off their heads and strike off every fingertip of them."

No God of Moral Perfection would ever teach 8:12. Beheading people as a law of God - cutting off their finger tips - this is truly evil - truly blasphemy against God. How can any rational person believe that God wrote the Quran and a copy of this monstrosity is in heaven? "I will cast terror into the hearts of those who disbelieve." God - the creator of the universe - a being of immeasurable power - is the greatest terrorist of the universe - who takes pleasure inflicting fear and pain into the hearts of his creations. If you believe that such a God exists then you are truly deranged. Muhammad spoke these words. He is the monster of the universe - an evil, hateful, murderous, being who demands obedience and worship by holy acts of torture, terror, slaughter, beheading etc. No normal person can believe in Muhammad and his false Allah (the AntiGod). By worshipping Allah (the AntiGod) Muslims have forsaken God, and are worshipping evil. Only a God of Moral Perfection is God. Furthermore, as already shown, all teachings of a God of Moral Perfection must be Moral Perfection; otherwise they are the teachings of evil men usurping the divine authority of God for their own evil designs. For a detailed listing of the 75 evil beheading teachings of Surah 8 go to the University of Southern California website;

http://www.usc.edu/schools/college/crcc/engagement/resources/texts/muslim/quran/008.qmt.html

VERSE 47:4 OF WAR TO KILL KAFIRS

YUSUFALI: "Therefore, when ye meet the Unbelievers (in fight), smite at their necks; At length, when ye have thoroughly subdued them, bind a bond firmly (on them): thereafter (is the time for) either generosity or ransom: Until the war lays down its burdens. Thus (are ye commanded): but if it had been Allah's Will, He could certainly have exacted retribution from them (Himself); but (He lets you fight) in order to test you, some with others. But those who are slain in the Way of Allah, - He will never let their deeds be lost."

PICKTHAL: "Now when ye meet in battle those who disbelieve, then it is smiting of the necks until, when ye have routed them, then making fast of bonds; and afterward either grace or ransom till the war lay down its burdens. That (is the ordinance). And if Allah willed He could have punished them (without you) but (thus it is ordained) that He may try some of you by means of others. And those who are slain in the way of Allah, He rendereth not their actions vain."

SHAKIR: "So when you meet in battle those who disbelieve, then smite the necks until when you have overcome them, then make (them) prisoners, and afterwards either set them free as a favor or let them ransom (themselves) until the war terminates. That (shall be so); and if Allah had pleased He would certainly have exacted what is due from them, but that He may try some of you by means of others; and (as for) those who are slain in the way of Allah, He will by no means allow their deeds to perish."

Here, the creator of the universe is instructing Muhammad and his Muslim army in the field of battle. Behead the disbelievers. Chop people's heads off as a holy duty from God. The Quranic God, therefore, is acting as the commander-in-chief on the battlefield, for defeating the enemy and taking the latter captive, for ransoming them in order to generate revenue. What a fantastic plan from the creator of the universe. Napoleon is nothing in comparison to the military genius of the Quranic god as displayed in verse 47.4. Of course, if Muslims can become victorious or martyred by following those military commands of Allah, he will reward those Jihadists with hoards of celestial virgins in paradise "(as for) those who are slain in the way of Allah, He will by no means allow their deeds to perish." (See page 47 for Quranic verse 9:111)

Osma bin laden and all the beheaders of Islam are following the Quran. They are following the obscene laws of Muhammad. If you believe such evil then your soul is lost forever. For the true God of Moral Perfection, the epitome of sanity and justice, to engage in such actions is nothing but madness. Only people with truly evil souls can believe in such insanity.

We are the slaves of God:- God does as He wills:- we cannot question the commandments of God:- we must obey God, whatever He orders us to do:- God is a fascist, God is a terrorist, God is the Supreme Dictator:- if God orders us to kill, we must kill:- if God orders us to oppress women & kafirs, we must do that too:- we cannot even look for the wisdom in God's instructions, there doesn't have to be any:- it is enough that God is our Lord & Master. Our only duty is to serve & obey, instantly. By definition; everything that God wants is good, & resistance is futile. If such a God exists then this God is not God but an evil being. More teachings of war from both Quran and Hadith are listed at:
http://www.islamreform.net/new-page-5.htm

VERSES 4:74 and 2:207: OF SUICIDE ATTACKS

Verse 4:74
YUSUFALI: "Let those fight in the cause of God Who sell the life of this world for the hereafter. To him who fighteth in the cause of God, - whether he is slain or gets victory - Soon shall We give him a reward of great (value)."

PICKTHAL: "Let those fight in the way of Allah who sell the life of this world for the other. Whoso fighteth in the way of Allah, be he slain or be he victorious, on him We shall bestow a vast reward."

SHAKIR: "Therefore let those fight in the way of Allah, who sell this world's life for the hereafter; and whoever fights in the way of Allah, then be he slain or be he victorious, We shall grant him a mighty reward."

Verse 2.207
YUSUFALI: "And there is the type of man who gives his life to earn the pleasure of God: And God is full of kindness to (His) devotees."

PICKTHAL: "And of mankind is he who would sell himself, seeking the pleasure of Allah; and Allah hath compassion on (His) bondmen."

SHAKIR: "And among men is he who sells himself to seek the pleasure of Allah; and Allah is Affectionate to the servants."

Christians are sanctified by the blood of Christ which they receive in Holy Communion. Muslim men are sanctified by the blood of murdered kafirs guaranteeing them accession to Paradise. Muhammad maintained that death in jihad not only blots out all sins including sexual ones but actually gratifies them.

"The martyr is special to Allah. He is forgiven [of all sins] from the first drop of blood [that he sheds]. He sees his throne in paradise, where he will be adorned in ornaments of faith. He will wed the 'Aynhour [a.k.a. "voluptuous women"] and will not know the torments of the grave, and safeguards against the greater terror [hell]. . And he will copulate with 72 'Aynhour" (see The Al Qaeda Reader, p. 143).

Suicide is a crime in Islam but martyrdom is a holy act guaranteeing entrance to Paradise. This is the Orwellian double speak of the AntiGod Allah. Place on a vest loaded with bombs and explode it in a crowed mall, load a track/car full of bombs and explode it in a farmer's market, seize a plane and fly it into skyscrapers are acts of martyrdom not mass murder. You are giving your life in the service of the AntiGod to ensure victory over the kafirs. "Fight in the way of Allah, who sells this world's life for the hereafter"; is an horrendous collection of words. Your life is a gift from God. In the endless deadness of the universe, you were born. Your birth was a true miracle. After 14 billion years of creation, you were created – the odds of any one of us being born is infinistemal. Our obligation is to live our life as good, moral human beings making our present and our children's future better. Our great moral duty is to care for our fellow man and ensure that every child is fed, every child is clothed, every child has a decent home, and every child can attend school. Taking our life and destroying it – blowing up our bodies to kill others in the name and to the greater glory of God is such a heinous crime as to be unspeakable. Islam is a heinous unspeakable crime against God. It must be rejected. There are 43 teachings of the glorification of suicide at: http://www.islamreform.net/new-page-6.htm

VERSES 8:60 and 3:151 OF TERRORISM

Bukhari: V4B52N220 "Allah's Apostle said, 'I have been made victorious with terror.'"

Verse 8:60

YUSUFALI: "Against them make ready your strength to the utmost of your power, including steeds of war, to strike terror into (the hearts of) the enemies, of God and your enemies, and others besides, whom ye may not know, but whom God doth know. Whatever ye shall spend in the cause of God, shall be repaid unto you, and ye shall not be treated unjustly"

PICKTHAL: "Make ready for them all thou canst of (armed) force and of horses tethered, that thereby ye may dismay the enemy of Allah and your enemy, and others beside them whom ye know not. Allah knoweth them. Whatsoever ye spend in the way of Allah it will be repaid to you in full, and ye will not be wronged."

SHAKIR: "And prepare against them what force you can and horses tied at the frontier, to frighten thereby the enemy of Allah and your enemy and others besides them, whom you do not know (but) Allah knows them; and whatever thing you will spend in Allah's way, it will be paid back to you fully and you shall not be dealt with unjustly."

Verse 3:151
YUSUFALI: "Soon shall We cast terror into the hearts of the Unbelievers, for that they joined companions with God, for which He had sent no authority: their abode will be the Fire: And evil is the home of the wrong-doers!"

PICKTHAL: "We shall cast terror into the hearts of those who disbelieve because they ascribe unto Allah partners, for which no warrant hath been revealed. Their habitation is the Fire, and hapless the abode of the wrong-doers."

SHAKIR "We will cast terror into the hearts of those who disbelieve, because they set up with Allah that for which He has sent down no authority, and their abode is the fire, and evil is the abode of the unjust."

   Terrorism in Islam is the striking of fear and terror into the hearts of kafirs. Blow up their subway stations and trains. Send suicide bombers to blow up malls and theatres. These attacks demonstrate to kafirs the total impotency of their governments to protect them. Rape and gang raping are a form of terrorism meant to terrorize kafir women and demonstrate the total helplessness of their men folk to protect their families. At the massacre of Banu Qurayza, Muhammad by beheading the Jewish male population struck sheer terror into the hearts of all kafir communities in Saudi Arabia sending a very clear message - surrender or share the same fate. Convert or die. As Mao **Tse**-Tung said intimidate one to intimidate millions to which we can change to terrorize many to terrorize many. This tactic is working in both Europe and the United States. Governments are singing the praises of Islam. They are busy bringing in Sharia Law and teaching Islam to their children. Fear works. Terror works. Violence works. You no longer need armies of millions to conquer. Britain which held out against the might of Hitler's armies standing alone for years has surrendered to the forces of the AntiGod with just one subway bombing. The USA is being Islamized at a rapid pace. As stated - 9/11 was the greatest victory ever achieved by the AntiGod. It struck real terror into the very centre of the political and military heart of the USA. There now is in office a President espousing the wonderful religion of peace telling us that the USA is also a Muslim country. The President is absolutely correct. The AntiGod is a military genius. For 11 pages of terrorism sanctioned by the AntiGod a.k.a Muhammad and his prophet a.k.a. Allah go to http://www.islamreform.net/new-page-7.htm

VERSES 9:39, 3:169/170 and 8:16 OF HELL

Verse 9:39
YUSUFALI "Unless ye go forth, He will punish you with a grievous penalty, and put others in your place; but Him ye would not harm in the least. For God hath power over all things."

PICKTHAL "If ye go not forth He will afflict you with a painful doom, and will choose instead of you a folk other than you. Ye cannot harm Him at all. Allah is Able to do all things."

SHAKIR "If you do not go forth, He will chastise you with a painful chastisement and bring in your place a people other than you, and you will do Him no harm; and Allah has power over all things."

Verse 3:169/170

YUSUFALI "Think not of those who are slain in God's way as dead. Nay, they live, finding their sustenance in the presence of their Lord; They rejoice in the bounty provided by God: And with regard to those left behind, who have not yet joined them (in their bliss), the (Martyrs) glory in the fact that on them is no fear, nor have they (cause to) grieve."

PICKTHAL "Think not of those, who are slain in the way of Allah, as dead. Nay, they are living. With their Lord they have provision. Jubilant (are they) because of that which Allah hath bestowed upon them of His bounty, rejoicing for the sake of those who have not joined them but are left behind: That there shall no fear come upon them neither shall they grieve."

SHAKIR "And reckon not those who are killed in Allah's way as dead; nay, they are alive (and) are provided sustenance from their Lord; Rejoicing in what Allah has given them out of His grace and they rejoice for the sake of those who, (being left) behind them, have not yet joined them, that they shall have no fear, nor shall they grieve."

Verse 8:16

YUSUFALI "If any do turn his back to them on such a day - unless it be in a stratagem of war, or to retreat to a troop (of his own)- he draws on himself the wrath of God, and his abode is Hell, - an evil refuge (indeed)!"

PICKTHAL "Whoso on that day turneth his back to them, unless manoeuvring for battle or intent to join a company, he truly hath incurred wrath from Allah, and his habitation will be hell, a hapless journey's end."

SHAKIR "And whoever shall turn his back to them on that day -- unless he turn aside for the sake of fighting or withdraws to a company -- then he, indeed, becomes deserving of Allah's wrath, and his abode is hell; and an evil destination shall it be."

Muslims believe in judgment day whereby their good deeds will be measured against their sins. However Allah (the AntiGod) in His great wisdom and mercy has given to His exalted Muslim men followers a **Stay Out of Hell Card.**

All kafirs both men and women are doomed to the fires of hell for all eternity for rejecting the AntiGod. The vast majority of Muslim women will be sent to hell for being born Muslim women instead of Muslim men. According to verse 9:39 those Muslim men who refuse to fight and kill kafirs will be sent to hell. Teaching 8:16 allows Muslim men who kill kafirs to avoid hell. Verses 3:169/170 allow martyrs to go directly from life to paradise, where they wait for those Muslim men who must first go through the Day of Judgment. (Again murdering, torturing, terrorizing, raping, enslaving etc. kafirs are not sins but blessed acts.)

Muhammad, Hitler and Stalin were the 3 greatest monsters of history. All three committed the second greatest crime against God – murder, kill, and slaughter their fellow human beings but only one of the three – Muhammad committed the greatest act of evil against God – to murder, kill, and slaughter in the name of and to the greater glory of God. Never has there been a more evilier man then Muhammad. He set in motion forces of evil that have murdered 270,000,000 humans sacrificed to God's glory. If there is a hell and a Satan – Muhammad is sitting at his right side. What of all the tens and tens of millions of Muslim men who obey the teachings of the Quran and live their lives according to the example set by Muhammad in the Hadith and Sira? It won't do them any good when they stand before God and discover that there is no Allah to greet them and reward them for the carnage they have brought to mankind. It won't do them any good when they start to cry tears that they believed that Muhammad was God's last prophet and killed, raped, and pillaged according to what they believed were God's teachings. Having been born with a free will to do good or evil, they chose evil and will suffer the consequences. Fortunately, 98% of Muslim women will ascend to heaven and be with God for living the hell on earth which is their fate for being born a Muslim woman. Unfortunately most of their fathers, brothers, sons and husbands will be with their leader prophet roasting and playing pocket polo with each other for all eternity and dream forlornly of their promised paradise full of virgins. For 48 teachings of hell go to:http://www.islamreform.net/new-page-9.htm and http://www.islamreform.net/new-page-21.htm Now we come to the most diabolical, evil teaching of all Islam and all human history. (This teaching is so critical that it was partially presented in Excerpts. It is repeated here with a much more complete analysis.)

MOST DIABOLICAL EVIL TEACHING IN ALL HUMAN HISTORY

EVIL, DEMENTED DEPRAVED SEXUAL ISLAMIC PARADISE AS LAWS OF GOD

Islam teaches that if Muslims slay or are slain (kill or are killed) in the service of God, they are guaranteed accession to a deviant sexual paradise. Islam's Paradise is filled with whorish virgins possessing voluptuous breasts and lustrous eyes. Muslims, blessed with an access to Paradise, will have 72 such virgins to engage in incessant copulation. Furthermore, Muslim's surest way of getting a passport to Paradise, says Allah, is to get slain while trying to kill the kafirs. The Quran is no more a holy book than Playboy, Penthouse, and Hustler are holy books. Indeed, Playboy, Penthouse and Hustler would make better holy books than the Quran in that the former does not incite murder of any persons whatsoever.

VERSE 9:111 – MUSLIM'S PASSPORT TO PARADISE

YUSUFALI: "Allah hath purchased of the believers their persons and their goods; for theirs (in return) is the garden (of Paradise): they fight in His cause, and slay and are slain: a promise binding on Him in truth, through the Law, the Gospel, and the Qur'an: and who is more faithful to his covenant than Allah? then rejoice in the bargain which ye have concluded: that is the achievement supreme."

PICKTHAL: "Lo! Allah hath bought from the believers their lives and their wealth because the Garden will be theirs: they shall fight in the way of Allah and shall slay and be slain. It is a promise which is binding on Him in the Torah and the Gospel and the Qur'an. Who fulfilleth His covenant better than Allah? Rejoice then in your bargain that ye have made, for that is the supreme triumph."

SHAKIR: "Surely Allah has bought of the believers their persons and their property for this, that they shall have the garden; they fight in Allah's way, so they slay and are slain; a promise which is binding on Him in the Taurat and the Injeel and the Quran; and who is more faithful to his covenant than Allah? Rejoice therefore in the pledge which you have made; and that is the mighty achievement."

Here is what the Paradise of Allah looks like:
"As for the righteous (Muslims)... We (Allah) shall wed them to beautiful virgins with lustrous eyes" [Quran 44:51-54]

"The righteous (Muslims) they shall triumph... Theirs shall be voluptuous women." [Quran 78:31-33].

Other verses in the Quran—such as 37:40-48, 44:51-55, 52:17-20, 55:56-58, 70-77, 56:7-40 and 78:31 (listed further)—describe the Paradise to be an alluring whorehouse. Additionally, never-molested (virgin) young boys like pearls will be available in abundance in the Muslim paradise (Surat 52:24, 56:17, and 76:19) for the blessed Muslim men to engage in sodomy. For Muhammad—who was a master of indulging in carnal pleasures with a dozen wives and at least two concubines in his harem—would obviously suit such a depraved whorehouse in the afterlife. Allah (the AntiGod), in pliant servitude, provided what Muhammad wanted.

Quranic verse 9:111 is the most evil, depraved, diabolical, immoral teaching in all of Islam. Indeed in all human history.

Verse 9:111 means what it means. A Muslim who dies while trying to murder kafirs fulfilling teachings 9:5, 9:29 and all the other teachings of murder, rape, terror, torture of kafirs in the Quran ARE GUARANTEED MARTYRDOM AND ACCESSION TO AN EVIL, LEWD, DEPRAVED PARADISE FILLED WITH ETERNAL VIRGINS OF EXQUISITE BEAUTY WHO REGENERATE AS VIRGINS AFTER EACH SEX ACT AND WHOM THESE KILLERS AND MURDERERS OF ISLAM CAN SEXUALLY MOLEST IN ENDLESS COPULATION FOR PERPETUAL ENJOYMENT FOR ALL ETERNITY.

In the laws of Allah (the AntiGod) as discussed above and earlier chapters, kafirs are not human beings to Muslims. They have absolutely no humanity. They have no right to life and must be killed by Muslims in Allah's cause [Jihad] for gaining Paradise. In the holy wars of Allah, for Muslims, it is a holy religious duty to murder kafirs who have grown pubic hair. The kafirs women and children will be enslaved and sold as prophet Muhammad did with the Jews of Banu Quraiza (coming discussion).

Allah takes away from Muslims all rights and ownership of their life. Muslims will engage Allah's stratagems of wars without any questions asked, and kill and get killed. This is the only mode of actions that will earn them Paradise. Allah is the peerless master of incitement of violence and bloodbath.

This evil Paradise for murderers is an outrageous affront and sin against God. It turns God into a pimp, the great whoremaster of the universe making a mockery of everything God stands for. This obviously is barbaric craziness. Islam's God – Allah is a depraved, deranged psychopath – the AntiGod. He is commander of mass-murder, rape, enslavement and plunder. His inhuman teachings have inspired the slaughter of an estimated 270,000,000 kafirs, over the last 1400 years, by Muslims in their aim to fulfill the teaching of Quran 9:111 for gaining a place in his whorehouse Paradise. Muslim Jihadists did the same on 9/11 ramming the twin towers in New York City slaughtering 2,976 people. They did the same in the London subway/bus massacres. They did the same in the Mumbai slaughter. Major Hasan did the same at Ft. Hood. You cannot ascend to Paradise by climbing on the corpses of the murdered. Those who kill in the name of and to the greater glory of God will ascend not to Paradise but descend into the fires of hell.

On 9/11 those 19 Muslim Saudi killers who rammed the twin towers in New York City slaughtering human beings were true, good Muslims obeying the teachings of Allah (the AntiGod) and by killing themselves murdering kafirs believed they would ascend to this sexual place of evil. These deaths were ordered by Allah (the AntiGod) in teaching Quran 9:5. Major Hasan who murdered 13 soldiers at Ft. Hood is a true, good Muslim obeying exactly the teachings of the Quran.

These depraved murderers died in the fulfillment of Allah's command to conquer the nations of the world for Islam. God is the greatest mass murderer in history. He is the great avenger of the sword, slaughtering entire populations, leaving behind a path of blood and destruction across entire continents, wailing women and children being led away in chains by the millions for a life of sexual abuse and slavery. This is not a God of Moral Perfection but a being of psychopathical evil.

The horrid reality of 9/11 is that if these Saudi holy killers had possessed nuclear weapons, they would have gladly detonated them killing 30 million kafirs.

Verse 9:111 is the teaching that has been used by Muhammad and his lieutenants to mobilize the suicide bombers, the beheaders, the jihadists to kill and slaughter millions. No God would ever teach 9:111 for if God gave such a law, He would be the greatest killer in all the universe – not a God of mercy, love, peace and goodness – not a God of Moral Perfection but a mass murderer on the scale of a Hitler or Stalin or Muhammad. Promising those who kill in the name of God, whose hands are coated with blood - the Islamic Paradise of sexual depravity – virgins who re-generate as virgins after each sex act - created by God for the sole purpose of servicing the righteous Muslim killers and murderers of God who are blessed with eternal erections and are permitted by God to engage in all forms of orgies, group sex, and sexual depravity is an obscenity against God.

Can you imagine a more deviant, immoral, depravity being taught to anyone whatever their age in this the 21st century?

The Quranic teachings of this morally corrupt and despicable Paradise with God acting as brothel master and slut director demonstrates the supreme evilness of Islam. Millions are being murdered in the name of and to the greater glory of God so these killers can ascend to this Paradise of madness. No normal, rational person can believe that God – the Creator of the Universe – a God of all goodness, mercy, love – could create such an evil Paradise. The modern Islamist preachers calling for young Muslims to sacrifice their lives in order to kill kafirs are calling for the blood of human beings. Quran 9:111 is an Eternal Law of God. It is timeless. The superb erections promised to Muslim men who achieve martyrdom are a powerful motivation.

Again and again, there is no way God would create such a demented Paradise. Only a sick psychopath could imagine such a place – that evil, sick mind is Muhammad.

How can anyone believe in Islam with such a pagan Paradise, believe in such evil, and pray to such an evil book – the Quran?

With its offer of eternal erections and gratifying heavenly sex with virgins who "re-virginate" after sex, its little wonder Muslim terrorists, suicide bombers and other Islamic martyrs are dying to enter Islam's brothel paradise.

God as a depraved, sexual lunatic.

The teachings of mass-murder of kafir men and women, their whole-sale enslavement, plundering and confiscating their wealth and properties and rewarding the blessed believers with a place in a Paradise of depraved sexual orgy are not befitting of a God of Moral Perfection - a God of pure love, mercy and nonviolence. As stated and re-stated, in reality, such an evil God does not exist for if such a being existed, he would not be Moral Perfection and therefore not God.

The teaching of Allah only represents Muhammad barbarous personality. This evil paradise is the creation of Muhammad to entice his followers to murder, rape, torture, terrorize kafirs and loot their property promising these holy killers eternal sexual delights. Allah was a creation in Muhammad's imagination in his own image. Allah of Quran simply represented Muhammad's own characteristics, personality, desires and ambitions.

Again, no rational, normal person can believe in such an evil, sexually depraved, irrational Paradise. If anyone believed in such a Paradise filled with virgins to be sexually molested for all eternity in the presence of God, and all they need to do to enter this paradise is kill or be killed in the service of God - we would declare them criminally insane.

However, as we have already learnt - ALL Muslims MUST believe the Quran is the ETERNAL divine word of God - the LAWS OF GOD - that God authored the Quran and a copy of the Quran is in heaven. It is valid for all times and places FOREVER; its ideas are absolutely true and beyond all criticism. To question it is to question the very word of God, and hence blasphemous. A Muslim's duty is to believe it and obey its divine commands without question.

Therefore, ALL Muslims must believe in verse 9:111 and ALL other teachings of the Quran, otherwise they are no longer Muslims but apostates of Islam and must themselves be killed. This means that 1.2 billion Muslims believe in this Islamic paradise filled with virgin sluts.

Needless to say NO SUCH SEXUALLY DEPRAVED ISLAMIC PARADISE EXISTS. Verse 9:111 is the incarnation of evil. It is not a teaching of Moral Perfection of a God of Moral Perfection but a teaching of moral depravity AND THEREFORE, SINCE EVERY WORD OF THE QURAN MUST BE MORAL PERFECTION TO BE THE WORD OF A GOD OF MORAL PERFECTION - THE QURAN IS NOT THE WORD/TEACHINGS OF ANY GOD AND THEREFORE, ISLAM IS TOTALLY AND COMPLETELY FALSE - A SHAM AND A FRAUD.

The God worshipped by Christians and Jews and His paradise is dramatically different. There is a vast difference ascending to a paradise of angels to be in the eternal presence of God and ascending to voluptuous, lustrous eyed virgins.

If God exists then Islam is a total and complete rejection of God and His teachings. Again, those Muslims who kill and are killed in the service of this bogus Allah are not going to ascend to paradise but will descend and join their founder Muhammad and his master Satan in the fires of hell.

Following are Muhammad's fictional Allah's teachings in the Quran describing this sexually depraved Islamic Paradise. Don't forget, Muslims believe that God wrote the Quran and therefore wrote these ridiculous evil teachings.

God, the creator is teaching that women are sexual objects whose sole purpose is to service men. The perfect woman will be young, bashful, dark eyed, full breasted, and most important untouched – VIRGINS.

Quran: (37:40-48): -they will sit with bashful, dark-eyed virgins, as chaste as the sheltered eggs of ostriches.

God is truly a man's man. He appreciates the sexual alluring qualities of women. And why not. He created them.

And what is the reward for Muslim men "who fight in His cause and slay and are slain" "they will sit with bashful, dark eyed virgins as chaste as the sheltered eggs of ostriches."

Quran (56: 35-36): "Verily, We have created them (maidens) of special creation. And made them Virgins."

Quran (56:34-37): "-we created the houris and made them virgins, loving companions for those on the right hand-."

Quran (55:70-77): "In each there shall be virgins chaste and fair-.dark eyed virgins sheltered in their tents whom neither man or Jinn have touched before-"

Quran (78: 33-34):"And young full-breasted (mature) maidens of equal age, and a full cup of wine."

Isn't God fantastic? "Bashful, dark eyed virgins" "virgins chaste and fair – eyed ... whom neither man or Jinn have touched before" "young, full breasted maidens" are these killers eternal reward. The words "dark eyed, full breasted, virgins" belong in sex magazines not in a so called book of God.
Needless to say, all these teachings are completely evil and not from A God of Moral Perfection. In sum, Allah of the Quran represents anything but the ideals of a supreme creator of Moral Perfection. Allah is no God, period!

SEX IN ISLAM AND ISLAMIC PARADISE

Quranic verses that promise Heaven with Houris, Sex, and Wine for the pious Muslim killers who slay and are slain in God's almighty service. (So you can truly understand true moral depravity, I have listed 39 teachings describing these virgin Paradise delights.)

Quran: (2:25): "And give glad tidings to those who believe and do righteous good deeds, that for them will be Gardens under which rivers flow (Paradise) ---.and they will be given these things in resemblance (i.e., in the same form but different in taste) and they shall have therein Azwajun Muhtahharatun (purified mates and wives) and that they will have abide therein foreer".

Quran 3:15 "Virgins await those who enter paradise."

Quran 4.57 "Virgins await those who enter paradise. "

Quran: (37:40-48): "-they will sit with bashful, dark-eyed virgins, as chaste as the sheltered eggs of ostriches."

Quran 37:40 "Those of the right hand-how happy will be those of the right hand! ...Who will be honored in the Garden of Bliss;

Quran 38:52 "Female companions await those who enter the Gardens of Eden on the Day of Reckoning."

Quran: (44:51-55): "As for the righteous (Muslims)...We (Allah) shall wed them to beautiful virgins with lustrous eyes"

Quran 44:54"So; and We shall join them to fair women with beautiful, big, and lustrous eyes."

Quran :(47:15): "The description of Paradise which the Muttaqun have been promised (is that) in it are rivers of water the taste and smell of which are not changed, rivers of milk of which the taste never changes, rivers of wine delicious to those who drink, and rivers of clarified honey---."

Quran 52:21 "Those who believe and whose families follow them in Faith, to them shall We join their offspring: Nor shall We deprive them of their works: (Yet) each individual is in pledge for his deeds. [Imagine that. Wives and children will be joined with husbands and fathers who are cavorting with virgins. That ought to be entertaining.] And We shall provide fruit and meat, anything they desire. There they shall pass from hand to hand a (wine) cup free of frivolity, free of all taint of vanity or cause of sin. Round about them will serve, (devoted) to them, young boy servants of their own (handsome) as well-guarded pearls. They will advance to each other, drawing near, engaging in mutual enquiry. They will say: 'We used to be afraid (of the punishment) in the midst of our families, but Allah has been good to us, and has delivered us from the torment of the Scorching Wind and Breath of Fire."

Quran 52:17 "Verily, the Muttaqun (those who fear) will be in Gardens and Delight. Enjoying the (bliss) which their Lord has provided, and their Lord saved them from the torment of the blazing Fire. 'Eat and drink with glee, because of what you used to do.' They will recline (with ease) on Throne Couches (of dignity) arranged in ranks; and We shall join them to beautiful Hur (female maidens) with big, lustrous eyes."

Quran (52:17-20): "They will recline (with ease) on thrones arranged in ranks. And We shall marry them to Huris (fair females) with wide lovely eyes." "There they shall pass from hand to hand a (wine) cup, free from any Laghw-."

Quran 55; 46 "For him who lives in terror of his Lord are two Gardens containing delights: shade, two fountains flowing, fruits in pairs. Reclining on carpets lined with silk brocade, fruits hanging low. In them virginal females with averted glances (desiring none but you), undeflowered by men or jinn. Is the reward of goodness aught but goodness?"

Quran (55:56): "Wherein both will be Qasirat-ut-Tarf (chaste females restraining their glances, desiring none except their husband) with whom no man or jinni has had tamth before them."

Quran (55:56-57):" In them will be bashful virgins neither man nor Jinn will have touched before. Then which of the favours of your Lord will you deny?"

Quran (55:57-58): "Then which of the blessings of your lord will you both (jinn and men) deny? (In beauty) they are like rubies and coral".

Quran 55:62 "And beside this, there are two other Gardens, rich green in color from plentiful watering. In them will be two springs, gushing forth, and fruits. And beautiful companions, virgins cloistered in pavilions, undefiled by men and jinn, reclining on green cushions and rich mattresses. Which of the favors of you Lord will you both deny?"

Quran (55:70-77): "In each there shall be virgins chaste and fair-.dark eyed virgins sheltered in their tents whom neither man or Jinn have touched before-"

Quran 55:71 "Allah will reward believing men with "fair ones" (beautiful women) in heaven."

Quran (55:72): "Hur (beautiful, fair females) guarded in pavilions;"

Quran 56:13 "A multitude of those from among the first, and a few from the latter, (will be) on couch-like thrones woven with gold and precious stones. Reclining, facing each other. Round about them will (serve) boys of perpetual (freshness), of never ending bloom, with goblets, jugs, and cups (filled) with sparkling wine. No aching of the head will they receive, nor suffer any madness, nor exhaustion. And with fruits, any that they may select: and the flesh of fowls, any they may desire. And (there will be) Hur (fair females) with big eyes, lovely and pure, beautiful ones, like unto hidden pearls, well-guarded in their shells. A reward for the deeds."

Quran 56:17 "Those in the Garden will be attended by immortal youths with wide, lovely eyes"

Quran 56:22: "And (there will be) Huris with wide, lovely eyes (as wives for the pious)"

Quran 56:33 "Unending, and unforbidden, exalted beds, and maidens incomparable. We have formed them in a distinctive fashion and made them virgins, loving companions matched in age, for the sake of those of the right hand." [Another translation reads:] "On couches or thrones raised high. Verily, We have created them (maidens) incomparable: We have formed their maidens as a special creation, and made them to grow a new growth. We made them virgins - pure and undefiled, lovers, matched in age."

Quran (56: 35-36): "Verily, We have created them (maidens) of special creation. And made them Virgins."

Quran (56:34-37): "-we created the houris and made them virgins, loving companions for those on the right hand-."

Quran 56:80 "Those of the right hand-how happy will be those of the right hand! ...Who will be honored in the Garden of Bliss;"

Quran 56:13 "A multitude of those from among the first, and a few from the latter, (will be) on couch-like thrones woven with gold and precious stones. Reclining, facing each other. Round about them will (serve) boys of perpetual (freshness), of never ending bloom, with goblets, jugs, and cups (filled) with sparkling wine. No aching of the head will they receive, nor suffer any madness, nor exhaustion. And with fruits, any that they may select: and the flesh of fowls, any they may desire. And (there will be) Hur (fair females) with big eyes, lovely and pure, beautiful ones, like unto hidden pearls, well-guarded in their shells. A reward for the deeds."

Quran 76:19 "Those in the Garden will be waited on by immortal youths, as beautiful as scattered pearls."

Quran 76:50 "As for the righteous, they will drink a cup of wine from a spring, making it gush forth abundantly." Quran 76:19 "And round them shall serve immortal boys of perpetual freshness, never altering in age. If you saw them, you would think they were scattered pearls." Quran 76:21 "Upon them will be green garments of fine green silk and heavy gold brocade. They will be adorned with bracelets of silver; their Lord will slack their thirst with wine."

Quran 77:41 "The righteous shall be amidst cool shades, springs, and fruits - all they desire. Eat and drink to your heart's content."

Quran 78:31 - 32 "Verily for those who follow Us, there will be a fulfillment of your desires: enclosed Gardens, grapevines, voluptuous full-breasted maidens of equal age, and a cup full to the brim of wine. There they never hear vain discourse nor lying - a gift in payment - a reward from your Lord."

Quran (78: 33-34):"And young full-breasted (mature) maidens of equal age, and a full cup of wine."

Quran 83:22 "The believers will be in Delightful Bliss: On couch-like thrones, gazing, their thirst will be slaked with pure wine."

Quran 85:11 "For those who believe and do good deeds will be Gardens; the fulfillment of all desires."

Quran (88:80) "Faces will be joyful, glad with their endeavour. In a lofty Garden they hear no harmful speech." Quran 88:12 "Therein will be a bubbling spring, raised throne-like couches, drinking cups ready placed, cushions set in rows, and rich silken carpets all spread out."

And what of Muslim women. Are they to be serviced by studs with eternal erections for all eternity? No such luck. The fate for most Muslim women is to burn in the fires of hell for all eternity.

"I (Mohammed) have seen that the majority of the dwellers of Hell-Fire were women... [because] they are ungrateful to their husbands and they are deficient in intelligence" (Sahih Bukhari: 2:18:161; 7:62:125,).

The only possible chance for a Muslim woman to ascend to Paradise is to completely obey her husband and even then her chances are very slim.

For the few Muslim women who do enter heaven, they will find a very bleak existence, for, according to Muhammad, they will spend eternity standing in the corners of Paradise, watching their husbands, fathers, brothers engaging in sexual orgies while they wait for the men to come and have sex with them.

Why did Muhammad create a Paradise of virgins that conveniently excluded Muslim wives? In order to get men to die for you, there must be either riches or sex offered to the stupid male believer. Allah teaches that Muslim women are deficient in intelligence but it is Muslim men who lack intelligence. What is not understandable about the species Homo sapiens is the absolute wiliness of males to die for the leader male. How little self esteem these poor pathetic Homo sapien men must possess to so willingly march off to slaughter and be slaughtered for the Hitler's and Muhammad's of the species.

Muhammad understood that if he created a Paradise filled with virgins that men would literally pound down the gates of Paradise to enter. A virgin is like a blank slate. They will never question, demand or disobey. You can create of her whatever you wish and once you get tried, you can dump her in the Paradise disposal bin and grab another without fear of losing out since God has supplied an eternal supply.

There was no way Muhammad was going to spoil Paradise for himself or his men by polluting it with Muslim wives. Muhammad understood that no matter how obedient Muslim wives are on earth, they would be nothing but trouble in Paradise. Corruption and mischief would enter Paradise. Having them sitting in a corner watching their husbands engaging in sex orgies with virgins, even for the most obedient of the obedient would lead to a slow smothering anger that would sooner rather then later explode into open rebellion. It would only be a matter of time before a wife started yelling and screaming epithets, grabbing a golf club or heaven forbid a sword and started chasing her husband from one end of Paradise to the other. Muslim wives would turn Paradise into a hell just as worse as the real hell. Better to send the wives to Hell then have them ruin eternal Paradise. They had done their duty by giving birth to Islam's warriors. Their wombs are all babied out. They are old and ugly. Time to throw them into the trash can of Hell.

All the above teachings of this immoral Paradise are totally immoral and evil and therefore, not from any God. They are an obscenity against humanity. They are an obscenity against God. Murder as a holy, divine act guaranteeing you eternal Paradise filled with virgins. 36 teachings of the Quran devoted to this monstrous Paradise have been presented in this chapter. How can 1.2 billion people believe such evil? This is the most stunning aspect of Islam that no normal person can ever comprehend. The Quran is not God's holy book. Only an AntiGod could create such depravity. The Quran is the book of Allah (the AntiGod) – the teachings of a fictional being. For more detailed description of this immoral, depraved Paradise go to: http://islamreform.net/new-page-44.htm and http://islamreform.net/new-page-45.htm

CHAPTER FIVE

ALLAH'S TEACHINGS CELEBRATING THE MASSACRE OF THE JEWS AT BANU QURAYZA
MUHAMMAD: THE FIRST ADOLF HITLER

In our quest of examining the claim of Muslims that the Quran is the divine word of God, a claim we have already proven to be fraudulent and therefore all Islam to be fraudulent, we will study next - the massacre of the Jews of Banu Qurayza.

Muhammad was one of the greatest criminals in history. He ordered 60 massacres and personally was involved in 27 atrocities. The most important massacre of Muhammad was at Banu Qurayza because it is cross referenced by Allah (the AntiGod) in the Quran. 600 to 900 Jewish men were beheaded at Banu Qurayza and the women and young Jewish girls (who were not selected as sex slaves by the Muslim SS killers known as the (Companions) were sold into slavery. Muhammad selected one of the Jewish women to rape and be his sex slave.

In Muhammad - God had selected - the perfect executioner for enforcing the will of God. Here was a true apostle who would show no mercy. Here was an apostle, who would not allow the crying of kafir women and children to touch his heart. Here was an apostle, who would stand as a moral example for all Muslim men to emulate through the ages - men like Osma bin Laden, Major Hasan, suicide bombers, jihadists, beheaders, etc who would follow the example set by the apostle of God at Banu Quraiza and enforce God's laws as set out in the Quran without mercy.

God, in all His merciful goodness celebrated this great victory and slaughter against the Banu Quraiza Jews through Quran passages 33.25, 33.26, 33.27, 8.67, 8.17 (listed below). But of course, it was not God who celebrated these immoral, evil acts but Allah (the AntiGod). By selling into slavery the women and children and seizing the property of this rich Jewish tribe great booty was obtained sanctioned by the AntiGod in the immoral Quranic verses 8.69, 8.1, 8.41.

BANU QURAIZA: BRIEF DESCRIPTION OF THE MASSACRE IN ISLAM'S OWN WRITINGS

ANGEL GABRIEL APPEARS TO MUHAMMAD INSTRUCTING HIM TO ATTACK THE JEWS OF BANU QURAYZA

As per sahi hadith (Buchari) – "when the Prophet returned from the battle of Al-Khandaq (i.e. Trench) and laid down his arms and took a bath, Gabriel came to the apostle wearing an embroidered turban and riding on a mule with a saddle covered with a piece of brocade and asked, " You have laid down your arms? By Allah, we angels have not laid them down yet and I have just come from pursuing the enemy. "God commands you, Muhammad, to go to Banu Qurayza. I am about to go to them to shake their stronghold (to terrorize Jews). So set out for them." The Prophet said, "Where to go?" Gabriel said, "Towards this side," pointing towards Banu Quraiza. So the Prophet went out towards them." Below is Sahi hadith proving the story:

Muslim: Volume 5, Book 59, Number 444:
Narrated by Anas:
"As if I am just now looking at the dust rising in the street of Banu Ghanm (in Medina) because of the marching of Gabriel's regiment when Allah's Apostle set out to Banu Quraiza (to attack them)."

These traditions about Gabriel's leadership are designed to give divine support for the atrocity that is about to be unleashed. Today, we may see this as fanciful, but to millions of Muslims this is real.

Muhammad Besieges Banu Quraiza For 25 Days. After The Jews Unconditionally Surrender All Men Are Beheaded, Women And Young Girls Raped And Sold Into Slavery. Their Property Is Looted.

Sahi Bukhari Volume 5, Book 59, Number 448:

"So Allah's Apostle went to them (i.e. Banu Quraiza) (i.e. besieged them). They then surrendered to the Prophet's judgment (unconditionally after 25 days of fierce resistance) but he directed them to Sad (ally) to give his verdict concerning them. Sad said, "I give my judgment that their warriors should be killed, their women and children should be taken as captives, and their properties distributed."

The Prophet said, "You have judged according to the King's (Allah's) judgment." (Hadith No. 447, Vol. 5). The sentence: Death by decapitation for around 600 men and pubescent boys, and enslavement for the women and children. Ibn Ishaq says that the number may have been as high as 800—900 (p. 464).

MERCIFUL MUHAMMAD ORDERS TRENCHES TO BE DUG FOR THE BEHEADED HEADS TO FALL INTO AND CONTROL THE BLOOD FLOW

The text of Sirat:

"Then they surrendered, and the apostle confined them in Medina in the quarter of d. al-Harith, a woman of B. al-Najjar. Then the apostle went out to the market of Medina (which is still its market today) and dug trenches in it. Then he sent for them and struck off their heads in those trenches as they were brought out to him in batches. Among them was the enemy of Allah Huyayy b. Akhtab and Ka`b b. Asad their chief. There were 600 or 700 in all, though some put the figure as high as 800 or 900. As they were being taken out in batches to the apostle they asked Ka`b what he thought would be done with them. He replied, 'Will you never understand? Don't you see that the summoner never stops and those who are taken away do not return? By Allah it is death!' This went on until the apostle made an end of them.

Huyayy was brought out wearing a flowered robe in which he had made holes about the size of the finger-tips in every part so that it should not be taken from him as spoil, with his hands bound to his neck by a rope. When he saw the apostle he said, 'By God, I do not blame myself for opposing you, but he who forsakes God will be forsaken.' Then he went to the men and said, "God's command is right. A book and a decree, and massacre have been written against the Sons of Israel." Then he sat down and his head was struck off." [Sirat, page 464]

As per the text of Sirat - Muhammad himself worked on the digging of the trench into which the massacred Jews were to be thrown. However, he did not only take part in those preparations, Muhammad also sent for them and STRUCK OFF their heads. Muhammad personally struck off at least the heads of those two mentioned men and maybe of more. Beheading 600-700 men one by one takes a substantial time and strength. Certainly, this was not done by one man alone but by many. Whoever was appointed to execute the bulk of this judgment, one has to be really numbed in ones conscience to strike off hundreds of heads, looking into the eyes of the victims to be killed.

BIG PROBLEM: How Did The SS Jihadist Executioners Decide On Which Jewish Boys To Slaughter Or Leave Alive To Be Sold Into Slavery

During this massacre, the apostle faced a very great problem. How to distinguish between young Jewish boys who could be sold into slavery and young Jewish men who had to lose their heads. Being a micro manager, the apostle came up with an ingenious solution. To separate adult men from the pre-pubescent boys, Muhammad had his devoted followers - the companions pull down the youngster's pants and each one examined SS style for pubic hairs around their genitals, and if they had grown any pubic hair, it was enough to behead them.

Book 38, Number 4390:
Narrated Atiyyah al-Qurazi:
"I was among the captives of Banu Qurayzah. They (the Companions) examined us, and those who had begun to grow hair (pubes) were killed, and those who had not were not killed. I was among those who had not grown hair."

One would expect this behavior from Hitler and his SS not from a prophet of God. Muhammad was no prophet. Again - **MUHAMMAD WAS THE FIRST HITLER**

Aisha Describes The Only Woman Murdered At Banu Qurayzah: She was Delirious Because Her Husband Had Just Been Beheaded. She Was Taken By An SS, Jihadist, Companion And Beheaded Putting Her Out Of Her Joyful Misery

Aisha said: "Only one of their women was killed. She was actually with me and was talking with me and laughing immoderately as the apostle was killing her man in the market when suddenly an unseen voice called her name. 'Good heavens,' I cried, 'What is the matter?' 'I am to be killed', she replied. 'What for?' I asked. 'Because of something I did,' she answered. She was taken away and beheaded." Aisha used to say, "I shall never forget my wonder at her good spirits and her loud laughter when all the time she knew that she would be killed" (Isahq 465). Book 14, Number 2665:

Narrated Aisha, Ummul Mu'minin: "No woman of Banu [tribe] Qurayzah was killed except one. She was with me, talking and laughing on her back and belly (extremely), while the Apostle of Allah . . . was killing her people with the swords. Suddenly a man called her name: Where is so-and-so? . . . I asked: What is the matter with you? She said: I did a new act. [Aisha] said: The man took her and beheaded her. [Aisha] said: I will not forget that she was laughing extremely although she knew that she would be killed." (Abu Dawud)

Muhammad Took One Of The Jewish Women As His Sex Slave

"The apostle had chosen one of their women for himself, Rayhana bint Amr . . . one of the women of . . . Qurayza, and she remained with him until she died, in his power. The apostle had proposed to marry and put a veil on her, but she said: "Nay, leave me in your power, for that will be easier for me and for you." So he left her. She had shown repugnance towards Islam when she was captured and clung to Judaism." (Ibn Ishaq p. 466)

The Looted Property And The Jewish Women And Children Were Divided Among the Muslims

More specifically, Ibn Ishaq says the spoils were divided among the Muslims thus:

"Then the apostle divided the property, wives, and children . . . among the Muslims, and he made known on that day the shares of horse and men, and took out the fifth. A horseman got three shares, two for the horse and one for the rider. A man without a horse got one share (p. 466). Then the apostle sent Sa`d b. Zayd al-Ansari brother of b. `Abdu'l-Ashhal with some of the captive women of B. Qurayza to Najd and he sold them for horses and weapons." [page 466]

Allah Allows Muhammad And His Jihadists To Have Sex With Their Sex Slaves

Allah also allows jihadists to have sex with female slaves. Sources: Ibn Ishaq, pp. 464—66; Tabari, vol. 8, pp. 27—41.

Muhammad Shows No Mercy:

Muhammad does not show any mercy, as the men and boys are handcuffed behind their backs and beheaded, and the women and children are enslaved. Instead, he takes one of the beautiful, recently 'widowed' Jewish women for himself.

Muhammad Enriches Himself:

Muhammad had huge spoils from this "final solution". Muhammad gets twenty percent of the Jewish property (movable, immovable and human), and the jihadists get eighty percent, to be distributed as he sees fit. At least 600 grown men are killed (those with the ability to fight). This represents probably something like 500 families, each of which on average would have at least a wife and a child, probably several. Consider, 1/5 of the possessions of a whole tribe (possessions of 100 families for Muhammad) plus the profit from selling the women as slaves.

Allah (the AntiGod) Shares In the Looting And Pillaging Of Murdered Jews Property

Quran 8:41— "And know that out of all the booty that ye may acquire (in war), a fifth share is assigned to Allah, - and to the Messenger, and to near relatives, orphans, the needy, and the wayfarer, - if ye do believe in Allah and in the revelation We sent down to Our servant on the Day of Testing, - the Day of the meeting of the two forces. For Allah hath power over all things."

Why Does Muhammad Not Show Mercy?

Muhammad needs to reward his jihadists, since they collected no spoils from the departed coalition - Allah gives him permission to do this in Quran 33:27. Booty from looted property and from the selling of women and children into slavery is utilized to pay his murderers and buy weapons to re-equip his army. And what makes this entire episode doubly heinous is that Muhammad and his jihadists could have had all of the wealth of the Jews after he banished them, but he still did not take this merciful option.

We need to recognize that Muhammad destroyed a large group that was challenging his sole authority and power over Medina, and which was in particular refusing to believe him to a true prophet from God. The latter was probably the more important. As long as there were people of the book who knew their scriptures, Muhammad's position of spiritual and subsequently political authority was challenged. We have seen in this story that the Jews would rather die than deny the word of God in the Torah and convert to Islam. The elimination of the challenge to his spiritual authority might well have been Muhammad's main motivation. Muhammad by this heinous act sent a powerful message throughout Arabia – surrender or die horribly with your women and children enslaved.

ALLAH (THE ANTIGOD) CELEBRATES THE MASSACRE OF BANU QURAYZA

Allah (the AntiGod) was overjoyed by the great victory of His apostle and celebrated this slaughter and enslavement of the Jewish kafirs of Banu Qurayza. Merciful Allah promptly sent Quranic teachings during that period of Banu Qurayza war to justify the cruelty of prophet Muhammad. Again, the hate of Allah pours like rivers of blood from these hideous words. The Quran is coated in the blood of the kafirs. Here are the Quranic teachings that are criminal in any concept of laws, but are valid in the eternal laws of Allah (the AntiGod) and must be obeyed by all Muslims for all eternity.

Quran-8:17—"It is not ye who Slew them; it is God; when thou threwest a handful of dust, it was not Thy act, but God's….." (Allah said, the killing of surrendered soldiers were done by the wish of Allah)

Quran-8:67—"It is not for any prophet to have captives until he hath made slaughter in the land. Ye desire the lure of this world and Allah desireth (for you) the Hereafter, and Allah is Mighty, Wise." (Allah insisting Prophet to kill all the prisoners, and should not keep any surrendered prisoners alive until He (Prophet) occupied entire Arabia.

How can you believe in a God who instructs the murder of all prisoners? These are CRIMES AGAINST HUMANITY. THESE ARE CRIMES AGAINST GOD. This law was an order from Allah (the AntiGod) to murder all prisoners until Arabia was conquered for Islam. Take no prisoners. Kill them all. "Make slaughter in the land." MASS MURDER. The word "slaughter" is so outrageous that only the insane can believe in Islam. As we have already seen - if God murdered human beings – just one human being, He would no longer be Moral Perfection and therefore, no longer God. He would be nothing more than just a murderer. IT WAS EVIL MUSLIMS WHO SLEW THE JEWS NOT GOD.

Quran-33:25- "Allah turned back the unbelievers [Meccans and their allies] in a state of rage, having not won any good, and Allah spared the believers battle. Allah is, indeed, Strong and Mighty."

Quran-33:26- "And He brought those of the People of the Book [Jewish people of Banu Qurayza] who supported them from their fortresses and cast terror into their hearts, some of them you slew (beheaded) and some you took prisoners (captive)"

Do you not hear the screaming and wailing of the women and children of the defenders as God brought their husbands, fathers and brothers (the defenders) down from their secured positions and cast terror into their hearts? Do you not feel the anguished torment of these women and their children? Do you not understand the terror instilled by God into the villagers, themselves the defenders against Muhammad's aggression?

Words of hate and terror stream out from the teaching 33:26: "in a state of rage" "he threw terror into their hearts" & "some you slew (beheaded)." Can you imagine the power of God, the creator of the universe—the full force of the sheer hatred of God striking fear and terror into the hearts and souls of men, women and children, the old and the infirm? Like a sadist, God enjoys torturing these people. Like a master terrorist, he reviles in the moment. God drove the Jews out of their secure forts in fear and terror, so that Muhammad and his co-jihadists could murder them and enslave the women and children.

Think about that for a moment. Can anybody in their right mind believe that God would commit such a brutal, immoral and hideous act? God as a criminal, mass murderer, sadist, psychopath—a deranged maniac. If at all, a perfect God will manifest himself only to show love and affection to his creatures - not to incite hate, violence and terror against any of them.

God never brought down the people of the book (Banu Quraiza Jews) from their secure positions for killing and enslaving them. God never cast terror into their hearts. It was Muhammad and his jihadi murderers that committed these evil acts. Indisputably, Quran 33:26 is a criminal and barbaric teaching. The Quran, therefore, is not a book of Moral Perfection, not authored by God, but by Allah (the AntiGod) and his messenger - Muhammad.

Again, says Allah:. Quran-8:17 – "It is not ye who Slew them; it is God; when thou threwest a handful of dust, it was not Thy act, but God's….."

How evil is the Quranic teaching that shifts the blame of Muhammad and his murderous followers' indiscriminate killing of kafirs onto God's shoulder. It is unacceptable even to invoke God in acts of evil. Verse 8:17 is one of the most despicable, immoral teachings of the Quran. In order to justify mass murder, in order to allay the pangs of conscience of his Muslim murderers, Muhammad fabricates that "it was not you who slew them, but it was God who killed them." In this verse, Allah advises Muhammad's followers: 'don't worry about those mindless murders; do not have any nightmares; do not have any feelings of remorse and regret - instead, steel your hearts against the enemies of God.' God did a good thing through your hands.

True God can never justify the killing and murdering of his own creations. It was Muhammad and his Muslim warriors who killed them, not God. This teaching of the Quran is truly evil, not authored by a God of Moral Perfection.

Does anybody in their right mind believe that God would order such a brutal, immoral, hideous act? God as a criminal. God as a mass murderer. All the above teachings are evil and immoral and not of God. Therefore, as already documented numerous times and will be further documented being not perfect – to say the least – the entire Quran is not a book of Moral Perfection – not a book of God but a book of evil.

ENJOY THE BOOTY

After killing, Allah (the AntiGod) now declares that Muhammad can take the defender's land, their homes, their money, and lands he never had stepped upon. God can do all things. It's now your land, your homes, your money. Take it all. Allah is not only a mass-murderer, but also a looter, a robber. Allah's prototypic teaching is: 'Attack and kill the kafirs, enslave the women and children and take possession of their property.'

How can acquiring earthly wealth and money through such immoral, barbaric and cruel means come into the equation of God's teaching? Indeed booty is so important to God that He titles an entire Surah in the Quran; Surah 8: "The Spoils of War Booty." This Surah was created to prevent fighting among Muslims for booty.

Ishaq: 307 "The 'Spoils of War' Surah came down from Allah to His Prophet concerning the distribution of the booty when the Muslims showed their evil nature. Allah took it out of their hands and gave it to the Apostle."

Bukhari V1B7N1331 "The Prophet said, 'I have been given five things which were not given to any one else before me. 1. Allah made me victorious by awe by His terrorizing my enemies. 2. The earth has been made for me. 3. Booty has been made lawful for me yet it was not lawful for anyone else before me. 4. I have been given the right of intercession. 5. Every Prophet used to be sent to his nation only but I have been sent to all mankind.'"

Following are the divine laws of Allah (the AntiGod) inviting Muslims to enjoy booty of Banu Qurayza Jews sanctioned for them. Below are some examples how Quran openly supported Islamic jihadi's immoral acts:

Quran-8:1— "They ask thee concerning (things taken as) spoils of war (booty). Say: "(such) spoils are at the disposal of Allah and the Messenger: So fear Allah, and keep straight the relations between yourselves: Obey Allah and His Messenger, if ye do believe."

Quran-8:41— "And know that out of all the booty that ye may acquire (in war), a fifth share is assigned to Allah, - and to the Messenger, and to near relatives, orphans, the needy, and the wayfarer, - if ye do believe in Allah and in the revelation We sent down to Our servant on the Day of Testing, - the Day of the meeting of the two forces. For Allah hath power over all things."

According to verse 8:41, a fifth share of the booty was taken by Muhammad some of which was distributed to near kin, etc. as stipulated in the verse. However, this distribution was at Muhammad's discretion. The booty included the captives, who were made slaves. After the first successful campaign, the Battle of Badr, Muhammad released the captives who were not ransomed by the Meccans. This clemency had been opposed by some Muslim leaders like Umar who wanted them executed. However, in later battles the general rule was that the men who refused to convert were executed while women and children where taken into slavery.

Quran-8:69—"But (now) enjoy what ye took in war (booty), lawful and good; but fear God..." (Allah encouraging Muslims to accept booty spoils of war) Had there not been a previous sanction from God, you would have been sternly punished for what you have taken. Therefore, enjoy the good and lawful things which you have gained in war, and fear God."

Quran-33:27- "And He made you heirs of their lands, their houses, and their goods, and of a land which ye had not frequented (before). And Allah has power over all things." [Merciful Allah asked Prophet Muhammad to confiscate entire properties of the surrendered Jews]

Can you imagine God teaching "And He made you heirs of their lands, their houses, and their goods, and of a land .."
Thou shalt steal.
Take all the property of the kafirs, steal it all, it's yours – looting, pillaging as holy duties of God.
All the booty received through all the teachings of the Quran from the sale of boys and women into slavery, and looting and pillaging the property of murdered kafirs were distributed as per instructions of Quran 8:41 - 1/5 went to Allah (the AntiGod) and of course his valiant partner in crime - Muhammad - leaving the remaining 80% to be divided among the murderous bandits. In this way, the prophet was able to raise an army, equip and finance his wars of conquest and extermination. Raping slaves, selling women and children, killing people for their property and sharing the proceeds with God is evil incarnate – these laws of God – are so morally outrageous – that too claim that these teachings in the Quran are the word of God – is the greatest sin that Muslims have committed against God. Again - the Quran is an evil book and an obscenity against God.
Of course, God in his infinite wisdom created a SPECIAL LAW OF GOD SOLELY FOR MUHAMMAD – that allowed his prophet to keep 100% of the booty if no fighting was involved. (Quran 59.5). One must obey Muhammad's decision (blindly and totally.) This is utter self serving nonsense.

Quran 59:6 "What God has bestowed on His Apostle (and taken away) from them - for this ye made no expedition with either cavalry or camelry: but God gives power to His apostles over any He pleases: and God has power over all things."

Quran 59:7 "Whatever booty goes to Muhammad belongs to Allah; it shall go to the relatives, the poor and the travelling alien; accept whatever booty Muhammad gives."

This is truly insane. How can any rational, reasonable, normal, moral person believe that God would have as his prophet - a killer, a murderer, a terrorist who slaughtered human beings, had the pants of young terrified boys pulled down to determine whether they lived or died, allowed the raping of the women and young girls, sold the women and young girls Muslims did not want as sex slaves into slavery, and took for himself one of the young beautiful women to be his sex slave. Can you imagine the horror of rape being divine, external laws of God? Can you imagine the horror of children being sold into slavery – their fathers beheaded – their mothers and sisters raped and gang raped. How can anyone belong to such a religion? Worship such an antiGod? Where is the humanity of Muslims? Where is our humanity that we can accept such barbarism as a religion? Again - where is our outrage?

How can any rational, reasonable, normal, moral person believe that God would celebrate such evil, heinous crimes with teachings for all eternity to be recorded in a so called holy book – the Quran?

How can any rational, reasonable, normal, moral person believe that God would share in the looting and pillaging of murdered Jew's property? God as the Mafia chieftain of Muhammad's Muslim crime family – that God would name an entire Surah of the Quran; "Spoils of War Booty." These are words of immoral imperfection - encouraging and promoting looting, stealing kafir property is the very essence of immorality. Murder the kafirs, torture them to hand over their property as Muhammad did to the Jewish chieftain of Khaybar, (page 99) and take their women and children as booty. These are not the divine acts a God of Moral Perfection would ever condone let alone glorify.

These acts are so evil as to be unspeakable. Again, by taking the concept of God - an all loving God of peace and goodness – a God of Moral Perfection and turning Him into the AntiGod of all evil - Muhammad has committed great crimes against God. Through his evilness, Muhammad has led himself and his followers into Hell. As with all humans, Muhammad was given a free will by God to do good or evil. By freely choosing a life of evil and never repenting, Muhammad has condemned himself to Hell for all eternity. For booty teachings:
http://www.islamreform.net/new-page-15.htm
http://www.islamreform.net/new-page-17.htm
http://www.islamreform.net/new-page-18.htm
http://www.islamreform.net/new-page-19.htm

CHAPTER SIX

JIHAD IS TREASON

GOD'S INCITEMENT TO WAR
JIHAD: UNHOLY WAR: WAR IN THE NAME OF AND TO THE GREATER GLORY OF GOD

We have examined 81 teachings that are totally immoral and therefore, not the teachings of a God of Moral Perfection. We will now examine 164 teachings of Jihad – unholy war - killing and murdering kafirs, conquering their nations, raping and enslaving their women and children and looting and pillaging their property – all these evil acts committed at the orders of Allah (the AntiGod) as recorded in the Quran.

Stated previously - as Moral Perfection God is Anti War. There is no Holy War. All war is UNHOLY and abhorrent to God - an affront to the intelligence He bestowed on mankind. God did not endow Homo sapiens with intelligence to war against fellow Homo sapiens like beasts in the jungle. War is an abomination, an obscenity against God. It is the greatest sin that man can commit against God. He never intervened in any battle, never lead an army into battle, changed the weather allowing (His) side to be victorious or any other form of divine intervention. There is no - "His side". War is AntiGod. War is anti-creation. War is the extermination of humanity. If God believes in violence, believes in war, believes in killing, terror, torture, maiming then God is no longer Moral Perfection and therefore, no longer God but the incarnation of evil. If God thought just one word of violence, ordered the killing or actually killed with His own hand just one human being or any other creature throughout the entire universe then God would be an immoral murderer. All teachings that pertain to be from God preaching, encouraging or engaging in war or any other act of violence are not from God but are the teachings of evil men.

Muhammad was a military leader, laying siege to towns, massacring the men, raping their women, enslaving their children, and taking what was once the property of others for his own. On several occasions, he rejected offers of surrender from the besieged inhabitants and killed those whom he could take prisoner. He inspired his followers to battle even when they did not feel it was right to fight, threatening them with Hell if they did not, promising them slaves and booty if they did. Muhammad allowed his men to rape traumatized women captured in battle. It is important to emphasize that Muslim armies waged aggressive campaigns, and it was the companions of Muhammad who made the most dramatic military gains in the decades following his death. The principle set in motion early on was that the civilian population of a town was to be destroyed (i.e. men executed, women and children taken as slaves) if they defended themselves.

It is the supreme duty of all Muslims to conquer the world for Allah and rid the earth of all kafirs until the only people left are Muslims and the only religion is Islam. In order to mobilize Muslims to fulfill this sacred duty, Allah (the AntiGod) and his messenger invented the concept of Jihad – sacred holy war – indiscriminate slaughter of kafirs who refuse to submit to Islam and raping and pillaging their women and property.

Allah (the AntiGod) has proclaimed that whatever wealth and riches that exist on the earth belong to Allah and His Messenger and Islam inspires its followers to wage a war against the kafirs, the unlawful occupiers of that wealth and riches, and bring them under the occupation of the legal owners - the Muslims. So, for a Muslim, launching a jihad or war against the kafir, is the highest virtue; higher even than a pilgrimage to Mecca (hajj), not to speak of lower virtues like prayer (namaz) and fasting (roja).

In order to justify this criminality, Muhammad created through his imaginary God – Allah's AntiGod teachings justifying war, slaughter, mayhem.

"Fighting against the kafirs is beyond one's personal likings and dislikings as Allah has commanded to fight the pagans and all those who ascribe partners (shirk) with Allah" Quran (2.216).

Allah also says,

"Verily, Allah loves those who fight in His cause in rows and ranks as if they were a solid mass" (61.4).

"Verily, those who are serving allegiance to you (O Mohammad), they are in fact serving allegiance to Allah" (48.10).

In this war against the kafirs, Allah promises divine assistance and guarantees victory for the Muslims and says,

"As a divine help, Allah will provide five thousand angles as fighters and victory for the Muslims" (3.124-125).

"So don't become weak and be not sad and you are superior if you are indeed believers. ...Allah helps those who remain steadfast" (3.139-142).

"Oh you who believe; when you meet the enemy force, take a firm stand against them and mention the name of Allah both with the tongue and mind, so that you may be successful" (8.45).

"If Allah helps you, none can overcome you and if He forsakes you, who is there after Him that can help you?" (3.160).

Allah also says, "... thousands believers will overpower two thousand non-believers" (8.66) and if they are properly inspired "twenty believers will overpower two hundred and a hundred believers will overpower one thousand non-believers" (8.65).

God, the supreme creator did not create mankind to engage in violence, war and bloodbaths. As previously stated - a true God will never intervene or will not take any side in any battle, never lead an army into battle, or any other form of divine intervention etc. All war is an abomination against God. War extinguishes life that God creates with love. God can never murder his creatures nor order anyone to kill any human being. A true God will be against sending calamity to destroy any human being. All the teachings of the Quran ordering killing, destruction and war are truly immoral and AntiGod.

Quran 2:190 "fight in the cause of god against those who fight you, but do not transgress, god does not like the aggressors."

2:191 "kill them wherever you find them, and expel them from where they expelled you, and know that persecution is worse than being killed. Do not fight them at the restricted temple unless they fight you in it; if they fight you then kill them. Thus is the reward of those who do not appreciate."

2:192 "if they cease, then god is forgiving, compassionate."

2:193 "fight them so there is no more persecution, and so that the system is god's. If they cease, then there will be no aggression except against the wicked."

2:194 "the restricted month is for the restricted month. The restrictions are mutual. Whoever attacks you, then you shall attack him the same as he attacked you; and be conscientious of god, and know that god is with the righteous."

"Fight in the cause of God", " Kill them wherever you find them, and expel them from where they expelled you, and know that persecution is worse than being killed... if they fight you then kill them..." "fight them so there is no more persecution, and so that the system is god's."

Fight, kill, expel, - God never wrote these words. Fight in the cause of God. There is no cause of God that a God of Moral Perfection would ever want you to fight in his name. Love thy neighbor not kill thy neighbor. The cause of God is love not hate, life not death, forgiveness not retribution, mercy not torture. You live the cause of God not by fighting but by being a true example of a good person living a moral life respecting people, not robbing and killing them in the name of God.

Persecution is worse than being killed. This is a crazy concept of a psychopathic personality. Muslims should aspire to acquiring spoils by launching jihad against kafirs – to kill them, loot their property, rape their women, enslave them, and if they are killed in committing these acts of terror then they can ascend to Allah's Paradise brothel. The Quran never teaches that, if you lead an honest, moral, ethical and a decent life, you will come into the presence of God after death.

The almighty God can bring any disobedient human being to his path just by a simple wish. He need not instruct Muslims to unleash violence, bloodbath and war against non-Muslims. These verses of the Quran, urging Muslims to engage in killing, bloodbath and war, do not come from a true God of Moral Perfection. Again, the content of the Quran, therefore, are not the teachings of God.

For the true God, the epitome of sanity and justice, to engage in such actions are nothing but insanity.

164 Jihad Unholy War Verses in The Quran

Following are 164 verses of Jihad in the Quran. These are the most important collection of Quranic verses in Islam. So critical are these teachings that rather then discuss a few, I have recorded them here enmass. All these teachings are truly UNHOLY, and evil. Being teachings of war, violence, death and destruction, terror ALL these verses are not MORAL PERFECTION and therefore, not from of a God of MORAL PERFECTION and therefore, Islam is a total fraud perpetrated on Muslims and humanity. These are the teachings that motivate Jihadists/suicide bombers to commit mass murder. All the suicide bombers in Iraq, Pakistan etc are following EXACTLY these teachings. Again, all Muslims believe that God wrote these verses. You cannot ignore these Quranic verses. 270,000,000 kafirs have perished, murdered in the name of God by good, pious Muslim men quoting these teachings. These suiciders are not misinterpreting these teachings – they understand Islam. (Again, there is an excellent web site that will give 10 translations of any Quranic teaching including the original Arabic. Just go to http://qb.gomen.org/QuranBrowser/ punch in a teaching like 2.178 and receive 10 simultaneous translations with the original displayed. Utilize this facility throughout this book.)

[*2.178]...retaliation is prescribed for you in the matter of the slain...

[*2.179] ...there is life for you in (the law of) retaliation, O men of understanding, that you may guard yourselves.

[*2.190] ...fight in the way of Allah with those who fight with you...

[*2.191] And kill them wherever you find them, and drive them out from whence they drove you out, and persecution is severer than slaughter, and do not fight with them at the Sacred Mosque until they fight with you in it, but if they do fight you, then slay them; such is the recompense of the unbelievers.

[*2.193]...fight with them... [194]...whoever then acts aggressively against you, inflict injury on him according to the injury he has inflicted on you...

[*2.216] Fighting is enjoined on you...

[*2.217]... fighting in it. Say: Fighting in it is a grave matter...persecution is graver than slaughter...

[*2.218]...strove hard in the way of Allah…

[*2.244] ...fight in the way of Allah

[*3.121]...to lodge the believers in encampments for war...

[*3.122] When two parties from among you had determined that they should show cowardice [about Jihad]...

[*3.123]...Allah did certainly assist you at [the Battle of] Badr...

[*3.124]... [*3.125] Yea! if you remain patient and are on your guard, and they come upon you in a headlong manner, your Lord will assist you with five thousand of the havoc-making angels.

[3.126] ...victory is only from Allah...

[*3.140] If a wound has afflicted you (at [the Battle of] Uhud), a wound like it has also afflicted the (unbelieving) people; and We bring these days to men by turns, and that Allah may know those who believe and take witnesses from among you...

[3.141] ...that He [Allah] may purge those who believe and deprive the unbelievers of blessings.

[3.142] Yusuf Ali: Did ye think that ye would enter Heaven without God testing those of you who fought hard (in His Cause) and remained steadfast?

[3.143] Pickthall: And verily ye used to wish for death before ye met it (in the field). Now ye have seen it [death] with your eyes!

[3.146] Yusuf Ali: How many of the prophets fought (in Allah's way) [Jihad], and with them (fought) large bands of godly men? But they never lost heart if they met with disaster in Allah's way [lost a battle], nor did they weaken (in will) nor give in.

[3.152]...you slew them by His [Allah's] permission [during a Jihad battle]...

[3.153] Pickthall: ...the messenger, in your rear, was calling you (to fight)...that which ye missed [war spoils]...

[3.154]...They say: Had we any hand in the affair, we would not have been slain here [in a Jihad battle]. Say: Had you remained in your houses, those for whom slaughter was ordained [in a Jihad battle] would certainly have gone forth to the places where they would be slain..

. [*3.155] (As for) those of you who turned back on the day when the two armies met...

[3.156] O you who believe! be not like those who disbelieve and say of their brethren when they travel in the earth or engage in fighting: Had they been with us, they would not have died and they would not have been slain...

[3.157]...if you are slain in the way of Allah...mercy is better than what they amass [what those who stay home from Jihad receive – no booty on earth and no perks in heaven].

[3.158] ...if indeed you die or you are slain, certainly to Allah shall you be gathered together.

[*3.165]...you [Muslims] had certainly afflicted (the unbelievers) with twice as much [in a Jihad battle]...

[*3.166]...when the two armies met ([the Battle of] Uhud)...

[*3.167]...Come, fight in Allah's way, or defend yourselves...If we knew fighting, we would certainly have followed you...

[*3.169] ...reckon not those who are killed in Allah's way as dead; nay, they are alive (and) are provided sustenance from their Lord [meaning they are enjoying their 72 virgins in heaven];

[3.172] ...those who responded (at [the Battle of] Uhud) to the call of Allah and the Apostle after a wound had befallen them...shall have a great reward.

[*3.173] Those to whom the people said: Surely men have gathered against you [in battle], therefore fear them, but this increased their faith, and they said: Allah is sufficient for us and most excellent is the Protector.

[*3.195] ...who fought and were slain...I will most certainly make them enter gardens beneath which rivers flow; a reward from Allah, and with Allah is yet better reward.

[*4.71] ...go forth in detachments or go forth in a body [to war].

[*4.72] ...hang back [from Jihad] ...not present with them [in Jihad].

[*4.74] Therefore let those fight in the way of Allah, who sell this world's life for the hereafter; and whoever fights in the way of Allah, then be he slain or be he victorious, We shall grant him a mighty reward.

[*4.75]...fight in the way of Allah...

[*4.76] Those who believe fight in the way of Allah, and those who disbelieve fight in the way of the Satan. Fight therefore against the friends of the Satan...

[*4.77] ...when fighting is prescribed for them... Our Lord! why hast Thou ordained fighting for us? ...

[*4.84] Fight then in Allah's way...rouse the believers to ardor maybe Allah will restrain the fighting of those who disbelieve...

[*4.89] ...take not from among them friends until they fly (their homes) in Allah's way; but if they turn back [to their homes], then seize them and kill them wherever you find them...

[4.90] Allah has not given you a way against them [Allah supposedly does not allow Muslims to fight people friendly to Muslims].

[*4.91]...seize them and kill them wherever you find them...

[*4.94]...when you go to war in Allah's way...

[*4.95] ...those who strive hard [Jihad] in Allah's way with their property and their persons are not equal...Allah shall grant to the strivers [i.e., Jihadist] above the holders back a mighty reward.

[*4.100] ...whoever flies in Allah's way [forsakes his home to fight in Jihad], he will find in the earth many a place of refuge and abundant resources, and whoever goes forth from his house flying to Allah and His Apostle, and then death overtakes him [in Jihad], his reward is indeed with Allah...

[4.101] Rodwell: And when ye go forth to war in the land, it shall be no crime in you to cut short your prayers, if ye fear lest the infidels come upon you; Verily, the infidels are your undoubted enemies!

[*4.102] ...let them take their arms...let them take their precautions and their arms...there is no blame on you, if you are annoyed with rain or if you are sick, that you lay down your arms...

[4.103] Khalifa: Once you complete your Contact Prayer (Salat), you shall remember GOD while standing, sitting, or lying down. Once the war is over, you shall observe the Contact Prayers (Salat); the Contact Prayers (Salat) are decreed for the believers at specific times.

[*4.104] ...be not weak hearted in pursuit of the enemy...

[4.141] Sher Ali: …If you have a victory [in Jihad] from Allah…

[*5.33] The punishment of those who wage war against Allah and His apostle and strive to make mischief in the land is only this, that they should be murdered or crucified or their hands and their feet should be cut off on opposite sides or they should be imprisoned [Pickthall and Yusuf Ali have "exiled" rather than "imprisoned"]

[*5.35] … strive hard [at Jihad] in His way that you may be successful.

[5.82] ……you will find the most violent of people in enmity for those who believe (to be) the Jews [compare with "whenever Jews kindle fire for war, Allah [Muslims] puts it out" (K 005:064)] and those who are polytheists [while they are converted to Islam on pain of death]…

[8.1] Pickthall: …the spoils of war…The spoils of war belong to Allah and the messenger

[*8.5] Even as your Lord caused you to go forth from your house with the truth, though a party of the believers were surely averse;

[*8.7].. …Allah promised you one of the two (enemy) parties, that it should be yours: Ye wished that the one unarmed should be yours, but Allah willed to justify the Truth according to His words and to cut off the roots of the Unbelievers.

[*8.9] …I will assist you [in Jihad] with a thousand of the angels following one another [see K 008:012].

[8.10] …Allah only gave it as a good news and that your hearts might be at ease thereby; and victory is only from Allah; surely Allah is Mighty, Wise.

[*8.12] ……make firm those who believe. I will cast terror into the hearts of those who disbelieve. Therefore strike off their heads and strike off every fingertip of them.

[*8.15] …when you meet those who disbelieve marching for war, then turn not your backs to them.

[*8.16] …for the sake of fighting…

[*8.17] So you did not slay them, but it was Allah Who slew them, and you did not smite when you smote (the enemy), but it was Allah Who smote [Allah gets the credit for Jihad]…

[*8.39] Shakir: ...fight with them until there is no more persecution and religion should be only for Allah...

[8.40] Yusuf Ali: If they [unbelievers] refuse [to stop fighting], be sure that God is your Protector...

[8.41] Shakir: ...whatever thing [loot] you gain, a fifth of it is for Allah and for the Apostle...the day on which the two parties met [in a Jihad versus anti-Jihad battle]...

[*8.42]...Allah might bring about a matter which was to be done, that he who would perish might perish by clear proof [bring success to Muslims engaged in robbing a caravan near Badr against all the odds]...

[8.43]...Allah showed them [the Mekkans] to you in your dream as few [fighters]; and if He had shown them [the Mekkans] to you as many [fighters] you would certainly have become weak-hearted [i.e., hearts. See the similar discussion in K 002:249 about how a smaller army can defeat a larger army]...

[8.44]...when you met, as few [fighters] in your eyes and He made you to appear little [few fighters] in their eyes, in order that Allah might bring about a matter which was to be done [a Jihad versus anti-Jihad battle brought on by overconfidence in each side]...

[*8.45]...when you meet a party [in battle], then be firm...

[8.46]...obey Allah and His Apostle and do not quarrel for then you will be weak in hearts [demoralized] and your power [to execute Jihad] will depart...

[8.47]...be not like those [Mekkans] who came forth from their homes [to fight Muslims]...

[8.48]...when the two parties [Muslims versus Mekkans] came in sight of each other he [Satan] turned upon his heels...

Pickthall: [8.57] If thou come on them in the war, deal with them so as to strike fear in those who are behind them, that haply they may remember.

[8.57] Khalifa: When you are betrayed by a group of people, you shall mobilize against them in the same manner. GOD does not love the betrayers.

[*8.59] Shakir: ...let not those who disbelieve think that they shall come in first; surely they will not escape.

[8.60] And prepare against them what force you can and horses tied at the frontier, to frighten thereby the enemy of Allah and your enemy and others besides them, whom you do not know (but) Allah knows them; and whatever thing you will spend in Allah's way [for Jihad]...

[*8.65] O Prophet! urge the believers to war; if there are twenty patient ones of you they shall overcome two hundred, and if there are a hundred of you they shall overcome a thousand of those who disbelieve, because they are a people who do not understand [in other words, "do not understand totalitarian ideologies like Islam"].

[8.66] ...if there are a hundred patient ones of you they shall overcome two hundred, and if there are a thousand they shall overcome two thousand by Allah's permission...

[*8.67] It is not fit for a prophet that he should take captives unless he has fought and triumphed in the land; you desire the frail goods [i.e., ransom money] of this world...

[8.68] ...ransom...

[*8.69] Eat then of the lawful and good (things) which you have acquired in war [war spoils]...

[8.70] O Prophet! say to those of the captives [non-Muslims] who are in your hands: If Allah knows anything good in your hearts, He will give to you better than that which has been taken away from you [in Jihad]...

[*8.71] Yusuf Ali: But if they have treacherous designs against thee, (O Apostle!)...He [Allah] given (thee) power over them...

[*8.72] Yusuf Ali: Those who ...fought for the Faith, with their property and their persons, in the cause of God...

[8.73] Yusuf Ali: The Unbelievers are protectors, one of another: Unless ye do this, (protect each other), there would be tumult and oppression on earth, and great mischief.

[*8.74] [*8.75] Yusuf Ali:...fight for the Faith...

[*9.5] ...slay the idolaters wherever you find them...take them captives and besiege them and lie in wait for them in every ambush...

[*9.12] ...fight the leaders of unbelief...

[*9.13] What! will you not fight a people...

[*9.14] Fight them, Allah will punish them by your hands and bring them to disgrace, and assist you against them and heal the hearts of a believing people.

[*9.16] ......those of you who have struggled hard [in Jihad]

[*9.19] ...strives hard in Allah's way?...

[*9.20]...strove hard [Jihad] in Allah's way with their property and their souls...

[*9.24] ...striving in His way [Jihad]:, then wait till Allah brings about His command [to go on Jihad]: ...

[*9.25] Certainly Allah helped you in many battlefields and on the day of [the Battle of] Hunain, when your great numbers made you vain, ...

[*9.26] ...chastised those who disbelieved [Muhammad gives credit to angels and Allah for the actions of Jihadists]...

[*9.29] Fight those who do not believe in Allah...nor follow the religion of truth, out of those who have been given the Book, until they pay the tax in acknowledgment of superiority and they are in a state of subjection.

[*9.36] ...fight the polytheists all together as they fight you all together...

[*9.38] ...Go forth in Allah's way [to Jihad]...

[*9.39] If you do not go forth [to go on Jihad], He will chastise you with a painful chastisement and bring in your place a people other than you [to go on Jihad]...

[*9.41] Go forth light [lightly armed] and heavy [heavily armed], and strive hard in Allah's way [Jihad] with your property and your persons...

[*9.44] ...striving hard with their property and their persons [Jihad]...

[*9.52]...Allah will afflict you with punishment from Himself or by our hands...

[*9.73] ...strive hard [Jihad] against the unbelievers and the hypocrites and be unyielding to them...

[*9.81] ...they were averse from striving in Allah's way [Jihad] with their property and their persons, and said: Do not go forth [to Jihad] in the heat...

[*9.83] ... shall you fight an enemy with me [in Jihad]...[*9.86] ...strive hard [in Jihad] along with His Apostle

[*9.88] ...strive hard [in Jihad] with their property and their persons...

[*9.92] Yusuf Ali: Nor (is there blame) on those who came to thee to be provided with mounts [saddles on which to go to war], and when thou said, "I can find no mounts for you," they turned back, their eyes streaming with tears of grief that they had no resources wherewith to provide the expenses [to go on Jihad].

[*9.111] ...they fight in Allah's way, so they slay and are slain...

[*9.120] Yusuf Ali:...whether they suffered thirst, or fatigue, or hunger, in the cause of Allah [while on a march to Jihad], or trod paths to raise the ire of the Unbelievers [invade their territory], or received any injury whatever from an enemy [during a Jihad battle] ...

[*9.122] Pickthall:...the believers should not all go out to fight. Of every troop of them, a party only should go forth...

[*9.123] ...fight those of the unbelievers who are near to you and let them find in you hardness...

[*16.110] Yusuf Ali:...who thereafter strive and fight for the faith and patiently persevere...

[*22.39] Permission (to fight) is given to those upon whom war is made...

[22.58] Sher Ali: ...those who leave their homes for the cause of Allah, and are then slain or die, Allah will, surely, provide for them a goodly provision...

[*22.78]...strive hard [in Jihad] in (the way of) Allah, (such) a striving a is due to Him...

[24.53]...they would certainly go forth [to Jihad (see K 024:055)]...

[24.55] Allah has promised to those of you who believe and do good that He will most certainly make them rulers in the earth [as a reward for going on Jihad (see K 024:053)]...

[25.52] Palmer: ...fight strenuously with them in many a strenuous fight.

[*29.6]...whoever strives hard [in Jihad], he strives only for his own soul...

[*29.69] ...(as for) those who strive hard [in Jihad] for Us...

[33.15] Pickthall: ...they had already sworn unto Allah that they would not turn their backs (to the foe) [in Jihad battle]...

[*33.18] ...they come not to the fight [Jihad] but a little... [*33.20] they would not fight save a little [in Jihad].

[33.23] Pickthall: ...Some of them [Jihadists] have paid their vow by death (in battle), and some of them still are waiting...

[*33.25]...Allah sufficed the believers in fighting...

[*33.26]...some [Jews] you killed and you took captive another part.

[33.27]...He made you heirs to their [Jewish] land and their dwellings and their property, and (to) a land which you have not yet trodden...

[33.50]...those [captive women] whom your right hand possesses [i.e., by virtue of the sword used in Jihad] out of those whom Allah has given to you as prisoners of war...

[42.39] Sale:...and who, when an injury is done them, avenge themselves...

[47.4] ...when you meet in battle those who disbelieve, then smite the necks until when you have overcome them, then make (them) prisoners, and afterwards either set them free as a favor or let them ransom (themselves) until the war terminates...(as for) those who are slain in the way of Allah...

[*47.20] ...fighting [allusion to Jihad] is mentioned therein ...

[47.35] Rodwell: Be not fainthearted then; and invite not the infidels to peace when ye have the upper hand: for God is with you, and will not defraud you of the recompense of your works.

[48.15] Pickthall: ...when you set forth to capture booty...

*48.16]...You shall soon be invited (to fight) against a people possessing mighty prowess; you will fight against them until they submit...

[48.17] Pickthall: There is no blame...for the sick (that they go not forth to war). And whoso obeys Allah and His messenger [by going on Jihad], He will make him enter Gardens underneath which rivers flow; and whoso turns back [from Jihad], him will He punish with a painful doom.

[48.18] Certainly Allah was well pleased with the believers when they swore allegiance to you under the tree, and He knew what was in their hearts, so He sent down tranquility on them and rewarded them with a near victory,

[48.19] And much booty that they will capture. Allah is ever Mighty, Wise.

[48.20] Allah promised you many acquisitions which you will take, then He hastened on this one for you and held back the hands of men from you, and that it may be a sign for the believers and that He may guide you on a right path.

[48.21] Sale: And [he also promiseth you] other [spoils], which ye have not [yet] been able [to take]: But now hath God encompassed them [for you]; and God is almighty.

[*48.22] And if those who disbelieve fight with you, they would certainly turn (their) backs, then they would not find any protector or a helper.

[48.23] Such [i.e., the Jihad mentioned the previous verse] has been the course [practice] of Allah that has indeed run before, and you shall not find a change in Allah's course.

[48.24] And He [Allah] it is Who held back...your hands from them [in Jihad] in the valley of Mecca...

[49.15] Sale: ...true believers ...employ their substance and their persons in the defense of God's true religion...

[*59.2] ...the hands of the believers [i.e. Muslims demolished Jewish homes] ...

Pickthall:[*59.5] Whatsoever palm-trees you cut down or left standing on their roots [during a Jihad siege of the Jews at Madina], it was by Allah's leave, in order that He might confound the evil-livers [Jews].

[*59.6] ...that which Allah gave as spoil unto His messenger from them, you urged not any horse or riding-camel for the sake thereof, but Allah gives His messenger lordship over whom He will...

[*59.7] That which Allah gives as [war] spoil unto His messenger from the people of the townships [Jews], it is for Allah and His messenger...whatsoever [spoils] the messenger gives you, take it...

[*59.8] ...who seek bounty [war spoils] from Allah...

[*59.14] They will not fight against you in a body save in fortified towns or from behind walls...

[*60.9] Allah only forbids you respecting those who made war upon you on account of (your) religion [no fraternizing with the enemy]...

[*61.4] ...Allah loves those who fight in His way in ranks as if they were a firm and compact wall.

[61.11] ...struggle hard in Allah's way [Jihad] with your property and your lives...

[61.13] ...victory [in Jihad] near at hand...

[63.4] ...they think every cry to be against them. They are the enemy, therefore beware of them; may Allah destroy them, whence are they turned back? [This verse speaks of internecine Jihad against Muslims deemed infidels or "hypocrites."]

[64.14] ...surely from among your wives and your children there is an enemy to you; therefore beware of them [collaborators with the enemy, especially if the women were once war spoils]...

[66.9] O Prophet! strive hard against the unbelievers and the hypocrites, and be hard against them.   [73.20] ...others who fight in Allah's way...

Quran 9.123 "O ye who believe! Fight those of the disbelievers who are near to you, and let them find harshness in you, and know that Allah is with those who keep their duty (unto Him.)"

How can any rational person believe that God wrote teaching 9.123? "Fight those of the disbelievers who are near you" "let them find harshness in you" Go to war against your kafir neighbor and be harsh with the non-believers so they will know you mean business. There is no love here. There is no mercy in this teaching. A Muslim can kill his nearest Kafir neighbor and then move on to the next. A God of Moral Perfection would never command killing your neighbor. The very essence of civilization is neighbor helping neighbor not killing them. If your neighbor is a Muslim you have no right to attack them. Know that you are keeping your duty unto God by killing your kafir neighbor is such a ridiculous, laughable concept if it were not for the reality that 1.2 billion Muslims believe in the Quran as the divine, timeless word of God.

Quran 4.75,, 84 "Those who believe fight in the way of Allah and those who disbelieve fight in the way of Taghut (idols). So fight the friends of Satan. So fight in the way of Allah. You are not responsible but for yourself. Allah is the strongest in war and the mightiest in punishment."

Quran 8.55-57 "Surely, the worst of all living, in the sight of Allah, are those who reject Faith, so they do not believe (the message of Islam). So, if you find them in war, make them an example (deterrent) for those behind them, so that they take a lesson."

It is a Muslim's sacred duty to attack all those who reject Islam and make an example of these kafirs by punishing and disgracing these enemies of God. Osama bin Laden and Major Hasan made an example of their kafir victims. They delivered the divine punishment of God as an example to all the other kafirs. Osma used planes and Major Hasan a gun to deliver the punishment of God upon the evil kafirs by the hand of a Muslim. In the case of Major Hasan, we will now have to suffer the endless indignity of listening to an endless assortment of psychiatrists diagnosing the psychological motivation of a .psychiatrist. We will listen to next door neighbors and relatives telling us how shocked they are that their nice wonderful neighbor/relative could kill. Hasan's teachers and school friends will be interviewed. His childhood will be analyzed. We will learn what he ate for breakfast that morning. His every action before the shooting. How he was ill treated as a Muslim by the evil American society. We will be told how society caused this good American to lose control. We will be told how the army failed this man. How the murdered, murdered caused their own murder.

The true victim here is Hasan.

Imams will be brought forward to explain the beauty and peace of Islam – that Hasan was mentally disturbed and in his mental disturbances misinterpreted the 4,000 teachings of murder, slaughter, and hate that is Islam. Of course, we will not be told how this good, Muslim American (of sound mind and body) was motivated by murderous teachings of the Quran to kill unbelievers (Quran 9.5, 5.33. 8.12 etc) so they can ascend as martyrs to a Paradise filled with virgins. Society, the army and the 13 killed were the problem. What of Osama bin Laden and his many video taped addresses to kafir America? Here we have the greatest misunderstander of the Quran.

Osama preaches the peace and love of the religion of peace. He quotes the divine unadulterated, pure word of God, eternal and perfect. This is a true Muslim who truly understands the Quran and the commandments of God. This is a holy man who obeys the commands of God to the letter. Osama quotes Muhammad's belief that "I have been sent with the sword between my hands to ensure that no one but Allah is worshiped." Osama then concluded that "The ruling to kill the Americans and their allies -- civilians and military -- is an individual duty for every Muslim who can do it in any country in which it is possible to do it." In addition to Quran 9.5 Verse of The Sword and 47.4 following are some of the wonderful gems bin Laden has preached from the book of peace and love.

Quran 2.154 "And say not of those who are slain in the way of God: "They are dead." Nay, they are living, though ye perceive (it) not."

Quran 4.76 "Those who believe, fight in the Cause of Allah, and those who disbelieve, fight in the cause of Taghut (anything worshipped other than Allah e.g. Satan). So fight you against the friends of Satan; ever feeble is indeed the plot of Satan"

Quran 9.14 "Fight them, and God will punish them by your hands, cover them with shame, help you (to victory) over them, heal the breasts of Believers/"

Quran 22.39 "Permission to fight (against disbelievers) is given to those (believers) who are fought against, because they have been wronged and surely, Allah is Able to give them (believers) victory"
In his Letter To America, Osama bin Laden quoted from the Quran 9.12 – 9.14:

9:12 "And if they break their pledges after their treaty (hath been made with you) and assail your religion, then fight the heads of disbelief - Lo! they have no binding oaths - in order that they may desist."

9:13 "Will ye not fight a folk who broke their solemn pledges, and purposed to drive out the messenger and did attack you first? What! Fear ye them? Now Allah hath more right that ye should fear Him, if ye are believers"

9:14 "Fight them! Allah will chastise them at your hands, and He will lay them low and give you victory over them, and He will heal the breasts of folk who are believers."

" Slain in the way of God" " Those who believe fight in the Cause of Allah, and those who disbelieve, fight in the cause of Taghut" "So fight you against the friends of Satan" "Fight them, and God will punish them by your hands" ""Permission to fight (against disbelievers)" " Allah is able to give believers victory."

These are not the ramblings of a deranged individual. God wrote these words. God wrote these teachings. They are all the divine word of God. Only someone totally deranged could believe that the Quran is from God. If Osama bin Laden and Major Hasan are deranged then all Muslim men are deranged. What we have in the Quran are teachings that will destroy the very essence of Homo sapiens. Mankind is not a species of killer apes killing on the bequest of the head killer ape – God. Deranged teachings can only come from a deranged, diseased mind. That evil mind was Muhammad.

We no longer have one word or one teaching that is not Moral Perfection but 233 Quranic teachings that are immoral, evil depravity. We haven't even started yet. There are over 320,000 derogatory statements and commandments in Islamic scriptures to kill, humiliate, torture, terrorize, subjugate non-Muslims. For a listing of hadith promoting immoral Jihad murder in the name of God go to: http://www.islamreform.net/new-page-10.htm

Again, these Quranic verses are not historical oddities with no present day consequences. As we have shown, for Muslims, these verses are divine, timeless, instructions from the one, true God. When Muslims are weak, they infiltrate kafir societies and utilize the goodwill of the non-Muslims to start the process of imposing their vision of Sharia Law on society – the process of islamification. Once their numbers have increased through immigration and childbirth, and they are strong enough to conquer their kafir neighbors, Muslims then utilize the Quranic teachings of murderous jihad. Kafirs who ignore this reality are inviting their own destruction.

If you want to copy these Jihad teachings go to: http://www.islamreform.net/new-page-121.htm

CHAPTER SEVEN

WHERE IS THE OUTRAGE

HORROR OF RAPE: A HOLY ACT ORDAINED BY GOD AS A WEAPON OF WAR

God in his infinite wisdom and divine creative genius has created two categories of Homo sapien women: Kafir women and Muslim women. A kafir woman has absolutely no humanity. A Muslim man has the full right granted by God to murder her husband, father, brother, boy friend and then rape and gang rape the kafir woman and her daughter(s) no matter what their age. The Muslim can then keep the kafir woman/child as his sex slave or sell her into slavery. In Islam, these are all holy acts to be rewarded by accession to previously described sexual Paradise.

The second greatest crime a man can commit against a woman is to rape her (murder being the greatest crime.) In Islam - rape is not only a sexual weapon – it is a weapon of war. Having murdered the kafir woman's man, Muslims can now - sanctioned by the law of God complete their final humiliation and domination of her body. Rape instills fear and subjugation in the kafir. A God of Moral Perfection would never allow any man to commit such a heinous crime – rape of any woman. He would never permit the sexual enslavement of kafir women/children. There are no such laws of God.

Following are some of the IMMORAL EVIL LAWS OF ALLAH (the ANTIGOD) of RAPING SEX SLAVES. These laws are ETERNAL AND FOR ALL TIME.

Men can marry up to four women if they treat them equally; unlimited forcible concubines (rape) permitted.

In Islam, not only are men allowed to practice polygamy, but they may also capture women in war and use them as sex slaves. This is considered morally legitimate according to the Quran. In other words, non-Muslim women have no right to be free from the horror of slavery and serial rape by Muslim men. Note the term "whom your right hand possess" means slaves.

Quran 4.24

YUSUFALI: " (prohibited are) women already married, **except those whom your right hands possess: Thus hath Allah ordained (Prohibitions) against you: Except for these**, all others are lawful, provided ye seek (them in marriage) with gifts from your property,- desiring chastity, not lust, seeing that ye derive benefit from them, give them their dowers (at least) as prescribed; but if, after a dower is prescribed, agree Mutually (to vary it), there is no blame on you, and Allah is All-knowing, All-wise."

PICKTHAL: "And all married women **(are forbidden unto you) save those (captives) whom your right hands possess**. It is a decree of Allah for you. Lawful unto you are all beyond those mentioned, so that ye seek them with your wealth in honest wedlock, not debauchery. And those of whom ye seek content (by marrying them), give unto them their portions as a duty. And there is no sin for you in what ye do by mutual agreement after the duty (hath been done). Lo! Allah is ever Knower, Wise."

SHAKIR: "And all married women **except those whom your right hands possess** (this is) Allah's ordinance to you, and lawful for you are (all women) besides those, provided that you seek (them) with your property, taking (them) in marriage not committing fornication. Then as to those whom you profit by, give them their dowries as appointed; and there is no blame on you about what you mutually agree after what is appointed; surely Allah is Knowing, Wise."

You can't have sex with married women, unless they are slaves obtained in war (with whom you may rape or do whatever you like).

4:3 "Marry women of your choice, Two or three or four; but if ye fear that ye shall not be able to deal justly (with them), then only one, or (a captive) that your right hands possess, that will be more suitable, to prevent you from doing injustice."

4:25 "If any of you have not the means wherewith to wed free believing women, they may wed believing girls from among those whom your right hands possess."

"Whom your right hand possess" is one of the most evil diabolical set of words ever written in any text. God has written in quite clear language that a Muslim can own another human being. Read the words: "your right hand possess" truly only Allah (the AntiGod) could conceive of such a wording. Slavery equated to – your right hand. Truly ingenious. Truly Allah. Not a God of Moral Perfection. It's impossible for any reasonable person to conceive of a God that permits slavery. A God that not only permitted slavery but allowed as a holy duty the sheer horror of unlimited raping of women. In all human history – in all human thinking – there has never been a more vile institution ever created than slavery. 120 million blacks were murdered by Islam in the slave trade – truly one of the greatest holocausts in history. Black male slaves were castrated by their Muslim overlords to ensure that they would not breed. Many died after castration.

However, slavery in Islam applies not only to blacks but to ALL kafirs. Millions of Europeans were enslaved by Muslims. "Whom your right hand possess" is so evil as to be unspeakable. These words are not Moral Perfection but immoral imperfection. Islam is the greatest criminal ideology in history. God as a slave trader profiting on 20% of the profits earned from breeding and selling human beings. How can 1.2 billion people believe in such craziness? Unfortunately, they do and the number is growing daily.

Sura 23 (The Believers), Verses 1-6

23.1-6: "Successful indeed are the believers, Who are humble in their prayers, And who keep aloof from what is vain, And who are givers of poor-rate, And who guard their private parts, Except before their mates or those whom their right hands possess, for they surely are not blameable."

This is the Sura which gives the slave owner the right of sexual access to his female slaves. The term "guarding the private parts" is a synonym for sexual intercourse.

The Quran not only allows slavery and sex with captured women and slave girls, it says God may even pardon those who forced their slave girls to sell their bodies.

Quran 24.33: "Force not your slave-girls to whoredom that ye may seek enjoyment of the life of the world, if they would preserve their chastity. And if one force them, then (unto them), after their compulsion, lo! Allah will be Forgiving, Merciful.s said that this is not blameable if indulges with wives and slaves."

Sura 70 (The Ways of Ascent) verses 29-35

70: 29-35 "And those who guard their private parts, Except in the case of their wives or those whom their right hands possess -- for these surely are not to be blamed, But he who seeks to go beyond this, these it is that go beyond the limits -- And those who are faithful to their trusts and their covenant And those who are upright in their testimonies, And those who keep a guard on their prayer, Those shall be in gardens, honored."

These verses give the right to slave owners to have sexual relation with female slaves.

70:22-30: "Not so the worshippers, who are steadfast in prayer, who set aside a due portion of their wealth for the beggar and for the deprived, who truly believe in the Day of Reckoning and dread the punishment of their Lord (for none is secure from the punishment of their Lord); who restrain their carnal desire (save with their wives and their slave girls, for these are lawful to them: he that lusts after other than these is a transgressor..." This verse shows that Muslim men were allowed to have sex with their wives (of course) and their slave girls.

Muhammad can go beyond the four-wife restriction, can treat his own wives and sex slaves unequally.

33:50-52 "O Prophet! We have made lawful to thee thy wives to whom thou hast paid their dowers; and those whom thy right hand possesses out of the prisoners of war whom God has assigned to thee; and daughters of thy paternal uncles and aunts, and daughters of thy maternal uncles and aunts, who migrated (from Makka) with thee; and any believing woman who dedicates her soul to the Prophet if the Prophet wishes to wed her;- this only for thee, and not for the Believers (at large); We know what We have appointed for them as to their wives and the captives whom their right hands possess;- in order that there should be no difficulty for thee. And God is Oft- Forgiving, Most Merciful. Thou mayest defer (the turn of) any of them that thou pleasest, and thou mayest receive any thou pleasest: and there is no blame on thee if thou invite one whose (turn) thou hadst set aside. This were nigher to the cooling of their eyes, the prevention of their grief, and their satisfaction - that of all of them - with that which thou hast to give them: and God knows (all) that is in your hearts: and God is All-Knowing, Most Forbearing. It is not lawful for thee (to marry more) women after this, nor to change them for (other) wives, even though their beauty attract thee, except any thy right hand should possess (as handmaidens): and God doth watch over all things."

This verse 33:50-52 is for Muhammad. God allows Muhammad to own and rape his slave girls.

The above verses are only a few out of numerous such verses scattered throughout the Quran. What could be more unethical than owning slaves and raping slave girls? God graciously allowed Muslims to own and rape slave girls. prophet Muhammad himself and his disciples routinely raped their slave girls. Muslim men were permitted unlimited raping of their slaves and even gang rape. Sex slaves were one of the main factors in the spread of Islam. This is the evil that is Islam.

Islam is a morally bankrupt and unethical ideology. Repeating, the reality of Islam previously discussed in this work - slavery, raping slave girls, owning slaves, murdering kafirs, killing apostates of Islam, selling boys and women as trophies of war, looting and pillaging the property of murdered kafirs, sharing the booty obtained from the sale of boys and women and the proceeds of looting with God - Himself, the subjugation and beating of women, martyrdom for those who kill and are killed for God, a depraved Paradise filled with virgins who re – generate as virgins after sex as the sex slaves of the killers of Islam – these are just some samples of utterly unethical and evil teachings in the Quran.

Can you tell us if you find some man in any civilized country who owned slaves let alone raping slaves, what will be your conclusion about that guy? Can you tell us how a man who Muslims claim was the apostle of God – the prophet of peace – was authorized by God – to own and rape slaves – a God who created evil laws that allowed the ownership of slaves, their purchase and sale, and their sexual abuse?

Islam codifies and legalizes the diabolical evil of rape. God and his messenger Muhammad not only endorsed the institution of slavery but also the raping and sexual molestation of female slaves. The very proposition that God would make rape a divine, holy act and have as his prophet a man who raped, allowed his male followers to attack their female captives is simply outrageous.

Where is the outrage?

Muhammad lived the Quran to the letter. Being a holy man, a symbol of perfection for all mankind, Muhammad obeyed the teachings of Allah (the AntiGod). Rape is Sunna – following the ideal behavior of Muhammad. After their battles, the jihadists partook in the pleasure of raping the wives and daughters of the conquered men. There is a total correlation between the Quran and the hadith recording Muhammad acts. One is the mirror image of the other.

Following hadiths describing the Massacre of Kaibyr show that the prophet of Islam and other jihadis used to capture women in raids and had sex with them (raping of helpless captives) and sold the ones they did not want as sex slaves into the dungeon of horrors that is slavery where they would become the sex slaves of their new Muslim master.

CHAPTER EIGHT

THE MASSACRE OF KHAYBAR

THE ASSASSINATION OF PROPHET MUHAMMAD

Muhammad Attacks The Rich Jewish Settlement Of Khaybar Without Warning. Muhammad Takes Safiya As His Sex Slave After Murdering Her Father, Brothers, And Torturing And Murdering Her Husband

Sahih Bukhari, Volume 5, Book 59, Number 512:
Narrated by Anas:
"The Prophet offered the Fajr Prayer near Khaybar when it was still dark and then said, "Allahu-Akbar! Khaybar is destroyed, for whenever we approach a (hostile) nation (to fight), then evil will be the morning for those who have been warned." Then the inhabitants of Khaybar came out running on the roads. The Prophet had their warriors killed, their offspring and woman taken as captives. Safiya was amongst the captives, She first came in the share of Dahya Alkali but later on she belonged to the Prophet. The Prophet made her manumission as her 'Mahr'."

Muhammad was sixty (60) when he married Safiyyahh, a young girl of seventeen. She became his eighth wife.

Distribution of War Booty OF Khaybar:

Sahi Buchari Hadith #143, page-700: SulaImam Ibne Harb...Aannas Ibne Malek (ra) narrated, "in the war of Khayber after the inhabitants of Banu Nadir were surrendered, Allah's apostle killed all the able/adult men, and he (prophet) took all women and children as captives (Ghani mateer maal).. Among the captives Safiyya Bint Huyy Akhtab was taken by Allah's Apostle as booty whom He married after freeing her and her freedom was her Mahr."

At first Dihyah al-Kalbi, a Muslim Jihadist asked for Safiyyah. But when Muhammad saw the unparallel beauty of her, he chosen her for himself and gave her two cousin sisters to Dihyah.

Muhammad Has Safiya Husband Horribly Tortured To Try And Force Him To Reveal Where He Hid The Gold Treasure Of The People of Khaybar. He Was Beheaded After He Refused To Give Up The Treasure

Prophet Muhammad accused Safiyyah's husband, Kinanah and his cousin of hiding some of their properties in contravention of the terms of surrender. He was especially angered that Kinanah had hidden the wealth (worth about ten thousad Dinars; i.e., US$ 500,000, approximately) that he received from his marriage to a B. Nadir girl (i.e. Safiyyah). A renegade Jew divulged the secret of Kinanah's hidden gold treasures. That Jew went and fetched the hidden treasures. Kinanah and his cousin were promptly arrested by the Muslims. Then Kinanah b. al-Rabi, Safiyyah's husband was brought to Muhammad. Muhammad charged him of hiding his wealth in some underground storage. When Kinanah denied this allegation, Muhammad ordered to inflict torture on him. He was tormented by branding his chest with a heated stake and then he was beheaded in Islamic style.

Sourcing Ibn Ishak, Tabari writes:

'Kinanah b. al-Rabi b. al-Huqyaq who had the treasure of B. Nadir was brought to the Messenger of God, who questioned him; but he denied knowing where it was. Then the messenger of God was brought a Jew who said to him, "I have seen Kinanah walk around this ruin every morning." The Messenger of God said to Kinanah: "What do you say? If we find it in your possession, I will kill you." "All right," he answered. The Messenger of God commanded that the ruin should be dug up, and some of the treasure was extracted from it. Then he asked him for the rest of it. Kinanah refused to surrender it; so the Messenger of God gave orders concerning him to al-Zubayr b. al-'Awwam, saying, "torture him until you root out what he has." Al-Zubayr kept twirling his firestick in his breast until Kinanah almost expired; then the Messenger of God gave him to Muhammad b. Maslamah, who beheaded him to avenge his brother Mahmud b. Maslamah.'"

The Looted Property And Women And Children Were Distributed Among The Jihadists:

Muhammad now allowed the Muslim Jihadists to take possession of the women and children of the Jews of Khaybar.

Allah's Messenger occupied Jewish land: Sahih Muslim writes: Book 010, Number 3759:

"Ibn Umar (Allah be pleased with them) reported: Allah's Messenger (may peace be upon him) handed over the land of Khaibar (on the condition) of the share of produce of fruits and harvest, and he also gave to his wives every year one hundred wasqs: eighty wasqs of dates and twenty wasqs of barley. When 'Umar became the caliph he distributed the (lands and trees) of Khaibar, and gave option to the wives of Allah's Apostle (may peace be upon him) to earmark for themselves the land and water or stick to the wasqs (that they got) every year. They differed in this matter. Some of them opted for land and water, and some of them opted for wasqs every year. 'A'isha and Hafsa were among those who opted for land and water."

Enjoying Special Booty (Gani-maater-maal): Muhammad Takes Safiya As Booty To Be His Sex Slave

Safiya bint Huyai/Huyayy was a captive Mohammed married after slaughtering her father, brother, husband and the men at Khaibar, according to Bukhari vol.2 book 14 ch.5 no.68 p.35; vol.4 book 52 ch.74 no.143 p.92; vol.4 book 52 ch.168 no.280 p.175 and Tabari vol.39 p.185.

Muhammad Attacks And Rapes Seventeen Year Old Safiya: Muhammad Was Sixty

After securing paragon beautiful Safiyaah daughter of Huyayy Prophet Muhammad has had sex with this young Safiyya in the tent, on their way back to Medina on the same night. Here is the precarious story: Merciful Prophet asked Bilal, the Negro crier of prayer to fetch Safiyyah to his (Muhammad's) camp. Bilal brought Safiyyah and her cousin straight across the battlefield strewn with dead and close by the corpses of Kinana and his cousin. The two cousin sisters of Safiyyah shrieked in terror when they witnessed the grotesque scene of the slain dead bodies of their dearest relatives that they had to cross over. They tremulously begged a stone-hearted Bilal for mercy but to no avail. When they were brought to Muhammad, he cursed the panic-stricken cousins as devilish and cast his mantle around Safiyyah indicating that she was to be his own. Muhammad consoled a frustrated Dhiya by giving him Safiyyah's cousin sisters. According to Ibn Sa'd Prophet Muhammad purchased Safiyyah from Dhiyah for seven camels (around US$ 2,450). On the same night (during the day her husband and all relatives were slaughtered) that Muhammad took possession of Safiyyah, he hastened to his tent to sleep with her. This was of course a holy character of Prophet of Islam!

Here is what Ibn Sa'd writes: "-.when it was night, he (Muhammad) entered a tent and she entered with him. Abu Ayyub came there and passed the night by the tent with a sword keeping his head at the tent."

To hide the lascivious character of Muhammad, Muslim biographers often mention that he married Safiyyahh before he slept with her. But they forget to mention that Muhammad did not follow the rule of waiting period (three monthly periods) to sleep with Safiyyahh. He slept with her in the same day she was captured.

Above writings from Sahi Hadith clearly and undoubtedly have confirmed at least three things: (1) Prophet killed all those surrendered unarmed Jews in cold blood, (2) Prophet was attracted by Safiyya's alluring beauty and he had sex with her (I really don't care after marriage or before marriage) in a period when that poor Safiyya was in terrible grief after the murder of her father, brother, husband and relatives and before the blood of her relatives was even dry. By what yardstick can we measure the mercifulness and compassionateness of Muhammad? (3) These evil acts of Muhammad: rape, torture, terrorism, murder, looting, enslaving are Sunna (holy acts) to be emulated for all time by Muslim men.

The Muslims who committed the slaughter and torture of hotel guests and the Jewish Rabbi family at Mumbai India (see Chapter 36) were following the example of the most merciful, perfect human being who ever lived – Muhammad. The torture of the Jewish Rabbi and his wife emulated the torture by Muhammad of Kinanah. As already stated countless times, and will be stated again - the actions of these killers are not crimes in Islam but divine, holy acts guaranteeing these Muslim murderers accession to Paradise. Muhammad's massacres were evil acts committed against God. The massacre of Mumbai was a crime against God. Muhammad and the Mumbai killers were following the teachings of Allah (the AntiGod). Islam is a crime against God.

It was at Khaybar that Prophet Muhammad was assassinated by a Jewish woman (Zaynab) who fed him a poisoned leg of lamb as revenge for killing her father, uncle and husband. Bishr, Muhammad's commander died immediately. Zaynab was taken away and beheaded. Quoting from Islam's holy book;

From Ibn Sa'd pages 251, 252: [different narrator] " Bishr did not rise form his seat but his color changed to that of "taylsan" (a green cloth)..........The apostle of Allah sent for Zaynab and said to her, "What induced you to do what you have done?" She replied, "You have done to my people what you have done. You have killed my father, my uncle and my husband, so I said to myself, "If you are a prophet, the foreleg will inform you; and others have said, "If you are a king we will get rid of you.""..... Zaynab was a great courageous Jewish woman.

The apostle of Allah lived three years till in consequence of his pain he passed away. During his illness he used to say, "I did not cease to find the effect of the (poisoned) morsel, I took at Khaibar and I suffered several times (from its effect) but now I feel the hour has come of the cutting of my jugular vein."

From Ibn Sa'd page 265

    The apostle of Allah fell ill and he i.e. Gabriel, chanted on him, saying, "In the name of Allah I chant on to ward off from you every thing that harms you and (to ward off you) against every envier and from every evil eye and Allah will heal you."

From Ibn Sa'd page 265 [Different narrator]

    Aisha, the wife of the prophet used to say, "When the apostle of Allah fell ill, Gabriel chanted on him saying, "In the name of Allah Who will cure you and Who will heal you from every malady (and will ward off) the evil of envier who envies and from smite of the evil eye.""

From Ibn Sa'd page 322

    Verily, whenever the apostle of Allah fell ill, he asked for recovery, from Allah. But in the illness as a result of which he died, he did not pray for recovery; he used to say, "O soul! What has happened to thee that thou are seeking refuge in every place of refuge?"

From Ibn Sa'd page 322:

    When the last moment of the prophet was near, he used to draw a sheet over his face; but when he felt uneasy, he removed it from his face and said: "Allah's damnation be on the Jews and the Christians who made the graves of their prophets objects of worship."

    Muhammad died a horrible death. He suffered for three years. There was no Angel Gabriel to cure him. Allah did not wave his magic wand and heal the prophet because there was no Allah. At no time did Muhammad ever repent his great crimes and beg forgiveness from God for the evil life he lead and the tens of thousands of Muslim men he led into evil and the hundreds of millions more that were to follow his bogus prophethood and Muhammad's fraudulent Allah. To the very end, Muhammad cursed the Jews and Christians who had rejected his false prophethood. As one of his final acts of revenge he ordered that they all be expelled from Arabia – ethnic cleaning at its worst. 270,000,000 kafirs were to perish in the next 1400 years all murdered in the name of and to the greater glory of God. There is an incomprehensible evil at work here.

CHAPTER NINE

THE MASSACRE OF BANI MUSTALIQ

Muhammad Attacks The Jewish Settlement Of Bani Mustaliq: He Captures And Rapes A Twenty Year Old Jewish Girl – Juwairiya

Bukhari yol 3,Book46, No. 717
"Narrated Ibn Aun: "Prophet had suddenly attacked Bani Mustaliq without warning while they were heedless and their cattle were being watered at the places of water. Their fighting men were killed and their women and children were taken as captives; the Prophet got Juwairiya on that day and raped her."

Juwairiya bint Harith/al-Harith was a captive. Bukhari vol.3 book 46 ch.13 no.717 p.431-432. Sahih Muslim vol.2 no.2349 p.520 says that Mohammed attacked the Bani Mustaliq tribe without any warning while they were heedlessly grazing their cattle. Juwairiya was a daughter of the chief. Sahih Muslim vol.3 no.4292 p.942 and Abu Dawud vol.2 no.227 p.728 and al-Tabari vol.39 p.182-183 also say Juwairiya/Juwairiyyah was captured in a raid on the Banu Mustaliq tribe. She had been married to Musafi' bin Safwan, who was killed in battle.

"Juwayriyyah bint al-Harith bin Abi Birar bin Habib, great grandson of Jadhimah al-Mustaliq of the Khuza'ah group, was taken as booty when Muslims raided the al-Mustaliq tribe. Her husband, Musafi' bin Safwan Dhu al-Shuir bin Abi Asrb bin Malik bin Jadhimah was killed in the battle. She was a prisoner of war who agreed to marry Mohammed." al-Tabari vol.39 p.182-183; al-Tabari vol.9 p.133.

Juwayriyya married Mohammed when she was 20 years old. al-Tabari vol.39 p.184

CHAPTER TEN

SEX SLAVES: MUHAMMAD AND THOSE HIS RIGHT HAND POSSESSES IN ISLAM'S OWN WRITINGS

To Muslims, the life of Muhammad is Sunna to be emulated as the perfect example of a man of perfection. All the actions of Muslim men today – the massacres, beheadings, torture, terrorism, assassinations, rape jihad of kafir women epically in Europe, are not only Muslim men following the teachings of Allah (the AntiGod) as ordered in the Quran to the letter but are also Sunna following the way Muhammad lived his life as ordered in the two other holy books of Islam: the Sira and the Hadith.

Following are just a few of the hundreds of teachings of the prophet and his sex slaves.

Sahih Bukhari: Volume 9, Book 93, Number 506:Narrated Abu Said Al-Khudri: "That during the battle with Bani Al-Mustaliq they (Muslims) captured some females and intended to have sexual relation with them without impregnating them. So they asked the Prophet about coitus interrupt us. The Prophet said, "It is better that you should not do it, for Allah has written whom He is going to create till the Day of Resurrection." Qaza'a said, "I heard Abu Sa'id saying that the Prophet said, 'No soul is ordained to be created but Allah will create it."

Sahih Muslim Book 008, Number 3371:
"Abu Sirma said to Abu Sa'id al Khadri (Allah he pleased with him): O Abu Sa'id, did you hear Allah's Messenger (may peace be upon him) mentioning al-'azl? He said: Yes, and added: We went out with Allah's Messenger (may peace be upon him) on the expedition to the Bi'l-Mustaliq and took captive some excellent Arab women; and we desired them, for we were suffering from the absence of our wives, (but at the same time) we also desired ransom for them. So we decided to have sexual intercourse with them but by observing 'azl (Withdrawing the male sexual organ before emission of semen to avoid-conception). But we said: We are doing an act whereas Allah's Messenger is amongst us; why not ask him? So we asked Allah's Messenger (may peace be upon him), and he said: It does not matter

if you do not do it, for every soul that is to be born up to the Day of Resurrection will be born."

Sunan Abu Dawud Book 11, Number 2166:Narrated AbuSa'id al-Khudri:
"A man said: Apostle of Allah, I have a slave-girl and I withdraw the penis from her (while having intercourse), and I dislike that she becomes pregnant. I intend (by intercourse) what the men intend by it. The Jews say that withdrawing the penis (azl) is burying the living girls on a small scale. He (the Prophet) said: The Jews told a lie. If Allah intends to create it, you cannot turn it away."

"He [Mohammed] replied, 'Conceal your private parts except from your wife and from whom your right hands possess (slave-girls).'" Abu Dawud vol.3 no.4006 p.1123

As was typical of wealthy Arab men, Muhammad had slave girls. See Bukhari vol.7 book 64 ch.6 no.274 p.210.

Muhammad briefly had a "very beautiful" captive before he gave her to Mahmiyah b. Jaz' al-Zubaydi. al-Tabari vol.8 p.151

In general, Abu Dawud vol.3 no.4443-4445 p.1244 teaches that having sex with a slave-girl a man owns is OK, but a man will be flogged for having sex with his wife's slave-girl.

But, having sex with a wife's slave girl is OK if the wife made her lawful for him. Note that he did not have to be married to the slave girl. Ibn-i-Majah vol.4 no.2551 p.12

Muhammad "had intercourse with her [Mary] (Coptic Christian sex slave) by virtue of her being his property." al-Tabari vol.39 p.194. Footnote 845 explains, "That is, Mariyah was ordered to veil herself as did the Prophet's wives, but he did not marry her."

Ishaq:499 "The Apostle provided some compensation that included a castle, some property, a portion of the zakat tax, and a Copt slave girl."

No normal, rational person can believe in a prophet that had sex slaves or a God that encouraged rape. To a God of Moral Perfection, rape is a crime not a holy act. To allow the sexual abuse of kafir women and young girls is evil.

CHAPTER ELEVEN

WOMEN ARE EQUAL OF MEN: GOD IS NOT A SEXIST: GOD IS NOT A MALE CHAUVINIST PIG

As Moral Perfection, (and repeating from our earlier description of a God of Moral Perfection) God created women as the equal of men. God is not a sexist. God is not a male chauvinist pig. Women and men are equal in the eyes of God. Women are not valued by God as worth 50% of men. God did not create women to be the chattel or slaves of men. Females have full rights in society before the law, under the rule of law, can dress any way they freely desire without fear of death, walk the streets without a male relative escort, do any occupation, have the right to vote, the full right to participate in the governance of any society, be the leader or member of government of any country, receive all educational rights, drive planes, trains, automobiles, fly to the stars, choose their own husbands, do not have to accept arranged, forced or child marriages etc. No man, whether husband, father, brother, relative, boyfriend, or stranger has the right to beat or mistreat a woman. Men who beat women are the lowest of the low. No woman can be forced to endure female circumcision. The equal rights of women in society to complete educational, economic, legal, and political equality - are very important. There is absolutely no way the West would be enjoying its modern prosperity without the full and equal participation of women. All teachings of the inferiority of women in any holy book/text/teaching are not the word/teachings of God but the word/teachings of man. If God is a sexist then God is no longer Moral Perfection and therefore, no longer God.

In Islam's Own Writings: Allah and His Messenger's Extreme Hatred of Women

Allah despises women, both Muslim and kafir, with such a deep hatred and loathing that one would wonder why he even bothered to create women. Being God, why didn't he just create man with both a penis and vagina and reproductive organs? He could have created bisexual men with reproductive organs. But Allah was not God. He was Muhammad and therefore never created anything.

In the laws of Allah (the AntiGod), a Muslim woman is worth half a man. Muslim women are dirty, vile, evil creatures that must be kept hidden. Following are a few examples demonstrating Muslim women's horrible status and treatment in Islam's own writings. All these teachings from the Quran and Hadith are immoral and not from a God of Moral Perfection. Being immoral, they represent the hate of Muhammad for Muslim women and are therefore false rendering ALL Islam fraudulent but still after 1400 years - the very unfortunate daily reality for 600,000,000 Muslim women.

Following are just a miniscule sample of Quranic and Hadith teachings that give religious justification for the enslavement of both Muslim and kafir women. It is astonishing that Western women's rights groups are not fighting for the freedom of Muslim women. Being kafirs - they and their daughters face a very grim future with the rapid Islamization of Western societies

A Muslim woman is first the possession of her father and then her husband. Fathers may offer their baby daughters to Muslim men of any age who are entitled to consummate the union. Subjugation, degradation and oppression of Muslim women, rape and enslavement of kafir women are central to Islam. There is no concept of adultery between a Muslim man and a kafir woman. There is no concept of rape of kafir women or Muslim wives being a crime. If a Muslim woman accuses a Muslim man of rape, she must have 4 male witnesses otherwise she is guilty of adultery and will be stoned to death. Rape jihad is rampant throughout Europe. Honor killing is exploding in the West. Unlimited sex with sex slaves, unlimited sex with Muslim wives, unlimited sex for all eternity with virgins. **ISLAM IS ALL ABOUT SEX STUPID KAFIR**

Muslim Women Are Dirty Polluting Creatures

The Quran:

- Sura (2:222) "They ask thee concerning women's courses. Say: They are a hurt and a pollution: So keep away from women in their courses, and do not approach them until they are clean."
- Sura 4:43 "Muslims, draw not near unto prayer…(if) ye have touched women…then go to high clean soil and rub your face and your hands." (Muslim women are pariahs and dirty)."
- Sura (5:6) - "…if ye have had contact with women, and ye find not water, then go to clean, high ground and rub your faces and your hands with some of it."

Women are polluting. Men purify themselves following a casual contact with a woman.

Muslim Women Are Inferior, Slave To Men

A Muslim woman is first the *possession* of her father and then her husband. Fathers may offer their baby daughters to Muslim men of any age who are entitled to consummate the union.

The Quran:

- Sura (2:228) - "And women shall have rights similar to the rights against them, according to what is equitable; but **men have a degree (of advantage) over them**. And God is Exalted in Power, Wise."
- Sura (4:11) – "God (thus) directs you as regards your Children's (Inheritance): **to the male, a portion equal to that of two females**." (see also Sura 4:176)
- Sura (4:176) "They ask thee for a legal decision. Say: God directs (thus) about those who leave no descendants or ascendants as heirs. ... if there are brothers and sisters, (they share), **the male having twice the share of the female**."
- Sura (53:27) - "Those who believe not in the Hereafter, name the angels with female names." (i.e., Angels, the sublime beings, can only be male.)
- Sura (37:149-155) "Now ask them their opinion: Is it that thy Lord has (only) daughters, and they have sons?- Or that We created the angels female, and they are witnesses (thereto)? Is it not that they say, from their own invention, "God has begotten children"? but they are liars! **Did He (then) choose daughters rather than sons?** What is the matter with you? How judge ye? Will ye not then receive admonition?"

Hadith: Bukhari (88:219)

Narrated Abu Bakra: "During the battle of Al-Jamal, Allah benefited me with a Word (I heard from the Prophet). When the Prophet heard the news that the people of the Persia had made the daughter of Khosrau their Queen (ruler), he said, "**Never will succeed such a nation as makes a woman their ruler**."

Bukhari (48:826) Narrated Abu Said Al-Khudri:

"The Prophet said, 'Isn't the witness of a woman equal to half of that of a man?' The women said, 'Yes.' He said, '**This is because of the deficiency of a woman's mind.**'"

Bukhari (72:715) - A woman seeks Muhammad's help in leaving an abusive marriage, but is ordered by the prophet to return to her husband and submit to his commands.

Tabri; I; 280 ' Allah said, " It is My obligation to make Eve bleed once every month as she made this tree bleed. I must also make Eve stupid, although I created her intelligent. Because Allah afflicted Eve, all of the women of this world menstruate and are stupid.

Bukhari 6:301 "[Muhammad] said, 'Is not the evidence of two women equal to the witness of one man?' They replied in the affirmative. He said, 'This is the **deficiency in her intelligence.**'"

"[Muhammad said] 'Isn't it true that a woman can neither pray nor fast during her menses?' The women replied in the affirmative. He said, 'This is the deficiency in her religion." Allah has made women deficient in the practice of their religion as well, by giving them menstrual cycles.)

Narrated Abu Said Al-Khudri:

"Once Allah's Apostle went out to the Musalla (to offer the prayer) o 'Id-al-Adha or Al-Fitr prayer. Then he passed by the women and said, "O women! Give alms, as I have seen that the majority of the dwellers of Hell-fire were you (women)." They asked, "Why is it so, O Allah's Apostle ?" He replied, "You curse frequently and are ungrateful to your husbands. I have not seen anyone more deficient in intelligence and religion than you. A cautious sensible man could be led astray by some of you." The women asked, "O Allah's Apostle! What is deficient in our intelligence and religion?" He said, "Is not the evidence of two women equal to the witness of one man?" They replied in the affirmative. He said, "This is the deficiency in her intelligence. Isn't it true that a woman can neither pray nor fast during her menses?" The women replied in the affirmative. He said, "This is the deficiency in her religion."

Bukhari (62:58) - A woman presents herself in marriage to Muhammad, but he does not find her attractive, so he "donates" her on the spot to another man.

Abu Dawud (2:704) - "...the Apostle of Allah said: When one of you prays without a sutrah, a dog, an ass, a pig, a Jew, a Magian, and a woman cut off his prayer, but it will suffice if they pass in front of him at a distance of over a stone's throw."

God reduces one half of humanity to the status of a dog, a pig, a monkey, or an ass Sahih Bukhari – 1.9.490, 493, 498 Sahih Muslim – 4.1039; Sunaan Abu Dawud – 11.2155; Mishkat ul-Masabih – vol 2, p.114, Hadis no.

Ishaq 593 - "From the captives of Hunayn, Allah's Messenger gave [his son-in-law] Ali a slave girl called Baytab and he gave [future Caliph] Uthman a slave girl called Zaynab and [future Caliph] Umar another." (Even in this world, Muhammad treated women like party favors, handing out slave girls to his cronies for sex.)

Ishaq 969 - "Men were to lay injunctions on women lightly, for they were prisoners of men and had no control over their persons." - This same text also justifies beating women for flirting.

Muslim Women Are Sex Object For Men's Enjoyment

From Quran:

Sura (2:223) - "Your wives are as a tilth unto you; so approach your tilth when or how ye will." Wives are to be sexually available to their husbands in all ways at all times. They serve their husbands at his command. This verse refers to anal sex (see Bukhari 60:51), and was "revealed" when women complained to Muhammad about the practice. The phrase "when and how you will" means that they lost their case. Islam considers a wife to be a sex object who must submit to sex whenever, wherever and however her husband wants it. The concept of spousal rape does not exist in Islam. Muslim women are the property of Muslim men.

From Hadith: Bukhari (60:51)

Narrated Jabir: Jews used to say: "If one has sexual intercourse with his wife from the back, then she will deliver a squint-eyed child." So this Verse was revealed:-- "Your wives are a tilth unto you; so go to your tilth when or how you will." (2.223)

Muhammad said: "If a husband calls his wife to his bed [i.e. to have sexual relation] and she refuses and causes him to sleep in anger, the angels will curse her till morning." -- Bukhari 4.54.460

"By him in Whose Hand lies my life, a woman cannot carry out the right of her Lord, till she carries out the right of her husband. And if he asks her to surrender herself [to him for sexual intercourse] she should not refuse him even if she is on a camel's saddle." -- Ibn Majah 1854

Bukhari (62:81)

"Narrated 'Uqba: The Prophet said: "The stipulations most entitled to be abided by are those with which you are given the right to enjoy the (women's) private parts (i.e. the stipulations of the marriage contract)."

Bukhari 7:62:132

Narrated 'Abdullah bin Zam'a:

The Prophet said, "None of you should flog his wife as he flogs a slave and then have sexual intercourse with her in the last part of the day." (Ideally when you flog one of your wives, let her recuperate that day and sleep with your other wives or your slave girls.)

Muslim Men Can Capture Kafir Women As Sex-slave Booty

Islam is the only religion in the world that condones, even encourages, rape of female captives taken as slaves or held for ransom as a tactic of war and a reward for victorious soldiers who conquer kafirs. (Repeating these sex slave teachings:)

The Quran:

Sura (4:24) "All married women (are forbidden unto you) save those (captives) whom your right hands possess." You can't have sex with married women, unless they are slaves obtained in war (with whom you may rape or do whatever you like). A man is permitted to take women as sex slaves outside of marriage.

Sura (4:25) "If any of you have not the means wherewith to wed free believing women, they may wed believing girls from among those whom your right hands possess." In Islam the phrase " Whom your right hand possesses" means – sex slave.

Sura (23:5,6) "...who restrain their carnal desires (except with their wives and slave girls, for these are lawful to them..." Again, Muslim men were allowed to have sexual relations with their wives and slave girls:

Sura (33:52) "It is not allowed thee to take (other) women henceforth, nor that thou shouldst change them for other wives even though their beauty pleased thee, save those whom thy right hand possesseth. And Allah is ever Watcher over all things."

Sura (24:34) "Force not your slave-girls to whoredom (prostitution) if they desire chastity, that you may seek enjoyment of this life. [And here's the freedom-to-pimp card:] But if anyone forces them, then after such compulsion, Allah is oft-forgiving."

Sura (70:29-30,35) "And those who guard their chastity, Except with their wives and the (captives) whom their right hands possess,- for (then) they are not to be blamed, ... Such will be the honored ones in the Gardens (of Bliss)."

A Muslim Woman's Testimony Is Worth Only Half Of A Man's

The Quran:

Sura 2:282 – "Get two witnesses, out of your own men, and if there are not two men, then a man and two women, such as ye choose, for witnesses, so that if one of them errs, the other can remind her." Establishes that a woman's testimony is worth only half that of a man's in court (there is no "he said/she said" gridlock in Islam).

From the Hadith:

Bukhari (5:59:462) - The background for the Qur'anic requirement of four witnesses to adultery. Muhammad's favorite wife, Aisha, was accused of cheating [on her polygamous husband]. Three witnesses corroborated the event, but Muhammad did not want to believe it, and so established the arbitrary rule that four witnesses are required.

It is virtually impossible for raped women to prove it under Islamic law (Sharia). If the man claims that the act was consensual sex, there is very little that the woman can do to refute this. Islam places the burden of avoiding sexual encounters of any sort on the woman. Without four witnesses, rape victims in Muslim countries are commonly accused of adultery and stoned to death, thus punishing the victim simply because she is a woman.

Brutal Punishment For Muslim Women

Sura 4:15 - Lewd women should be punished with life imprisonment until death: "If any of your women are guilty of lewdness, Take the evidence of four (Reliable) witnesses from amongst you against them; and if they testify, confine them to houses until death do claim them, or God ordain for them some (other) way."

But men can get away with the same crime if they simply repent:

"If two men among you are guilty of lewdness, punish them both. If they repent and amend, Leave them alone; for God is Oft-returning, Most Merciful." (Quran 4:16)

Fewer Seats for Muslim Women in Allah's Paradise

Islamic Scriptures inform us that most Muslim women will go to hell.

The Quran:

Sura (37:22-23) "Those who "did wrong" will go to hell, and their wives will go to hell with them (no matter how they behaved)."

From Hadith: Bukhari (2:28) - Women comprise the majority of Hell's occupants. This is important because the only women in heaven ever mentioned by Muhammad are the virgins who serve the sexual desires of men. (A weak Hadith, Kanz al-`ummal, 22:10, even suggests that 99% of women go to Hell).

"Narrated Ibn 'Abbas: The Prophet said:

"I was shown the Hell-fire and that the majority of its dwellers were women who were ungrateful." It was asked, "Do they disbelieve in Allah?" (or are they ungrateful to Allah?) He replied, "They are ungrateful to their husbands and are ungrateful for the favors and the good (charitable deeds) done to them. If you have always been good (benevolent) to one of them and then she sees something in you (not of her liking), she will say, 'I have never received any good from you."

"Among the inmates of Heaven women will be the minority" (Sahih Muslim 36: 6600)

"I (Mohammed) have seen that the majority of the dwellers of Hell-Fire were women...[because] they are ungrateful to their husbands and they are deficient in intelligence" (Sahih Bukhari: 2:18:161; 7:62:125,).

Ishaq: 185 " In hell I saw women hanging by their breasts. They had fathered bastards."

Narrated 'Abdullah bin Abbas:

.The Prophet replied, "I saw Paradise and stretched my hands towards a bunch (of its fruits) and had I taken it, you would have eaten from it as long as the world remains. I also saw the Hell-fire and I had never seen such a horrible sight. I saw that most of the inhabitants were women." The people asked, "O Allah's Apostle! Why is it so?" The Prophet replied, "Because of their ungratefulness." It was asked whether they are ungrateful to Allah. The Prophet said, "They are ungrateful to their companions of life (husbands) and ungrateful to good deeds. If you are benevolent to one of them throughout the life and if she sees anything (undesirable) in you, she will say, 'I have never had any good from you.' "

The Tyranny Of Muslim Men Over Muslim Women

The Quran:

Sura (24:31) - "And say to the believing women that they cast down their looks and guard their private parts and do not display their ornaments except what appears thereof, and let them wear their head-coverings over their bosoms, and not display their ornaments except to their husbands or their fathers, or the fathers of their husbands, or their sons, or the sons of their husbands, or their brothers, or their brothers' sons, or their sisters' sons, or their women, or those whom their right hands possess, or the male servants not having need (of women), or the children who have not attained knowledge of what is hidden of women; and let them not strike their feet so that what they hide of their ornaments may be known." The woman is not only supposed to cover herself, except with relatives, but to look down, so as to avoid making eye-contact with men.

Sura (33:59) – "O Prophet! Tell your wives and your daughters and the women of the believers to draw their cloaks (veils) over their bodies (when outdoors). That is most convenient that they should be known and not molested."

Sura (24:60) "Such elderly women as are past the prospect of marriage,- there is no blame on them if they lay aside their (outer) garments, provided they make not a wanton display of their beauty: but it is best for them to be modest: and God is One Who sees and knows all things."

Sura (33:32-33) "O Consorts of the Prophet! ... stay quietly in your houses, and make not a dazzling display, like that of the former Times of Ignorance" (i.e., Muhammad's wives should stay in their houses)

Sura (33:30) "O Consorts of the Prophet! If...any of you are devout, obedient, and submissive in the service to Allah and His Messenger, and does good, to her shall We grant her reward twice. We have prepared for her a generously rich provision."

Sura (33:53) "And when ye ask (his ladies) for anything ye want, ask them from before a screen: that makes for greater purity for your hearts and for theirs. Nor is it right for you that ye should... marry his [Muhammad's] widows after him at any time. Truly such a thing is in God's sight an enormity." (i.e., Nobody can marry Muhammad's widows after he is dead.)

Sura (33:54) "You must not speak ill of God's apostle, nor shall you ever wed his wives after him; this would be a grave offense in the sight of Allah." The great adulterer/fornicator condemned his wives to a life of loneliness.

From the Hadith:

Bukhari (6:321) - Muhammad is asked whether it is right for a young woman to leave her house without a veil. He replies, "She should cover herself with the veil of her companion."

Bukhari (60:282) - After Muhammad issued the command (Sura 24:31) for women to cover themselves, the women responded by tearing up sheets to cover their faces.

Narrated Safiya bint Shaiba:

'Aisha used to say: "When (the Verse): "They should draw their veils over their necks and bosoms," was revealed, (the ladies) cut their waist sheets at the edges and covered their faces with the cut pieces."

Abu Dawud (2:641) – "The Prophet (peace_be_upon_him) said: 'Allah does not accept the prayer of a woman who has reached puberty unless she wears a veil.'"

Bukhari (52:250) - [The Prophet said] "It is not permissible for a man to be alone with a woman, and no lady should travel except with a Muhram (i.e. her husband or a person whom she cannot marry in any case for ever; e.g. her father, brother, etc.)." - Neither is a woman allowed to travel by herself.

Narrated Ibn Abbas:

"That he heard the Prophet saying, "It is not permissible for a man to be alone with a woman, and no lady should travel except with a Muhram (i.e. her husband or a person whom she cannot marry in any case for ever; e.g. her father, brother, etc.)." Then a man got up and said, "O Allah's Apostle! I have enlisted in the army for such-and-such Ghazwa and my wife is proceeding for Hajj." Allah's Apostle said, "Go, and perform the Hajj with your wife."

Polygamy:

The Quran:

Sura (4:3) - (Wife-to-husband ratio) "Marry women of your choice, Two or three or four; but if ye fear that ye shall not be able to deal justly (with them), then only one, or (a captive) that your right hands possess, that will be more suitable, to prevent you from doing injustice."

Sura (4:129) - "Ye are never able to be fair and just as between women, even if it is your ardent desire" (but don't let that stop you, husbands, because your need come first anyway).

Muslim Wife Swapping:

Sura (4:20) "And if ye wish to exchange one wife for another and ye have given unto one of them a sum of money (however great), take nothing from it. Would ye take it by the way of calumny and open wrong?"

(You can change your wives. Islamic wife-swapping requires saying "talaq" three times to one of the four wives, and replacing her with another wife.) The woman will be removed from the household with no legal rights to visit the children or financial rights to any shared property.

Muslim Wives as slaves:

Sura (66:5) - "Maybe, his Lord, if he divorce you, will give him in your place wives better than you, submissive, faithful, obedient, penitent, adorers, fasters, widows and virgins"

(A disobedient wife can be replaced. A man can only have up to four wives, but he can rotate as many women as he pleases in and out of the lineup.)

From Bukhari (62:2)

Narrated 'Ursa: "that he asked 'Aisha about the Statement of Allah: 'If you fear that you shall not be able to deal justly with the orphan girls, then marry (other) women of your choice, two or three or four; but if you fear that you shall not be able to deal justly (with them), then only one, or (the captives) that your right hands possess. That will be nearer to prevent you from doing injustice.' (4.3) 'Aisha said, "O my nephew! (This Verse has been revealed in connection with) an orphan girl under the guardianship of her guardian who is attracted by her wealth and beauty and intends to marry her with a Mahr less than what other women of her standard deserve. So they (such guardians) have been forbidden to marry them unless they do justice to them and give them their full Mahr, and they are ordered to marry other women instead of them."

Bukhari (5:268) - "The Prophet used to visit all his wives in a round, during the day and night and they were eleven in number." I asked Anas, "Had the Prophet the strength for it?" Anas replied, "We used to say that the Prophet was given the strength of thirty men." Muhammad had special rules that allowed him at least eleven wives. (His successors had more than four wives at a time as well.)

Bukhari (62:6) - "The Prophet used to go round (have sexual relations with) all his wives in one night, and he had nine wives."

Bukhari (77:598) - "Allah's Apostle said, "No woman should ask for the divorce of her sister (Muslim) so as to take her place, but she should marry the man (without compelling him to divorce his other wife)"

Narrated Abu Huraira:

"Allah's Apostle said, "No woman should ask for the divorce of her sister (Muslim) so as to take her place, but she should marry the man (without compelling him to divorce his other wife), for she will have nothing but what Allah has written for her." Polygamy is firmly established in the Islamic tradition.

Muslim Wife Beating

The Quran:

Sura (4:34) - "Men are the maintainers of women because Allah has made some of them to excel others and because they spend out of their property; the good women are therefore obedient, guarding the unseen as Allah has guarded; and (as to) those on whose part you fear desertion, admonish them, and leave them alone in the sleeping-places and beat them; then if they obey you, do not seek a way against them; surely Allah is High, Great."

A husband has the legal right and religious obligation to beat a wife if she disobeys him, is disloyal to him or simply does not please him. The concept of wife abuse does not exist in Islam. According to Islamic law, a husband may strike his wife for any one of the following four reasons:

- She does not attempt to make herself beautiful for him (i.e. "let's herself go")
- She refuses to meet his sexual demands
- She leaves the house without his permission or a "legitimate reason"
- She neglects her religious duties

Any of these are also sufficient grounds for divorce.

From the Hadith:

Muslim (4:2127) - Muhammad struck his favorite wife, Aisha, in the chest one evening when she left the house without his permission. Aisha narrates, "He struck me on the chest which caused me pain."

Bukhari (7:72:715) - A woman came to Muhammad and begged her to stop her husband from beating her. Her skin was bruised so badly that she it is described as being "greener" than the green veil she was wearing. Muhammad did not admonish her husband, but instead ordered her to return to him and submit to his sexual desires.

Abu Dawud (2141) - "Iyas bin 'Abd Allah bin Abi Dhubab reported the Apostle of Allah (may peace be upon him) as saying: Do not beat Allah's handmaidens, but when 'Umar came to the Apostle of Allah (may peace be upon him) and said: Women have become emboldened towards their husbands, he (the Prophet) gave permission to beat them. Then many women came round the family of the Apostle of Allah (may peace be upon him) complaining against their husbands. So the Apostle of Allah (may peace be upon him) said : Many women have gone round Muhammad's family complaining against their husbands. They are not the best among you." At first, Muhammad forbade men from beating their wives, but he rescinded this once it was reported that women were becoming emboldened toward their husbands. Beatings are sometimes necessary to keep women in their place.

Abu Dawud (2142) - "The Prophet said: A man will not be asked as to why he beat his wife."

MUSLIM WOMEN: ISLAM'S DOMESTIC ANIMALS

"Now then, O people, you have a right over your wives and they have a right over you. You have [the right] that they should not cause anyone of whom you dislike to tread your beds, and that they should not commit any open indecency (fahishah). **If they do, then God permits you to shut them in separate rooms and to beat them, but not severely. If they abstain from [evil], they have the right to their food and clothing in accordance with custom (bi'l-maruf). Treat women well, for they are [like] domestic animals ('awan) with you and do not possess anything for themselves.** You have taken them only as a trust from God, and you have made the enjoyment of their persons lawful by the word of God, so understand and listen to my words, O people. I have conveyed the Message, and have left you with something which, if you hold fast to it, you will never go astray: that is, the Book of God and the sunnah of His Prophet. Listen to my words, O people, for I have conveyed the message and understand [it]... It was reported [to me] that **the** people said, "O God, yes." And the Messenger of God said, "O God, bear witness.""

Reference: Al-Tabari, Abu Ja'far Muhammad b. Jarir. The History of al-Tabari. Vol.IX: The Last Years of the Prophet. Translated and annotated by Ismail K. Poonawala. State University of NewYork Press, Albany, 1990. (Pages 112-114. Bold emphasis is mine)

Eve was created from the rib of Adam but all of humankind is created from the womb of women. Women therefore deserve equal, if not greater, respect and right than men in society. Reducing women to a vile, psychologically impaired and inferior being to men is a criminal injustice against women's natural place in society. Muhammad, a sex-crazed, brutal, criminal engendered 1,400 years of repression and degradation of billions of Muslim mothers and daughters. Because these Quranic teachings are eternal, this repression and degradation of both Muslim and kafir women will continue forever.

It is important to understand that a Muslim man has the full right to obedience from his Muslim wife including beheading her if she continues to displease him. Verse 4:15 states that a disgraced woman is condemned to a solitary confinement till death. The alternative is the judgment of Allah. The Qur'an is not clear what that judgment of Allah could be. There are various interpretations on this. Therefore, a Muslim man may do to his woman whatever he wishes, including ending her life.

According to Islam, if a Muslim woman disobeys her husband she is disgraced. Therefore, when a Muslim woman resorts to the Western justice system to seek protection from her menacing husband, she has certainly broken the Islamic tenet of complete surrender to the wishes of her husband. Thus, she has dishonored her husband, his reputation and, most importantly, the Islamic code of conduct for an obedient wife. Therefore, it is not surprising that her husband can end her life islamically, to restore his pride, honor and religious conviction.

Please note that in verse 4:34 Allah permits a husband to punish his disobedient wife. It is worthy to observe that this verse says if the husband suspects or fears disobedience and rebellion; that the actual acts might not have taken place. This verse also says that the men are the protectors of women. Thus, islamically, a Muslim wife, foolish enough to seek the protection of man's law is a clear violation of Quranic injunction of verse 4:34, a challenge to Islam. And, as per the Islamic law, if anyone violates the Quranic command the only punishment is death by beheading. Thus, we may conclude that a Muslim man beheading his wife has acted in the manner that Quran commands him.

So vile, depraved, unjust and deplorable are the position and treatment of women in Islamic scriptures and teachings. Allah (the AntiGod) and his messenger Muhammad are male, chauvinist, pigs. A God of Moral Perfection is not a sexist. He believes in the complete equality of men and women. A God permitting the murder of Muslim women and the rape/enslavement of kafir women is not a God but a beast. All these teachings are morally and therefore, not from a God of Moral Perfection and therefore (repeating countless times) being not the teachings of a God of Moral Perfection Islam is totally and completely fraudulent.

For article: Islam and Submission of Women go to
http://islamreform.net/new-page-72.htm

CHAPTER TWELVE

SEXUAL PERVERSIONS OF PROPHET MUHAMMAD NECROPHILIA WITH HIS DEAD AUNT

This is from a book called "Kanz Al Umal" (The Treasure of the Workers), in the chapter of "The issues of women", authored by Ali Ibn Husam Aldin, commonly known as Al-Mutaki Al-Hindi. He based his book on the hadith and sayings listed in "Al-Jami Al-Saghir," written by Jalal ul-Din Al-Suyuti.

Narrated by Ibn Abbas:

"I (Muhammad) put on her my shirt that she may wear the clothes of heaven, and I SLEPT with her in her coffin (grave) that I may lessen the pressure of the grave. She was the best of Allah's creatures to me after Abu Talib"... The prophet was referring to Fatima, the mother of Ali.

The Arabic scholar Demetrius explains : "The Arabic word used here for "slept" is "Id'tajat," and literally means "lay down" with her. It is often used to mean, "lay down to have sex." Muhammad is understood as saying that because he slept with her she has become like a wife to him so she will be considered like a "mother of the believers." This will supposedly prevent her from being tormented in the grave, since Muslims believed that as people wait for the Judgment Day they will be tormented in the grave. "Reduce the pressure" here means that the torment won't be as much because she is now a "mother of the believers" after Muhammad slept with her and "consummated" the union."

SUCKING THE TONGUES OF HIS DAUGHTER AND COUSIN'S SONS

According to Father Botros (see notes) there are no less than 20 Islamic sources—such as the hadith of Ahmad bin Hanbal— that Muhammad used to suck on the tongues of boys and girls" A hadith relayed by Abu Hurreira describes Muhammad sucking on the tongues of his cousin (and future caliph) Ali's two boys, Hassan and Hussein. Muhammad sucked on the tongue of his own daughter, Fatima.

Muhammad would not sleep until he kissed his daughter Fatima and nuzzled his face in her bosom.

MUHAMMAD WOULD DRESS IN WOMAN'S CLOTHES

The prophet displayed "transvestite" tendencies. There are no less than 32 different references to this phenomenon in Islam's books—wherein Muhammad often laid in bed dressed in women's clothes, specifically his child-bride Aisha's.

Sahih Bukhari (2/911), "Revelations [i.e., the Quran] never come to me when I'm dressed in women's clothing—except when I'm dressed in Aisha's," implying that it was something of a habit for the prophet to dress in female clothing.

BREAST FEEDING GROWN MEN BY MUSLIM WOMEN AND THE BILLY GOAT

Just when you think you have reached the bottom of the depravity that is Islam, there is revealed even crazier, depraved, evil, madness.

In order to circumvent the prohibition on a male and a Muslim female who are not married to each other from working together in private is for the Muslim women to allow the man to suck her breasts becoming her foster child, and then they can be together without a chaperone. From Father Botos website www.fatherzakaria.com

From Islam's Unholy Books

- Narrated Ibn Shehab: when he was asked about adult suckling he said; "Abe Hozaifa one of the companions of the messenger of God has adopted a boy named Salem, then when God descended a verse in his book concerning Zaied Ibn thabet abating the adoption saying: call them after their fathers (meaning that to attribute those adopted sons to their biological fathers), Salma the wife of Abe Hozaifa came to the messenger of God saying: we had an adopted son named Salem ,he was getting into my house while I was wearing one dress , after the adoption was abated , my husband Abe Hozaifa hated to see him getting into my home, while I am in such way, so what do you think?, how can I deal with that? The prophet replied her: then let him suck from you five times, and then he will be forbidden to you (as it was thought that if one sucks from a woman, he will be like her son)? She said surprisingly: how could I suckle him while he is a full grown man? Then the prophet smiled and said: I know that he is a full grown man.

She went out and followed that advice and allowed the man to suck from her, she came back to the prophet saying I suckled him, now I don't find anything wrong with my husband any more."

This story about Adult suckling was mentioned in:

- Sahih Muslim , converse number 3663, 3674
- Mawtte' malek
- Sonan Al-Nyssa'y
- Sonan Al-Bayhaky
- Sonan Ibn Majah
- The abrogator and abrogated by Abe-Gaefar Al-Mansour, page124
- And other exegesis

- Ibn Shehab continued his narration about the Adult suckling saying;" and so, Aeisha the mother of believers followed the prophet's advice, when she wanted some men to get into her house, she was asking her sister Om' Kolthoum, the daughter of Abe-Baker, and her niece to suckle those men, so by that way she will be like the aunt of them, and they can get into her house freely and be with her."

- Narrated Zainab Bent Om Salma: Om Salma said to Aeisha, "I am seeing the full grown men getting into your house, which I hate to see from you, Aeisha replied: didn't you hear about Salma the wife of Abe Hozaifa? who came to the messenger of God complaining to him that Salem was getting into her house and her husband Abe Hozaifa hated to see that ,and the prophet said to her: then let him suck from you, to be permissible for him to get into your house freely, so don't you follow the advice of the messenger of God ?"

- It was mentioned that Aeisha remained in her attitude towards the adult suckling issue, and she was practicing it

- Aeisha supported her attitude saying: there was among the descended verses of the Quran, verses saying about giving ten known suckling, then that verse was abrogated by another one saying that they are five known suckling, ant till the messenger of God died, this verse was among the recited verses of the Quran.

- Narrated Aeisha;"the verse concerning the adult suckling was in a paper under my bed, when the prophet of God was very sick (before he died), we were very busy looking after him, then a goat came into the house, and ate that paper, and till the messenger of God died, this verse was among the recited verses of the Quran."

Breast feeding of grown men was a law of God until a billy goat ate this law of God. Aisha also claimed that there was a law of God that Muslim women were to be murdered i.e. beheaded for adultery until a goat thankfully ate the scrap of paper it was written on. Too bad the billy goat didn't devour the entire Quran.

For Father Zakeria Botras teachings on the sexual pervasions of prophet Muhammad go to : http://www.islamreform.net/new-page-69.htm

Father Zakaria Botras Sexual Pervasions of Muhammad Part I:
http://www.islamreform.net/new-page-35.htm

Father Zakaria Botras Sexual Pervasions of Muhammad Part II
http://www.islamreform.net/new-page-34.htm

Father Zakaria Botras Sexual Pervasions of Muhammad Part III
http://www.islamreform.net/new-page-33.htm

Father Zakaria Botras Sexual Pervasions of Muhammad Part IV
http://www.islamreform.net/new-page-31.htm

Father Zakaria Botras Sexual Pervasions of Muhammad Part V
http://www.islamreform.net/new-page-32.htm

More sexual pervasions of Islam:

Quoting Ayatollah Khomeini: " A man can have sex with animals such as sheep's, cows, camels and so on. However he should kill the animal after he has his orgasm. He should not sell the meat to the people in his own village, however selling the meat to the next door village should be fine."From Khomeini's book,"Tahrirolvasyleh", fourth volume, Darol Elm, Gom, Iran, 1990

"If one commits the act of sodomy with a cow, a ewe, or a camel, their urine and their excrements become impure, and even their milk may no longer be consumed. The animal must then be killed and as quickly as possible and burned." The little green book, Sayings of Ayatollah Khomeini, Political, Phylosophica, Social and Religious with a special introduction by Clive Irving, ISBN number 0-553-14032-9, page 47

CHAPTER THIRTEEN

WHERE IS THE OUTRAGE

ALLAH IS A PEDIPHILE MONSTER

BABY TILTHS:

The most important duty of any species is the care and protection of its young. The prime duty of mankind is to raise children in a safe environment, care and educate them, so they can progress into responsible adults. There is no worse crime than the sexual abuse and exploitation of children. By sexually abusing a child, you totally destroy the child's self esteem and mentally condemn the child to a life of psychological torment. Having murdered their souls, they become part of the living dead.

As we have already seen, Allah (the AntiGod) has created two types of Homo sapiens - Muslims and kafirs. Again as previously stated, on the human evolutionary scale, kafirs are sub-humans - they have no humanity and can be murdered, tortured, terrorized etc. with impunity. In Islam, these are not crimes but holy acts deserving of Paradise provided, they are perpetrated on kafirs. While kafir women have no humanity, Muslim women are only slightly higher on the evolutionary scale having evolved to the status of a dog.

Seeking to please the sexual desires of his male Muslims, Allah (the AntiGod) has decreed verse (65.4) that Muslim baby girls can be sexually molested condemning them to a life of sexual and mental anguish. Quran 65.4 sets the prescribed period for divorce. You can marry (and divorce) little girls who have not yet reached menstruation age. As if Islam was not morally depraved enough, we now sink to the true essence of the evil that is Islam: Allah (the AntiGod) IS **A PEDIPHILLE MONSTER**.

Quran 65:4 "And those of your women as have passed the age of monthly courses, for them the 'Iddah (prescribed divorce period), if you have doubts (about their periods), is three months, <u>and for those who have no courses [(i.e. they are still immature) their 'Iddah (prescribed period) is three months likewise</u>, except in case of death] . And for those who are pregnant (whether they are divorced or their husbands are dead), their 'Iddah (prescribed period) is until they deliver (their burdens) (give birth) and whosoever fears Allah and keeps his duty to Him, He will make his matter easy for him."

Allah loved little girls and he wished that all his Jihadist Muslim men could love little girls.
Quran 65.4 states that the Iddah period for Muslim men to divorce PRE PUBERCENT Muslim girls is 3 months. This means that Muslim men were allowed to marry girl children. THIS IS AN ETERNAL LAW OF GOD. Muslim men can marry and have sex with young female Muslim girls, and if they want to divorce them – they must wait 3 months. Think about it. Little Muslim baby girls being offered on a silver platter for a life of sexual abuse by old Muslim men. Isn't Allah wonderful.

Quoting Ayatollah Khomeini:

"It is better for a girl to marry in such a time when she would begin menstruation at her husband's house rather than her father's home. Any father marrying his daughter so young will have a permanent place in heaven. " From Khomeini's book, "Tahrirolvasyleh", fourth volume, Darol Elm, Gom,

Comment from an Iranian on the wisdom of the great, holy Ayatollah;

"I am ashamed of being born and raised in Iran, a country where they built a Mausoleum over his grave and had the greatest party for his 100th birthday. Shame on such people."

CHAPTER FOURTEEN

MUHAMMAD: A HUMAN BEING OF PERFECTION
MUHAMMAD: THE PERFECT HUSBAND AND FAMILY MAN

Baby Aisha And Muhammad: A Love Story For The Ages Between A 6 Year Old Child And A 50 Year Old Sexual Pervert: It Will Bring Tears Of Joy To Your Eyes And Heart: From The Holy Book Of Islam

MUHAMMAD AND HIS CHILD BRIDE BABY AISHA

Muhammad was one sick, evil man. He had fantasies of Baby Aisha. She came to his home with dolls at the age of 6, and he raped her when she was 9. In order to justify his criminality, he created through his phony God – Allah (the AntiGod) teaching 65.4.

Since girls at that age are not fully mature either physically, emotionally, or psychologically, we know that it is wrong for a man, regardless of his age, to engage a child in sexual relations. No other conclusion can be drawn. No one would expect a real prophet of a righteous God to engage in, justify, allow, and prescribe for his followers such a malignant act.

Muhammad established an appalling precedent for Islam, Muslims, and young girls. This was not based upon wisdom, knowledge, or science, but only upon his desires, actions, and teachings. He should be judged as a man who established child abuse as a norm in Islam

MUHAMMAD AND MOLESTATION OF BABY AISHA (FROM THE WRITINGS OF ISLAM)

Muhammad Fantasized About Baby Aisha Before Soliciting Her From Her Father.

Sahih Bukhari 9.140
Narrated 'Aisha:
"Allah's Apostle said to me, "You were shown to me twice (in my dream) before I married you. I saw an angel carrying you in a silken piece of cloth, and I said to him, 'Uncover (her),' and behold, it was you. I said (to myself), 'If this is from Allah, then it must happen."

Baby Aisha's Father Did Not Approve At First

Aisha's father, Abu Bakr, wasn't on board at first, but Muhammad explained how the rules of their religion made it possible. This is similar to the way that present-day cult leaders manipulate their followers into similar concessions.

Sahih Bukhari 7.18
Narrated 'Ursa: "The Prophet asked Abu Bakr for 'Aisha's hand in marriage. Abu Bakr said "But I am your brother." The Prophet said, "You are my brother in Allah's religion and His Book, but she (Aisha) is lawful for me to marry."

Muhammad Marries Baby Aisha At Age 6

Sahih Bukhari Volume 5, Book 58, Number 234
Narrated Aisha: "The Prophet engaged (married) me when I was a girl of six (years). We went to Medina and stayed at the home of Bani-al-Harith bin Khazraj. Then I got ill and my hair fell down. Later on my hair grew (again) and my mother, Um Ruman, came to me while I was playing in a swing with some of my girl friends. She called me, and I went to her, not knowing what she wanted to do to me. She caught me by the hand and made me stand at the door of the house. I was breathless then, and when my breathing became Allright, she took some water and rubbed my face and head with it. Then she took me into the house. There in the house I saw some Ansari women who said, "Best wishes and Allah's Blessing and a good luck." Then she entrusted me to them and they prepared me (for the marriage). Unexpectedly Allah's Apostle came to me in the forenoon and my mother handed me over to him, and at that time I was a girl of nine years of age."

Baby Aisha Sat On The Prophet's Lap And Was Raped
Tabari IX:131 "My mother came to me while I was being swung on a swing between two branches and got me down. My nurse took over and wiped my face with some water and started leading me. When I was at the door she stopped so I could catch my breath. I was

brought in while Muhammad was sitting on a bed in our house. My mother made me sit on his lap. The other men and women got up and left. The Prophet CONSUMMATED his marriage with me in my house when I was NINE years old."

Sahih Bukhari Volume 7, Book 62, Number 64:

Narated By 'Aisha : "That the Prophet married her when she was six years old and he *consummated his marriage* when she was nine years old, and then she remained with him for nine years" (i.e., till his death).

Sahih Bukhari Volume 8, Book 73, Number 151

Narrated 'Aisha: "I used to play with the dolls in the presence of the Prophet, and my girl friends also used to play with me. When Allah's Apostle used to enter (my dwelling place) they used to hide themselves, but the Prophet would call them to join and play with me." (The playing with the dolls and similar images is forbidden, but it was allowed for 'Aisha at that time, as she was a little girl, not yet reached the age of puberty.) (Fateh-al-Bari page 143, Vol.13)

Dear Reader - think about what you just read. 1400 years ago Baby Aisha was a happy young girl of six playing with her dolls and swinging on her swing with her girl friends.

Muhammad Would Thigh with Baby Aisha

The permanent committee for the scientific research and fatwahs (religious decrees) reviewed the question presented to the grand Mufti Abu Abdullah Muhammad Al-Shemary, the question forwarded to the committee by the grand scholar of the committee with reference number 1809 issued on 3/8/1421 (Islamic calendar).

After the committee studied the issue, they gave the following reply:

"As for the prophet, peace and prayer of Allah be upon him, thighing his fiancée Aisha. She was six years of age and he could not have intercourse with her due to her small age. That is why [the prophet] peace and prayer of Allah be upon him placed HIS [MALE] MEMBER BETWEEN HER THIGHS AND MASSAGED IT SOFTLY, as the apostle of Allah had control of his [male] member not like other believers."

Muhammad Reserved Baby Aisha For Himself Because She Was A Virgin And He Wanted a Virgin

(Sahih Al-Bukhari, Volume 7, Book 62, Number 17)

Narrated Jabir bin 'Abdullah:
"When I got married, Allah's Apostle said to me, "What type of lady have you married?" I replied, "I have married a matron." He said, "Why, don't you have a liking for the virgins AND FOR FONDLING THEM?" Jabir also said: Allah's Apostle said, "Why didn't you marry a young girl so that you might play with her and she with you?"

Muslim (8:3460) - *"Why didn't you marry a young girl so that you could sport with her and she could sport with you, or you could amuse with her and she could amuse with you?"* Muhammad posed this question to one of his followers who had married an "older woman" instead.

Hence, Muhammad's comments indicate that his reason for marrying Aisha while a young virgin is so that he could fondle and sexually play with her!

Baby Aisha Was Not The Only Baby Girl Muhammad Fantasized About

In the classic history of "The Life of Muhammad" (Sirat Rasul Allah) by Ibn Ishaq, there is an account in which Muhammad expressed a marital interest in a crawling baby. This event seems to have occurred around the time of the Battle of Badr which would have made Muhammad approximately 55 years old. He had married Aisha two years earlier, when he was 53 years of age.

(Suhayli, ii. 79: In the riwaya of Yunus I. "I recorded that the apostle saw her (Ummu'lFadl) when she was a baby crawling before him and said, 'If she grows up and I am still alive I will marry her.' But he died before she grew up and Sufyan b. al-Aswad b. 'Abdu'l-Asad al-Makhzumi married her and she bore him Rizq and Lubab…"(Ibn Ishaq, The Life of Muhammad: A Translation of Ishaq's Sirat Rasul Allah, translated by A. Guillaume [Oxford University Press, Karachi], p. 311)

Muhammad saw Um Habiba the daughter of Abbas while she was fatim (age of nursing) and he said, "If she grows up while I am still alive, I will marry her." (Musnad Ahmad, Number 25636)

Muhammad Would Bath With and Fondle Baby Aisha

Bukhari (6:298) - Muhammad would take a bath with the little girl and fondle her.

Narrated 'Aisha: "The Prophet and I used to take a bath from a single pot while we were Junub. During the menses, he used to order me to put on an Izar (dress worn below the waist) and used to fondle me. While in Itikaf, he used to bring his head near me and I would wash it while I used to be in my periods (menses)."

Baby Aisha Would Wash Semen Stains off Muhammad's Clothes

Bukhari (4:232) – Muhammad's wives would wash semen stains out of his clothes, which were still wet from the spot-cleaning even when he went to the mosque for prayers.

Sahih Bukhari Volume 1, Book 4, Number 231:

Narrated SulaImam bin Yasar:
"I asked 'Aisha about the clothes soiled with semen. She replied, "I used to wash it off the clothes of Allah's Apostle and he would go for the prayer while water spots were still visible."

Muhammad Would Lie With Baby Aisha

Sunaan Abu Dawud: Book 11, Number 2161:
Narrated Aisha, Ummul Mu'minin:
"I and the Apostle of Allah (peace_be_upon_him) used to lie in one cloth at night while I was menstruating. If anything from me smeared him, he washed the same place (that was smeared), and did not wash beyond it. If anything from him smeared his clothe, he washed the same place and did not wash beyond that, and prayed with it (i.e. the clothe)."

Muhammad Would Recite Quran While Lying With Menstruating Baby Aisha

Bukhari (93:639) - The Prophet of Islam would recite the 'Holy Qur'an' with his head in Aisha's lap, when she was menstruating.

Baby Aisha Understood That Muhammad's Teachings Were Phoney

Bukhari (60:311) - *"I feel that your Lord hastens in fulfilling your wishes and desires."* These words were spoken by Aisha within the context of her husband having been given 'Allah's permission' to fulfill his sexual desires with a large number of women in whatever order he chooses. (It has been suggested that Aisha may have been speaking somewhat wryly).

Captured Kafir Women Are Slave Booty

Tabari IX:137 - *"Allah granted Rayhana of the Qurayza to Muhammad as booty."* Muhammad considered the women that he captured and enslaved to be God's gift to him.

Muhammad – The Womanizer

Tubari IX:139 - *"You are a self-respecting girl, but the prophet is a womanizer."* Words spoken by the disappointed parents of a girl who had 'offered' herself to Muhammad

Muhammad Would Sexually Abuse His Wives

Bukhari (6:300) - Muhammad's wives had to be available for the prophet's fondling even when they were having their menstrual period.

Bukhari Volume 1, Book 6, Number 299: Narrated 'Abdur-Rahman bin Al-Aswad: ...(on the authority of his father) 'Aisha said: "Whenever Allah's Apostle wanted to fondle anyone of us during her periods (menses), he used to order her to put on an Izar and start fondling her." 'Aisha added, "None of you could control his sexual desires as the Prophet could."

In the *Hadith* of Sahih Muslim, Vol. I, page 590, Muslim says, that Aisha said: "If anyone of us was having her menstrual period, Allah's Messenger ordered her to come to him for sexual intercourse while she is on the peak of her period." Maymuna said: "The Messenger of Allah used to have sexual intercourse with me during my menstrual period, while a piece of garment is between us."

You tell me what kind of man would stick his hand in his wives menstruating vagina. You tell me what kind of man would force a menstruating woman to have sex. This is rape and sexual molestation.

The Prophet Would Do All His Wives In One Night

Bukhari (62:6) - "The Prophet used to go round (have sexual relations with) all his wives in one night, and he had nine wives." Muhammad also said that it was impossible to treat all wives equally - and it isn't hard to guess why.

Bukhari (5:268) - "The Prophet used to visit all his wives in a round, during the day and night and they were eleven in number." I asked Anas, 'Had the Prophet the strength for it?' Anas replied, 'We used to say that the Prophet was given the strength of thirty men. "

Allah (the AntiGod) Promoted This Immoral Behavior:

"Your women are a tilth for you (to cultivate) so go to your tilth as ye will" Quran (2:223) Likens a woman to a field (tilth), to be used by a man as he wills:

As we have already shown - this is an Eternal teaching of God allowing Muslim men to perform anal sex on Muslim women.

As we have already seen, according to Islam, Muhammad is the perfection of humanity and the prototype of the most wonderful human conduct. He raped a nine year-old child and leaves an enduring legacy for old Muslim men to fulfill their carnal desires contrary to natural law and to the life-long devastation of young girls. On the other hand, Muhammad passed down revelations from Allah that clearly condoned sleeping with underage girls, even by the standard of puberty.

THIS SICKNESS OF ISLAM AND RAPING MUSLIM BABY GIRLS IS AN EVIL APPROVED BY ALLAH (the ANTI GOD) FOR ALL TIME

When you are living in a totalitarian system, the fantasies, nightmares and sexual pervasions of the dictator become the daily reality for the population living under his control. In this spirit - Ayatollah Khomeini issued a fatwa about Quran 65.4 and Quran 2:223.

Fatwas by the late Ayatollah Khomeini of Iran.

Ayatollah Ruhollah Khomeini, The Supreme Leader of Iran, the Shia Grand Ayatollah, 1979-89 said in his official statements:

"A man can marry a girl younger than nine years of age, even if the girl is still a baby being breastfed. A man, however is prohibited from having intercourse with a girl younger than nine, other sexual acts such as foreplay, rubbing, kissing and sodomy is allowed. Sodomizing the baby is halal (allowed by sharia). A man having intercourse with a girl younger than nine years of age has not committed a crime, but only an infraction, if the girl is not permanently damaged. If the girl, however, is permanently damaged, the man must provide for her all her life. But this girl will not count as one of the man's four permanent wives. He also is not permitted to marry the girl's sister."

What you are reading is a well reasoned religious Edith of immoral monstrousness. Islam is a bottomless well of moral depravity.

Khomeini, "Tahrirolvasyleh" fourth volume, Darol Elm, Gom, Iran, 1990

"It is not illegal for an adult male to 'thigh' or enjoy a young girl who is still in the age of weaning; meaning to place his penis between her thighs, and to kiss her."

Ayatu Allah Al Khumaini's "Tahrir Al wasila" p. 241, issue number 12

"Young boys or girls in full sexual effervescence are kept from getting married before they reach the legal age of majority. This is against the intention of divine laws. Why should the marriage of pubescent girls and boys be forbidden because they are still minors, when they are allowed to listen to the radio and to sexually arousing music?"

WHY QURAN 65:4 IS NOT THE WORD/TEACHING OF GOD AND THEREFORE THE ENTIRE QURAN IS NOT THE WORDS/TEACHINGS OF GOD

The AntiGod Allah in his infinite wisdom and mercy decided that the sexual pleasure of sex with baby Muslim girls should not only be reserved for his prophet but be enjoyed by all Muslim men.. He therefore created verse 65.4.

No normal, rational, moral human being can believe that God would ever have created Verse 65.4. No God would ever allow the marriage and divorcing of little girls. Verse 65.4 is so evil, so immoral, so outrageous, so corrupt – God authorizing the rape and molestation of young girls – GOD AS A PEDIPHILE MONSTER. No such God exists. The PEDIPHILLE MONSTER is Allah (the AntiGod.) But since Allah never existed - the pedophile monster is Muhammad.

God as Moral Perfection is the protector of children. He would never sanction the abuse of a child. Again, the very essence of a God of MORAL PERFECTION IS MORAL PERFECTION. GOD IS NOT AN IRRATIONAL, IMMORAL, EVIL, BEING. IF GOD IS IRRATIONAL, IMMORAL, EVIL THEN GOD IS NOT MORAL PERFECTION AND THEREFORE, SINCE GOD CANNOT BE MORAL IMPERFECTION AN IRRATIONAL, IMMORAL, EVIL GOD IS NOT GOD.

As we have demonstrated repeatedly, in order for the Quran to be the word/teachings of God - every word - every teaching must be Moral Perfection - the morally perfect words and teachings of a God of Moral Perfection. If only one word is not Moral Perfection then the entire Quran is not the word/ teachings of God. Quran 65.4 is not Moral Perfection to say the least. It is an immoral, brutal, heartless, evil teaching of an immoral, brutal, heartless, evil, AntiGod - Allah. Quran 65.4 is so evil, so immoral that it must be rejected without equivocation. Therefore, repeating again - the entire Quran is not the word/teachings of God but the word/teachings of Allah (the AntiGod) - the word/teachings of Muhammad- who is the antiGod of Islam – the anti religion.

VERSE 65.4 IS SO EVIL - SUCH AN AFFRONT TO GOD – SUCH A GREAT SIN AGAINST GOD – THE RAPE AND MOLESTATION OF LITTLE GIRLS – ALLAH THE MONSTER ANTI GOD – AS TO BE UNSPEAKABLE. For detailed analysis of the immoral horror of Baby Aisha marriage to Muhammad go to http://islamreform.net/new-page-68

CHAPTER FIFTEEN

WHERE IS THE OUTRAGE

CRUELITY, TORTURE

In Islam's Own Writings: Muhammad, the Most Merciful Prophet

In Islam, Muhammad, the apostle of Allah, was the most merciful human being ever born as says the Quran: "And We have not sent you except as a mercy to mankind" (21:107).

Both Muhammad and Allah (the AntiGod) showed their mercy to Kafirs by murdering, torturing, terrorizing and raping them as holy duties in Islam. As explained over and over previously, if Muslims kill or are killed in performing these holy acts, then Allah guarantees them accession to a paradise filled with eternal sexual delights.

During his life-time, Muhammad meted out such merciful treatments to the first Muslims, who dared criticize him, or who in his opinion were hypocrites in their worship or committed adultery or fornication. The full wrath of merciful Muhammad and his Allah was directed against these deviants of Islam.

The merciful prophet had Muslims tortured, children beaten and families burnt alive in their homes for not fulfilling prayer duties, homosexuals and apostates murdered, alcoholics beaten, thieves' hands chopped off, adulterers stoned to death, and fornicators lashed.

When murdering adulterous women, the merciful prophet used to have them buried in a hole covering up to the breasts, then mercifully stoned until their life extinguished.

Following, in Islam's own words/writings, are examples of Muhammad, the most merciful man who ever lived on earth.

TORTURE

Hands Must Be Cut Off For Theft

The Quran says:

5:38 "Cut off the hands of thieves, whether they are male or female, as punishment for what they have done-a deterrent from God: God is almighty and wise." 39 "But if anyone repents after his wrongdoing and makes amends, God will accept his repentance: God is most forgiving and merciful. (Haleem)"

      As Moral Perfection, God is all pure mercy. God is all pure compassion. God is all pure forgiveness.
      Commanding that hands be cut off for stealing is draconian punishment that does not fit the crime. In fact, there is no crime imaginable that gives us the right to cut off any human body part. Not murder. Not rape. No crime. To leave a human being a cripple for life is cruelty beyond comprehension. How can a person earn a living without the use of both hands? To leave someone an amputee cripple depending on begging to survive is ridiculous. This is barbarism belonging to the dark ages of humanity. Quran 5:38 is not a moral teaching of a God of Moral Perfection.

Volume 8, Book 81, Number 779:

Narrated 'Aisha: "The Quraish people became very worried about the Makhzumiya lady who had committed theft. They said, "Nobody can speak (in favor of the lady) to Allah's Apostle and nobody dares do that except Usama who is the favorite of Allah's Apostle. " When Usama spoke to Allah's Apostle about that matter, Allah's Apostle said, "Do you intercede (with me) to violate one of the legal punishment of Allah?" Then he got up and addressed the people, saying, "O people! The nations before you went astray because if a noble person committed theft, they used to leave him, but if a weak person among them committed theft, they used to inflict the legal punishment on him. By Allah, if Fatima, the daughter of Muhammad committed theft, Muhammad will cut off her hand.!"

Volume 8, Book 81, Number 780:

Narrated 'Aisha: The Prophet said, "The hand should be cut off for stealing something that is worth a quarter of a Dinar or more."

Muhammad Ordered Feet And Hands Cut Off And Eyes Burnt Out, And Left To Suffer A Horrendous Death

From Sahih Bukhari, 1.234

Narrated Abu Qilaba: Anas said, "Some people of 'Ukl or 'Uraina tribe came to Medina and its climate did not suit them. So the Prophet ordered them to go to the herd of (Milch) camels and to drink their milk and urine (as a medicine). So they went as directed and after they became healthy, they killed the shepherd of the Prophet and drove away all the camels. The news reached the Prophet early in the morning and he sent (men) in their pursuit and they were captured and brought at noon. He then ordered to cut their hands and feet (and it was done), and their eyes were branded with heated pieces of iron. They were put in 'Al-Harra' and when they asked for water, no water was given to them." Abu Qilaba said, "Those people committed theft and murder, became infidels after embracing Islam and fought against Allah and His Apostle."

Beat The Children If They Do Not Pray

First, children are to be beaten if they refuse to pray after they reach the age of 10: Sunan Abu-Dawud Book-2 Book 2, Number 0495:

Narrated Abdullah ibn Amr ibn al-'As:

The Apostle of Allah (peace be upon him) said: "Command your children to pray when they become seven years old, and beat them for it (prayer) when they become ten years old; and arrange their beds (to sleep) separately."

Burnt Alive For Missing Prayers

Muhammad was so merciful that he instructed his followers to burn people alive who missed prayers according to Sahih Bukhari hadith.

Volume 1, Book 11, Number 617:

Narrated Abu Huraira: Allah's Apostle said," By Him in Whose Hand my soul is I was about to order for collecting fire-wood (fuel) and then order Someone to pronounce the Adhan for the prayer and then order someone to lead the prayer then I would go from behind and burn the houses of men who did not present themselves for the (compulsory congregational) prayer. By Him, in Whose Hands my soul is, if anyone of them had known that he would get a bone covered with good meat or two (small) pieces of meat present in between two ribs, he would have turned up for the 'Isha' prayer."

Volume 1, Book 11, Number 626:

Narrated Abu Huraira: The Prophet said," No prayer is harder for the hypocrites than the Fajr and the 'Isha' prayers and if they knew the reward for these prayers at their respective times, they would certainly present themselves (in the mosques) even if they had to crawl." The Prophet added," Certainly I decided to order the Mu'adh-dhin (call-maker) to pronounce Iqama and order a man to lead the prayer and then take a fire flame to burn all those who had not left their houses so far for the prayer along with their houses."

Homosexuals Are To Be Killed

Ibn Abbas, Muhammad's cousin and highly reliable transmitter of hadith, reports the following about early Islam and Muhammad's punishment of homosexuals:

"... If you find anyone doing as Lot's people did, kill the one who does it, and the one to whom it is done." (Abu Dawud no. 4447)

This hadith passage says that homosexuals should be burned alive or have wall pushed on them:

Ibn Abbas and Abu Huraira reported God's messenger as saying, "Accursed is he who does what Lot's people did." In a version . . . on the authority of Ibn Abbas it says that Ali [Muhammad's cousin and son-in-law] had two people burned and that Abu Bakr [Muhammad's chief companion] had a wall thrown down on them. (Mishkat, vol. 1, p. 765, Prescribed Punishments).

Apostates Must Be Murdered

Apostates, who leave a religion like Islam, such as Salman Rushdie, are supposed to be killed according to the Quran, the hadith, and later legal rulings. Sahih Bukhari 9:83:17: Narrated 'Abdullah:
Allah's Apostle said, "The blood of a Muslim who confesses that none has the right to be worshipped but Allah and that I am His Apostle, cannot be shed except in three cases: In Qisas for murder, a married person who commits illegal sexual intercourse and the one who reverts from Islam (apostate) and leaves the Muslims."

Stoned to Death

Narrated Abu Huraira and Zaid bin Khalid Al-Juhani:

"A bedouin came and said, "O Allah's Apostle! Judge between us according to Allah's Laws." His opponent got up and said, "He is right. Judge between us according to Allah's Laws." The bedouin said, "My son was a laborer working for this man, and he committed illegal sexual intercourse with his wife. The people told me that my son should be stoned to death; so, in lieu of that, I paid a ransom of one hundred sheep and a slave girl to save my son. Then I asked the learned scholars who said, "Your son has to be lashed one-hundred lashes and has to be exiled for one year." The Prophet said, "No doubt I will judge between you according to Allah's Laws. The slave-girl and the sheep are to go back to you, and your son will get a hundred lashes and one year exile." He then addressed somebody, "O Unais! go to the wife of this (man) and stone her to death" So, Unais went and stoned her to death."

Volume 7, Book 63, Number 196:

Narrated Abu Huraira: "A man from Bani Aslam came to Allah's Apostle while he was in the mosque and called (the Prophet) saying, "O Allah's Apostle! I have committed illegal sexual intercourse." On that the Prophet turned his face from him to the other side, whereupon the man moved to the side towards which the Prophet had turned his face, and said, "O Allah's Apostle! I have committed illegal sexual intercourse." The Prophet turned his face (from him) to the other side whereupon the man moved to the side towards which the Prophet had turned his face, and repeated his statement. The Prophet turned his face (from him) to the other side again. The man moved again (and repeated his statement) for the fourth time. So when the man had given witness four times against himself, the Prophet called him and said, "Are you insane?" He replied, "No." The Prophet then said (to his companions), "Go and stone him to death." The man was a married one. Jabir bin 'Abdullah Al-Ansari said: I was one of those who stoned him. We stoned him at the Musalla ('Id praying place) in Medina. When the stones hit him with their sharp edges, he fled, but we caught him at Al-Harra and stoned him till he died."

Volume 8, Book 82, Number 803:

Narrated Ash-Sha'bi: "from 'Ali when the latter stoned a lady to death on a Friday. 'Ali said, "I have stoned her according to the tradition of Allah's Apostle."

Volume 8, Book 82, Number 813:

Narrated Ibn 'Abbas: "When Ma'iz bin Malik came to the Prophet (in order to confess), the Prophet said to him, "Probably you have only kissed (the lady), or winked, or looked at her?" He said, "No, O Allah's Apostle!" The Prophet said, using no euphemism, "Did you have sexual intercourse with her?" The narrator added: At that, (i.e. after his confession) the Prophet ordered that he be stoned (to death)."

From Sahih Muslim

Book 017, Number 4191: "Ubada b. as-Samit reported: Allah's Messenger (may peace be upon him) as saying: Receive (teaching) from me, receive (teaching) from me. Allah has ordained a way for those (women). When an unmarried male commits adultery with an unmarried female (they should receive) one hundred lashes and banishment for one year. And in case of married male committing adultery with a married female, they shall receive one hundred lashes and be stoned to death."

Book 017, Number 4194:

"'Abdullah b. 'Abbas reported that 'Umar b. Khattab sat on the pulpit of Allah's Messenger (may peace be upon him) and said: Verily Allah sent Muhammad (may peace be upon him) with truth and He sent down the Book upon him, and the verse of stoning was included in what was sent down to him. We recited it, retained it in our memory and understood it. Allah's Messenger (may peace be upon him) awarded the punishment of stoning to death (to the married adulterer and adulteress) and, after him, we also awarded the punishment of stoning, I am afraid that with the lapse of time, the people (may forget it) and may say: We do not find the punishment of stoning in the Book of Allah, and thus go astray by abandoning this duty prescribed by Allah. Stoning is a duty laid down in Allah's Book for married men and women who commit adultery when proof is established, or it there is pregnancy, or a confession."

Rape Sanctioned By God

Sunan Abu Dawud: Abu Sa'id al-Khudri said: The Apostle of Allah (may peace be upon him) sent a military expedition to Awtas on the occasion of the battle of Hunain. They met their enemy and fought with them. They defeated them and took them captives. Some of the Companions of the Apostle of Allah (may peace be upon him) were reluctant to have intercourse with the female captives in the presence of their husbands who were unbelievers. So Allah, the Exalted, send down the Qur'anic verse: "And all married women (are forbidden) unto you save those (captives) whom your right hand possess."[Surah 4:24] ...Sunan Abu Dawud, Book V, Chapter 711, Number 2150

What kind of savages could commit such barbarism – barbarism sanctioned and indeed ordered by the greatest savage of the universe Allah (the AntiGod.) and his monster messanger. To truly understand the sheer barbarism of this barbarism go to page xxix and re-read the Hadith of the poor pregnant woman stoned to death in the presence of her newborn baby.after giving birth. **WHERE IS THE OUTRAGE?**

These are teachings and acts of the most merciful human being and the prophet of Islam, who was guided 24/7 by the Islamic deity, Allah (the AntiGod).

And forget not, these were what Muhammad meted out to his own followers. How merciful could his actions towards the kafirs be?

For teachings of Muhammad's moral depravity go to:
http://www.islamreform.net/new-page-19.htm
http://www.islamreform.net/new-page-26.htm

CHAPTER SIXTEEN

WHERE IS THE OUTRAGE

ALLAH IS A BARBARIC BARBARIAN

Adultery and fornication must be punished by flogging with a hundred stripes

24:2 "The woman and the man guilty of adultery or fornication, - flog each of them with a hundred stripes: Let not compassion move you in their case, in a matter prescribed by God, if ye believe in God and the Last Day: and let a party of the Believers witness their punishment."

This verse leaves no other option for Muslims who believe in the divine origin of the Quran. It specifically says they must not have mercy on people who have committed adultery or fornication, and that this brutal punishment of 100 lashes is "prescribed by God." However, since other verses in the Quran specifically allow men to have sex slaves, the horrible crime of serial rape against a non-Muslim woman is not considered adultery or fornication and would not be punished if the woman is considered a concubine.

No God would ever teach 24.2. To beat someone with 100 lashes is barbaric. Allah (the AntiGod) is a barbarian. No God would ever state "flog each of them with a hundred stripes: Let not compassion move you in their case, in a matter prescribed by God, if ye believe in God and the Last Day: and let a party of the Believers witness their punishment."

No God would ever write - "Let not compassion move you in their case". Stating these words as God's words is evil and repugnant. As we have already demonstrated - A God of Moral Perfection is pure mercy and compassion. God is all mercy and all compassion. He would never allow anyone to beat any other human being - not with a whip, not with a stick, not even with a toothbrush.

No God would ever speak - " in a matter prescribed by God, if ye believe in God and the Last Day" to force someone to put aside his natural human feelings of compassion - do it because I God have prescribed it - no matter what your own personal feelings of mercy may be - do it if you believe in Me and the Last day. This is truly evil - commit a brutal evil act to prove you believe in Me. God would never order anyone to commit evil - to go against what he knows in his heart to be morally wrong.

You tell me what kind of person could flog a woman 100 times and not be an immoral brute. For God to force someone to commit this evil is truly evil incarnate.

You tell me what kind of barbaric, barbarian God would be to order the whipping of a human being.

"let a party of the Believers witness their punishment." Not only brutality flog but do it in front of Believers to make sure, they get the message. God wrote these words. God spoke this teaching. Who can believe in such immoral nonsense?

No normal, rational human being can believe that God would ever utter Quran 24:2.

Quran 24.2 is not the word or the teaching of God. It is the word and teaching of Allah (the AntiGod). Allah is the AntiGod of pure hate – a brutal barbarian without mercy, without compassion. But of course this teaching is not from Allah – since Allah never existed. The brutal, barbaric, barbarian – the evil mind that produced this teaching is Muhammad.

WHY QURAN 24:2 IS NOT THE WORD/TEACHING OF GOD AND THEREFORE THE ENTIRE QURAN IS NOT THE WORDS/TEACHINGS OF GOD

As has been shown - A God of Moral Perfection is the very essence of pure love. The very existence of God is pure love. If God is not the embodiment of pure love then God does not exist. God has never spoken one violent word. If God spoke just one word of violence - God would no longer be Moral Perfection and therefore, no longer God. God is not a violent being. God is the very essence of non-violence. If God committed just one act of violence or ordered an act of violence be committed, he would no longer be Moral Perfection and therefore, no longer God.

Quran 24.2 is not Moral Perfection, It is a hateful, violent, brutal, heartless, immoral, evil teaching of an immoral, brutal, hateful, violent, heartless, evil, barbarian AntiGod - Allah. Therefore, stating again for the countless time - the entire Quran is not the word/teachings of God and Islam is fraudulent. Although we are stating and re-stating the morally obvious in this book, and presenting teachings enmass, we must continue to state "Quran is not the word/teachings of God and Islam is fraudulent" to expose and destroy without question the propaganda that the Quran is the divine word of God, Islam is a religion of peace and Muhammad – the prophet of mercy and peace.

CHAPTER SEVENTEEN

OWNING SLAVES ARE ETERNAL LAWS OF GOD

No man is the property of any other man - God is not a slaver. All human beings are created equal. All races are created equal. God does not wish that any human be a slave. No one person is the lesser of the other. Slavery is one of the vilest institutions ever created by man. Slavery is an obscenity to God. All human beings (no matter their race, color, creed, ethnic origins) have the full right to protection of their human rights and human dignity. To use religion to spread hate against other races and other religions in places of worship, employing television or any other medium, teaching hatred to young in schools - this is evil incarnate. To use religion as an instrument of persecution and violence stands as an affront to the very concept of a God of pure love and pure mercy. If God is a racist, believes in persecution, slavery and violence then God is immoral and therefore, no longer God.

Slavery is one of the most evil, vile institutions ever devised by man. To allow one human being to be the property of another human being stands against everything that mankind stands for. Human beings being bred as property to be bought and sold, people being reduced to the status of cattle, beasts of burden to work the fields, toil underground in mines, clean the master's home, cater to the master's wife and children is the very essence of inhumanity.

Now to take man's creation of slavery and turn it into an institution sanctioned by ETERNAL LAWS OF GOD – is so outrageous as to defy reason. God allowing the enslavement of kafirs is the total essence of immorality. For God to share 20% of the proceeds from the sale of women and children into slavery as an eternal law of God is so far outside the realm of rationality that anyone who can believe in such evil is evil themselves.

Following are some of the ETERNAL SLAVERY LAWS OF GOD. All these laws are not the teachings of God – indeed these teachings blaspheme against the very essence of God - the Quran is not the word/teachings of God – Islam is pure evil.

Sura 2 (The Cow) Verse 178

Quran 2.178: "O you who believe! retaliation is prescribed for you in the matter of the slain, the free for the free, and the slave for the slave, and the female for the female, but if any remission is made to any one by his (aggrieved) brother, then prosecution (for the bloodwit) should be made according to usage, and payment should be made to him in a good manner; this is an alleviation from your Lord and a mercy; so whoever exceeds the limit after this he shall have a painful chastisement."

Retaliation for murder and other crimes was sanctioned by Arabian usage and accepted by Muhammad. Here it is said that a free (man) can be killed for the murder of a free (man) and similarly for a (free) woman and a slave. The mention of these three categories quite casually indicates that slavery is accepted along with the other two categories as an acceptable state for a human being. What is not clear is whether the person put to death is the person responsible for the killing. While this may be true of free persons this is not necessarily true of slaves. Thus if a slave is killed then it is not the killer of the slave that has to be killed but a slave of the killer! What this shows is that slaves are treated as pure merchandise of the slave owner. If a slave is killed then it is a loss to its owner and the retaliation for this is the killing of a slave belonging to the offender. Of course the slave killed may be quite innocent.

Of course it may be argued that the free people may have been responsible for the crime but to a kill an innocent slave for the crime of his master is truly a perversion of justice. The casual way in which slaves as a category of humans are mentioned along with free men and women in the application of this law shows that Muhammad completely accepted the slave status of humans to be a perfectly normal status.

Again, as a human being I have absolutely no right to own another human being. No God would ever teach "the free for the free, and the slave for the slave, and the female for the female". There is no free, slave, female that belong to any man. The "free" possess their own humanity. They are free from the very moment of their conception. No human can ever be born into slavery, become the property of a Muslim and then be granted a non-slavery status of the "free" later. This is truly criminal. There is no such human category as "slave". Slavery is an abomination against God. You kill one of my slaves and I'll kill one of your slaves. No God would ever speak or grant any such right. The same for "female." No woman is the property of any man. This teaching is immoral depravity and a sin against God. All these teachings of slavery in this chapter are evil. Islam renounces God.

Sura 24 (The Light), Verse 31

24.31: "And say to the believing women that they cast down their looks and guard their private parts and do not display their ornaments except what appears thereof, and let them wear their head-coverings over their bosoms, and not display their ornaments except to their husbands or their fathers, or the fathers of their husbands, or their sons, or the sons of their husbands, or their brothers, or their brothers' sons, or their sisters' sons, or their women, or those whom their right hands possess, or the male servants not having need (of women), or the children who have not attained knowledge of what is hidden of women; and let them not strike their feet so that what they hide of their ornaments may be known; and turn to Allah all of you, O believers! so that you may be successful."

This is the famous Sura enjoining the veiling of women. Amongst those before whom the women need not be covered are slaves (who under included in those that "the right hand possess" a term that we have already seen is used throughout in the Quran as a synonym for slaves). This is probably because slaves were such a common occurrence in Muslim households that they are taken for granted and women need not use the dress code prescribed for outside wear while they are at home even in front of their slaves.

Sura 23 (The Believers), Verses 1-6

23.1-6: "Successful indeed are the believers, Who are humble in their prayers, And who keep aloof from what is vain, And who are givers of poor-rate, And who guard their private parts, Except before their mates or those whom their right hands possess, for they surely are not blameable."

This is the Sura which gives the slave owner the right of sexual access to u\his female slaves. The term "guarding the private parts" is a synonym for sexual intercourse.

Sura 24 (The Light), Verse 32

24.32: "And marry those among you who are single and those who are fit among your male slaves and your female slaves; if they are needy, Allah will make them free from want out of His grace; and Allah is Ample-giving, Knowing."

This is said to sanction marriages of slaves with slaves and slaves with free persons (including the owner). Owners did not usually marry slaves as they could use them for sexual purposes at will. This dispensation has been used to make slaves marry other slaves. In Islam a child born to a slave couple also is a slave from birth, so this verse gives a great incentive to slave owners to bredslaves. This is another obnoxious aspect of Islamic slavery. Whatever be the other circumstances in which people are made into slaves to make a new-born infant a slave is one of the most cruel and callous. Ye this did not evoke a protest from the Prophet and has been extensively resorted to by Muslims.

Sura 16 (The Bee), verse 75

16.75 "Allah sets forth a parable: (consider) a slave, the property of another, (who) has no power over anything, and one whom We have granted from Ourselves a goodly sustenance so he spends from it secretly and openly; are the two alike? (All) praise is due to Allah!"

This is one of the clearest instances where the institution of slavery is justified in the Quran as a divine dispensation. It deserves close scrutiny. This "parable" contrasts two people a slave who is owned by another and is completely powerless and a freeman on whom Allah has granted "a goodly sustenance" which he can spend openly or secretly as he pleases (perhaps acquiring slaves for himself). Since Allah claims for himself the position of the granter of all benefits (or lack of them) both the freeman's fortune and the slave's misfortune are ultimately determined by Allah. By his rhetorical question "Are the two alike?" Muhammad is actually justifying the inequality between the slave and the freeman as if it was a natural thing. Thus a Muslim will have no compunctions or qualms in employing and exploiting slaves (subject only to any conditions that Muhammad may have imposed) because it is what Allah has ordained and "all praise is due to Allah".

Sura 33 (The Clans), Verse 50

33.50: "O Prophet! surely We have made lawful to you your wives whom you have given their dowries, and those [slaves] whom your right hand possesses out of those whom Allah has given to you as prisoners of war, and the daughters of your paternal uncles and the daughters of your paternal aunts, and the daughters of your maternal uncles and the daughters of your maternal aunts who fled with you; and a believing woman if she gave herself to the Prophet, if the Prophet desired to marry her -- specially for you, not for the (rest of) believers; We know what We have ordained for them concerning their wives and those whom their right hands possess in order that no blame may attach to you; and Allah is Forgiving, Merciful".

As stated before - here, as elsewhere, the term "possessions of the right hand" mean slaves. It is expressly stated that Muhammad's slaves are given to him by Allah himself to be taken out of his share of the captives in war. It also records the special dispensation given to Muhammad, not available to other Muslims, in the number of wives

Sura 39 (The Companions), Verses 29

39.29: "Allah sets forth an example: There is a slave in whom are (several) partners differing with one another, and there is another slave wholly owned by one man. Are the two alike in condition? (All) praise is due to Allah. Nay! most of them do not know."

The example set out here compares joint ownership of a slave by many owners and the single ownership by one person. Muhammad asks rhetorically whether the two cases are the same. Of course they are not and it is clear that Muhammad prefers single ownership. In fact this is why he established the rule that after a military campaign the captives were allocated to each of his soldiers individually not collectively, with himself keeping a fifth of the captives as his personal slaves.

Sura 70 (The Ways of Ascent) verses 29-35

70: 29-35 "And those who guard their private parts, Except in the case of their wives or those whom their right hands possess -- for these surely are not to be blamed, But he who seeks to go beyond this, these it is that go beyond the limits -- And those who are faithful to their trusts and their covenant And those who are upright in their testimonies, And those who keep a guard on their prayer, Those shall be in gardens, honored."

These verses are similar to Sura 23.93-96 and gives the right to slave owners to have sexual relation with female slaves. The only difference is that the earlier reference may leave some doubt as to whether both males and female slaves are meant. These verses clearly show that it is only female slaves that are meant.
A God of Moral Perfection would never permit slavery. The ownership, raping and murder of human beings as chattel sanctioned by God are so abhorrent that it defies all reason. All these teachings are very essence of evil. Again, Islam is an immoral, bottomless, black hole. **WHERE IS THE OUTRAGE AGAINST ISLAM?** For article titled; Islam, Slavery and Rape go to: http://www.islamreform.net/new-page-62.htm

CHAPTER EIGHTEEN

THE QURAN IS A BOOK FILLED WITH HATE

All hate is abhorrent to God. As Moral Perfection, God has never spoken a word of hate. As the essence of pure love, as a being whose very existence is pure love God is totally incapable of hate. If God is not pure love then God is not God. If God had just one hateful thought, spoke just one hateful word, committed/ordered just one hateful act, then God would no longer be Moral Perfection but since God cannot be immoral imperfection and still be God a hateful God is no longer God. Again, ALL teachings of violence, hate, war, extermination, genocide, retaliation, terror, torture, maiming, rape, slavery, inequality, intolerance, in any holy book are not the word/teachings of God but the word/teachings of man.

What can we say that has not already been said about this ridiculous and very dangerous ideology? Allah hates kafirs, Christians, Jews, women, children, families, apostates of Islam. He is one AntiGod of pure hate. Let us do a short comparison between the three great monsters of history – the Fuehrer Adolf Hitler, the Fuehrer Prophet Muhammad and Allah (the AntiGod.)

HITLER: THE FINAL SOLUTION OF THE JEWISH QUESTION AND MUHAMMAD: THE FIRST, "FINAL SOLUTION" OF THE JEWISH AND CHRISTIAN QUESTION OF ARABIA

MEIN KAMPF VERUS THE QURAN

As stated previously, before there was a Hitler, Mein Kampf, the SS, concentration camps and final solution of the Jewish question, there was Muhammad, the Quran, the SS Jihadists and the first, final solution – the murder and forced exile of Jews/Christians from Arabia. Repeating these two paramount teachings of Muhammad ordering the mass murder of Jews:

"the Apostle of Allah said, 'Kill any Jew that falls into your power." Ibn Ishaq, Siratul Rasul, v. 553

Bukhari Volume 4, Book 52, Number 176 Narrated 'Abdullah bin 'Umar: Allah's Apostle said, "You (i.e. Muslims) will fight with the Jews till some of them will hide behind stones. The stones will (betray them) saying, 'O 'Abdullah (i.e. slave of Allah)! There is a Jew hiding behind me; so kill him.' "

HITLER AND THE "FINAL SOLUTION" OF THE JEWISH QUESTION

In any process of extermination and mass murder of human beings, the first step is to blame them for all of societies ills, demonize the selected victims as dangerous, then as the enemy, then dehumanize and reduce them to the status of sub-humans - evil creatures – that must be destroyed. Once human beings are robbed of their humanity – mass murder becomes the final solution.
Following is just a very small sample of Hitler's teachings demonizing the Jews and laying the intellectual foundation for their extermination.

HITLER'S HATRED OF THE JEWS

"The struggle for world domination will be fought entirely between us, between Germans and Jews. All else is facade and illusion. Behind England stands Israel, and behind France, and behind the United States. Even when we have driven the Jew out of Germany, he remains our world enemy." - Rauschning, Hitler Speaks, p. 234

"The Ten Commandments have lost their validity. Conscience is a Jewish invention, it is a blemish like circumcision." - Rauschning, Hitler Speaks, p. 220

- "If only one country, for whatever reason, tolerates a Jewish family in it, that family will become the germ center for fresh sedition. If one little Jewish boy survives without any Jewish education, with no synagogue and no Hebrew school, it [Judaism] is in his soul. Even if there had never been a synagogue or a Jewish school or an Old Testament, the Jewish spirit would still exist and exert its influence. It has been there from the beginning and there is no Jew, not a single one, who does not personify it." - Robert Wistrich, Hitler's Apocalypse, p. 122; from a conversation with Croatian Foreign Minister General Kvaternik, July 21, 1941

"The internal expurgation of the Jewish spirit is not possible in any platonic way. For the Jewish spirit as the product of the Jewish person. Unless we expel the Jewish people. Unless we expel the Jewish people soon, they will have judaized our people within a very short time." - Jackel, Hitler's Worldview, p. 52; from a speech at Nuremberg, January 13, 1923

- "The Jew has always been a people with definite racial characteristics and never a religion." -Adolf Hitler (Mein Kampf)

"If we consider how greatly he has sinned against the masses in the course of the centuries, how he has squeezed and sucked the blood again and again; if furthermore, we consider how the people gradually learned to hate him for this, and ended up by regarding his existence as nothing but punishment of Heaven for the other peoples, we can understand how hard this shift must be for the Jew." - Adolf Hitler (Mein Kampf)

"But even more: all at once the Jew also becomes liberal and begins to rave about the necessary progress of mankind." -Adolf Hitler (Mein Kampf)

'The Jew almost never marries a Christian woman; it is the Christian who marries a Jewess." -Adolf Hitler (Mein Kampf)

- " the personification of the devil as the symbol of all evil assumes the living shape of the Jew.' -Adolf Hitler (Mein Kampf)

- " With satanic joy in his face, the black-haired Jewish youth lurks in wait for the unsuspecting girl whom he defiles with his blood, thus stealing her from her people." -Adolf Hitler (Mein Kampf)

"And so he [the Jew] advances on his fatal road until another force comes forth to oppose him, and in a mighty struggle hurls the heaven-stormer back to Lucifer." -Adolf Hitler (Mein Kampf)

Hitler's final solution was the concentration camps and the industrialization of mass murder.

MUHAMMAD AND THE FIRST, "FINAL SOLUTION" OF THE JEWISH/CHRISTIAN QUESTION OF ARABIA

Unlike Hitler who had a very deep hatred of Jews as a young man, Muhammad spent the early part of his life (13 years) trying to convince the Jews and Christians that he was the final prophet of Allah and that his Allah was the one and same God that the Jews and Christians worshipped. The Jews and Christians realized that he was a false prophet and totally rejected Muhammad and his Allah. It was after this rejection that Muhammad turned to sheer hatred.

As stated earlier - having failed as a preacher, Muhammad fled to Medina. It was here that Muhammad re–invented his Allah. Gone was the Allah of peace that preached tolerance and in was the Allah – the AntiGod of murder, extermination, terror, torture, looting. Repeating, in the new reformed Islam, deceit, torture, murder, assassination, massacre, genocide, pillage, robbery, enslavement and rape are halal (legal) acts, deserving of paradise, as long as they were perpetrated on kafirs. The new Allah permitted polygamy, temporary marriages (muta), pedophilia, marriage with adopted son's wives, wife beating, and sex with slave girls.

In Medina, the teachings of the Quran exploded into hatred and rage against Jews, Christians and all other kafirs. The hatred of Muhammad and his Allah was directed against the peoples of the book – Jews and Christians, who had dared to reject his prophethood. Because of their rejection, they remained a direct challenge to the authority of Muhammad and the legitimacy of Islam. Due to the danger posed by the peoples of the book – their destruction became imperative. The first, "final solution" of the Jews and Christians – their murder and mass exile from Arabia, the looting of their rich towns, the rape and enslavement of their women by Muhammad and his Allah was set in motion.

MUHAMMAD'S TEACHINGS OF PURE HATE FROM THE HADITH

MASS EXILE FROM SAUDI ARABIA

Book 019, Number 4366:

"It has been narrated by 'Umar b. al-Khattib that he heard the Messenger of Allah (may peace be upon him) say: "I will expel the Jews and Christians from the Arabian Peninsula and will not leave any but Muslim." [This single sahi hadith tells everything about Islamic intolerance]

Bukhari Volume 4, Book 52, Number 288

Narated By Said bin Jubair : Ibn 'Abbas said, ..."On Thursday the illness of Allah's Apostle was aggravated and he said, "Fetch me writing materials so that I may have something written to you after which you will never go astray." ...The Prophet on his death-bed, gave three orders saying, "Expel the pagans from the Arabian Peninsula..."

     Is it a rational, reasonable. normal, moral human thought of a rational, reasonable, normal, moral person that 700 years after Christ and his teachings of peace and love that allowed the peoples of the Roman Empire to embrace Christianity throughout the Middle East, Turkey, Iraq, Syria, Egypt, North Africa that God would send another prophet who after 13 years of trying to convince Jews/Christians of his prophecy by teachings of peace would then turn to teachings of extermination and set them in motion by raising armies to terrorize, conquer and make slaughter in the land?

     If anyone can believe that God would have as His prophet – such an evil man who ordered extermination and genocide of entire peoples, can believe that such a God exists who would order and celebrate such slaughter, then they have forsaken God and embraced evil.

MUHAMMAD'S TEACHINGS OF HATE FROM THE QURAN

     Just as Hitler demonized the Jews and called for their destruction in Mein Kampf so to Allah (the AntiGod) dehumanized the Jews and demanded their total destruction in the Quran.

     As described earlier as part of the first, final solution, Muhammad conquered the Jewish settlement of Banu Qurayzah and ordered that all Jewish men be beheaded and their women raped and sold into slavery. The SS companions with Muhammad's assistance beheaded 600 to 900 Jews. To separate young Jewish men from young Jewish boys, the difference between keeping the young Jewish boys heads attached to their bodies while beheading the young Jewish men, Muhammad in his infinite genius and mercy had his Muslim men SS killers pull down the pants of these Jewish boys/men and behead only those who had pubic hair on their groin. 1400 years later, the German SS would separate Jews at the concentration camps into those able bodied to work and the weak to be gassed. Beheading or gassing – dead is dead.

     In order to do a comparison between the Quran and Mein Kampf, let us again review, the Quranic teachings that celebrated the great massacre and mass murder at Banu Qurayza. You tell me what is the difference between the Quran and Mein Kampf. If Jesus was the son of God then Hitler would certainly qualify as the second son of Allah (the AntiGod) Muhammad being the first son. Don't forget these teachings are the word of God and were written by God himself.

The Quran Celebrated The Massacre Of The Jews Of Banu Qurayza

Quran-33:25- "Allah turned back the unbelievers [Meccans and their allies] in a state of rage, having not won any good, and Allah spared the believers battle. Allah is, indeed, Strong and Mighty."

Quran-33:26- "And He brought those of the People of the Book [Jewish people of Banu Qurayza] who supported them from their fortresses and cast terror into their hearts, some of them you slew (beheaded) and some you took prisoners (captive)"

Quran-33:27- "And He made you heirs of their lands, their houses, and their goods, and of a land which ye had not frequented (before). And Allah has power over all things." [Merciful Allah asked Prophet Muhammad to confiscate entire properties of surrendered Jews]

Quran-8:67-" It is not for any prophet to have captives until he hath made slaughter in the land. Ye desire the lure of this world and Allah desireth (for you) the Hereafter, and Allah is Mighty, Wise." (Allah insisting Prophet to kill all the prisoners, and should not keep any surrendered prisoners alive until He (Prophet) occupied entire Arabia.

Quran- 8:17 "It is not ye who Slew them; it is God; when thou threwest a handful of dust, it was not Thy act, but God's….." (Allah said, the killing of surrendered soldiers were done by the wish of Allah)

As already discussed - Allah (the AntiGod) teaches raping sex slaves, selling women and children into slavery, killing people for their property and sharing 20% of the proceeds with God and keeping 80% of the booty for the holy killers.

But what of Hitler and the German SS robbing and looting the property of murdered Jews. When Hitler came to power, Jewish businesses, bank accounts and property were confiscated. Everything was seized from expensive paintings to exclusive furniture. Jewish women and children were stripped of their clothing, forced into slavery, and after slaughter in the ovens – gold teeth were extracted from their burnt out skulls. At the concentration camps Jewish women were raped and gang raped by the SS guards.

How dare we compare Hitler – a monster of history with the prophet Muhammad, the apostle of Peace, the prophet of God. The protype of human perfection. The most merciful man who ever existed?

Hitler was a brutal killer who showed absolutely no mercy to his Jewish victims. His SS murdered all Jews equally no matter their age or sex. 7 month old Jewish babies were pulled from their mother's arms and heads smashed into the ground. 7 months, 7 years, 14, 21, 51, 77 it didn't matter. All were forced to strip naked, march to dug out graves and stand at attention while SS executioners placed a gun to the back of their heads and blew their brains out. There was no mercy.

Muhammad was a true man of mercy. He valued Jewish women no matter their age as sex slaves. Rather then behead them, his SS were allowed to mercifully rape and gang rape them. If any of the SS did not want to keep any of the women as their sex slave then they were sold into slavery to be bred like cattle. Such was the mercy of the prophet. Indeed Muhammad set a divine example for all eternity for all Muslim men to copy by personally raping and then marrying young Jewish women of the Jewish men he murdered. This was a true prophet of God. This was no Hitler. The Fuehrer would never have permitted such a display of mercy.

Muhammad was a hands on Fuehrer who murdered Jewish men by personally chopping off their heads and raping his sex slaves.

The only difference between Muhammad and his Allah, and Hitler was that Muhammad created a God to give divine sanction to his great acts of evil. He wrapped up his evil in religious trappings.

What if Hitler had declared that God appeared to him and instructed that as his last, true prophet he must rid the world of all non-Aryan peoples to prevent the mongolization of the Aryan race? All believers in Hitler and his god - Aryan must bring war, death and destruction to the mongoloided races of the world. All non-Aryans peoples must be exterminated. The followers of Aryan and his prophet, Hitler demonstrated their holiness by praying 5 times a day, fastening one month/year, and going on pilgrimages at least once in their lifetime. Their women showed submission and obedience to Aryan and his SS holy men by covering up. We would categorically state that all followers of Hitler and his god Aryan were evil people. (Of course, all followers of Hitler and Hitler himself never pretended that his teachings were God inspired.)

Jesus taught "For what will it profit a man if he gains the whole world and forfeits his soul?" Both men sold their souls to evil for power and glory. Their male followers sacrificed their souls for promised riches, sex and power over their victims. If there is a hereafter, Muhammad/Hitler are together with their master Satan roasting in the oven of hell for all eternity. Unfortunately hundreds of millions of their male followers are burning with them. For teachings of intolerance go to: http://www.islamreform.net/new-page-11.htm

Anti-Jewish Hate Teachings in The Quran:

Mein Kampf is the word and teachings of Hitler. As has already been shown, ALL Muslims believe that the Quran is the word and teachings of God. The Quran is God talking to us – teaching us how to be better people, how to lead better victorious lives.

Such wonderful teachings of love and peace that only God could create fill the Quran like: 5.60 "God has cursed the Jews, transforming them into apes and swine and those who serve the devil." Isn't this a wonderful teaching to quote to your children around the kitchen table? Such noble wisdom to live their lives by.

Does any rational, reasonable, normal. moral person believe that Quran 5.60 is God speaking to us – imparting to us moral wisdom? "God cursed the Jews transforming them into apes and swine and those who serve the devil." The words "ape" and "swine" are evil words meant to dehumanize Jews, robbing them of their humanity. Jews are the lowest of the low. Apes and swine. No longer human. Sub-humans. Once deprived of their humanity, they can be killed with impunity just as apes and swine can be killed.

The Quran is no more the word/teaching of God then Mein Kampf is the word/teaching of God. You tell me the difference between the two books. There is none. Both books are books of pure hate that reflect the hateful souls and minds of their authors - Hitler and Muhammad. The Koran was the word and teachings of Muhammad. Mein Kampf was the word and teachings of Adolf Hitler. Both men who hated Jews with a passion. Both men who sought their total dehumanization and extermination from the history of humanity.

All of the teachings listed below are evil. None of these teachings are from God. These are the teachings that prepare the Muslim mind for genocide. I list them all here so you can understand the sheer hatred Muhammad had for the Jews. They dared reject his prophecy. They knew he was a false prophet. For more teachings of Jewish hate; http://www.islamreform.net/new-page-16.htm

2.61 Wretchedness and baseness were stamped on the Jews and they were visited with wrath from Allah.

2.65 And ye know of those of you who broke the Sabbath, how We said unto them: Be ye apes, despised and hated!

2:96 Jews are the greediest of all humankind. They'd like to live 1000 years. But they are going to hell.

4:160-1 For the wrongdoing Jews, Allah has prepared a painful doom.

4.16 And for the evildoing of the Jews, we have forbidden them from some good things that were previously permitted them.

5.59 Say: O People of the Scripture! Do ye blame us for aught else than that we believe in Allah and that which is revealed unto us and that which was revealed aforetime, and because most of you are evil-livers?

5.60 God has cursed the Jews, transforming them into apes and swine and those who serve the devil.

5.82 Indeed you will surely find that the most vehement of men in enmity to those who believe are the Jews and the polytheists.

7.166 So when they took pride in that which they had been forbidden, We said unto them: Be ye apes despised and loathed!

9.29 Fight against such of those have been given the Scriptures, Jews and Christians, as believe not in Allah nor the last Day.

9.30 The Jews say that Ezra is the son of Allah, and the Christians say the Messiah is the son of Allah. Allah attack them! How perverse they are!

9.34 Many of the rabbis and the monks devour the wealth of mankind and wantonly debar men from the way of Allah.

33:26 "And He brought those of the People of the Book [Jewish people of Banu Qurayza] who supported them from their fortresses and cast terror into their hearts, some of them you slew (beheaded) and some you took prisoners." (captive)

33:27 "And He made you heirs of their lands, their houses, and their goods, and of a land which ye had not frequented (before). And Allah has power over all things." [Merciful Allah asked Prophet Muhammad to confiscate entire properties of surrendered Jews]

62:5 A hypocritical Jew looks like an ass carrying books. Those who deny the revelations of Allah are ugly.

Again, it is important to understand that Islam is not anti Jewish. Islam is anti kafir – the Jews being just one category of kafirs (of course the most reviled of kafirs.) Allah hates all kafirs no matter their race or color.
Repeating, - how can any rational, reasonable, normal. moral person believe that God would have as his prophet a killer, a murderer, a terrorist who slaughtered human beings, had the pants of young terrified boys pulled down to

determine whether they lived or died, allowed the raping of women and young girls, sold the women/girls Muslims did not want as sex slaves into slavery, and took for himself young beautiful women to be his sex slaves?

How can any rational, reasonable, normal. moral person believe that God would celebrate such evil, heinous crimes with teachings for all eternity to be recorded in a holy book – the Quran?

How can any rational, reasonable, normal, moral person believe that God would share in the looting and pillaging of murdered Jew's property? God as the Mafia chieftain of Muhammad's Muslim crime family.

Again, these teachings are evil and not from God. They are the teachings of Allah (the AntiGod). The teachings of Muhammad. Since not one of these teachings is Moral Perfection, the Quran is not the word/teachings of God. To truly understand this very great evil, we need to reiterate that the Quran is not a holy book but a book of evil. Islam is the total and complete rejection of God, the total and complete rejection of all teachings of God. The teachings of the Quran are a very great sin and crime against God. It is a book that blasphemes against and makes a farce of everything God stands for. Islam is totally and completely fraudulent. **ISLAM IS EVIL IN THE NAME OF GOD.**

Take your pen right now and write the word ALLAH on a piece of paper, crumple the paper up and throw it into the trash can. That's where this evil being belongs. In the trash can to be taken out with all the other garbage to the historical dump to rot for all eternity.

Following From The Quran Are 55 Teachings Not Of Pure Love But of Pure Hate. Not The Teachings Of A God Of MORAL PERFECTION

Verses That Show Intolerance Of And Incite Violence Against Non-Muslims And Other Religions.

These teachings are listed enmass so you can understand that we are not cherry picking Islam picking out the odd worst one. As we have done with the teachings of Jihad and Jewish hatred, we list them all. It is mind numbing and nauseating to read thru them. Don't forget God wrote these wondrous words. Maybe you should wear shaded glasses to protect your eyes, so these beautiful words strung together into beautiful verses don't blind your eyes from the miraculous miracle that is the Quran.

Don't marry non-Muslims: 2:221 "Do not marry unbelieving women (idolate.rs), until they believe: A slave woman who believes is better than an unbelieving woman, even though she allures you. Nor marry (your girls) to unbelievers until they believe: A man slave who believes is better than an unbeliever, even though he allures you. Unbelievers do (but) beckon you to the Fire. But God beckons by His Grace to the Garden (of bliss) and forgiveness, and makes His Signs clear to mankind: That they may celebrate His praise."

3:24 "They [Christians and Jews] say: The Fire will not touch us save for a certain number of days. That which they used to invent hath deceived them regarding their religion." (The Fire will burn them forever.)

3.28 "Let believers not make friends with infidels in preference to the faithful. He that does this has nothing to hope for from God."

3:54 "Lord, we believe in Your revelations (the Torah and Gospels) and follow this Apostle (Jesus). Enroll us among the witnesses.' But the Christians contrived a plot and Allah did the same; but Allah's plot was the best."

3:56 "As for those disbelieving infidels, I will punish them with a terrible agony in this world and the next. They have no one to help or save them."

3.85 He that chooses a religion other than Islam... in the world to come he will be one of the lost.

3.118 Believers, do not make friends with anyone but your own people.

4.101 The unbelievers are your inveterate enemies.

4.156 "They denied the truth and uttered a monstrous falsehood against Mary. They declared, "We have put to death the Messiah Jesus, the son of Mary, the apostle of Allah." They did not kill him, nor did they crucify him, but they thought they did."

4:171 "O people of the Book (Christians), do not be fanatical in your faith, and say nothing but the truth about Allah. The Messiah who is Isa (Jesus), son of Mariam, was only a messenger of Allah, nothing more. He bestowed His Word on Mariam and His Spirit. So believe in Allah and say not Trinity for Allah is one Ilah (God)...far be it from His Glory to beget a son".

5.14 "With those who said they were Christians...we stirred among them enmity and hatred which shall endure until the day of Resurrection. "

5:37 "The (Christian) disbelievers will long to get out of the Fire, but never will they get out there from; and theirs will be an enduring torture."

5.51 "O you who believe! Take not the Jews and Christians for friends, they are friends one to another. He among you who takes them for friends is one of them."

5.72 "Unbelievers are those who say "God is the Messiah, the son of Mary"..Unbelievers are those who say: "God is one of three."

5:72 Christians will be burned in the Fire.

8.14 The scourge of the Fire awaits the unbelievers.

8.39 Make war on them until idolatry shall cease and God's religion shall reign supreme.

8:55 Surely the vilest of animals in Allah's sight are those who disbelieve.

8:71 "And if they intend to act unfaithfully towards you, so indeed they acted unfaithfully towards Allah before, but He GAVE YOU MASTERY OVER THEM."

9.28 "O you who believe! the idolaters are nothing but unclean, so they shall not approach the Sacred Mosque (Mecca) after this year; and if you fear poverty then Allah will enrich you out of His grace if He please; surely Allah is Knowing Wise."

9:31 "They have taken their doctors of law and their monks for lords besides Allah, and (also) the Messiah son of Marium and they were enjoined that they should serve one God only, there is no god but He; far from His glory be what they set up (with Him)."

9:32 "They desire to put out the light of Allah with their mouths, and Allah will not consent save to perfect His light, though the unbelievers are averse."

9:33 "He it is Who sent His Apostle with guidance and the religion of truth, that He might cause it to prevail over all religions, though the polytheists may be averse."

9:34 Give tiding of a painful doom to Christians and Jews.

9.39 If you do not fight he will punish you severely, and replace you with other men.

9.5 Slay the idolators wherever you find them...lie in ambush everywhere for them.

9.73 "Prophet, make war on the unbelievers and the hypocrites and deal rigorously with them . Hell shall be their home, an evil fate."

9:113 Don't pray for idolaters (not even for your family) after it is clear they are people of hell-fire.

16: 27-29 Disbelievers are evil and will dwell in hell forever.

16:94 Those who oppose Islam will face an awful doom.

18:52 Christians will cry out to Allah's "partners", but they won't hear them; Allah will send them to their doom.

19:35-37 Jesus was not the Son of God. Those who say he was (Christians) are going to hell.

20:127 Those who do not believe Allah's revelations will face doom in the Hereafter.

21:15 The people cried out for mercy, but Allah killed them anyway.

22:25 Allah will provide the disbelievers with a painful doom.

22:25 How many towns Allah has destroyed!

22:51 Those who disregard Allah's revelations are the owners of the Fire.

22:57 Those who disbelieve Allah's revelations will have a shameful doom.

22:72 Those who disbelieve Allah's revelations will burn in the Fire.

22.9 Garments of fire have been prepared for the unbelievers. Scalding water shall be poured upon their heads, melting their skins and that which is in their bellies. They shall be lashed with rods of iron.

28:62-64 Allah will taunt Christians on the day of their doom, saying: Where are My partners whom ye imagined?

30:13-14 Allah will tear Christians apart for ascribing partners to him.

30:28 It's OK to own slaves.

33:25-26 Allah cast panic into the hearts of the disbelievers. He killed some, and enslaved others. 35:26 Allah hates disbelievers.

36-7 Disbelievers will burn forever in the fire of hell. Allah will keep them alive so that he can torture them forever. When they repent and ask for mercy, he will ignore them.

40:73 Allah will taunt the Christians in hell, saying: Where are all my parnters that you used to believe in?

47.4 When you meet the unbelievers in battle strike off their heads.

48:13 Those who "believe not in Allah and His Messenger, He has prepared, for those who reject Allah, a Blazing Fire!

63:4 Disbelievers are perverted. They are the enemy, confounded by Allah.

98.6 The unbelievers among the People of the Book, Christian and Jews, and the pagans shall burn forever in the fire of Hell. They are the vilest of creatures.

      How's your eyes. Are they filled with tears of joy at these divine revelations? Only God could write such magnificent literary teachings that will shrine as moral instructions for humanity to ponder for all time. Christians, Jews, all other kafirs are the people of hell fire – "the vilest of creatures." "Disbelievers will burn in the fires of Hell. Allah will keep them alive so he can torture them forever" What kind of twisted mind could conceive of such instructions from God. Disbelievers are to be tortured with hell fire by God Himself. "When they repent and ask for mercy, he will ignore them" Such will be their fate willed not by God but by Muhammad. In his diseased mind, this will be the punishment for Christian/Jews and pagan Arabs for having rejected him. In his mind, Muhammad really believes that Hell will be their fate because he has willed it to be so. Being teachings of hate and intolerance ALL the above Quranic verses are fraudulent. We are destroying Islam not with just one word or one teaching but with thousands of immoral words and four thousand teachings of immoral depravity For 691 teachings of intolerance and persecution go to http://www.islamreform.net/new-page-23.htm

CHAPTER NINTEEN

ISLAM DEVOURS ITS YOUNG

In every totalitarian system, control of the human mind by the dictator and complete submission and slavery to the totalitarian ideology is demanded of all. Any questioning of the ideology, any denigrating of the dictator means immediate imprisonment and execution. To ensure there is a totalitarian future after the death of the dictator, indoctrination of children is paramount.

In a dictatorship, every citizen must watch and spy on every other citizen – their friends, relatives, wives, brothers, sisters, parents on their children and children on their parents. No one is immune and no one is safe.

Children belong to the dictator not the parents. They are his children to be raised in his image and to his greater glory. In this way, the ideology ensures its future.

Under Communism, children were constantly questioned in their class rooms by their teachers;

What do your mother and father think about the Communist Party? Heaven forbid if the poor child answered – my mother says that the President is a criminal and the Communist Party is a collection of criminals robbing the state. The parents would be immediately arrested, jailed (sometimes murdered) and stripped of their children.

In Islam, Muhammad set up a totalitarian ideology in which every aspect of his Muslim follower's life was dictated and controlled. There are 3 pages in Islamic texts on how to defecate. Epically the actions of women were totally controlled to prevent them from developing into independent human beings.

God greatest gift to mankind besides his human brain was the concept of family. A man and a woman join in love and respect for each other's humanity to create children in an environment of protection and security. Can you imagine the very first human families living in a cave while outside hungry beasts hunted for prey? Can you imagine how many died from lions/wolves/snakes?

It was the family unit that allowed mankind to survive. The grouping together of multiple families led to the creation of tribes and eventually nation states. A God of Moral Perfection loves children. He could never teach hate towards any human being let alone children. No parent has the right to disown their children. The true test of parental love is the care and comfort given to their child even if that child has grievously wronged them.

"Don't make be friends with your disbelieving family members. Those who do so are wrong-doers." 9:23

You tell me how 1.2 billion people called Muslims can believe in Quran teaching 9:23. Don't forget EVERY Muslim must believe that all teachings of the Quran are the written word of God to be obeyed without question. "Don't make friends with your disbelieving family members" in short disown them if they do not believe in Islam.

Does this disowning include the Muslim's children, parents, brothers, sisters – of course it does. Quran 9:23 means what it says – ALL family members who disbelieve must be disowned.

"On the Last Day good Muslims will not love their non-Muslim friends and family members, not even their fathers, sons, or brothers (or their mothers, daughters, or sisters)." Quran 58:22

Quran 58:22 says it all. In order to be "good Muslims "they" will not love their non– Muslim friends and family members, not even their fathers, sons, or brothers (or their mothers, daughters or sisters.) How can any normal person believe that God spoke/wrote these words? Quran 58:22 is abhorrent. To be a good person you must not love. To be a good person you must disown your own flesh and blood. Because they have rejected the evil of Islam, the teachings of extermination, murder, violence, hate, they are to be not loved. For a God of Moral Perfection to be a good person you must love not only your family but your neighbor as you would love yourself.

"Your wives and children are your enemies. They are to you only a temptation." Quran 64:14-15

"Your wives and children are your enemies" This is the very essence of evil. "Your wives and children are your enemies" – these words border on lunacy. Your wives and your children are you – your children are your own flesh and blood, they are the carriers of your genes, your humanity into the epochs to come.

They are your future and the future of humanity. To call them your "enemies" is AntiGod. Anti human.

"Don't let your children distract you from your duty to Allah." Quran 63:9

Your duty to God is to raise your children. To be a father and mother to them. To show them constant love and caring. You should be not distracted from the caring and raising of your children.

"Those who refuse to fight for Allah will be treated (along with their children) as unbelievers." Quran 9:85

It is against a God of Moral Perfection to "fight" any other human being in His name. This is a sin against God. It makes a farce of the human intelligence gifted to man to overcome his primitive evolutionary past and live with his fellow human in peace and love. There is no cause of God that a God of Moral Perfection would ever want you to fight violently for. God could never condemn a person for refusing to engage in violence. It is the duty of every parent to instill in their children love and respect for all human kind no matter their race, color, and creed or ethic origin.

"Don't pray for idolaters (not even for your family) after it is clear they are people of hell-fire." Quran 9:113

On the contrary "idolaters" are your friends. They are not people of hellfire. They are human beings deserving of God's love and your love and respect. Quran (9:113) and all the Quranic teachings of this chapter are a fraud committed against human intelligence. To believe any of these teachings is to show a complete lack of the qualities that make us human – love and respect. A God of Moral Perfection is love and respect. Allah (the AntiGod) is a barbaric entity that threatens the qualities of peace and love and respect that make mankind, mankind.

CHAPTER TWENTY

HONOR THY FATHER OR BE MURDERED

What is honor killing?

Honor killing is the bone chilling horrific cruelty committed by the family members- father, mother, brothers, brother-in-laws, even in some cases own sisters also. In this terrible episode the victim is always the daughter/sister or other blood related young women who get killed. Perpetrators are always the family members stated above. Family honor is one of the core values of Arab society. Anything from speaking with an unrelated man, to rumored pre-marital loss of virginity, to an extra-marital affair, refuses forced marriages; marry according to their will; or even women and girls who have been raped—can stain or destroy the family honor. Therefore, family members (parents, brothers, or sisters) kill the victim in order to remove the stain or maintain, and protect the honor of the family. Killers are given light sentences, sometimes with little or no jail time at all. The killers mainly defend their act of murder by referring to the Quran and Islam. Family guardian will say that they are merely following the directives set down in their Islamic ethical beliefs.

These barbaric killings occur only to save the honor of the family, and not for any animosity or for wealth or gold. In 100% of cases- the killers have no animosity, rather they love the girl as their own daughter or sister, but they kill the girl anyway upon their ethical compulsion to save their family honor, or to erase family stigmas. The victims cry, beg for their life but the family members become merciless (out of their ethical prejudices and also religious burden of fear) and kill the victim. After killing family members usually mourn and cry for the victim (usually loving daughter or sister) but feel solace that they have done the right thing to save their family honor.

And this kind of cruel killings to save family honor had happened, still happening, and will remain to happen - only to a Muslim family. Honor killings happen only to some designated Muslim nations such as Saudi Arabia, Jordan, Syria, Yemen, Lebanon, Egypt, Sudan, the Gaza strip and the West Bank

(Palestine), Jordan, Pakistan, Indonesia, Malaysia, Nigeria, Somalia, Turkey, Iran and some other south and central Asian countries. Bangladesh though a Muslim majority country- regular pattern of honor killings never happened as of today. But it is not unknown or impossible to record some stray incidences in Bangladeshi rural Muslim family (only) in which girl was poisoned by family members, or asked to commit suicide after being impregnated by unwed sexual intercourse. However, this same kind of case history was never heard, or recorded in the non-Muslim family of Bangladesh.

Honor killing is different from other killings

Honor killing should never be confused with wife beating, or wife killings by husbands or other relatives. Since pre-historic ancient time people assassinated, killed, or poisoned their wives or husbands, or other family members for either adultery, love affairs (Poro-keya prem) with other man besides her husband, or for property disputes—and these are simple homicide in English terminology. They are never called honor killing. This kind of homicides did occur, still occurs, and will occur in any nations, or race throughout the human history and these are not any race, or religion related happenings by any standard. Honor killings also should never be confused, or mixed up with killings for dowry, acid throwing by unsuccessful/disappointed love stalkers (as frequently happened in the Indian sub-continent), or any other violence against women. These are simply not honor killings, which is the topic of this essay.

Some sample cases of horrific honor killing:

Case-1: " When she tried to run away yet again, Kina (father of the girl) grabbed a kitchen knife and an ax and stabbed and beat the girl [his daughter] until she lay dead in the blood-smeared bathroom of the family's Istanbul apartment. He then commanded one of his daughters-in-law to clean up the mess. When his two sons came home from work 14 hours later, he ordered them to dispose of the 5-foot-3 corpse, which had been wrapped in a carpet and a blanket. The girl's head had been so mutilated, police said, it was held together by a knotted cloth."

Case-2: "Kifaya Husayn, a 16-year-old Jordanian girl, was lashed to a chair by her 32-year-old brother. He gave her a drink of water and told her to recite an Islamic prayer. Then he slashed her throat. Immediately afterward, he ran out into the street, waving the bloody knife and crying, 'I have killed my sister to cleanse my honor.' Kifaya's crime? She was raped by another brother, a 21-year-old man. Her judge and jury? Her own uncles, who convinced her eldest brother that Kifaya was too much of a disgrace to the family's honor to be allowed to live. The murderer was sentenced to fifteen years, but the sentence was subsequently reduced to seven and a half years, an extremely severe penalty by Jordanian standards."

Case-3: "A 25-year-old Palestinian who hanged his sister with a rope: "I did not kill her, but rather helped her to commit suicide and to carry out the death penalty she sentenced herself to. I did it to wash with her blood the family honor that was violated because of her and in response to the will of society that would not have had any mercy on me if I didn't . . . Society taught us from childhood that blood is the only solution to wash the honor."

Case-4: "Samia Sarwar, 29, mother of two boys aged 4 and 8, was shot dead today in lawyer Hina Jillani's office by a bearded man accompanying her mother and uncle. 'He's my helper, I can't walk,' said the mother, when Hina told the two men to get out. As the mother went to sit down in front of Hina's desk, and Saima stood up from her chair, the bearded man whipped out a pistol from his waistcoat and shot Saima in the head, killing her instantly."

Case-5: ABU QASH, Palestine: Amira Abu Hanhan Qaoud (mother of 9 children) killed her daughter 'Rofayda Qaoud' who had been raped by her brothers and was impregnated. Armed with a plastic bag, razor and wooden stick, Qaoud entered her sleeping daughter's room last Jan. 27, 2003. "Tonight you die, Rofayda," she told the girl, before wrapping the bag tightly around her head. Next, Qaoud sliced Rofayda's wrists, ignoring her muffled pleas of "No, mother, no!" After her daughter went limp, Qaoud struck her in the head with the stick. The 43-year-old mother of nine said. "I had to protect my children. This is the only way I could protect my family's honor."

Case-6: A 23 year old Rania Arafat, whose plight was broadcast live on national TV in Jordan. Rania was promised to her cousin as a very young child. Rania repeatedly told that she doesn't love him and she is in love with someone else. She pled with her family to allow her to marry her lover, instead. She ran away twice, including two weeks before her forced marriage. She wrote to her mother and pled for forgiveness and understanding. Her parents promised that she would not be harmed and she could return home. On August 19, 1997, Rania returned home. The same night, her younger brother, Rami, shot her five times in the head and chest, killing her immediately. Her youngest brother was chosen to commit the murder not only to allow his defense to find protection under the laws protecting so-called honor crimes, but also because he was a juvenile. Rami served six months in jail for his crime.

Case-7: Amal, another Arab woman and victim of honor killing was run away because she insisted on her independence. Her family said that they were ashamed because of that and the gossip of neighbors. One night, when she returned home and went sleep, her brother accompanied by Amal's father, strangled her. He said:

"I strangled her. She didn't fight back. I recited the "Holly Quran" as she was dying... it took a few minutes and she was dead." He and his father both given light sentences.

Case-8: Death of Aqsa Pervez: A reflection on Canadian Muslim-Pakistanis-Honor killing in Canada!, December 16, 2007

A young Mississauga teenager (16-year old) Aqsa Pervez, was killed by her father last week who later called the police and confessed. Mohammad Pervez is now in police custody and his case hearings have begun. The young girl was killed by strangulation for her refusal to wear the hijab.

Case- 9: Texas manhunt on for father of slain his two girls (January 3, 2008) Texas authorities continued a manhunt today for an Egyptian-born taxi driver accused of murdering his two teenage daughters. Yaser Abdel Said, 50, was wanted on a warrant for capital murder after police say he shot the girls Tuesday and left them to die in his taxi, which was found parked in front a hotel in Las Colinas, a suburb north of Dallas. Police said Mr. Said should be considered armed and dangerous.

Friends of Amina Yaser Said, 18, and Sarah Yaser Said, 17, described the girls to the Dallas Morning News as "extremely smart — like geniuses," saying the slain sisters had been enrolled in advanced placement classes and were active in soccer and tennis at suburban Lewisville High School. Family and friends told reporters that the girls' Westernized lifestyle caused conflict with their Muslim father, who emigrated from Egypt in the 1980s.

"He was really strict about guy relationships and talking to guys, as well as the things she wears," Kathleen Wong, a friend of the girls, told KTVT-TV, the Dallas CBS affiliate. Two boys who said they had been dating the sisters told KXAS-TV in Dallas that Mr. Said was upset that his daughters were involved with non-Muslims.

"She just wanted a normal life, like any American girl wanted," one of the boys told the NBC affiliate station, adding that Sarah "was always kind, gentle, always cheerful, always had a smile on her face."

Honor killing is an ETERNAL Law of Allah (the ANTI GOD) in Islam.

Dictums of Quran and Hadith which dictate/incite honor killing:

Quran- 4:15 "If any of your women are guilty of lewdness, take the evidence of four (reliable) witness from amongst you against them; if they testify, confine them to houses until death do claim them. Or God ordain for them some (other) way."

Quran - 24:2 "The woman and the man guilty of adultery or fornication—flog each of them with hundred stripes: Let no compassion move you in their case, in a matter prescribed by God, if ye believe in God and the last day."

Quran-17:32 " Nor come nigh to adultery: for it is a shameful (deed) and an evil, opening the road (to other evils)."

Quran-33:33 "stay quietly in your houses, and make not a dazzling display."

Now some sahih hadith:

Bukhari: Volume 7, Book 63, Number 196:

Narrated Abu Huraira: A man from Bani Aslam came to Allah's Apostle while he was in the mosque and called (the Prophet) saying, "O Allah's Apostle! I have committed illegal sexual intercourse." On that the Prophet turned his face from him to the other side, whereupon the man moved to the side towards which the Prophet had turned his face, and said, "O Allah's Apostle! I have committed illegal sexual intercourse." The Prophet turned his face (from him) to the other side whereupon the man moved to the side towards which the Prophet had turned his face, and repeated his statement. The Prophet turned his face (from him) to the other side again. The man moved again (and repeated his statement) for the fourth time. So when the man had given witness four times against himself, the Prophet called him and said, "Are you insane?" He replied, "No." The Prophet then said (to his companions), "Go and stone him to death." The man was a married one. Jabir bin 'Abdullah Al-Ansari said: I was one of those who stoned him. We stoned him at the Musalla ('Id praying place) in Medina. When the stones hit him with their sharp edges, he fled, but we caught him at Al-Harra and stoned him till he died.
(See also Bukhari: Volume 7, Book 63, Number 195.)
Sahi Bukhari: 8:6814:

Narrated Jabir bin Abdullah al-Ansari: "A man from the tribe of Bani Aslam came to Allah's Messenger [Muhammad] and informed him that he had committed illegal sexual intercourse; and he bore witness four times against himself. Allah's Messenger ordered him to be stoned to death as he was a married person."

Sahi Muslim No. 4206:

"A woman came to the prophet and asked for purification by seeking punishment. He told her to go away and seek God's forgiveness. She persisted four times and admitted she was pregnant. He told her to wait until she had given birth. Then he said that the Muslim community should wait until she had weaned her child. When the day arrived for the child to take solid food, Muhammad handed the child over to the community. And when he had given command over her and she was put in a hole up to her breast, he ordered the people to stone her. Khalid b. al-Walid came forward with a stone which he threw at her head, and when the blood spurted on her face he cursed her."

Sahih Al-Bukhari Vol 2. pg 1009; and Sahih Muslim Vol 2. pg 65: Hadhrat Abdullah ibne Abbaas (Radiallahu Anhu) narrates the lecture that Hadhrat Umar (Radiallaahu Anhu) delivered whilst sitting on the pulpit of Rasulullah (Sallallaahu Alayhi Wa Sallam). Hadhrat Umar (Radiallahu Anhu) said, "Verily, Allah sent Muhammad (Sallallaahu Alayhi Wa Sallam) with the truth, and revealed the Quran upon him. The verse regarding the stoning of the adulterer/ess was from amongst the verse revealed (in the Quraan). We read it, secured it and understood it. Rasulullah (Sallallaahu Alayhi Wa Sallam) stoned and we stoned after him. I fear that with the passage of time a person might say, 'We do not find mention of stoning in the Book of Allah and thereby go astray by leaving out an obligation revealed by Allah. Verily, the stoning of a adulterer/ress is found in the Quraan and is the truth, if the witnesses are met or there is a pregnancy or confession."

Al-Bukhari:
The Prophet (peace and blessings be upon him) said, "Whoever guarantees me that he will guard his chastity, I will guarantee him Paradise".

Al-Bukhari, Muslim, Abu Dawud, An-Nisa'i and others:

Abu Hurayrah reports that the Messenger of Allah said, "No one commits adultery while still remaining a believer, for faith is more precious unto Allah than such an evil act!" In another version, it is stated, "When a person commits adultery he casts away from his neck the bond that ties him to Islam; if, however, he repents, Allah will accept his repentance".

Al-Bayhaqi:
The Prophet (peace and blessings be upon him) said, "O mankind! Beware of

fornication/adultery for it entails six dire consequences: three of them relating to this world and three to the next world. As for the three that are related to this world, they are the following: it removes the glow of one's face, brings poverty, and reduces the life-span. As for its dire consequences in the next world they are: it brings down the wrath of Allah upon the person, subjects him to terrible reckoning, and finally casts him in hell-fire."

    The above Quranic verses and authentic sahih hadith clearly demonstrate beyond doubt that Prophet Muhammad, under Allah's direction, stoned adulterers to death and flogged fornicators. Allah's decree/choice of death for fornicators (Quran: 4:15) and flogging adulteress 100 times with no mercy (Quran: 24:2, which could lead to certain death) has clearly sanctioned/dictated dreadful punishment for sexual intercourse outside marriage. It is from these scriptural divine spirits Iranian fundamentalist Islamic government practices stoning and flogging adulterers today.The Iranian government/is closely following Allah's prophet. It is also quite prudent to consider that Muslim parents those who are practicing honor killing are directly motivated, or influenced by the above scriptural and historical (Hadith) support; hence they are able to commit heinous crime called 'honor killing' with (almost) impunity, exultantly and with ample satisfaction that they are following the strict Islamic ethical code to guard chastity, as the holy Prophet repeatedly cautioned Muslims so seriously to guard their women's chastity. Court sanctioned that an adulteress should be buried up to her chest and stoned to death. Mullahs of Iran know the hadith quite well.

    There is no honor in honor killings. Murder is murder. These heinous acts are cold blooded murder. Islam robs humanity of humanity – to kill a young daughter – to murder her in the name of God to protect the family honor is a grievous, barbaric act. These people have forsaken their humanity. They have forsaken God himself. They have embraced the AntiGod.

CHAPTER TWENTY ONE

TEACHING ISLAM TO CHILDREN IS CHILD ABUSE
(Recapitulation of Quranic Teachings Quoted In This Book)
(Why Teaching Islam To Children Is Child Abuse)

What people in the West do not understand is the very grave danger Islam presents to democracy and freedom.

There is absolutely no moral equivalence between Christianity/Judaism and Islam. We must oppose the establishment of Islamic schools in the West. In any campaign against Islamic schools, you will no doubt be challenged by the assertion that Jews and Catholics have their own schools so why can't Muslims.

Christianity and Judaism are religions that truly preach peace and love with democracy, freedom and human rights as central to their belief system. As we have proven, Islam is not a religion but a totalitarian ideology as evil as Nazism and Communism. Jews and Christians worship God. Muslims worship the AntiGod Allah.

In this chapter, we will recapitulate the teachings of the Quran already presented and categorize them along with the major tenets of this ideology and ask the question: How can any school allow the teaching of this evil to children?

As already stated, nobody cares if Islam is a religion in which people pray 5 times a day, go on a pilgrimage, fast for one month, do not use alcohol etc. That would be wonderful. HOWEVER, IT IS NOT. Islam is a declaration of war against kafirs. This war is permanent until all the kafirs have converted, paid a submission tax or been murdered.

Children are the very essence of innocence – the very essence of Moral Perfection.

Ask yourself - How can any Western school system allow the following Islamic teachings of evil be taught to children. Although, we have already listed these evil teachings from the view point of grown Muslims, to truly comprehend the sheer horror of these teachings - we re-present them here so you can understand that this evil is being taught to children indoctrinating them forever - murder, killing, death and destruction, violence, hate, violent jihad, terrorism, torture, brutality, savagery, maiming, inferiority of women, wife beating, women as instruments of sexual pleasure in paradise, honor killings, stoning, cutting off limbs, child sex, Sharia law, bigotry, intolerance, extortion, slavery, mutilations, looting, pillaging, slavery, inequality of kafirs, inequality of any human being, that kafirs can be murdered and their property stolen as a holy duty, that Muslims who renounce Islam can be killed, that Muslims (or anyone) who challenge the teachings of Islam can be murdered, etc. These teachings of the Quran are evil and irrational. Again, Islam is a morally bankrupt and unethical ideology.

Can you imagine teaching harmless, innocent children murder as the Law of God, owning slaves as a Law of God, raping slaves as A Law of God, looting and pillaging the property of murdered kafirs, selling their women and children into slavery and then sharing the immoral proceeds with God as a Law of God. As we have shown, all these evil crimes are the Laws of God in the Quran. Again, how could any school allow this evil to be taught to children?

HOW CAN ANY SCHOOL TEACH AN IDEOLOGY THAT OWNING SLAVES ARE ETERNAL LAWS OF GOD

Sura 2 (The Cow) Verse 178

2.178: "O you who believe! retaliation is prescribed for you in the matter of the slain, the free for the free, and the slave for the slave, and the female for the female, but if any remission is made to any one by his (aggrieved) brother, then prosecution (for the bloodwit) should be made according to usage, and payment should be made to him in a good manner; this is an alleviation from your Lord and a mercy; so whoever exceeds the limit after this he shall have a painful chastisement."

HOW CAN ANY SCHOOL TEACH AN IDEOLOGY THAT RAPING SLAVES ARE ETERNAL LAWS OF GOD

Raping slave girls:

Quran - 70:22-30: "*Not so the worshippers, who are steadfast in prayer, who set aside a due portion of their wealth for the beggar and for the deprived, who truly believe in the Day of Reckoning and dread the punishment of their Lord (for none is secure from the punishment of their Lord); who restrain their carnal desire (save with their wives and their slave girls, for these are lawful to them: he that lusts after other than these is a transgressor...*" This verse shows that Muslim men were allowed to have sex with their wives (of course) and their slave girls.

Quran - 23:5, 6: "*...who restrain their carnal desires (except with their wives and slave girls, for these are lawful to them...*" Again, Muslim men were allowed to have sexual relations with their wives and slave girls.

Quran - 4:24: "*And all married women are forbidden unto you save those captives whom your right hand possess. It is a decree of Allah for you.*" You can't have sex with married women, unless they are slaves obtained in war (with whom you may rape or do whatever you like).

Quran - 33:50: "*Prophet, We have made lawful to you the wives whom you have granted dowries and the slave girls whom God has given you as booty;...*"

HOW CAN ANY SCHOOL TEACH AN IDEOLOGY THAT TEACHES CHILDREN THAT AS MUSLIMS THEY CAN LOOT AND PILLAGE THE PROPERTY OF KAFIRS

The Ten Commandments state: "Thou shalt not steal."

It bears stating again that as a Law of God all the booty received from the sale of boys and women into slavery, and looting and pillaging the property of murdered kafirs must be shared with God. We cannot emphasize strongly enough as free people that raping slaves, selling women and children, killing people for their property and sharing the proceeds with God is evil incarnate – these timeless laws of God – are so morally outrageous – that too claim that these teachings in the Quran are the word of God – is the greatest sin that Muslims have committed against God. We cannot state strongly enough - the Quran is an evil book and an obscenity against God.

Following are some of the Laws of God inviting Muslims to enjoy booty sanctioned for them. Below are some examples how God openly supported Islamic jihadi's immoral acts.

Quran 8:1 "They ask thee concerning (things taken as) spoils of war (booty). Say: "(such) spoils are at the disposal of Allah and the Messenger: So fear Allah, and keep straight the relations between yourselves: Obey Allah and His Messenger, if ye do believe."

Quran 8:41 "And know that out of all the booty that ye may acquire (in war), a fifth share is assigned to Allah, and to the Messenger, and to near relatives, orphans, the needy, and the wayfarer, - if ye do believe in Allah and in the revelation We sent down to Our servant on the Day of Testing, - the Day of the meeting of the two forces. For Allah hath power over all things."

Quran 33:27 "And He made you heirs of their lands, their houses, and their goods, and of a land which ye had not frequented (before). And Allah has power over all things." [Merciful Allah asked Prophet Muhammad to confiscate entire properties of the surrendered Jews]

HOW CAN ANY SCHOOL TEACH AN IDEOLOGY THAT TEACHES CHILDREN THAT INFIDELS MUST CONVERT TO ISLAM OR PAY A JIZYA (SUBMISSION) TAX OR BE MURDERED AS ETERNAL LAWS OF GOD

The Ten Commandments teach: "Thou Shalt Not Kill." Can you imagine teaching children that it is a holy, religious duty to murder kafirs. We repeat here to drive into your mind the cold, hard reality that the Quran is written in the language of terrorism. It is filled with numerous verses urging the Muslims to terrorize the non-Muslims, kill them, and take possession of their lands and properties. 65% of the Quranic verses are teachings of murder, hate, terror etc. The important points to remember are that whatever Muhammad did to terrorize the kafirs was actually the actions of God. Among the many verses which exhort Islamist terrorism, the following verses stand out as naked aggression of God/Muhammad on the unbelievers: 2:63, 3:151, 8:12, 8:60, 8:59, 9:55, 11:102, and 17:59 These are the Eternal Laws of God authorizing murder as a holy, divine, blessed duty.

Quran-8:67 "It is not for any prophet to have captives until he hath made slaughter in the land. Ye desire the lure of this world and Allah desireth (for you) the Hereafter, and Allah is Mighty, Wise. " (Allah insisting Prophet to kill all the prisoners, and should not keep any surrendered prisoners alive until He (Prophet) occupied entire Arabia."

47:4 "Therefore, when ye meet the Unbelievers (in fight), smite at their necks; At length, when ye have thoroughly subdued them, bind a bond firmly (on them): thereafter (is the time for) either generosity or ransom: Until the war lays down its burdens. Thus (are ye commanded): but if it had been God's Will, He could certainly have exacted retribution from them (Himself); but (He lets you fight) in order to test you, some with others. But those who are slain in the Way of God, - He will never let their deeds be lost."

HOW CAN ANY SCHOOL TEACH AN IDEOLOGY THAT TEACHES THAT ALL OTHER RELIGIONS MUST SUBMIT TO ISLAM

God intends to enforce Muhammad's religion until it prevails in this world; Muslims can act for God.

48:28-29 "It is He Who has sent His Apostle with Guidance and the Religion of Truth, to proclaim it over all religion: and enough is God for a Witness. Muhammad is the apostle of God; and those who are with him are strong against Unbelievers, (but) compassionate amongst each other."

58:21 "God has decreed: "It is I and My apostles who must prevail": For God is One full of strength, able to enforce His Will."

HOW CAN ANY SCHOOL TEACH AN IDEOLOGY WITH AN EVIL, DEMENTED DEPRAVED SEXUAL ISLAMIC PARADISE

We have already described the evil Islamic Paradise in detail. We will give a partial, repeat rendition here. Again ask yourself, how is it possible that German, British, US, Canadian etc. schools are allowing the teaching of this obscene evil?
Islam teaches children that if they slay or are slain in the service of God, they will ascend to a deviant sexual paradise and will be awarded with 72 virgins with voluptuous breasts and lustrous eyes.

"Allah hath purchased of the believers their persons and their goods for theirs in return is the garden of Paradise they fight in his cause and slay and are slain a promise binding on him as truth." Quran 9:111

These virgins were created by God to service the righteous men of Islam in Paradise. These virgins re- generate as virgins every time a believer has sex with them. These righteous Muslim killers and murderers of God are blessed with eternal erections. They are permitted by God to engage in all forms of orgies, group sex, and sexual depravity. Can you imagine a more deviant, immoral, depravity being taught to anyone whatever their age?

As already demonstrated, 9:111 is the teaching that has been used by Muhammad and his lieutenants to mobilize the suicide bombers, the beheaders, the jihadists to kill and slaughter millions. An estimated 270,000,000 people have been murdered by Islam because of 9:111 over the past 1400 years.

Again, on 9/11 - the 19 Muslims on those planes that smashed into the World Trade Center were obeying 9:111, so they could ascend to the highest levels of Paradise and each be rewarded with 1000 virgins that they could molest and sexually abuse for all eternity.

"As for the righteous (Muslims)...We (Allah) shall wed them to beautiful virgins with lustrous eyes" - Q 44:51-54

In Iraq, bombs are strapped onto school children's bodies and then the children are tied in the back of cars which are driven into crowded markets and blown up. These children did not have a choice between choosing good over evil. The Muslim men who murdered and used them as instruments of mass murder studied Islam in schools and memorized the Quran. Young Muslim girls are raped by Muslim men and then sent as suicide bombers to wash away in blood and murder, the disgrace their rape caused their families. This is the crazy, evil, depravity of Islam.

HOW CAN ANY WESTERN SCHOOL SYSTEM ALLOW THE TEACHING OF AN IDEOLOGY CREATED BY AN EVIL INCARNATE CHILD ABUSER, WIFE ABUSER, RAPIST AND MURDERER - MUHAMMAD?

In our analysis of Muhammad, we have shown that Muslims regard prophet Muhammad as the perfect man and role model. In his life-time, Muhammad waged war, killed his enemies and critics. While his behavior was not unusual for a 7th century ruler, he did start a religion. To repudiate his example would be tantamount to rejecting Islam.

Allah's Apostle said, 'I have been made victorious with terror." Bukhari 4:52:220

It was Hitler who once said that when you tell a lie tell a big lie. The two biggest lies that have ever been told are that Islam is a religion of peace and Muhammad as a prophet of peace.

In his life, Muhammad was a megalomaniac; a self-appointed "prophet", using his self-serving revelations, supposedly from God, for personal gain, and to satisfy his own base nature. He was personally guilty of murder, including by beheadings and crucifixion, rape, torture, kidnapping, extortion, slavery, mutilations, theft, adultery, false witness, abuse of women, physically and sexually, and sexual abuse of at least one child. Muhammad slaughtered unbelievers and masterminded 60 massacres.

Convinced of his own status, he was intolerant of those who rejected him, assassinated those who criticized him, raided and looted those who did not believe in him, and massacred entire populations. He reduced thousands into slavery, raped and allowed his men to rape female captives. He was generous to those who accepted him, but vengeful towards those who didn't. Punishments for taking a stand against Muhammad included torture and death. Both men and women were brutally killed for criticizing Muhammad. Hundreds of Jewish men were beheaded for standing against him, while their wives and children were sold into slavery. Some early Muslims who apostatized were killed after Muhammad gave the command to kill all who turn away from Islam. He murdered numerous people whose only crime was writing poems against him.

As a child molester, among the earliest duties of Aisha as Muhammad's 9 year old wife was the task of washing semen stains off his clothes: "Aisha (may Allah be pleased with her) narrated: I used to wash the semen off the clothes of the prophet (the blessing and peace of Allah be upon him) and even then I used to notice one or more spots on them."

Muhammad ordered the assassinations of at least 10 people who mocked him. Muslim tradition also recounts that upon taking Mecca, Muhammad ordered the death of a poetess of the city, Asma daughter of Marwan, who had ridiculed him and who had pointed out that some of the material in the Quran had actually been stolen from her father, also a poet, and used by Muhammad. The traditions relate this story as follows,

"The Apostle of Allah said, 'Who will rid me of the daughter of Marwan?' "Upon hearing this, the Companion Umair ibn Udaj went to her house and killed her, reporting back to Mohammed of the deed the next day. It is then recorded,
"Then in the morning he was with the Apostle of Allah and said to him, 'O Apostle of Allah, verily I have killed her.' Then (Mohammed) said, 'Thou hast helped Allah and His Apostle, O Umair!'

Thus, this "prophet" ordered the death of a woman because of personal vendetta and to protect himself from charges of plagiarism!

Muhammad one time ordered the death of an old man who mocked the Muslim pride in their dirty foreheads. Muslims in Muhammad's day were proud of their method of prayer, placing their foreheads directly in the dirt. The elderly man, mockingly suggesting that there was more to prayer than mere outward form (having a dirty forehead), took some dirt, spread it on his own forehead, and stated that this was good enough for him. Muhammad ordered his Muslim followers to murder the old man, which they did. (For a description of Muhammad's assassinations go to http://www.islamreform.net/new-page-37.htm)

We have already described in detail that after defeating the Jews of Banu Qurayza, Muhammad ordered the beheading of all the adult males in the place, numbering anywhere from 600-900 individuals. The women and children were sold into slavery, and the town looted.

But this is not the end. There are more teachings of hate and evil in the Quran. Islam teaches the total inequality of women. We will re - list some of these sexist and degrading teachings.

HOW CAN ANY SCHOOL TEACH AN IDEOLOGY THAT PREACHES THE OPPRESSION AND SUBMISSION OF WOMEN TO MEN? THESE SCHOOLS ARE INDOCRINATING YOUNG GIRLS THAT THEY ARE INFERIOR TO AND THE PROPERTY OF MEN AND MUST ACCEPT THEIR INFERIORITY AS IT IS ALLAH'S WILL. YOUNG BOYS ARE BEING TAUGHT THEIR SUPERIORITY AND THAT MUSLIM WOMEN EXIST AS THEIR PROPERTY TO BE ENJOYED AT THEIR PLEASURE AND THAT KAFIR WOMEN ARE SUB-HUMANS TO BE RAPED, MOLESTED AND ENSLAVED FOR THEIR PLEASURE AND PROFIT

Women Are Sex Objects. Go and use them sexually whenever, however you want.

Likens a woman to a field (tilth), to be used by a man as he wills: "Your women are a tilth for you (to cultivate) so go to your tilth as ye will" (2:223) This teaching permits anal sex of Muslim women by their husbands.

Women Are Inferior To Men

Women have rights that are similar to men, but men are "a degree above them." 2:228

A woman is worth one-half a man. 2:282

Marry of the women two, or three, or four. 4:3

Males are to inherit twice that of females. 4:11

Women Are Deficient In Intelligence

Bukhari 6:301 "[Muhammad] said, 'Is not the evidence of two women equal to the witness of one man?' They replied in the affirmative. He said, **'This is the deficiency in her intelligence.'"**

Husbands Can Beat Their Disobedient Wives

Tells husbands to beat their disobedient wives: "Men are in charge of women, because Allah hath made the one of them to excel the other, and because they spend of their property (for the support of women). So good women are the obedient, guarding in secret that which Allah hath guarded. As for those from whom ye fear rebellion, admonish them and banish them to beds apart, and scourge them." 4:34

Women Are Dirty

"When it's time to pray and you have just used the toilet or touched a woman, be sure to wash up. If you can't find any water, just rub some dirt on yourself." 5:6

Most Women Are Going To Hell

Those who "did wrong" will go to hell, and their wives will go to hell with them (no matter how they behaved). Quran 37:22-23

"And it is said unto the angels): Assemble those who did wrong, together with their wives and what they used to worship." 37:22-23

Among the inmates of Heaven women will be the minority" (Sahih Muslim 36: 6600);........
"I (Mohammed) have seen that the majority of the dwellers of Hell-Fire were women... [because] they are ungrateful to their husbands and they are deficient in intelligence" (Sahih Bukhari: 2:18:161; 7:62:125, 1:6:301).

HOW CAN ANY SCHOOL PROCLAIM AN IDEOLOGY THAT TEACHES BRUTALITY AS ETERNAL LAWS OF GOD

Lewd" women should be punished with life imprisonment

4:15 "If any of your women are guilty of lewdness, Take the evidence of four (Reliable) witnesses from amongst you against them; and if they testify, confine them to houses until death do claim them, or God ordain for them some (other) way."

Stealing should be punished by amputation of hands

5:41 "As to the thief, Male or female, cut off his or her hands: a punishment by way of example, from God, for their crime: and God is Exalted in power."

Adultery and fornication must be punished by flogging with a hundred stripes

24:2 "The woman and the man guilty of adultery or fornication, flog each of them with a hundred stripes: Let not compassion move you in their case, in a matter prescribed by God, if ye believe in God and the Last Day: and let a party of the Believers witness their punishment."

HOW CAN ANY SCHOOL TEACH AN IDEOLOGY THAT PROCLAIMS THE FOLLOWING FAMILY VALUES

"Don't make be friends with your disbelieving family members. Those who do so are wrong-doers." 9:23

"Those who refuse to fight for Allah will be treated (along with their children) as unbelievers." 9:85

"Don't pray for idolaters (not even for your family) after it is clear they are people of hell-fire." 9:113

"On the Last Day good Muslims will not love their non-Muslim friends and family members, not even their fathers, sons, or brothers (or their mothers, daughters, or sisters)." 58:22

Don't let your children distract you from your duty to Allah. 63:9

"Your wives and children are your enemies. They are to you only a temptation." 64:14-15

How can any school teach children to not make friends with disbelieving family members? How can you teach Muslim children not to make friends with kafir children? One of the most important functions of schools is to bring together children of different backgrounds, races, religions and teach them the equality of their humanity – mutual respect and tolerance each for the other. How can you teach Muslim children to believe that their wife and children are their enemies not to be trusted?

HOW CAN ANY SCHOOL TEACH AN IDEOLOGY THAT TEACHES SEX (RAPE) WITH YOUNG FEMALE CHILDREN

ALLAH IS A PEDOPHILE MONSTER

Allah loved little girls and allows all his Jihadist Muslim men to love little girls

Quran 65:4 "And those of your women as have passed the age of monthly courses, for them the 'Iddah (prescribed divorce period), if you have doubts (about their periods), is three months, and for those who have no courses [(i.e. they are still immature) their 'Iddah (prescribed period) is three months likewise, except in case of death] . And for those who are pregnant (whether they are divorced or their husbands are dead), their 'Iddah (prescribed period) is until they deliver (their burdens) (give birth) and whosoever fears Allah and keeps his duty to Him, He will make his matter easy for him."

HOW CAN ANY SCHOOL TEACH AN IDEOLOGY THAT TEACHES CHILDREN HATE AND INTOLERANCE TOWARD JEWS, CHRISTIANS AND ALL OTHER KAFIRS

Anti-Jewish Hatred In The Quran:

We re-illustrate these teachings again because they make mass murder divine. These are some of the Quranic teachings that warp the minds of children and turn them into zombie killers. They rob these children of empathy – feeling the pain of others. Jews are apes and swine. It's not murder to kill apes and swine. It's not murder to kill Jews. It's not murder to kill Christians, Hindus or any kafir.

2.61 "Wretchedness and baseness were stamped on the Jews and they were visited with wrath from Allah."

2:96 "Jews are the greediest of all humankind. They'd like to live 4,000 years. But they are going to hell."

4:160 "For the wrongdoing Jews, Allah has prepared a painful doom."

5.60 "God has cursed the Jews, transforming them into apes and swine and those who serve the devil."

Intolerance Of And Incite Violence Against Non-Muslims And Other Religions: For these teachings go to pages 152 – 156

These are not teachings instructing children to love Jews and Christians. Hate breeds hate. All these teachings form the ideological, intellectual and religious foundations for extermination and genocide. It would be the same if German children were taught the sanctity of Adolf Hitler.

All these Quranic verses are not Moral Perfection and therefore not the teachings of God. They are the rantings of a manic – Muhammad. Therefore Islam is an immoral, fascist, ideology created by a sick, evil man. How can any school teach such evil to innocent children?

ANY SCHOOL SYSTEM THAT ALLOWS TEACHING ISLAM IN SCHOOLS IS GUILTY OF CHILD ABUSE AND CHARGES SHOULD BE BROUGHT.

CHAPTER TWENTY TWO

ISLAM IS TO BE SUPERIOR OVER ALL OTHER RELIGIONS

Quoting from the Declaration of Universal Rights and Freedoms of a God of Moral Perfection:

God is a non-religious being. For God, there exists no concept of believers or non-believers, no chosen people. God is God for all mankind. There is no one truth - no such thing as the one and only true religion. Belief in any religion does not make you a superior human being or give you any special privileges over any other human. It does not give you any God given right to enslave, discriminate against, kill, terrorize, rape, loot, non-believers in your faith in the name of God. All such teachings are not from God but are created by evil men to usurp God's divine power and utilize this power for evil justifying it as the will of God.

Everyone has the total and complete right to find his/her own way to God or not. Religious freedom is the unimpeachable right of all mankind. The right to build places of worship to practice non-violently one's religious beliefs - (the religious teachings of a God of pure love, peace, mercy - A God of Moral Perfection) should be a cornerstone of all civilized societies. The right to change one's religion without fear of death. The right to freely preach and practice one's religion without coercion or intimidation but with liberty and tolerance in any country. The right to explore the truth of any religious question, including the truth as to the origins, sources, and teachings of any religion. The unqualified liberty to question and differ from any religion and its teachings. The right to condemn all religious practices that violate human rights. The total and complete rejection of teachings of violence, intolerance and bigotry. The right not to believe in God. Only an evil being would order people put to death for not believing in religion or deciding to change one's beliefs from one religion to another, or believing in a different religion. God is a God of peace and love for all mankind. Again, any teaching that claims to be from God of hate, inequality, intolerance, bigotry, rape, war, terror, extermination, murder, slaughter, death and destruction - that orders people killed, terrorized, maimed or tortured are the teachings of man and not of God. Any religion that proclaims the above listed teachings as the timeless, eternal word of God is not Moral Perfection and therefore is not a religion but an evil ideology. Only a religion that worships a God of Moral Perfection is a religion.

Quoting From The Quran

Quran 9:33. - "It is He {Allah} Who has sent His Messenger (Muhammad) with guidance and the religion of truth (Islam), to make it superior over all religions even though the Mushrikun (polytheists, pagans, idolaters, disbelievers in the Oneness of Allah) hate (it)."

2:193 (or 2:189): "... Fight the unbelievers until **no other religion except Islam** is left."

2:259:- "As to those who **believe not,** ... they shall be given over to the **fire ... for ever.**"

2:286:- "... O our Lord! ... give us **victory** therefore over the **infidel nations.**"

3:19 (or 3:17):- "The **only religion approved** by Allah is Islam. Ironically, those who have **received the scripture** are the ones who dispute this fact, despite the knowledge they have received, due to jealousy. For such rejectors of Allah's revelations, Allah is **most strict** in reckoning."

3:85 -"Whoever seeks other than Islam as his religion, it will not be accepted from him, and in the hereafter he will be with the losers"

48:16:- "...Ye shall **do battle** with them, **or they** shall **profess Islam.** ..."

Muhammad said, "I have been ordered to fight with the people till they say, none has the right to be worshipped but Allah" (Al Bukhari vol. 4:196

Muhammad said, "Whoever changes his Islamic religion, kill him." (Hadith Al Buhkari vol. 9:57)

These teachings of the superiority of Islam are illegitimate and dangerous. Being not Moral Perfection, they are fraudulent and therefore Islam is fraudulent. The mission of Islam is quite clear – "Ye shall do **battle with them, or they shall profess Islam**" "O our Lord! ... give us **victory** therefore over the **infidel nations.**" "It is He {Allah} Who has sent His Messenger (Muhammad) with guidance and the religion of truth (Islam), to make it **superior over all religions**" "Fight the unbelievers until **no other religion except Islam** is left." "Fight" "do battle" are immoral words of violence.

The mission of Islam is not peace but war, death and destruction. Muslims must "do battle" with kafirs until they profess Islam. There must be victory over all kafir nations until Islam is superior over all religions and no other religion is left except Islam. These are not teachings of peace. There is no call to carry the Quran and preach door to door throughout the nations of the world and convince non-believers peacefully to convert. Oh no. Muslims must do battle and fight the unbelievers. The sword is to be blooded to spread the true religion of God - Islam. All of these teachings are AntiGod. No God of Moral Perfection would ever teach killing and murdering in his name. Being God, God would never condone murder of believers in other religions.

Islam seeks the total destruction of ALL other religions until they disappear from the earth. If there is a devil, a Satan then Islam is his religion. It gives this evil entity the religious cover to destroy Christianity, Judaism, Hinduism, Buddhism etc. – religions that seek to ascend to heaven through peace and love, mercy and kindness, respect and good works. Having the free will to do good or evil, Muslims by choosing the evil of Islam are condemning their souls not to a Paradise of virgin whores but to hell and damnation.

Personally, I do not believe that Satan exists. That there is an actual, living, breathing, being of demonic evil. However it is beyond curiosity that 700 years after God sent his son Jesus to earth to show us the way, to help us try to overcome our evolutionary development as a species that instilled in human kind seeds of self destruction, establishing Christianity throughout the entire Middle East with Egypt, Syria, Iraq, large parts of Saudi Arabia Christianized that there is born in Saudi Arabia a Muhammad who would dramatically reverse the work of Christ.

It's as if God and Satan are playing a universe game of chess. God checkmates Satan for 700 years with Jesus Christ spreading good throughout the world. During these long years, Satan stares at the chess board totally checkmated and then hits on an ingenious plan. He will duplicate God by sending not his son but an evil human being to initially imitate Jesus and then turn to evil creating a religion of evil. A religion of Satan. To deceive good people, he preaches peace and then teachings so diabolically evil that many will refuse to believe that anyone could believe in such evil allowing this evil to become accepted and intellectually rationalized as normal, peaceful good. People wanting to believe the best of others, hope that these true believers will come to their senses and in the end realize that they had been duped and reject evil. That the nightmare will pass. This creates complacency allowing evil to flourish and grow stronger and stronger becoming more powerful, more violent until it is too late. This was the tragedy of Germany. Satan is called the devil for a reason.

Again I do not believe any of this. I believe that Muhammad was an evil human being. He did not plan to start out teaching tolerance, peace and then cleverly turn to teachings of demonic evil. It was all accidental circumstances that caused Muhammad as a failed preacher to become a criminal totalitarian using revelations from his phony AntiGod to control his followers, reward his male Muslim killers with booty and sex, and set in motion this great evil - Islam that now threatens mankind

CHAPTER TWENTY THREE

OBEYING THE MESSANGER IS OBEYING ALLAH

Quran 4:80 "He who obeys the Messenger, obeys Allah."

Sahih Muslim (1:33) The Messenger of Allah said: "I have been commanded to fight against people till they testify that there is no god but Allah, that Muhammad is the messenger of Allah..." The last part is the Shahada, or profession of faith in Islam.

Bukhari (60:40) - "...: And fight them till there is no more affliction (i.e. no more worshiping of others along with Allah)." 'Affliction' of Muslims is explicitly defined here being a condition in which others worship a different god other than Allah. Muslims are commanded to use violence to 'rectify' the situation.

Sahih Muslim (19:4294) - "When you meet your enemies who are polytheists [Christians...], invite them to three courses of action. If they respond to any one of these, you also accept it and withhold yourself from doing them any harm. Invite them to (accept) Islam; if they respond to you, accept it from them and desist from fighting against them ... If they refuse to accept Islam, demand from them the Jizya. If they agree to pay, accept it from them and hold off your hands. If they refuse to pay the tax, seek Allah's help and fight them"

THE CRIMINALITY OF MUHAMMAD

Although we have already documented the criminality of Muhammad lets re–document the reality of this man.

How could any person be 'proud' to follow a man who was a child abuser, endorser of clitoridectomy, slave trader (Muhammad owned 40 slaves), rapist, polygamist, punched his child bride and endorsed whipping/beating women and ploughing them like fields, stoned women to death, flogged his slave women for fornication while he raped his slaves, propositioned women and passed them round to friends, denied women equal inheritance, or equality under the law etc. forever and abused and denigrated them in every way--not to mention his general sadism to others, mass murder, beheading captives, massacres, terror, torture, owning slaves and raping them, looting and pillaging, amputations, flogging, thievery, lying, hate, megalomania, had followers burned alive in their homes, the eyes burnt out of people's heads, ordered the pants pulled down of young Jewish boys and their genitals inspected for pubic hair. Just the slightest growth of hair and these poor young boys were taken away and beheaded --- unending horror.

Repeating as we have done throughout this work, how can any normal rational person believe that God would choose a criminal as His prophet and then allow this evil person to declare that obeying the messenger was obeying Allah and vice versa? The very proposition is ridiculous.

As we already have proven and stated over and over- all the Quranic teachings are the teachings of Muhammad. He created the Allah of the Quran. Muhammad invented Allah, and staged the revelations to give him authority over his followers and justification to war against the neighboring tribes of so called idolaters (pagan Arabs) and Jews and Christians – the first kafirs that faced the murderous onslaught of this killer and murderous conquering ideology. When Muhammad spoke, he was speaking the word of Allah – the laws of Allah - that had to be obeyed without question. How could the word of Allah be challenged? By morphing into Allah and His messenger, Muhammad set up the perfect totalitarian system whereby his rule could not be challenged. **MUHAMMAD WAS ALLAH and ALLAH WAS MUHAMMAD**. The Allah of the Quran never existed except in the mind of Muhammad.

In order to ensure his power could not be challenged Muhammad had his phony Allah create eternal laws of God that made it mandatory to obey Allah and His Messenger.

First, let us focus on a few verses of the Quran where Allah says a Muslim must emulate Muhammad's manners, traditions, and practices at all time.

In verses 3:132 and 4:80 (see listing next page) Allah says that obeying Him and Muhammad (i.e., Muhammad's examples) is mandatory. This means Muslims have no choice but to follow Muhammad's deeds, as this constitutes obeying the commands of Allah. A similar command is echoed in verse 33:36 where Allah stipulates that provisions (rules and examples, even toilet rules) set by Allah and Muhammad is binding to all Muslims; there are no alternatives. This verse is general in meaning and applies to all matters, i.e., if Allah and His Messenger decreed a matter, no one has the right to go against that, and no one has any choice or room for personal opinion on that case.

Allah decrees in verse 33:21 that He has made Muhammad an excellent example for the believers to follow and in verse 68:4 Allah reminds the Muslims that Muhammad is the exalted (ultimate/excellent) standard of character. Muhammad has great character traits with which Allah has honored him.

Allah promises great rewards for emulating Muhammad's habits, manners, and instructions. In verse 33:71 Allah declares that obeying Allah and Muhammad are the highest achievements, and in verse 3:31 Allah sets a condition that if any Muslim loves Allah then he/she must follow Muhammad, and Allah will forgive his/her sins. Verse 4:13 guarantees paradise for those who blindly obey Muhammad.

Allah prescribes severe punishment for not emulating Muhammad. In verse 47:33 Allah says that if Muslims do not obey Muhammad, then He will nullify all their good deeds. In verse 48:13, we read that Allah has prepared a blazing fire for those who reject Him and his apostle Muhammad. In verse 58:5 Allah has decreed that those who reject Allah and His messenger (Muhammad) will be reduced to dust.

Here is what Ash Shifa (p.316) writes about imitating Muhammad absolutely:

"It is also known that the Companions were in the habit of imitating the actions of the Prophet, whatever they were and in every way, just as they obeyed whatever he said. They threw away their signet rings when he threw his away. They discarded their sandals when he discarded his. They used as a proof for facing Jerusalem when going to the lavatory the fact that Ibn 'Umar saw him doing so. Others found a proof for other actions both in the category of worship and general custom by saying, "I saw the Messenger of Allah do it."

"Those who obey Allah and His Messenger will be admitted to Gardens to abide therein and that will be the supreme achievement. But those who disobey Allah and His Messenger and transgress His limits will be admitted to a Fire, to abide therein: And they shall have a humiliating punishment." Quran 4:12

In verse 4:12, God has declared in no uncertain terms that if you obey not just God – "but His Messenger" you will be admitted to Paradise, but if you challenge the authority of God and His Messenger i.e. Muhammad you will be sent to hell for all eternity.

28 FRAUDELENT TEACHINGS OF OBEYING ALLAH AND HIS MESSANGER

Again we will not cherry pick any of this category of Quranic teachings. All of these 28 teachings are totally false and not the word/teachings of a God of Moral Perfection but the teachings of Muhammad. God would never give instructions "Obey Allah and obey the Messenger and beware." Muhammad had created the perfect totalitarian system. By creating the verses of the Quran, and palming them off as God's word that had to be obeyed without question, there could be no threat to his political and economic power. Muhammad was in total dictatorial control. Since Allah did not exist he did have to worry that at some time God might decide to fire His present messenger and hire a new one. It was Muhammad who was the boss prophet. He had hired Allah to be his slave, follow his commands not the other way around. Allah was the slave of Muhammad. And what would be the fate for those who refused to obey the messenger and his Allah. You guessed it. Hell fire. "And so for him who believeth not in Allah and His messenger - Lo! We have prepared a flame for disbelievers." 48:13

"Believers, obey Allah, and obey the Messenger, and those charged with authority. If you dispute any matter, refer it to Allah and His Messenger. That is best, and most suitable for final determination." 4:59

"All who obey Allah and the Messenger are the ones whom Allah has bestowed favors [war booty]." 4:69

"Obey Allah and obey the Messenger, and beware!" 5:92

It is Muhammad who "commands them what is just and forbids them what is evil; he allows them as lawful what is good (and pure) and prohibits them from what is bad (and impure)" 7:157)

"They ask you about the benefits of capturing the spoils of war. Tell them: "The benefits belong to Allah and to His Messenger." 8:1

"O you who believe! Obey Allah and His Messenger. Do not turn away from him when you hear him speak. Do not be like those who say, 'We hear,' but do not listen. Those who do not obey are the worst of beasts, the vilest of animals in the sight of Allah. They are deaf and dumb. Those who do not understand are senseless. If Allah had seen any good in them, He would have made them listen. And even if He had made them listen, they would but have turned away and declined submission."8:20

"You have in (Muhammad) the Messenger of Allah a beautiful pattern of conduct for any one to follow." 33:21

"Say, (O Muhammad, to mankind): If ye love Allah, follow me; Allah will love you and forgive you your sins. Allah is Forgiving, Merciful." 3:31

"Say: Obey Allah and the messenger. But if they turn away, lo! Allah loveth not the disbelievers (in His guidance)." 3:32

"And obey Allah and the messenger, that ye may find mercy." 3:132

"These are the limits (imposed by) Allah. Whoso obeyeth Allah and His messenger, He will make him enter Gardens underneath which rivers flow, where such will dwell for ever. That will be the great success." 4:13

"And obey Allah and His messenger, and dispute not one with another lest ye falter and your strength depart from you; but be steadfast! Lo! Allah is with the steadfast." 8:46

"And the believers, men and women, are protecting friends one of another, they enjoin the right and forbid the wrong, and they establish worship and they pay the poor – due, and they obey Allah and His messenger. As for these, Allah will have mercy on them. Lo! Allah is Mighty, Wise." 9:71

"And they say: We believe in Allah and the messenger, and we obey; then after that a faction of them turn away. Such are not believers." 24:47

"The saying of (all true) believers when they appeal unto Allah and His messenger to judge between them is only that they say: We hear and we obey. And such are the successful." 24:51

"He who obeyeth Allah and His messenger, and feareth Allah, and keepeth duty (unto Him): such indeed are the victorious." 24:52

"Say: Obey Allah and obey the messenger. But if ye turn away, then (it is) for him (to do) only that wherewith he hath been charged, and for you (to do) only that wherewith ye have been charged. If ye obey him, ye will go aright. But the messenger hath no other charge than to convey (the message) plainly." 24:54

"Establish worship and pay the poor-due and obey the messenger, that haply ye may find mercy." 24:56

"And stay in your houses Bedizen not yourselves with the bedizenment of the Time of Ignorance. Be regular in prayer, and pay the poor-due, and obey Allah and His messenger. Allah's wish is but to remove uncleanness far from you, O Folk of the Household, and cleanse you with a thorough cleansing." 33:33

"It is not fitting for a Muslim man or woman to have any choice in their affairs when a matter has been decided for them by Allah and His Messenger. They have no option. If any one disobeys Allah and His Messenger, he is indeed on a wrong Path." 33:36

"He will adjust your works for you and will forgive you your sins. Whosoever obeyeth Allah and His messenger, he verily hath gained a signal victory." 33:71

"Believers, obey Allah, and obey the Messenger. Do not falter; become faint-hearted, or weak-kneed, crying for peace." And any treaties with Infidels can be broken anytime for any reason, they have no meaning." 47:33

"And so for him who believeth not in Allah and His messenger - Lo! We have prepared a flame for disbelievers." 48:13

"The wandering Arabs say: We believe. Say (unto them, O Muhammad): Ye believe not, but rather say "We submit," for the faith hath not yet entered into your hearts. Yet, if ye obey Allah and His messenger, He will not withhold from you aught of (the reward of) your deeds. Lo! Allah is Forgiving, Merciful." 49:14

"Lo! those who oppose Allah and His messenger will be abased even as those before them were abased; and We have sent down clear tokens, and for disbelievers is a shameful doom" 58:5

"Fear ye to offer alms before your conference? Then, when ye do it not and Allah hath forgiven you, establish worship and pay the poor - due and obey Allah and His messenger. And Allah is Aware of what ye do." 58:13

"So obey Allah, and obey His Messenger (Muhammad)." 64:12

"And thou (standest) on an exalted standard of character." 68.4

Obeying Muhammad is obeying Muhammad – a failed, evil, human being and renouncing God. If you cannot see the self serving nonsense of these fraudulent teachings then check the statistical analysis of the Quran in the next chapter. As the statistical analysis of the Quran will state, 83% of all Quranic teachings were about Muhammad and only 17% concerning God. All 100% of the Quran is a fraud perpetrated by the prophet For 91 teachings commanding Muslims to obey Muhammad: http://islamreform.net/new-page-41.htm For more teachings of Muhammad's megalomania and superiority of Islam go to http://www.islamreform.net/new-page-13.htm http://www.islamreform.net/new-page-12.htm http://www.islamreform.net/new-page-22.htm

CHAPTER TWENTY FOUR

VERY IMPORTANT STATISTICS CONCERNING QURAN

LOVE VERSUS FEAR IN THE QURAN: A STATISTICAL ANALYSIS

More statistical analysis. Muslims claim that Islam is a religion of peace and love but a statistical analysis of the teachings of the Quran completed by Bill Warner (www.politicalislam.com) display an Allah of hate, fear, terror, murder. 61 percent of the Quran talks ill of unbelievers or calls for their violent conquest and subjugation, but only 2.6 percent of it talks about the overall good of humanity.

While there are over 300 references in the Quran to Allah and fear, there are only 49 references to love. Of these love references, 39 are negative such as the 14 negative references to love of money, power, other gods and status.

Three verses command humanity to love Allah and 2 verses are about how Allah loves a believer. There are 25 verses about how Allah does not love kafirs (unbelievers)

This leaves 5 verses about love. Of these 5, 3 are about loving kin or a Muslim brother. One verse commands a Muslim to give for the love of Allah. This leaves only one quasi-universal verse about love: give what you love to charity and even this is contaminated by dualism since Muslim charity only goes to other Muslims. There are over 400 teachings of hate of all unbelievers: Jews, Christians, Idolaters, and Kafirs.

So much for love. Hate and fear are what Allah demands.

Islamic Hell is primarily political. As stated previously, hell is mentioned 146 times in the Quran. Only 9 references are for moral failings—greed, lack of charity, love of worldly success. The other 137 references to Hell involve eternal torture for not agreeing that Muhammad is right. That is a political charge, not a morals failure. Thus 94% of the references to Hell are as a political prison for dissenters. For detailed listing of Quranic verses describing Hell go to: http://islamreform.net/new-page-42.htm

There are 14 verses in the Quran that teach that a Muslim is not the friend of a kafir

MUHAMMAD VERSUS ALLAH: STATASTICAL ANALYSIS

More research on Islam by Bill Warner illustrates the Islamic focus on conformist behavior and beliefs. According to the Bill's analysis of the Quran, the Sira, and the Hadith, only 17% of the Islamic trilogy deals with the words of Allah. The remaining 83% refers to the words and deeds of Muhammad. As displayed above, of all the references to "hell" in the trilogy, 6% are for moral failings, while 94% are for the transgression of disagreeing with Muhammad. Statistical analysis of the trilogy revealed that 97% of references to "jihad" relate to war and a mere 3% to the concept of "inner struggle."

About 67% of the Quran of Mecca deals with punishing unbelievers for merely disagreeing with Muhammad. Over 50% of the Quran of Medina deals with hypocrites and jihad against unbelievers. Nearly 75% of the Sira deals with jihad. About 20% of the Hadith by Bukhari is about jihad. The majority of the doctrine is political, and it is all violent.

Most of the Koran is about kafirs, 64%, only 36% is about Muslims. About 37% of the Hadith is about kafirs and 81% of the Sira is about kafirs. Muhammad was fixated on kafirs and annihilated every kafir by violence, exile or conversion. When Muhammad died, there was not a person alive in Arabia who would argue with him.

JIHAD: STATISTICAL ANALYSIS

Again quoting from Bill Warner: - what is the real jihad, the jihad of inner, spiritual struggle or the jihad of war? Let's turn to Bukhari (the Hadith) for the answer, as he repeatedly speaks of jihad. In Bukhari 97% of the references to jihad are about war and 3% are about the inner struggle. So the statistical answer is that jihad is 97% war and 3% inner struggle. Is jihad war? Yes-97%. Is jihad inner struggle? Yes-3%.

WOMEN IN ISLAM: STATASTICAL ANALYSIS

In 4% of the teachings of the Quran regarding Muslim women, women were superior, in 91% of the cases they were inferior and in 5%, they were equal. However, there is a big catch. The only way that Muslim women are equal is after death on judgment day, when men and women will be judged on how well they followed the Quran and the Sunna. And guess what? The only way to follow the Quran and the Sunna is to obey men. Equality means obeying men.

Muslim women are superior by being a mother, who must obey her husband. Therefore, the perfect woman on judgment day will be a mother, who obeyed all the men in her life. So really, the Muslim women are subordinate to men in 100% of all of the Quran, Hadith and the Sira.

Kafir women can be raped, murdered, and enslaved. These are all holy acts ordained by Allah. Hell on earth is their fate at the hands of Muslim men.

These are not Moral Perfection but immoral hatred that only a phony AntiGod could teach. For 691 teachings of moral depravity go to: http://www.islamreform.net/new-page-23.htm

For article concerning the Golden Rule go to: http://islamreform.net/new-page-46.htm

For Sharia Law and the kafir go to http://www.islamreform.net/new-page-83.htm

CHAPTER TWENTY FIVE

ABSURD TEACHINGS OF THE QURAN – VERSES THAT ALLOWED MUHAMMAD TO ANNUL THE ADOPTION OF HIS ADOPTED SON AND MARRY HIS ADOPTED SON'S WIFE. CRAZY, CRAZY, CRAZINESS

MUHAMMAD SCREWING HIS ADOPTED SON'S WIFE

When Muhammad morphed into Allah (the AntiGod) becoming God - nothing could be denied to him. How could the desires of a god be denied? All Muhammad had to do was create a teaching to justify his manly desires and the teaching became instantly the eternal law of God.

So it passed that after a time - Muhammad developed the hots for his adopted son's wife. That's right. Muhammad – the poor, orphaned child who had ascended to become God wanted to screw and marry his adopted son's wife. However, this caused a huge problem for Muhammad because the Arabs regarded an adopted son as the adoptive father's true son and therefore, sexual relations with the wife of your son as incest. And rightfully so.

However, Muhammad as the man god of the universe came up with a solution to placate this nasty Arab tradition and fulfill his greatest desire of the moment which was to screw his daughter in law. He created a series of revelations received from himself to himself that authorized this sexual depravity and in the process abolished adoption for all time in Islam. That's right Muhammad as man god abolished adoption. In pre-Islamic Arab Custom, adoption of orphaned/helpless children was a very popular and moral practice among pre-Islamic Arabs. By adopting orphaned children, they used to consider the adopted child as their own. Furthermore, they used to pass onto them the adopter's genealogy and name, his investment of them with all the rights of the legitimate son including that of inheritance and the prohibition of marriage on grounds of consanguinity.

Adoption is one of the most beautiful gifts that a grown human being can grant to a helpless, abandoned child. To take a child into one's family, give that child your name, treat the child as your own flesh and blood, is an act of MORAL PERFECTION. To take this beauty and destroy it in the name of God is criminal and a very great tragedy for 1.2 billion human beings who believe in this Islamic evil.

The name of Muhammad's adopted son was Zayd bin Harithah who became upon adoption by Muhammad - Zayd bin Muhammad. Zayd wife's name was Zaynab bint Jahsh.

Don't forget, the following teachings were written by God to give moral justification to allow Muhammad to annul the adoption of Zayd bin Muhammad setting the stage for Muhammad to marry Zainab. Basically, in order to allay the consternation, in Arab society caused by Muhammad's sexual lust, Muhammad cleverly created a situation whereby God willed him to marry Zainab and therefore how could God's will be denied by his faithful prophet.

If you believe that God would ever create these following immoral teachings to justify moral depravity then you are a sick person. All these teachings are immoral nonsense formed in the diseased mind of an evil prophet. The fact that 1.2 billion people believe in Muhammad, Allah and Islam is a tragedy for them and all mankind.

33:4 "Allah hath not assigned unto any man two hearts within his body, nor hath He made your wives whom ye declare (to be your mothers) your mothers, nor hath He made those whom ye claim (to be your sons) your sons. This is but a saying of your mouths. But Allah saith the truth and He showeth the way."

In teaching 33:4 God is saying that no man can possess two hearts, nor can a man make his wife his mother, and therefore a man cannot make an adopted male child a real son.

33:5 "Proclaim their real parentage. That will be more equitable in the sight of Allah. And if ye know not their fathers, then (they are) your brethren in the faith, and your clients. And there is no sin for you in the mistakes that ye make unintentionally, but what your hearts purpose (that will be a sin for you). Allah is ever Forgiving, Merciful." Verse 33.5 is God telling mankind for all eternity that an adopted son must keep the name of his natural father and can never be considered the child of the adoptive family. Because Zayd was never Muhammad's son, he was free to marry Zaynab bint Jahsh who was never Muhammad's daughter – in – law. The marriage was not an act of incest.

33:36 "And it becometh not a believing man or a believing woman, when Allah and His messenger have decided an affair (for them), that they should (after that) claim any say in their affair; and whoso is rebellious to Allah and His messenger, he verily goeth astray in error manifest."

The stage has now been set by Muhammad for marriage. "when Allah and His messenger have decided an affair (for them), that they should (after that) claim any say in their affair;" God has decreed that Muhammad must marry Zaynab bint Jahsh and Muhammad must obey the will of God otherwise by refusing, he would be in rebellion against God "who so is rebellious to Allah and His messenger, he verily goeth astray in error manifest."

33:37 "And when thou saidst unto him on whom Allah hath conferred favour and thou hast conferred favour: Keep thy wife to thyself, and fear Allah. And thou didst hide in thy mind that which Allah was to bring to light, and thou didst fear mankind whereas Allah hath a better right that thou shouldst fear Him. So when Zeyd had performed that necessary formality (of divorce) from her, We gave her unto thee in marriage, so that (henceforth) there may be no sin for believers in respect of wives of their adopted sons, when the latter have performed the necessary formality (of release) from them. The commandment of Allah must be fulfilled."

In verse (33:37) God states that this revelation is not for Muhammad himself but for the future of the Muslim community. For all time, if a father-in-law wants to marry the divorced wife of an adopted son he may do so and vice versa. We permitted you to marry her so that it may hence be legitimate and morally blameless for a believer to marry the wife of his adopted son.
Can you imagine marrying your son's wife? It is sickening. Why in the world any father-in law will need to marry his adopted son's wife which is extremely unethical. How can any rational, moral, human being believe in such evil – that is Islam? DO YOU THINK FOR ONE MOMENT – IS IT A RATIONAL HUMAN THOUGHT THAT GOD WOULD CREATE A TEACHING TO ALLOW SUCH UNETHICAL BEHAVIOUR? THAT THE QURAN IS THE ETERNAL WORD OF GOD.

33:38 "There is no reproach for the Prophet in that which Allah maketh his due. That was Allah's way with those who passed away of old - and the commandment of Allah is certain destiny"

33:48 "And incline not to the disbelievers and the hypocrites. Disregard their noxious talk, and put thy trust in Allah. Allah is sufficient as Trustee."

In these teachings, God is telling Muhammad that he cannot be criticized for fulfilling the will of God.

Thus prophet Muhammad married Zainab to fulfill God's will in order to provide a good example of what the all-wise legislator was seeking to establish by way of rights and privileges for adoption.

All of this was turned into a farce to satisfy the sexual fantasies of Muhammad.

As already discussed and bears a short re–mention here - another humdinger of an ETERNAL LAW OF GOD – guess what – shock – surprise – the 4 wife restriction that Allah applied to Muslim men was not meant for the prophet – Muhammad after all was the messenger of Allah – he was someone special – he could have UNLIMITED WIVES AND SEX SLAVES FOREVER. Presenting again:

"O Prophet, We have made lawful for thee thy wives whom thou hast given their dowries; and those whom thy right hand owns out of the spoils of war (booty) that God has given thee; and daughters of thy paternal uncle, and daughters of thy paternal aunts, and daughters of thy maternal uncle, and daughters of thy maternal aunts, who have emigrated with thee, and any Believing woman, if she gives herself to the Prophet, provided the Prophet also desires to take her in marriage; it is exclusive for thee, apart from the Believers; We know what We have ordained for them concerning their wives and what their right hands own; it is so that there may be no blame on thee; and surely God is Forgiving, Merciful." 33:50

"You may put off whom you please, and you may take to you whomever you desire. You may defer any of them you please, and you may have whomever you desire; there is no blame on you if you invite one who you had set aside. It is no sin." 33:51

All the above Quranic verses are completely immoral. Not from a God of Moral Perfection. To have God sanction Muhammad's sexual lust and hedonic lifestyle is an affront to God.

CHAPTER TWENTY SIX

TEACHINGS REGARDING MUHAMMAD'S WIVES AS ETERNAL LAWS OF GOD: A TRAGIC SOAP OPHERA

Muhammad had many problems with his many wives. He was married at any one time to between 11 to 23 not counting all his sex slaves. Allah was always creating eternal laws of God threatening Muhammad's harem to try to keep his wives in submission.

33.28 "O Prophet! Say unto thy wives: If ye desire the world's life and its adornment, come! I will content you and will release you with a fair release."

33.29 "But if ye desire Allah and His messenger and the abode of the Hereafter, then lo! Allah hath prepared for the good among you an immense reward."

33.30 "O ye wives of the Prophet! Whosoever of you committeth manifest lewdness, the punishment for her will be doubled, and that is easy for Allah."

33.31 "And whosoever of you is submissive unto Allah and His messenger and doeth right, We shall give her her reward twice over, and We have prepared for her a rich provision."

33:53 "And when ye ask (his ladies) for anything ye want, ask them from before a screen: that makes for greater purity for your hearts and for theirs. Nor is it right for you that ye should... marry his [Muhammad's] widows after him at any time. Truly such a thing is in God's sight an enormity."

33:54 "You must not speak ill of God's apostle, nor shall you ever wed his wives after him; this would be a grave offense in the sight of Allah."

33; 59 "O Prophet! Tell your wives and your daughters and the women of the believers to draw their cloaks (veils) over their bodies (when outdoors). That is most convenient that they should be known and not molested."

Muhammad's wives need to be careful. If they criticize their husband, Allah will replace them with better ones.

66:40 "If you (women) turn in repentance to him, it would be better. Your hearts have been impaired, for you desired (the ban) [on how many girls Muhammad could play with at a time]. But if you back each other up against (Muhammad), truly Allah is his protector, and Gabriel, and everyone who believes - and furthermore, the angels will back (him) up."

66:5 "It may be that if he divorces you (all) his Lord may give him in exchange wives better than you surrendering, believing, obedient, penitent, serving, journeying, previously married and virgins."

66:10 "Allah citeth an example for those who disbelieve: the wife of Noah and the wife of Lot, who were under two of Our righteous slaves yet betrayed them so that they (the husbands) availed them naught against Allah and it was said (unto them): Enter the Fire along with those who enter."

66:11 "And Allah citeth an example for those who believe: the wife of Pharaoh when she said: My Lord! Build for me a home with thee in the Garden, and deliver me from Pharaoh and his work, and deliver me from evil-doing folk;"

66.10-11 "On one hand wives of Allah's prophets Noah and Lut misbehaved with their husbands and they were put in hell fire. On the other hand wife of the kafir Pharoah was well behaved and she was awarded paradise"

70:29-30,35 "And those who guard their chastity, Except with their wives and the (captives) whom their right hands possess,- for (then) they are not to be blamed, ... Such will be the honored ones in the Gardens (of Bliss)."

What is on display, here is the immorality of having more than one wife at a time.
As already stated - the relationship between a man and a woman is one of the most sacred. It's the love that comes from this relationship that produces a special psychological bond between the man and woman. Once that bond is broken, and you add other women or men to the relationship you are introducing jealously, loathing, and even hatred. You are creating a psychological disaster for the woman. It's no longer a human relationship but that of a bull servicing a bunch

of cows. Verse 33:50 is a Law sanctioning pure lust. This teaching stands against everything that God willed for Adam and Eve when they left Paradise. That a man Muhammad could possess unlimited wives. This is not what God willed for mankind. This is what Muhammad willed for himself – unlimited wives and unlimited sex with his sex slaves. A Muslim bull serving his harem of cows.

What also is on display is a man who as God created Laws of God to threaten his wives and keep them in line.

Muhammad's wives had to take revolving "turns" to be with their husband. Muhammad ignored his own system and had sexual relations with Mary the Copt on a day that was either Hafsah's or Aisha's "turn". Hafsah discovered Muhammad's breach of protocol and became upset. Muhammad promised her that he would not have sexual relations with Mary, probably out of fear that Hafsah would tell his favorite wife, Aisha - whom he married when she was a child of 6 years of age.

Hafsah and Aisha were, according to the traditions, often competitors for Muhammad's attention, and Hafsah told Aisha the entire sordid story. We can only imagine the anger of Aisha and the other wives of Muhammad. In retaliation, Muhammad boycotted the other wives, in respect to his sexual relations with them, and co-habitated exclusively with Mary. After one month, we are told by the traditions and the Quran that Almighty God intervened on Muhammad's behalf.

God tells Muhammad that it is acceptable for him to break his own oaths! Imagine Almighty God promoting and commending a breach of an oath made by Muhammad, especially under such circumstances as the satiation of Muhammad's carnal desires!

But wait, things become much worse! God warns Muhammad's wives against conspiring against the "Prophet". If they do not heed this warning, they will face Almighty God, the Archangel Gabriel and all of the angels, as well as all of the righteous. What chance would these poor women have against such opposition?

Another threat against the wives of Muhammad is that Almighty God will permit Muhammad to divorce his wives AND find prettier wives for him! But the intimidation does not end with the threats of divorce! God threatens the wives of Muhammad AND their families with the eternal fires of Hell! After Muhammad's lies and betrayal, his wives are commanded to repent (for what I am honestly not sure) and Muhammad is exhorted to fight against the unbelievers. We are told that Almighty God then gave the wives of Muhammad "positive role models" of female behavior, including Mary the mother of Jesus who is incorrectly called the daughter of Imran. But who cares about the details at a time like this?

God rushes head on into Muhammad's domestic disputes in order to intervene on Muhammad's behalf! Why would God permit His so called messenger to satisfy his own sexual fantasies? Why would God record these threats for all of eternity? What moral lesson are we to learn from all of this? Clearly, these "revelations" were "received" by Muhammad so that he could excuse himself from the consequences of his own moral weaknesses. I can understand why the people in Muhammad's day accepted this nonsense without question - they feared for their lives. I cannot understand why people accept such hypocrisy today as the alleged words of an Almighty and All-Righteous God!

Muhammad utilized God to mobilize his followers to drive people from their secured positions, strike terror into their hearts and kill them. He utilized God as a front to create his final solution to the kafir threat posed by Christians and Jews – the Mass Exile from Saudi Arabia. He utilized God as his accomplice to threaten his rebellious wives and allow him to indulge in sexual, sinful fantasies.

All the above teachings and the entire Quran are not the word/teachings of a God of Moral Perfection but of Muhammad and therefore, Islam is a farce.

Does anybody believe that God would spy on behalf of Muhammad? God being God knows the future. Does anybody believe that God would speak "then his Lord will substitute other wives in your place who are better than you; peacefully surrendering, acknowledging, devout, repentant, serving, active in their societies, responsive, and foremost ones?"

Does anybody believe that God would invoke his power to intervene and utilize angels to punish Muhammad's wives?

"If you (women) turn in repentance to him, it would be better. Your hearts have been impaired, for you desired (the ban) [on how many girls Muhammad could play with at a time]. But if you back each other up against (Muhammad), truly Allah is his protector, and Gabriel, and everyone who believes - and furthermore, the angels will back (him) up." 66:40

Muhammad was a very jealous, possessive, man who kept a firm grip on any wandering eyes. In his later years, Muhammad became impotent and could not get an erection. That's right the apostle of God, the prophet of Peace – the man with the sexual strength of 100 men could not get a hard on. In order to keep his wives from the clutches of his merry band of SS Companion killers, who were desperately waiting for him to die so they could grab his wives epically Aisha, Muhammad created laws of God requiring all Muslim women to cover up. Moreover, he banned his wives from ever marrying after his death.

"O Prophet! Tell your wives and your daughters and the women of the believers to draw their cloaks (veils) over their bodies (when outdoors). That is most convenient that they should be known and not molested." 33:59

Every time you see a Muslim woman all covered up from head to foot with a head scarf and heavy full length coat one of the reasons is because Muhammad could not get an erection.

Quoting from Ali Sina (faithfreedom.org) famous book: Understanding Muhammad " In the later years of his life Muhammad was affected by acromegaly, a disease caused by excessive production of a growth hormone, resulting in large bones, cold and fleshy hands and feet and coarse facial features such as enlarged lips, nose and tongue.

Acromegaly occurs after the age of 40 and usually kills the patient in his early 60s. It causes impotence, while it increases libido. This explains Muhammad's sexual vagaries in his old age and why in the later years of his life he had such an insatiable craving for sex. He would visit all his 9 wives in one night to touch and fondle them, without being satisfied. His impotence explains his insecurity, paranoia, and intense jealousy of his young wives. He ordered them to cover themselves, lest other men would cast a lusting eye on them. Today, half a billion Muslim women veil themselves, because Muhammad was impotent. Muhammad's illnesses explain a lot of mysteries of Islam."

MUHAMMAD'S SHEER HATRED OF DOGS

A SECOND TRAGIC SOAP OPERA

When Islam conquers the United States and Europe, dogs will join kafirs and blacks in the graveyard of history. Muhammad's hatred of dogs is only exceeded by his hatred of Muslim women whom he often compared to dogs. When Muslim taxi drivers refuse to transport blind people with seeing eye dogs they are following in the footsteps of their crazy prophet. For an understanding of Muhammad's sheer hatred of dogs go to: http://islamreform.net/new-page-40.htm

CHAPTER TWENTY SEVEN

MURDERING MUSICANS, SINGERS IN ISLAM

Muhammad murdered poets who opposed his rule. As a total totalitarian, he decreed that all music be destroyed from the human race. Music is one of the greatest gifts granted by God to mankind. It is one of the greatest achievements of mankind to utilize his ability to speak and turn words and thoughts into music. Islam will destroy the joy of humanity.

Hadith Qudsi 19:5: "The Prophet said that Allah commanded him to destroy all the musical instruments, idols, crosses and all the trappings of ignorance."

The Hadith Qudsi, or holy Hadith, are those in which Muhammad transmits the words of Allah, although those words are not in the Qur'an.
Muhammad also said:
(1) "Allah Mighty and Majestic sent me as a guidance and mercy to believers and commanded me to do away with musical instruments, flutes, strings, crucifixes, and the affair of the pre-Islamic period of ignorance."
(2) "On the Day of Resurrection, Allah will pour molten lead into the ears of whoever sits listening to a songstress."
(3) "Song makes hypocrisy grow in the heart as water does herbage."
(4) "This community will experience the swallowing up of some people by the earth, metamorphosis of some into animals, and being rained upon with stones." Someone asked, "When will this be, O Messenger of Allah?" and he said, "When songstresses and musical instruments appear and wine is held to be lawful."
(5) "There will be peoples of my Community who will hold fornication, silk, wine, and musical instruments to be lawful ...." -- **'Umdat al-Salik** r40.0

"Allah did not create man so that he could have fun. The aim of creation was for mankind to be put to the test through hardship and prayer. An Islamic regime must be serious in every field. There are no jokes in Islam. There is no humor in Islam. There is no fun in Islam. There can be no fun and joy in whatever is serious." -- The Ayatollah Khomeini.

CHAPTER TWENTY EIGHT

THE TEN COMMANDMENTS ARE NOT THE TEACHING OF A GOD OF MORAL PERFECTION

Sorry Charlton Heston I hope you don't get mad up there but the Ten Commandments are not from God. Moses never met God – God never carved with his almightily power the Ten Commandments into stone tablets.

How do we know that the Ten Commandments are not from God?

Remember for a teaching to be from God every word of the pertained teaching must be Moral Perfection. If only one word is not Moral Perfection then the entire teaching is not from God.

The Ten Commandments Catholic Version

I. <u>I am the LORD your God: you shall not have strange Gods before me!</u>

II. <u>You shall not take the name of the LORD your God in vain!</u>

III. Remember<u> to keep holy the LORD'S Day!</u>

IV. <u>Honor your father and your mother!</u>

V. <u>You shall not kill!</u>

VI. <u>You shall not commit adultery!</u>

VII. <u>You shall not steal!</u>

VIII. <u>You shall not bear false witness against your neighbor!</u>

IX. You shall not covet your neighbor's wife/husband!

X. You shall not covet your neighbor's goods!

The first three teachings of the Ten Commandments are bogus. They were never spoken to Moses by God.

I. I am the LORD your God: you shall not have strange Gods before me!
II. You shall not take the name of the LORD your God in vain!
III. Remember to keep holy the LORD'S Day!

As Moral Perfection, God is not an egotist. God does not seek your adoration nor does He demand it. God is not a rock/movie star. He is not a dictator ordering us to bow down before His greatness. All teachings of God basking in his own glory and ordering mankind to bask in His glory are the teachings of man.

These three commandments were recited by Moses to give him a position of power over his sometimes unruly Israelite flock. My God is the true God. There can be no other god's before him. I'm His prophet and therefore, you must obey and follow me.

If a tree growing in my back yard represents to me God, and I pay homage to my tree god – build a shrine – write a book praising my tree god – try to convert the entire world non-violently to my new religion of the tree god, I have not sinned. My tree god religion is just as valid as Christianity, Judaism etc. Notice in the first two commandments the implied threat. "You shall not have strange Gods before me." "You shall not take the name of the Lord your God in vain" This is not a God of Moral Perfection. These are the words of a man - perhaps Moses himself or one of his religious advisors who created these teachings.

Moses could have created a teaching of Moral Perfection changing the first three commandments to:

Thou shalt not rape.
Thou shalt not own slaves or countenance the ownership of slaves.
Thou shalt not make war.
Notice the change to commandment IX.
Now the Ten Commandments are Moral Perfection. However, even though the Ten Commandments are now Moral Perfection, they are obviously not from God. They are from me. Therefore, even though a teaching may be Moral Perfection does not necessarily mean that it is from God – it only raises the possibility that the teaching is from God.

CHAPTER TWENTY NINE

JESUS VERSUS MUHAMMAD

ISLAM IS A VERY GREAT SIN AND BLASPHEMY AGAINST GOD AND JESUS

One of the most important frauds that Islam attempts to perpetuate is that Islam is a direct continuation from Abraham through Jesus to Muhammad.

It is not.

Following is a short comparison between the life and teachings of Jesus and the life and teachings of Muhammad. Muhammad was no Jesus and Islam is not Christianity/Judaism and Allah is not God.

JESUS THE REVOLUTIONARY

We do not know if Christ existed or Not. If he did exist, we will never know if he truly was the son of God. The question of Christ is the question of timeless greatness.

What is greatness?

In my view, greatness is when you rise above your times and create an example of goodness and justice for all humanity for all time.

The teachings that Jesus brought to mankind are revolutionary and timeless. The Sermon On The Mount is such a moment of revolutionary greatness. It is one of the greatest writings in human history. During this time of the brutal oppression of the Roman Empire, Christ came with teachings not of violent uprisings, or forming armies to over throw the Romans but a message of peace and love – that the meek shall inherit the earth, turn the other cheek, love your enemies etc. In an era of man's inhumanity to man, to people's suffering under a cruel occupation, Jesus brought not a message of liberation by the sword but by words: Peace, Love, Mercy, Kindness, and Non-violence.

His simple message is for mankind to live according to the Sermon or go to extinction as a species. However, again, we do not know if the Sermon on The Mount was ever spoken by Christ or if spoken, the inspiration was received from God or even if God exists at all. However the person (Christ or someone else) who created The Sermon On The Mount is the greatest human being who has ever lived. (For The Sermon On The Mount go to:
http://www.goarch.org/ourfaith/ourfaith7110)tp://www.goarch.org/ourfaith/ourfaith7110)

JESUS WAS A TRUE PROPHET OF PEACE AND LOVE

Again, Jesus message for mankind was really very simple: follow my teachings of peace and love, the brotherhood of all man or go to extinction as a species.

Jesus never engaged in violence or retaliation against those who mocked and rejected his message. He never sent out assassins to seek vengeance and murder His critics.

Jesus never molested a child, raped or abused women, ordered raids to capture booty, owned slaves, kept sex slaves, sold women and children into slavery, formed armies to conquer towns and cities, engaged in massacres, beheaded captives, tortured and brutalized non-believers in His Messiah hood, called on the Angel Gabriel to wreak havoc against His enemies.

God never sent any revelations to His son commanding Him to hate, murder, rape, terrorize, torture, non-believers in Jesus' teachings. Christ never received any teachings from God to beat women, maim, stone, whip, sinners. He never received any revelations to commit or command his disciples to commit acts of terror, brutality, violence against any human being. God never sent revelations allowing His son Jesus (or His disciples) to marry unlimited women, own or rape slaves - that Christians (or anyone) who renounce Christ can be killed, that Christians (or anyone) who challenge the teachings of Christ can be murdered, that believers who slay and are slain in the service of God will ascend to a sexual Paradise of lustrous eyed, voluptuous breasted virgins who they can sexually molest for all eternity.

Instead of conversion by force, physically or otherwise, Christ said that His disciples did not fight because His kingdom was not of this world (John 18:36). Those who fight love this present world and the Bible says the love of the Father is not in them. Indeed, He told His disciples, "Love your enemies, bless them that curse you, do good to them that hate you, and pray for them which despitefully use you and persecute you" (Mt 5:44). There is nothing similar to this in the Quran.

Jesus message was of non-violence, mercy, forgiveness and redemption of mankind, respect for women, respect for all human beings and not their brutalization. His teachings were of dignity and freedom – the equality of all human beings. When Satan offered Jesus all the kingdoms of the world He completely rejected Satan.

Jesus was a moral example for human beings to emulate for all time.

The message of Christ is not – follow my teachings become a Christian or go to hell and damnation. This is an evil distortion and definitely not Moral Perfection. To condemn billions of Hindus, Buddhists, non – Christians to hell and damnation is frankly idiotic. If you are a Hindu and you commit acts of evil then you are an evil Hindu. If you die without begging forgiveness for your life as an evil Hindu then you will stand before God and be judged. This brings us to the next big question – How does a God of Moral Perfection judge us? How does a God of Moral Perfection judge failed evil human beings like Prophet Muhammad, Hitler, Stalin and all the other countless killers and murderers of history. What of their millions and millions of followers who aided these killers in their evil acts? These evil people choose a life of evil. They exercised their free will to commit evil. They utilized their God given brain to do evil.

If God does not exist then the answer is simple. They are all buried 6 feet under rotting away. That's it. But if God does exist then He cannot sentence them to hell fire and still be Moral Perfection. He cannot inflict pain and suffering. If God exists then He must be Moral Perfection and therefore Hell does not exist. And yet we cannot accept that Prophet Muhammad or Hitler get off scott free. To live an evil life and then walk. There has to be some form of punishment for their great crimes. It is my belief that when your soul stands before God you feel all the the pain and suffering you have inflicted on others, all the bad/evil you have ever committed torments your soul and then …… ????

Just as mankind was ascending out of the abyss of the darkness of its barbaric and bloody past into the light of Jesus teachings – there was born a man who would claim to be the last prophet of God and seek to destroy Jesus teachings and plunge mankind back into the abyss.

MUHAMMAD: A TRUE PROPHET OF MURDER, TORTURE, TERROR, MASSACRES, GENOCIDE – A TRUE PROPHET OF DEATH

A truly insane person cannot commit acts of evil but a truly evil person can commit insane acts of evil. As we have seen in this writing - when Muhammad started teaching in Mecca he sought to obtain the support of the Christians and Jews. Allah presented himself as the same God worshipped by Christians and Jews who now revealed himself through his chosen messenger - Muhammad. Islam was the same divine guidance sent to all prophets before Jesus. That Muhammad was sent for all mankind and was the last and final messenger sent to deliver the message of Islam.

The teachings of Muhammad during this Mecca period were benign and tolerant and presented as a continuation from Abraham through the previous prophets, Jesus and finally Muhammad. The teachings of the Quran of Jesus, Mary during these early years were designed to give legitimacy to Muhammad and the revelations of Allah.

The Christians and Jews soundly rejected Muhammad as a FALSE PROPHET and after 13 years Muhammad was forced to flee for his life to Medina with a mere handful of followers.

A COMPLETE REJECTION OF JESUS

As already discussed, once Muhammad obtained political and military power in Medina, Islam changed completely from a benign, tolerant belief system into a political - military ideology that sought the destruction of the Jews, Christians and all other kafirs and their submission to Islam as the one and only true religion or their death.

Islam would no longer teach respect and tolerance of Christians and Jews, but their total and complete destruction.

The new (Post Medina) Islam is a total and complete rejection of all Jesus teachings – a total and complete rejection of God – and a total and complete acceptance of violence, terror and war as holy instruments of religious terrorism.

Islam's mission as dictated by Allah is to bring all mankind into submission ("Islam") by what ever means necessary including the killing all "kafirs", if necessary (these are the unbelievers in Allah and Muhammad his prophet) (Sura 2:190-192;4:76; 5:33; 9:5, 29,41; 47:4).

As stated numerous times, the only guarantee for a Muslim to enter Paradise is to die in a Jihad. Sura 9:111 "God hath purchased of the believers their persons and their goods; for theirs (in return) is the garden (of Paradise): they fight in His cause, and slay and are slain: a promise binding on Him in truth, through the Law, the Gospel, and the Qur'an: and who is more faithful to his covenant than God? Then rejoice in the bargain which ye have concluded: that is the achievement supreme." "And if you are slain, or die in the way of Allah, forgiveness and mercy from Allah are far better than all they could amass." (Surah 3:157 Al-Imran 3:157)

While other religions offer entrance to heaven for good works and Christianity which offers it for free to those who believe and follow Jesus Christ, obedient Muslim men cannot be sure of their hereafter without martyrdom. Muslim men are offered a palace; in it are 72 mansions with 72 homes with 72 sheets on 72 beds with 72 virgins that never lose their virginity to sexually molest for all eternity. Muhammad said, "The person who participates in (Holy Battles) in Allah's cause and nothing compels him to do so except belief in Allah and His Apostle, will be recompensed by Allah either with a reward, or booty (if he survives) or will be admitted to paradise (if he is killed)." (Al Bukhari vol. 1:35.)

"They [true believers] will sit with bashful, dark-eyed virgins, as chaste as the sheltered eggs of ostriches" (Sura 37:48).

We cannot state strongly enough - this evil Islamic Paradise for Muslim killers and murderers who slay and are slain in the service of and to the greater glory of Allah is an obscenity against God.

Muhammad's unique contribution to history was to take the true God, of Peace and Love and Goodness, an all Wise, all Merciful, all Loving God for all mankind, a God of Moral Perfection and turn God - into a murderous Allah (the AntiGod) of hate, terror, violence, death and destruction, intolerance for the creation of a rigid, fundamentalist, totalitarian system. The two main tenets of this totalitarianism are the use of terror to maintain this dictatorial system and the oppression and subordination of women. No longer do we have Jesus' God of peace, love, non-violence, mercy – Moral Perfection but Muhammad's Allah (the AntiGod) of war, torture, terror, brutality, death and destruction.

In our comparison of Jesus Christ and Muhammad, go to the start of the book, and re-read THE CRIMES OF MUHAMMAD - the great crimes committed by Muhammad – these are crimes against humanity, crimes against the very essence of humanity – crimes against God. Again, none of these crimes were ever committed by Jesus or any of His apostles.

CONCLUSION:

The cold reality for the species Homo sapiens is that when confronted with evil doers the meek won't inherit anything except their heads unceremoniously chopped off. When Muslims invaded the east, Buddhist monks would meekly sit in their temples chanting prayers as the Muslim killers severed their heads. But the message of Christ is that if the meek do not inherit the earth mankind will go to extinction.

Islam is the total and complete rejection of Jesus – a total and complete rejection of all the teachings of Christ – a total and complete rejection of God.

Islam seeks the total destruction of Christianity and Judaism and replacement of the Bible and Torah with the Quran.

Islam hates Jews and Christians and all other kafirs. They must convert to Islam or submit to a devastating submission (jizya) tax becoming second class dhimini - virtual slaves of the Muslims or be murdered. That is the fate Allah has ordained for the People of The Book.

As already stated, Islam divides the world into dar al-Islam (the House of Islam, i.e., those nations who have submitted to Allah) and dar al-harb (the House of War, i.e., those who have not). It is this dispensation that the world lived under in Muhammad's time, and that it lives under today. Then as now, Islam's message to the unbelieving world is the same: submit or be conquered, convert or be killed. The choice is yours. If you decide to reject Islam then your death is your own doing.

Muhammad and Jesus

Bukhari: V4B55N657 "Allah's Messenger said, 'Isa (Jesus), the son of Mariam, will shortly descend amongst you Muslims and will judge mankind by the law of the Qur'an. He will break the cross and kill the swine (Jews) and there will be no Jizyah tax taken from non-Muslims. Money will be so abundant no one will accept it. So you may recite this Holy Verse: "Isa (Jesus) was just a human being before his death. On the Day of Resurrection he (Jesus) will be a witness against the Christians."

Quran 4:171 "O people of the Book (Christians), do not be fanatical in your faith, and say nothing but the truth about Allah. The Messiah who is Isa (Jesus), son of Mariam, was only a messenger of Allah, nothing more. He bestowed His Word on Mariam and His Spirit. So believe in Allah and say not Trinity for Allah is one Ilah (God)…far be it from His Glory to beget a son."

Quran 61:14 "O Muslims! Be helpers of Allah: As Jesus the son of Mary said to the Disciples, 'Who will be my helpers (in the Cause) of Allah?' Said the disciples, 'We are Allah's helpers!' Then a portion of the Children of Israel believed, and a portion disbelieved: But We gave power to those who believed against their enemies, and they became the victorious."

Muhammad despised the Jesus/Mary/God trinity relationship and the Christian worship of them as polytheism.

Quran 9:31 "They have taken their doctors of law and their monks for lords besides Allah, and (also) the Messiah son of Marium and they were enjoined that they should serve one God only, there is no god but He; far from His glory be what they set up (with Him)."

Quran 9:32 "They desire to put out the light of Allah with their mouths, and Allah will not consent save to perfect His light, though the unbelievers are averse."

Quran 9:33 "He it is Who sent His Apostle with guidance and the religion of truth, that He might cause it to prevail over all religions, though the polytheists (Christians) may be averse."

Hadith in al-Siyuti (6/395), Muhammad asserts that, "In heaven, Mary mother of Jesus, will be one of my wives."

CHAPTER THIRTY

WESTERN CIVILIZATION: THE GREATEST CIVILIZATION IN WORLD HISTORY

Europe and America must understand that Islam has declared war against Western Civilization. That Islam is an evil ideology as evil as Nazism and Communism. It cannot be appeased. The more appeasement – the more violence will be committed against kafir societies. As I have stated over and over - Nobody cares if Islam is a religion in which people pray 5 times a day, go on pilgrimages, fast for one month, do not use alcohol etc. That would be wonderful. BUT AGAIN IT IS NOT.

Polls in the US and worldwide have consistently shown that 20% of Muslims support suicide bombers – this means worldwide 300 million people – the population of the US.

The Western World has created the Greatest Civilization the world has ever known. We have invited into our countries tens of millions of people from 5200 different nations, tribes, clans, ethnic origins, religions, religious sects etc. They emigrate and live their lives in freedom and equality. Practice their customs and religion without interference. We grant them full protection of the Rule of Law. Citizenship is offered with very few if any restrictions. Unlike the Roman Empire which brought people acquired by conquest to their cities as slaves, the Western World has welcomed immigrants from all corners of the world. This integration of humanity on such a grand scale - on our soil has never been attempted in the history of mankind.

It is rightfully stated that the Greatest Generation was the generation that fought the Second World War. As citizen soldiers, they came from the farms, towns, villages, cities aged 17, 18, 19 … to offer their lives to save civilization from the threat of Nazi/Fascist racial dictatorship. Furthermore, after that great victory, these patriots were immediately plunged into defending Western

Civilization from the evil ideology of Communism. They were the Greatest Generation in human history.

WE – their descendents by bringing together - the people of the world into our cities, into our neighborhoods, into our schools, - we are the Second Greatest Generation in history. The evolution of mankind has instilled in us a FEAR of other humans who are different from us – different races, tribes, religions. This survival mechanism was instilled through millions of years of evolution. Overcoming this deeply ingrained fear of difference is not easy. Our willingness to attempt this great project – the integration of the world – is the Greatest Endeavour of our time. It is both heroic and historic. Unfortunately, there are those who rather than get down on their hands and knees and kiss the ground of their new countries, their new homelands – rather than welcoming with open arms the freedom and democracy, equality and human rights, being offered to them - want instead to set the ground of their new national homes on fire and destroy the very foundations of Western Civilization.

During the Cold War, we welcomed millions of East Europeans who fled Communism for democracy and freedom. At no time did we ever have to worry about them blowing up planes or buses/subways. They brought their culture/customs and integrated into our society. Not so with Muslims. The greatest danger we face is that a Muslim will smuggle a nuclear device into a major Western/Indian city and kill millions in the name of and to the greater glory of Allah. The second greatest danger we face is the drip, drip loss of our freedoms through this process of Islamic appeasement (Islamification).

Tonight hundreds of thousands of a new generation of young Americans are engaged in another life and death struggle defending Western Civilization against another evil ideology – a 7th century barbarism based on an AntiGod called Allah and a book called the Quran.

Unlike the Second World War were after the attack on Pearl Harbor the political and military elites of the nation rallied in support of defeating both Germany and Japan, after the attack on 9/11 present day elites are either ignoring the grave danger posed by Islam or activity supporting the enemy

It is the height of political and military criminal irresponsibility that American military and political leaders have no idea what is contained in their enemy's manual of war – the Quran. Thousands of American soldiers/citizens have already died and more are dying daily because of the murderous teachings of the Quran.

Again, we must face the cold, hard reality that Islam is an evil ideology that directly threatens our democracy and freedom. Our society is assimilating to Islam. Muslims are not assimilating to democracy and freedom. IT IS NOT US WHO MUST CHANGE. WE MUST DEMAND THAT MUSLIMS ABANDON ISLAM

Throughout history - all the dictators and proponents of evil ideologues have hated the West with a passion. They despise everything we in the West stand for: democracy and freedom, the rule of law, equality of all human beings, the equality of women but they have ALL craved one thing from the West: RESPECT.

Furthermore, the West trying to be Mr. Nice Guy, trying to be politically correct has always granted these evil people respect.

By so doing - The West creates its own monsters. By trying desperately to avoid war through appeasement – the West all but guarantees war. By trying to placate evil – the West allows this evil to grow in power to the point that it threatens the very existence of freedom and democracy – the very existence of the West.

Quoting Winston Churchill: "Want of foresight, unwillingness to act when action would be simple and effective, lack of clear thinking, confusion of counsel until the emergency comes, until self-preservation strikes its jarring gong - these are the features which constitute the endless repetition of history." Speech House of Commons May 2, 1935

It was Ronald Reagan by refusing to grant the Soviet Union and Communism – **RESPECT** when he stated -The Soviet Union was an evil empire and **YOU ARE NOT US** that lead directly to the defeat and collapse of this very evil empire.

When the leaders of all the world's religions and its political leaders stand up against this Islamic evil as Reagan stood against the evil empire, refuse to be cowed by political correctness, this will be the start of the liberation of Muslims from the evil of Islam.

The story of the Second World War was not only the liberation of occupied Europe from Nazism but the liberation of the German people. The story of our victory of the Cold War was the liberation of the Soviet peoples from Communism. The story of standing against Islam will be the liberation of 1.2 billion Muslims from the clutches of Allah (the AntiGod) and by turning them to the teachings of peace and love, mercy and goodness of God - the saving of their souls from the fires of hell damnation.

Following is a very important study by Dr. Peter Hammond of the consequences for Western countries of allowing Islam to function unrestricted in their societies.

CHAPTER THIRTY ONE

WHAT ISLAM ISN'T

The following is adapted from Dr. Peter Hammond's book: Slavery, Terrorism and Islam: The Historical Roots and Contemporary Threat:
Islam is not a religion nor is it a cult. It is a complete system.
Islam has religious, legal, political, economic and military components. The religious component is a beard for all the other components.
Islamization occurs when there are sufficient Muslims in a country to agitate for their so-called 'religious rights.'
When politically correct and culturally diverse societies agree to 'the reasonable' Muslim demands for their 'religious rights,' they also get the other components under the table. Here's how it works (percentages source CIA: The World Fact Book (2007)).
As long as the Muslim population remains around 1% of any given country they will be regarded as a peace-loving minority and not as a threat to anyone. In fact, they may be featured in articles and films, stereotyped for their colorful uniqueness:

United States -- Muslim Norway -- Muslim 1.8%1.0%
Australia -- Muslim 1.5%
Canada -- Muslim 1.9%
China -- Muslim 1%-2%
Italy -- Muslim 1.5%

At 2% and 3% they begin to proselytize from other ethnic minorities and disaffected groups with major recruiting from the jails and among street gangs:

Denmark -- Muslim 2%
Germany -- Muslim 3.7%
United Kingdom -- Muslim 2.7%
Spain -- Muslim 4%
Thailand -- Muslim 4.6%

From 5% on they exercise an inordinate influence in proportion to their percentage of the population.

They will push for the introduction of halal (clean by Islamic standards) food, thereby securing food preparation jobs for Muslims. They will increase pressure on supermarket chains to feature it on their shelves -- along with threats for failure to comply. (United States).

France -- Muslim 8%
Philippines -- Muslim 5%
Sweden -- Muslim 5%
Switzerland -- Muslim 4.3%
The Netherlands -- Muslim 5.5%
Trinidad &Tobago -- Muslim 5.8%

At this point, they will work to get the ruling government to allow them to rule themselves under Sharia, the Islamic Law. The ultimate goal of Islam is to convert the world and establish Sharia law over the entire world.

When Muslims reach 10% of the population, they will increase lawlessness as a means of complaint about their conditions (Paris --car-burnings). Any non-Muslim action that offends Islam will result in uprisings and threats (Amsterdam - Mohammed cartoons).

Guyana -- Muslim 10%
India -- Muslim 13.4%
Israel -- Muslim 16%
Kenya -- Muslim 10%
Russia -- Muslim 10-15%

After reaching 20% expect hair-trigger rioting, jihad militia formations, sporadic killings and church and synagogue burning:

Ethiopia -- Muslim 32.8%

At 40% you will find widespread massacres, chronic terror attacks and ongoing militia warfare:
Bosnia -- Muslim 40%
Chad -- Muslim 53.1%
Lebanon -- Muslim 59.7%

From 60% you may expect unfettered persecution of non-believers and other religions, sporadic ethnic cleansing (genocide), use of Sharia Law as a weapon and Jizya, the tax placed on infidels:

Albania -- Muslim 70%
Malaysia -- Muslim 60.4%
Qatar -- Muslim 77.5%
Sudan -- Muslim 70%

After 80% expect State run ethnic cleansing and genocide:

Bangladesh -- Muslim 83%
Egypt -- Muslim 90%
Gaza -- Muslim 98.7%
Indonesia -- Muslim 86.1%
Iran -- Muslim 98%
Iraq -- Muslim 97%
Jordan -- Muslim 92%
Morocco -- Muslim 98.7%
Pakistan -- Muslim 97%
Palestine -- Muslim 99%
Syria -- Muslim 90%
Tajikistan -- Muslim 90%
Turkey -- Muslim 99.8%
United Arab Emirates -- Muslim 96%

100% will usher in the peace of 'Dar-es-Salaam' -- the Islamic House of Peace -- there's supposed to be peace because everybody is a Muslim:

Afghanistan -- Muslim 100%
Saudi Arabia -- Muslim 100%
Somalia -- Muslim 100%
Yemen -- Muslim 99.9%

Of course, that's not the case. To satisfy their blood lust, Muslims then start killing each other for a variety of reasons.

'Before I was nine I had learned the basic canon of Arab life. It was me against my brother; me and my brother against our father; my family against my cousins and the clan; the clan against the tribe; and the tribe against the world and all of us against the infidel. – Leon Uris, 'The Haj'

It is good to remember that in many, many countries, such as France, the Muslim populations are centered around ghettos based on their ethnicity. Muslims do not integrate into the community at large. Therefore, they exercise more power than their national average would indicate.

CHAPTER THIRTY TWO

SUMMARIZING
IS IT A RATIONAL, REASONABLE NORMAL, MORAL THOUGHT

Does anyone truly believe that God would have as His prophet for His one and only true religion a criminal – Muhammad and teachings of slavery, rape, murder, terror, torture, etc. Is this a rational, reasonable, normal, moral human thought that God chose such a criminal to represent him on earth and not only represent Him but God Himself - a criminal actively involved in these evil, criminal acts perpetrated by His prophet? (Although these questions have been asked throughout the book lets summarize them here.)

We can never prove or disprove that God exists. When it comes to questions of God/religion we must ask the question: Is it a rational, reasonable normal, moral human thought of a rational, reasonable, normal, moral human being that God exists? And the answer is yes. It is rational, reasonable and normal to believe in God's existence. However it is not rational, reasonable, normal, moral to believe in a criminal God. Let us now give a short rendition of what we have learnt so far about Islam and again ask the question - Is it a rational, reasonable, normal moral human thought?

Is it a rational human thought that God would create a religion that allowed His followers (believers) in His one and only true religion to murder unbelievers after giving them a warning to convert or pay a submission tax? Is this rational, reasonable, normal, moral?

Is it a rational human thought that God would create a religion that allowed His followers (believers) in His one and only true religion who slay and are slain in His service to ascend to an evil Paradise of voluptuous breasted, lustrous eyed virgins that they can sexually molest with eternal erections for all eternity in the presence of God who teaches you how to engage in orgies, group sex. Virgins that re-generate as virgins after each sex act. Is this rational, reasonable, normal, moral? How can you be a normal, moral person and believe that by fulfilling Quranic teaching 9:111 (quoting again) - "...the Garden will be theirs: they shall fight in the way of Allah and shall slay and be slain" you will go to this demented sexual whorehouse of God and not directly to hell.

Is it a rational human thought that God would create a religion with such an evil sexually depraved Paradise? Is this rational, reasonable, normal, moral?

Is it a rational human thought that God would create a religion that allowed His followers (believers) in His one and only true religion to enslave the unbelievers, breed and sell them? Is this rational, reasonable, normal, moral?

Is it a rational human thought that God would create a religion that allowed His male followers (believers) in His one and only true religion to rape unbelievers and gang rape them? Is this rational, reasonable, normal, moral?

Is it a rational human thought that God would create a religion that allowed His followers (believers) in His one and only true religion to marry up to 4 women and His prophet to marry as many women as he desired and own and rape his sex slaves? Is this rational, reasonable, normal, moral?

Is it a rational human thought that God would create a religion where women are evil, vile, stupid creatures - ½ human beings? Is this rational, reasonable, normal, moral?

Is it a rational human thought that God would create a religion that required His followers (believers) in His one and only true religion to share the booty gained from the looted property of the unbelievers and from the sale of slaves 20% with God Himself and allowing his criminal believers to keep 80%? In addition, if no fighting was involved then allowing His prophet of peace to obtain 100% of the booty. Is this rational, reasonable, normal, moral?

Is it a rational human thought that God would allow Muslims to finance war (jihad) by selling slaves and looted property? Is this rational, reasonable?

Is it a rational human thought that God would order Muslims to declare unending war against kafirs, torture, terrorize and murder them until the entire world had been conquered for God and his true religion – Islam? Is this rational, reasonable, normal, moral?

Is it a rational human thought that God would create a religion that allowed His followers (believers) in His one and only true religion to amputate hands or flog to death (100 lashes is death) people for robbery or adultery? Is this rational, reasonable, normal, moral?

Is it a rational human thought that God would create a religion that allowed His followers (believers) in His one and only true religion to murder freemen, slaves and women in retaliation for someone killing one of their freemen, slaves, and women? Is this rational, reasonable, normal, moral?

We can go on and on.

ANSWER IS ABSOLUTELY NOT. IT IS NOT A RATIONAL, REASONABLE, NORMAL, MORAL HUMAN THOUGHT. NO SUCH CRIMINAL GOD EXISTS.

As we have demonstrated throughout this text - Islam was the invention and creation of Muhammad. There was no Allah. The Quranic verses are the teachings of Muhammad and not of any God. Repeating over and over - being teachings of immoral depravity and not of Moral Perfection Islam is totally fraudulent.

CHAPTER THIRTY THREE

REFORM OF ISLAM

WHAT TURKEY MUST DO BEFORE BEING ALLOWED TO JOIN THE EU: THE 36th CHAPTER

Reforming Islam: A Tough Impossible Call

Reform is to destroy and renew. How can you reform the word of God? There are some Muslims trying to reform Islam, although there should not be anything reformable in the final and perfected religion of Allah. Many believe that Islam cannot be reformed at all.

The reformists, however, must undertake not a phony but a tough-love approach towards reforming Islam eradicating all the unethical and dangerous teachings that pollute the Quran. There can be no choice here.

Kemal Attaturk, the father of the Turkey Republic (1923) stated that Islam was "a rotting corpse" and attempted to change Turkey into a modern secular state with separation of mosque and state. Unfortunately his legacy is being rapidly destroyed by Prime Minister Edrogen and President Gul of the Islamist AKP Party who are step by step re–imposing Quranic teachings and Sharia Law on the country. They are using democracy to create an Islamic state. Turkey is on the verge of becoming another Iran.

Turkey is in the process of trying to join the EU. In order to join, Turkey must complete 35 chapters bringing its legal, commercial and political structures up to EU standards by adopting some 80,000 pages of EU law. There is an historical opportunity for the EU to demand that Turkey reform Islam before being allowed to join: **THE 36TH CHAPTER.**

The first step in reforming Islam is a declaration that the Quran is not the eternal word/teaching of God, and that it is not valid for all times and places. It must be declared that a good part of the Quran is unacceptable to the civilized society, which must be expunged from it. The Turkish Parliament must pass into law the Declaration of A God of Moral Perfection. Turkey must declare that Allah is not God and that all Quranic teachings that are not Moral Perfection must be renounced, denounced and removed from the Quran. Of course, as we have already demonstrated once a Muslim challenges just one word of the Quran let alone the thousands of words/teachings of immoral imperfection filling this very evil book then he is no longer a Muslim but an apostate of Islam and must be murdered. Since Islam is evil, once you remove the evil teachings you no longer have Islam. Reforming Islam would be like reforming Nazism. You cannot reform evil. Therefore Islam is impossible to reform and Muslims must embrace God, abandon the fictional AntiGod and his psychotic prophet Muhammad creating a totally new religion adopting the teachings of a God of Moral Perfection while keeping the 4 pillars of Islam. Following are just a few issues the reformists must meticulously work on.

WHAT TURKEY MUST DO BEFORE BEING ALLOWED TO JOIN THE EU: THE 36th CHAPTER

Again, the very first step for Turkey is a written admission that the Quran is not the word of God and adoption into law of the Declaration of a God of Moral Perfection. As we have shown in this work, Islam is a 7th century ideology whose prime directive is the extermination of ALL kafirs from face of the earth. In addition to the above declarations, the EU must demand the following reforms of Islam by Turkey. This chapter is a stand alone summary that should be photocopied and sent to all EU governments:

1. Bring to an end the 1400 year old war against the kafirs. As stated previously, it is the prime directive of Islam to conquer the nations of the world for Allah by whatever means necessary. Allah seeks the extermination of all kafirs. By refusing to convert to Islam, kafirs are a danger to Allah and must be destroyed. Islam is a declaration of war against kafirs. The Quran is not a holy book but a book of war. A book of genocide. Allah is a god of war. This war is permanent until all kafirs convert to Islam or agree to pay a devastating jizya (submission tax) or be murdered.

This means the renouncing, denouncing and removing from the Quran the close to 4,000 fascist teachings that are not Moral Perfection of violence, terror, war, death and destruction, violent jihad, murder, which we have already explained are holy acts guaranteeing accession to Paradise as long as they are perpetrated against kafirs

A true God will be against sending the calamity of war to destroy any human being. As we have noted, the teachings of the Quran are ridden with instructions for killing, destruction and war that Turkey would have to condemn and remove before being allowed EU membership.

2. Renouncing, denouncing and removing from the Quran all teachings of the oppression, subjugation and repression of women.

The total and complete protection of all baby and young girls from the sexual abuse /molestation sanctioned by the AntiGod and Muhammad.

The total and complete equality of women and their legal protection in a democratic society without equivocation is absolutely essential to the reform of Islam. Nothing less is acceptable.

3. Renouncing, denouncing and removing from the Quran all teachings of rape of kafir women:

4. Renouncing, denouncing and removing from the Quran all teachings of slavery. Again - slavery is the most vile, evil institutions ever invented by man. Slavery is an immortal, eternal, divine institution of God in the Quran.

5. Renouncing, denouncing and removing from the Quran all teachings of looting and pillaging and sharing the profit received from selling looted property and slaves with God.

We have asked before - How can acquiring earthly wealth and money through such immoral, barbaric and cruel means come into the equation of God's teaching?

6. Renouncing, denouncing and removing from the Quran all teachings of brutality.

Stealing should be punished by amputation of hands

Adultery and fornication must be punished by flogging with a hundred stripes.

7. Renouncing, denouncing and removing from the Quran all teachings of hate, inequality and racism. All human beings are created equal. Islam must denounce all teachings of the inferiority and sub-humanness of kafirs. All teachings calling for the murder, torture, terrorization of kafirs must be renounced and removed from the Quran.

8. Renouncing, denouncing and removing from the Quran (and Islam) all teachings of murdering apostates of Islam. The total and complete right of Muslims to leave Islam.

9. Renouncing, denouncing and removing from the Quran all teachings of polygamy.

10. The complete eradication of the sexually depraved Islamic Paradise of virgins who are to service the Men of Allah for all eternity.

11. The total and complete destruction of Sharia Law and its replacement by separation of religion and state and democracy and freedom. All democratic constitutions are man made and therefore evil to Allah. This means the constitutions of the US, Canada, Britain, France, Germany, etc. must be torn up and replaced by the totalitarianism of Sharia Law - a governing system based on barbarism. Turkey must destroy Sharia Law before being allowed into the union.

12. The complete implementation of the Golden Rule in Islam and applying the Ten Commandments to kafirs. The removal of all teachings of hate.

13. As has been clearly demonstrated in this work, Islam is not a religion but a political - military ideology with religious trappings. Again, only 10% of Islam has anything to do with religion - the other 90% is political. Before Turkey can join the EU, it must eradicate political Islam and change Islam into a true religion of peace in which Muslims pray 5 times a day, observe Ramadan, go on pilgrimages, abstain from alcohol, donate to charity and women wear headscarf's of their own free will. And that's it.

14. Renouncing, denouncing and removing from the Quran all teachings of honor killing. Murdering one's child is murdering all mankind.

15. Establishment of the rule of law including:
(a) All humanity are created equal.
(b) Women are equal to men.
(c) Kafirs are equal to Muslims.
(d) All humanity regardless of race or color are equal.

Without addressing these points rigorously, there can never be any meaningful reformation of Islam. Anything less will be nothing more then putting a happy face on a dangerous evil, essentially changing nothing. Turkey cannot be allowed to join the EU until it renounces the Quran and turns Islam from a murderous, evil, fascist ideology into a religion of true peace – a religion of Moral Perfection worshipping a God of Moral Perfection. Just as there is an historical opportunity to challenge Islam by calling on Turkey to complete the 36th chapter so to Israel's Netanyahu can change history by demanding that the 36th chapter changing the notation "Turkey" to "Palestinians" be an integral part of any peace agreement with the Palestinians. This will be a stunning moment in Middle East history. This proposal is detailed in the letter to President Obama on website.

CHAPTER THIRTY FOUR

EUROPE'S FINAL, "FINAL SOLUTION" OF THE JEWISH AND CHRISTIAN QUESTION: FINISHING THE WORK OF MUHAMMAD AND HITLER

LETS GIVE A RED CARD TO THE CITY OF COLOGNE, GERMANY

HITLER, MUHAMMAD AND COLOGNE'S EMBRACE FROM NAZI TO ISLAMIC FINAL SOLUTION

CONCENTRATION CAMPS WILL RETURN TO GERMANY

As already stated in "Hitler The First, Final Solution ..." before there was Hitler, Mein Kampf, the SS, concentration camps, Nazism and Aryan, - the Nazi God; there was Muhammad, the Quran, the SS Companions, slavery, Islam, Muhammad's fictional AntiGod Allah and the first, final solution of the Jewish and Christian question - the murder and forced exile of Jews/Christians from Arabia. (The comparison between the careers of Hitler and Muhammad is so important that we will repeat from Chapter 18 and will re-repeat in Chapter 39 in much more detail the concepts of Hitler/Nazism and Muhammad/Islam proving that they are virtually one and the same totalitarian ideology.)

The City of Cologne, Germany - which just allowed the building of one of Europe's largest mosques complete with sky - touching minarets and viciously suppressed a peaceful anti-Islamization rally (Sept 20, 2008) - has a long history of Jewish oppression.

The first pogrom of the Jews in Cologne was in 1349. In 1424, they were evicted from the city and had to wait nearly four centuries to be allowed back in 1798.

When the Nazis came to power in 1933, the Jewish population of Cologne was about 20,000. By 1939, some 40% of the Jews had emigrated. The vast majority of those who remained were deported to concentration camps by 1941. The Jewish population used to be herded together at the trade-fair grounds next to the Deutz Train Station for deportation to death-camps and for the disposal of their household goods by public auction. On Kristallnacht in 1938, Cologne's synagogues were set on fire.

Mr. Erdogan, the current Prime Minister of Turkey cited a poem with the following text: "The minarets of mosques are our bayonets, the domes our helmets, the mosques our barracks and the faithful our soldiers."

In the 1990s, as the mayor of Istanbul, Erdogan expressed his opposition to secularism in no uncertain terms:

"You cannot be both secular and a Muslim! You will either be a Muslim, or secular!... It is not possible for a person who says 'I am a Muslim' to go on and say 'I am secular too.' And why is that? Because Allah, the creator of the Muslim, has absolute power and rule!"

The City of Cologne has set in motion the completion of Hitler's mission—the final, final solution of the Jewish, and also Christian, question of modern Germany. They have set in motion the destruction of Western civilization in Germany.

In order to truly understand the grave future consequences of the actions of supporting Islam not only by the City of Cologne but many other cities throughout Germany and Europe let us repeat from the earlier chapter " Mein Kampf Versus The Quran" what Adolf Hitler and Muhammad taught:

Adolf Hitler (Mein Kampf): "...the personification of the devil as the symbol of all evil assumes the living shape of the Jew."

Muhammad the Fuehrer of the Muslim SS taught:

Tabari VIII: 130 " The Messanger said during his final illness, ' Two religions cannot coexist in the Arabian Peninsula. ' Umar investigated the matter, then sent to the Jews, saying: 'Allah has given permission for you to be expelled; for I have received word that the Prophet said that two religions cannot coexist in Arabia."

Allah, the Nazi-like God of Muslims, teaches His followers concerning the Jews:

Quran 2:43 "(Jews) Perform prayer; pay the zaket tax; bow down and prostrate yourself with At-Raki'un (the obedient bowers). You read recite, and study the Scripture. Why don't you understand? Nay, seek [Islamic prostration] prayer. It is indeed hard heavy, and exacting for those who obey in submission."

Allah orders Jews to submit to the supremacy of Islam. and in willing humiliation, pay jizya tax to Muslims. (For more teachings of Jewish hatred of Allah aka Muhammad go to http://www.islamreform.net/new-page-16.htm)

As we already know - the prophet himself had inaugurated the first holocaust of Jews by exterminating the entire adult men, 600 to 900 of them (judged by pubic hair growth Abu Dawud 38:4390), of the Jewish tribe of Banu Qurayzah in 627 CE. He had exiled the Jewish tribes of Banu Qainuqa and Banu Nadir of Medina, confiscating their homes and properties. Prophet Muhammad, on his death-bed, had ordered the extermination of the Jews and Christians from Arabia, which was completed by second Caliph Omar. Let us not forget that, despite Hitler's genocide of the Jews, they still live in Germany in good numbers and quite honorably. But it is from the Arab lands that the Jews have been wiped out most extensively.

At the far-left organized pro-mosque rally on 20th September, the mayor of Cologne, pointing to the anti-Islamization Conference, declared: **"We're here to show racism the red card."**

Make no mistake Mr. Mayor and your violent ultra-left allies, you have shown red card, not to racism, but to democracy, to liberty, to freedom of speech, to Jews and Christians, to gays, to equality of races, to equality of men and women, to human rights and dignity, to the rule of law. In order to realize this, you just have to look back at history and to what's been happening all over the Muslim world. You may well look at what's happening in Muslim dominated areas in Europe, the no-go zones in European cities for non-Muslims.

The Mayor has shown the green card to wife-beating [Quran 4:34], honor killing [4:15], public flogging for fornication and stoning for adultery [Quran 24:2], amputation of hands and feet [Quran 4:51]. These are all standard laws in Sudan, North Nigeria and Arab countries. Germany is already a fertile land for barbarous acts like wife-beating and honor-killing amongst Muslim immigrants.

Let us have a look at a few parallels between Islam and Nazism:

Both Hitler and Muhammad were born on April 20th - 1319 years apart.

1. On April 20, 1889, there was born a psychotic named Adolf Hitler who was to set in motion the extermination of 6 million Jews and start a war that killed 55 million people. He created an ideology called Nazism that sought the total destruction of Western Civilization and wrote a book detailing his vision of the New Europe called - Mein Kampf (My Struggle). Hitler utilized terror as a political weapon to instill fear into the hearts of Germans and create chaos in the streets. He was never elected to power by the German people but was granted the Chancellorship by the political, economic, intellectual elites. In the year 570, April 20th there was born in Mecca, Saudi Arabia a psychotic who was to become known as the prophet Muhammad. He created a murderous ideology named Islam that he masqueraded as a religion giving divine sanction to criminality. Muhammad set in motion a firestorm that engulfed much of the world and has murdered to date 270,000,000 kafirs. He utilized terror as Laws of God to instill fear into

kafirs. As did Hitler, Islam's followers are utilizing violence to create chaos in the streets. As did Hitler, they have formed an alliance with Western political, religious and intellectual elites who are determined to destroy Christians, Jews and Western Civilization.

2. Hitler instructed his followers to exterminate the Jews, so did Islam and prophet Muhammad. It is the Islamic lands that have achieved the most complete extermination of the Jews. Islam and prophet Muhammad wanted extermination of the Christians too from Arabia. It was executed most successfully. Both men created such diabolical evil that is incomprehensible to normal people. Hitler industrialized mass murder with concentration camps that Churchill and Roosevelt could never imagine Jews being gassed by the millions. That is why they never ordered the bombing of the trains and rail lines leading to these camps of horror. Muhammad cloaked his diabolical evil in religious practices that sanctified mass murder and is so incomprehensibly evil that most people dismiss it as harmless foolishness and do not see the very grave danger Islam represents until it will be too late when they will be offered the choice of becoming Muslims and losing their souls or fighting a civil war in their streets for their democracy and freedom.

3. Hitler's Nazis seized and looted Jewish homes, businesses, lands, paintings and bank accounts; so did the Muslims under prophet Muhammad and throughout history well into the 20th century. Hitler used the looted proceeds to finance his wars. When Muhammad's SS jihadists [his Companions] murdered Jews and Christians their property was looted with 20% of the pillaged proceeds going to Allah and his Messenger - Muhammad (later to the state or caliphal treasury) and the remaining 80% to the jihadis [Quran-8:41]. Muhammad used these looted proceeds plus the money obtained from selling woman and children into slavery to finance his jihadist armies.

4. When the trains arrived at the concentration camps, the Nazi SS would select Jewish women to rape and keep as sex-slaves and the rest sent to be massacred. So did prophet Muhammad and Muslims. Having murdered the men of Banu Qurayzah, and their homes and property confiscated, Muhammad and his SS Companions raped the young and beautiful Jewish women and kept them as sex-slaves. It happened throughout the history of Muslim conquest as Allah allowed capturing women in wars for rape and sex-slavery: "And all married women are forbidden unto you save those captives whom your right hand possess. It is a decree of Allah for you." You can't have sex with married women, unless they are slaves obtained in war (with whom you may rape or do whatever you like) [Quran 4:24].

5. Hitler and his SS ran a huge slave-market in Germany. Millions of people from the East were enslaved and sold in Germany, and worked as slaves for their German masters in factories, farms, homes etc. So did Islam! Prophet Muhammad himself enslaved the kafir in large numbers, such as the women and children of Banu Qurayzah and Khaybar. Prophet Muhammad also sold the Banu Qurayzah Jews he did not want into slavery. Islam created the most extensive slave-market around the world for selling millions of the enslaved kafirs. Muslims had sold up to 20 million enslaved Blacks from Africa to the Muslim world and up to six times that number perished in the process of their capture and transportation. Black men were castrated so they could not reproduce. Many died. Millions of Europeans were also captured and taken away to a life of slavery. Again, both Muhammad and Hitler used the slave trade money to finance their armies.

6. Hitler had opponents of his dictatorship brutality tortured and then hung alive on meat hooks. The SS would videotape the torture for Hitler's private viewing. Muhammad had kafirs tongues seared with hot metal, their eyes burnt out of their heads and their bodies cut open and limbs cut off and then left to die without water in the hot desert sun. He built a fire on the chest of a Jewish chieftain to torture him into revealing where he had hidden gold.

All in all, the Mayor and the City of Cologne have shown the green card to Sharia Law, the inviolable constitution of the Islamic God, which is brutally oppressive to non-Muslims and even utterly cruel to Muslims. Given that Europe is slated to be dominated by Muslims in the next 3-5 decades, if everything goes as of now; Sharia, the divine constitution of God, is coming to Europe for sure to replace its abhorrent manmade secular-liberal constitutions. Make no mistake about that. Sharia is the legal code ordained by Allah for all mankind. To violate Sharia or not to accept its authority is to commit rebellion against Allah, which Allah's faithful are required to combat.

The City of Cologne has renounced civility and embraced a barbarous deity, Allah. Given that anti-Semitism is on an alarming rise in Europe, overwhelming committed by its minuscule Muslim immigrants, make no mistake that the holocaust of the Jews of Cologne (and of wider Europe is most likely coming again; just as Colognean's ancestors did in 1349, 1424, and 1939. This time, it will be a complete one; look at the Arab world to make a grasp of it. The final solution of the Jews will be truly final this time round. The same fate will extend to the Christians as well unless they choose to pay jizya in willing humiliation and become the dhimmi slaves of the Muslims.

Although Hitler came close in his historical mission to rid Europe of Jews, and destroy Western Civilization, Europe's political, intellectual, and cultural elites are determined to succeed. The dirty little secret of the Second World War is that in virtually every country conquered by Hitler, their national elites were heavily involved aiding the SS in their extermination projects.

Islamization is rapidly progressing throughout all Europe not just the City of Cologne. Rape Jihad has been declared on European kafir women. Seventy five % of all rapes in Norway, Sweden are being committed by Muslim men. British women are unsafe in their cities. Judges in Britain treat rapes with minor prison sentences if at all. In Belgium, a Brussels' woman was viciously raped at the main train station by 6 Muslim men. The police asked the woman what she was wearing that provoked the attack. In Germany and France, Jews have been attacked, beaten, killed. Many Jews have left France for their safety. Young German boys (16 years) have been killed for dating young Turkish, German girls. A Turkish, German who had been sent by her father at age 14 to Turkey to marry a relative eventually ran away and returned to Germany. She went into hiding from her father. At age 18, she was lured to the Berlin train station under the guise of family reunion. Her younger brother met and shoot her 5 times. At his murder trial, the father gave him a boutique of flowers. There have been hundreds of these so called honor killings throughout Europe and now even America and Canada. Muslim women brutalized by their husbands who fled their homes to seek the protection of German courts cannot find lawyers to represent them because their husbands and his family threaten to kill the lawyers and their families. Entire sections of major European cities including Berlin/London//Amsterdam are now off limits to police and the rule of law becoming no go zones. Kafirs living in these zones including the old and crippled are attacked on the streets in an organized campaign to force them out. Gays are attacked and beaten on European streets. There was a meeting of a Grand Muslim Counsel in France to decide if gays should be killed. They decided that Muslims were not powerful enough right now so it would be problematic. It's just a matter of time before Gays will be legally murdered. It's just a matter of time before cranes come into the center of European cities and hang adulterers. In Denmark, Christian churches are paying a form of jizya tax to Muslims. Sharia Law is now law in Britain. As already noted - it is expected that Sharia will be Europe wide in our life time. The AntiGod is on the march. The ruling elites of Britain, France, Germany, Netherlands, Sweden, Norway have renounced God and embraced Allah (the AntiGod). These elites are the driving force behind implementation of the Final, Final Solution of the Jewish and Christian Question that has plagued the West ever since the West was the West. Hitler's vision is now Europe's vision. Muhammad's vision will be Europe's reality. Muhammad's vision will be America's reality.

HOW STEALTH CENSORSHIP IS DESTROYING FREEDOM OF SPEECH

In his recent book "Stealth Jihad" Robert Spencer describes how Muslims are utilizing US law to undermine the rule of law leading to the Islamization of America through stealth.

This Islamization is being aided by media organizations that are imposing stealth censorship on society ensuring that the population remains totally ignorant of the evil teachings of Islam and the very grave danger this evil ideology poses to the security of the state.

Publishing houses including many self publishing enterprises are refusing to publish books critical of Islam. Any author who quotes directly from the Quran/Hadith/Sira in Islam's own words and writings (as I have done) is immediately labeled a racist, hate monger and refused publication on the basis of hate speech. Think about this hypocrisy. The Quran is a book that preaches hate and is freely available throughout the world. When you quote from this book, you are spreading hate and are a politically incorrect racist.

Letters to newspaper editors quoting from the Quran are erased from the internet. Bloggers are denied access to sites. Internet providers shut down websites that condemn Islam and expose this very great evil for the evil that it is. Google has recently banned all searches bringing up criticism of Islam when you search the term Islam. This is a complete denial of freedom of speech. Google and all other media organizations are offering a filtered portrayal of Islam disguising the evil reality.

YouTube removes videos of Muslim clerics recorded on Arabic TV calling for the murder of Jews or the beating of Muslim women posted by mainly ex-Muslims not out of any noble concern of the evil nature of these clerics but because YouTube does not want to be declared as anti-Islam and lose Muslim revenues.

In Europe, bloggers/ web site owners are sent to jail for up to 5 years for standing against the Islamization of their societies and exercising their democratic right of freedom of expression by opposing the AntiGod. TV commentators refuse to invite onto their programs anyone who opposes Islam. Universities do the same. There is now a movement in both the United Nations and the United States to criminalize any criticism of Islam as hate speech making it a very serious felony. This is done under the guise of condemnation of racism. We are no longer a free people.

CHAPTER THIRTY FIVE

THE BOYS FROM MUMBAI: THE MUSLIM KILLERS OF MUMBAI MASSACRE: SOON TO BE FOLLOWED BY THE BOYS FROM NEW YORK CITY AND THE BOYS FROM LONDON

IT'S ALL ABOUT THE QURAN STUPID KAFIR

Islam is the disaster that will destroy civilization as we know it. It will dramatically change human history forever. The stakes are that high.

All acts of terrorism being committed by Muslims are not an aberration of Islam but ARE Islam. There are NO such creatures as Islamic terrorists. As we have pointed out - these are Muslim men who are following EXACTLY the teachings of the Quran and are following EXACTLY the Sunnah – the example set by Muhammad in the Hadith/Sira as to how Islam was to be lived and practiced.

The Muslim killers, who carried out the Mumbai massacre, were not perverted murderers or religious zealots/crazies but NORMAL SANE Muslim men following **EXACTLY** the teachings of Islam as stated by Allah in the Quran and examples set by prophet Muhammad in the Hadith and Sira. What these Muslims did in Mumbai was not "evil" but "holy acts" sanctioned by Allah to be rewarded by accession to a Paradise filled with sensuous virgins.

The first Mumbai was the beheading of 600 to 900 Jewish men by Muhammad at Banu Quiraiza in 627.

The brutal torturing of the Jewish Rabbi and his family in the Mumbai Jewish Center that entailed their sexual mutilation were not acts deviant to Islam but obeying Allah's commandments to the letter. The Jewish male genitals were cut off and the female Jewish vagina was cut open as a knife or sword was plunged into her vagina. The Indian Mumbai police said that they had never witnessed such bloody acts of human depravity. These Muslim killers followed the example set by the prophet Muhammad at the Massacre of Khayber when he ordered the Jewish chieftain Kinanah brutally tortured until he revealed where he had buried the treasure of the city. When Kinanah refused to disclose the treasure whereabouts he was taken away and beheaded.

Sourcing Ibn Ishak, Tabari writes:
"...Kinanah refused to surrender it; so the Messenger of God gave orders concerning him to al-Zubayr b. al-'Awwam, saying, "torture him until you root out what he has." Al-Zubayr kept twirling his firestick in his breast until Kinanah almost expired; then the Messenger of God gave him to Muhammad b. Maslamah, who beheaded him to avenge his brother Mahmud b. Maslamah."

The killers of Mumbai were not murdering human beings but kafirs - the abhorrent rejecters of Allah - despicable sub-human creatures. They were obeying Allah's commands in the Quran to attack kafirs, murder the men, and rape the women. They were also following the perfect Sunna example of the prophet.

9/11, Ft. Hood and Mumbai Massacres are Quran 9:111

In their delusion to have a direct landing in Allah's erotic whorehouse, millions of Muslims (men) have given their lives to embrace martyrdom; they have killed hundreds of millions of kafirs, 80 million in India, since the time of Muhammad. The killers of Mumbai are only continuing that grand jihadi tradition of Islam. The Boys from Mumbai will soon be followed by The Boys From New York City and The Boys From London. The nightmare scenario that these jihadis will get their hands on nuclear weapons killing millions causing a major mayhem upon the kafirs is the cold hard evil reality of Islam.

CHAPTER THIRTY SIX

ISLAM THE RELIGION OF PEACE

THE BLOODY EXPANSION OF ISLAM

Muslims want us to believe that Islam was spread peacefully by Muslims travelling from country to country, city to city, door to door preaching the teachings of peace and love and goodness from Allah and His Messenger.

This is not what happened.

Obeying the teachings of Islam – Muslims fell upon the kafir civilizations and peoples with unimaginable savagery and rivers of blood flowed across the pages of human history.

Islam is coated in blood of the murdered. As stated at the start of this book, in the past 1400 years, Islam has slaughtered 270,000,000 kafirs:

80 million Hindus killed.

60 million Christians /Jews/ Zoroastrians/Others

10 million Buddhists

120 million Africans butchered

and the tens of millions of Hindu, Negro, European, Asian women raped, brutalized and enslaved by most evil ideology ever created by man. Unlimited sex and booty were powerful motivations for Muslims to grab their swords, climb on their horses and ride off into the sunset to bring war, death and destruction to the kafirs.

Before there was a West there was an East. Muslim hordes fell upon the East bringing devastation. India paid a horrific price. The world famous historian,

Will Durant has written in his Story of Civilization that "the Mohammedan conquest of India was probably the bloodiest story in history".
Buddhism was devastated.
Persia's civilization disappeared from history.
Christianity was destroyed in Turkey, Iraq, Syria, and Egypt. The cultures and historical memory of these countries were totally destroyed. 57 countries have been conquered and are now ruled by the AntiGod.
Before there was a West, there was a South. The holocaust of Islamic slavery was imposed on large parts of black Africa. Islam was a major player in the black African slave trade – a historical fact not well known today. Black civilization was devastated. Slavery has been an integral part of Islam since its creation by Muhammad. Islam institutionalized slavery and made its existence legal and an Eternal Law of Allah (the AntiGod). In addition, not taught is the fact that up to 3 million Europeans were taken as slaves by Muslims. Seventy five percent of all Islam slaves died on the way to market. Black male slaves were castrated to ensure they could not reproduce. This is why there are no blacks in the Middle East.
Islam expanded by financing its armies thru imposing a devastating jizya criminal extortion tax on the kafirs forcing many of them to convert to Islam, looting and plundering kafir property, mass raping their women captives to produce new jihadists, and enslaving tens of millions of kafir women and children. Rather then see their children born into slavery many women converted to Islam. The descendents of present day Pakistan and the Muslims of India were for the most part products of rape and slavery.

EXTORTION

From the Hadith:

Muslim (19:4294) - There are many places in the hadith where Muhammad tells his followers to demand the jizya of non-believers. Here he lays down the rule that it is to be extorted by force: "If they refuse to accept Islam, demand from them the Jizya. If they agree to pay, accept it from them and hold off your hands. If they refuse to pay the tax, seek Allah's help and fight them"

Bukhari (53:386) - The command for Muslims to spread Islamic rule by force, subjugating others until they either convert to Islam or pay money, is eternal: Our Prophet, the Messenger of our Lord, has ordered us to fight you till you worship Allah Alone or give Jizya (i.e. tribute); and our Prophet has informed us that our Lord says:-- "Whoever amongst us is killed (i.e. martyred), shall go to Paradise to lead such a luxurious life as he has never seen, and whoever amongst us remain alive, shall become your master." This is being recounted during the reign of Umar, Muhammad's companion and the second caliph who sent conquering armies into non-Muslim Persian and Christian lands (after Muhammad's death).

Ishaq 956 & 962 - "He who withholds the Jizya is an enemy of Allah and His apostle." The words of Muhammad.

This lucrative extortion was practiced down through the centuries and was a part of the brutal Ottoman rule over Christians, Jews and others. The Serbs of Europe were particularly hard hit and often had to hand over their children to satisfy the collector. The children were then converted to Islam and trained as Jihad warriors for use in foreign campaigns (the so-called Janissaries).

In India, well into the 17th century, Muslim tax collectors would also take the wives and children of impoverished Hindus and sell them into slavery for the Jizya requirement. The only way for many to avoid losing their families was to convert to Islam. This tremendous discrimination is how Islam made inroads into populations that wanted nothing to do with it.

Technically, there is no such thing in Islam as an innocent non-Muslim, which makes those ballyhooed condemnations of "terror against innocent people" even more useless. There is a basis for protecting the "People of the Book" (originally Jews and Christians, but later extended to Hindus when Muslim leaders realized that killing them was not as profitable as taxing them). These would be those who place themselves completely under the rule of Muslims, relinquishing all rights and agreeing to finance the Muslim expansion. Unfortunately, even this has not been enough to spare religious minorities from extreme persecution and massacre.

Traditionally the collection of the jizya occurs at a ceremony that is designed to emphasize the subordinate status of the non-Muslim, where the subject is often struck in a humiliating fashion. M.A. Khan recounts that some Islamic clerics encouraged tax collectors to spit into the mouths of Hindu dhimmis during the process. He also quotes the popular Sufi teacher, Shaykh Ahmad Sirhindi:

"The honor of Islam lies in insulting the unbelief and the unbelievers (kafirs). One who respects kafirs dishonors Muslims... The real purpose of levying the Jizya on them is to humiliate them... [and] they remain terrified and trembling." Islamic Jihad

BOOTY

Ishaq: 510 "We ask Thee for the booty of this town and its people. Forward in the name of Allah. 'He used to say this of every town he raided."

Ishaq:327 "Allah said, 'A prophet must slaughter before collecting captives. A slaughtered enemy is driven from the land. Muhammad, you craved the desires of this world, its goods and the ransom captives would bring. But Allah desires killing them to manifest the religion.'"

Ishaq:592 "The Apostle held a large number of captives. There were 6,000 women and children prisoners. He had captured so many sheep and camels they could not be counted."

Ishaq:321 "The Spoils of War surah was handed down because we quarreled about the booty. So Allah took it away from us and gave it to His Apostle. When He did, we learned to fear Allah and obey his Messenger.... For in truth, our army had gone out with the Prophet seeking the caravan because we wanted its booty."

SLAVERY WAS PART OF BOOTY AND PLUNDER

From the Hadith:

Bukhari (80:753) - "The Prophet said, 'The freed slave belongs to the people who have freed him.'"

Bukhari (52:255) - The slave who accepts Islam and continues serving his Muslim master will receive a double reward in heaven.

Bukhari (41.598) - Slaves are property. They cannot be freed if an owner has outstanding debt, but rather used to pay off the debt.

Bukhari (62:137) - An account of women taken as slaves in battle by Muhammad's men after their husbands and fathers were killed. The woman were raped with Muhammad's approval.

Bukhari (34:432) - Another account of females taken captive and raped with Muhammad's approval. In this case it is evident that the Muslims intend on selling the women after raping them because they are concerned about devaluing their price by impregnating them. Muhammad is asked about coitus interruptus.

Bukhari (47.765) - A woman is rebuked by Muhammad for freeing a slave girl. The prophet tells her that she would have gotten a greater heavenly reward by giving her to a relative (as a slave).

Bukhari (34:351) - Muhammad sells a slave for money. He was thus a slave trader.

Bukhari (72:734) - Some contemporary Muslims in the West, where slavery is believed to be a horrible crime, are reluctant to believe that Muhammad owned slaves. This is just one of many places in the Hadith where a reference is made to a human being owned by Muhammad. In this case, the slave is of African descent.

Muslim 3901 - Muhammad trades away two black slaves for one Muslim slave.

Muslim 4112 - A man freed six slaves on the event of his death, but Muhammad reversed the emancipation and kept four in slavery to himself. He cast lots to determine which two to free.

Bukhari (47:743) - Muhammad's own pulpit - from which he preached Islam - was built with slave labor on his command.

Bukhari (59:637) - "The Prophet sent Ali to Khalid to bring the Khumus (of the booty) and I hated Ali, and Ali had taken a bath (after a sexual act with a slave-girl from the Khumus). I said to Khalid, 'Don't you see this (i.e. Ali)?' When we reached the Prophet I mentioned that to him. He said, 'O Buraida! Do you hate Ali?' I said, 'Yes.' He said, 'Do you hate him, for he deserves more than that from the Khumlus.'" Muhammad approved of his men having sex with slaves, as this episode involving his son-in-law, Ali, clearly proves. This hadith refutes the modern apologists who pretend that slaves were really "wives," since Muhammad had forbidden Ali from marrying another woman as long as Fatima (his favorite daughter) was living.

Abu Dawud (2150) - "The Apostle of Allah (may peace be upon him) sent a military expedition to Awtas on the occasion of the battle of Hunain. They met their enemy and fought with them. They defeated them and took them captives. Some of the Companions of the Apostle of Allah (may peace be upon him) were reluctant to have intercourse with the female captives in the presence of their husbands who were unbelievers. So Allah, the Exalted, sent down the Qur'anic verse: (Qur'an 4:24) 'And all married women (are forbidden) unto you save those (captives) whom your right hands possess.'" This is the background for verse 4:24 of the Qur'an. Not only does Allah grant permission for women to be captured and raped, but allows it to even be done in front of their husbands.

Ibn Ishaq (734) - A slave girl is given a "violent beating" by Ali in the presence of Muhammad, who does nothing about it.

Ibn Ishaq (734) - "Then the apostle sent Sa-d b. Zayd al-Ansari, brother of Abdu'l-Ashal with some of the captive women of Banu Qurayza to Najd and he sold them for horses and weapons." Muhammad trades away women captured from the Banu Qurayza tribe to non-Muslim slave traders for property. (Their men had been executed after surrendering peacefully without a fight).

Umdat al-Salik (Reliance of the Traveller) (o9.13) - According to Sharia, when a child or woman is taken captive by Muslims, they become slaves by the fact of their capture. A captured woman's previous marriage is immediately annulled.

The fact that throughout Islam's history, this slaughter in the worst ways imaginable, murdered in the name of and to the greater glory of God is an obscenity. The so called men of Allah (the AntiGod) responsible for this carnage who have - through the millenniums - for power, domination, and control of society unleashed this evil deserve to be in Hell.

To take man's natural concept of God, a conception of peace and love and goodness - an all wise, all merciful God for all mankind, - A God of Moral Perfection and turn God - by bastardizing his teachings into a murderous Allah (the AntiGod) of hate, terror, intolerance, death and destruction is one of the greatest sins that can be committed against God. Islam will remain forever a black historical stain smearing all human history.

Following is the bloody history of Jihad.

HISTORY OF JIHAD

The Jihad against Arabs (622 to 634)
The Jihad against Zoroastrian Persians of Iran, Baluchistan and Afghanistan (634 to 651)
The Jihad against the Byzantine Christians (634 to 1453)
The Jihad against Christian Coptic Egyptians (640 to 655)
The Jihad against Christian Coptic Nubians - modern Sudanese (650)
The Jihad against pagan Berbers - North Africans (650 to 700)
The Jihad against Spaniards (711 to 730)
The Reconquista against Jihad in Spain (730 to 1492)
The Jihad against Franks - modern French (720 to 732)
The Jihad against Sicilians in Italy (812 to 940)
The Jihad against Chinese (751)
The Jihad against Turks (651 to 751)
The Jihad against Armenians and Georgians (1071 to 1920)
The Crusade against Jihad (1096 – 1291 ongoing)
The Jihad against Mongols (1260 to 1300)
The Jihad against Hindus of India, Pakistan and Bangladesh (638 to 1857)
The Jihad against Indonesians and Malays (1450 to 4,000)
The Jihad against Poland (1444 to 1699)
The Jihad against Romania (1350 to 1699)
The Jihad against Russia (4,000 to 1853)
The Jihad against Bulgaria (1350 to 1843)
The Jihad against Serbs, Croats and Albanians (1334 to 1920)
The Jihad against Greeks (1450 to 1853)
The Jihad against Albania (1332 - 1853)
The Jihad against Croatia (1389 to 1843)
The Jihad against Hungarians (4,000 to 1683)
The Jihad against Austrians (1683)
Jihad in the Modern Age (20th and 21st Centuries)
The Jihad against Israelis (1948 – 2004 ongoing)

The Jihad against Americans (9/11/2001)
The Jihad against the British (1947 onwards)
The Jihad against the Germans (1945 onwards)
The Jihad against the Filipinos in Mindanao(1970 onwards)
The Jihad against Indonesian Christians in Malaku and East Timor (1970 onwards)
The Jihad against Russians (1995 onwards)
The Jihad against Dutch and Belgians (2003 onwards)
The Jihad against Norwegians and Swedes (2003 onwards)
The Jihad against Thais (2003 onwards)
The Jihad against Nigerians (1965 onwards)
The Jihad against Canadians (2001 onwards)
The Jihad against Latin America (2003 onwards)
The Jihad against Australia (2002 onwards)
The Global Jihad today (2001 – ongoing)
The War on Terror against Jihad today (2001– ongoing

For a detailed description of the bloody expansion of Islam, I recommend the following books:
The Truth About Muhammad: Founder of the World's Most Intolerant Religion by Robert Spencer available at Amazon.
Islamic Jihad: A Legacy of Forced Conversion, Imperialism and Slavery by MA Khan available at Barnes & Noble, Amazon.

MUHAMMAD THE PROPHET OF PEACE:
Chronology of Muhammad's Life

For a detailed chronology of Muhammad's life go to:
http://www.islamreform.net/new-page-37.htm

CHAPTER THIRTY SEVEN

BLACKS CALLING THEMSELVES MUSLIMS SHOULD BE ASHAMED

We have examined slavery in this work from the view point of the Quran. We have shown that slavery is one of the vilest institutions ever created by man. Islam institutionalized slavery. Allah, the Islamic God, created ETERNAL LAWS allowing Muslims to own and rape their slaves. Muslims can enslave kafirs and keep the female captives as sex-slaves.

Slavery in Islam is not restricted to any one race or color. ALL kafirs no matter what their color are slaves of the Muslims. However, blacks are treated with special racist contempt.

If Islam succeeds in conquering the world, there will rise again Islamic corporations for breeding, raising, and trading slaves in tens of millions as was done until the late 19th century. Kafir women will again become the sex-slaves of Muslim masters. This evil, horrid treatment, which so characterized the fate of tens of millions of kafirs at the hands of Muslims, will make a comeback on the world-stage.

Muhammad, the apostle of God, the Islamic prophet of peace, was a slaver. He owned 40 slaves some of them blacks. Muhammad had kept his female slaves as concubines, so did his comrades and pious companions.

Mahran, one of Muhammad's black slaves, was made to carry the belongings of Muhammad and his companions while on a journey through the burning desert as Muhammad said: "Carry them, for you are a ship." Thereafter, he became known by that surname, Safina ('ship'). Relating this own story, Mahran said:

"The apostle of God and his companions went on a trip. (When) their belongings became too heavy for them to carry, Muhammad told me, 'Spread your garment.' They filled it with their belongings, then they put it on me. The apostle of God told me, 'Carry (it), for you are a ship.' Even if I was carrying the load of six or seven donkeys while we were on a journey, anyone who felt weak would throw his clothes or his shield or his sword on me so I would carry that, a heavy load. The prophet told me, 'You are a ship'" (refer to Ibn Qayyim, p. 115–116; al-Hulya, Vol. 1, p. 369, quoted from Ahmad 5:222).

Islamic 'Black Slave' Trade

The awful truth is that Arabs ravaged Africa for nearly a millennium engaging in enslavement of Africans on a grand scale before the Europeans began exporting black slaves. In fact, the Arabic word for 'black' ("abed") is also the same word for 'slave'. This is because; the black Africans became synonymous with slaves to Arabs. As we have already stated, over 120 million black Africans were killed by Muslims in one of the greatest holocausts in history. Some 75% of slaves perished on their way to markets thousands of miles away. To ensure that black men could not have children Muslims castrated them; many died in this barbaric cruelty.

Slavery is a divine institution in Islam, enshrined in the Quran and unchangeable for all time. To admit that slavery is a mistake is to admit the fallibility of the Quran and bring its divine origin into question.

Muhammad Owned and Sold Black Slaves

Muhammad owned several black slaves. Muslim scholar Ibn Qayyim al-Jawziyya relies heavily on the prophet's biographies written by great early Islamic scholars. He is regarded by Muslims as an authority, a primary source and a leader amongst Islamic scholars. He tells us in his book, "Zad al-Ma'ad" (part 1, pp. 114-116), the following:

"These are the names of Muhammad's male slaves: Yakan Abu Sharh, Aflah, 'Ubayd, Dhakwan, Tahman, Mirwan, Hunayn, Sanad, Fadala Yamamin, Anjasha al-Hadi, Mad'am, Karkara, Abu Rafi', Thawban, Ab Kabsha, Salih, Rabah, Yara Nubyan, Fadila, Waqid, Mabur, Abu Waqid, Kasam, Abu' Ayb, Abu Muwayhiba, Zayd Ibn Haritha, and also a black slave called Mahran."

Still to this day in Saudi Arabia, the heartland of Islam, the common word for "Black" is "Abd", also meaning "slave" as it was in Muhammad's time.

Muhammad's position on freeing slaves

In one instance, a man freed a slave that he kept as a sexual partner. When Muhammad heard what happened, he auctioned the boy and sold him for 800 *dirhams* to Na-eem Ebn Abdullah Al- Nahham. (Sahih Moslem vol. 7, page 83)

According to Muhammad, the punishment for committing adultery is different with a free-woman and a slave-woman. The man must be flogged one-hundred stripes and be exiled for one year. The free woman must be stoned to death. But the slave-woman (since she has a monetary value) will not be exiled or killed, she is to be flogged one-hundred stripes. If the violation is repeated, the slave-woman is to be sold. (Sahih Al Bukhari vol. 8:821 & 822)

We have already documented many teachings in the Quran, in which Allah promotes the sexual and physical brutalization of human beings. Following are two teachings of slavery, we have examined previously that form part of the foundation of slavery in the Quran.

Quran 2:178: "O you who believe! retaliation is prescribed for you in the matter of the slain, the free for the free, and the slave for the slave, and the female for the female, but if any remission is made to any one by his (aggrieved) brother, then prosecution (for the bloodwit) should be made according to usage, and payment should be made to him in a good manner; this is an alleviation from your Lord and a mercy; so whoever exceeds the limit after this he shall have a painful chastisement."

Quran 4:3: "Marry women of your choice, Two or three or four; but if ye fear that ye shall not be able to deal justly (with them), then only one, or (a captive) that your right hands possess, that will be more suitable, to prevent you from doing injustice."

Again, you can have sex with married women and female slaves obtained in war (with whom you may rape or do whatever you like). The divine institution of Islamic slavery, including the sex-slavery, is the vilest of institutions ever created in history.

Islam Looked Down on Blacks

Islam is an ideology, whose sacred Scriptures contain explicit denigrating remarks about black people.

Muhammad referred to Blacks as "raisin heads". (Sahih al-Bukhari vol. 1, no. 662 and vol. 9, no. 256).

In another Hadith, Muhammad is quoted as saying that Blacks are, "pug-nosed slaves". (Sahih Moslem vol. 9, p. 46-47).

A Slave Is Not Entitled to Property or Money

Ibn Hazm says in Vol. 6, Part 9,

"The slave is not permitted to write a will when he dies, nor can he bequeath (anything) because his entire possessions belong to his master."

The Testimony of Slaves is Not Admissible

In Vol. 35, p. 409 Ibn Timiyya remarks,

"The Shafi'i, Malik, and Abu Hanifa, who are the legists of Islam, assert that the testimony of the slave is not acceptable."

The "Ordinances of the Qur'an" by the Shafi'i (part II, p. 142), stipulates that,

"The witnesses must be from among our freeman, not from our slaves, but from freeman who belong to our religion!"

Black Slaves on Matters of Sex and Marriage

1. The Slave cannot choose for himself.

This was confirmed by all the Muslim scholars on the authority of Muhammad. In Vol. 6, Part 9, p. 467, Ibn Hazm said,

"If a slave gets married without the permission of his master, his marriage will be invalid and he must be whipped because he has committed adultery. He must be separated from his wife. She is also regarded as an adulteress because Muhammad said, 'Any slave who gets married without the approval of his master is a prostitute.'"

The same text is quoted by Ibn Qayyim al-Jawziyya (Part 5, p. 117 of "Zad al-Maad"), as well as Ibn Timiyya (Vol. 32, p. 201). Malik Ibn Anas relates (Vol. 2, Part 4) more than that. He says (pp. 199, 201, 206),

"The slave does not get married without the approval of his master. If he is a slave to two masters, he has to obtain the approval of both men."

2. The male slave and the female slave are forced to get married.

Malik Ibn Anas says explicitly,

"The master has the right to force his male or female slave to marry without obtaining their approval" (Vol. 2, p. 155).

"The master does not have the right to force the female slave to wed to an ugly black slave if she is beautiful and agile unless in case of utmost necessity" (refer to Ibn Hazm, Vol. 6, Part 9, p. 469).

In matters of sex and marriage, Ibn Timiyya states:

"The one who owns the mother also owns her children. Being the master of the mother makes him the owner of her children whether they were born to a husband or they were illegitimate children. Therefore, the master has the right to have sexual intercourse with the daughters of his maid-slave because they are his property, provided he does not sleep with the mother at the same time" (Vol. 35, p. 54).

Price of Slaves

"If an owned slave assaults somebody and damages his property, his crime will be tied to his neck. It will be said to his master, `If you wish, you can pay the fine for the damages done by your slave or deliver him to be sentenced to death.' His master has to choose one of the two options - either the value of the slave and his price or the damage the slave has caused" (Vol. 32, p. 202, Ibn Timiyya).

Racism From The Hadith

Ishaq:243 "I heard the Apostle say: 'Whoever wants to see Satan should look at Nabtal!' He was a black man with long flowing hair, inflamed eyes, and dark ruddy cheeks.... Allah sent down concerning him: 'To those who annoy the Prophet there is a painful doom." [9:61] "Gabriel came to Muhammad and said, 'If a black man comes to you his heart is more gross than a donkey's.'"

Ishaq:144 "A rock was put on a slave's chest. When Abu Bakr complained, they said, 'You are the one who corrupted him, so save him from his plight.' I will do so,' said Bakr. 'I have a black slave, tougher and stronger than Bilal, who is a heathen. I will exchange him. The transaction was carried out."

Tabari II:11 "Shem, the son of Noah was the father of the Arabs, the Persians, and the Greeks; Ham was the father of the Black Africans; and Japheth was the father of the Turks and of Gog and Magog who were cousins of the Turks. Noah prayed that the prophets and apostles would be descended from Shem and kings would be from Japheth. He prayed that the African's color would change so that their descendants would be slaves to the Arabs and Turks."

Tabari II:21 "Ham [Africans] begat all those who are black and curly-haired, while Japheth [Turks] begat all those who are full-faced with small eyes, and Shem [Arabs] begat everyone who is handsome of face with beautiful hair. Noah prayed that the hair of Ham's descendants would not grow beyond their ears, and that whenever his descendants met Shem's, the latter would enslave them."

Ishaq:450 "It is your folly to fight the Apostle, for Allah's army is bound to disgrace you. We brought them to the pit. Hell was their meeting place. We collected them there, black slaves, men of no descent."

Bukhari:V4B52N137 "The Prophet said, 'Let the negro slave of Dinar perish. And if he is pierced with a thorn, let him not find anyone to take it out for him.... If he [the black slave] asks for anything it shall not be granted, and if he needs intercession [to get into paradise], his intercession will be denied.'"

Already demonstrated and re-listed here - slavery, raping slave girls, owning slaves, selling boys and women as trophies of war, sharing the booty (including slaves) obtained in raids and wars with Allah are all central teachings of Islam. Slavery was one of the major driving forces behind the expansion of Islam.

Asking again the question - what will be one's conclusion about a man found to own slaves in a civilized country, let alone raping slaves? Prophet Muhammad, aided by Allah, created the institution of slavery: he enslaved in large numbers, owned dozens of slaves as the Prophet of Islam; he used the female captives as sex-slaves on top his dozen wives; he traded in slaves.

Such an evil incarnate is eulogized by world's 1.2 billion Muslims as the perfect human being, the greatest apostle of God, a man of peace. Tens of millions of Blacks—who were given the worst treatment by Muhammad, who suffered the most devastating treatment at the hands of Muslims—also eulogize this man, call themselves proud Muslims. There cannot be anything more shameful than this.

CHAPTER THIRTY EIGHT

WHY A MUSLIM CAN NEVER BE ALLOWED TO BE PRESIDENT OF THE UNITED STATES EVER

COLIN POWELL: THE UTLIMATE DHIMMI'S DHIMMI

People ask how was it possible that a country as cultured as Germany could have allowed a Hitler to come to power? People ask how was it possible that Germans at the time sat back and allowed the evil of Nazism to function: the arrest, killing, murdering, torturing and extermination of their fellow Jewish citizens, the enslavement of millions of conquered people dying, laboring in German factories, on German farms, mass murder of millions of Jews in concentration camps, mass murder of conquered peoples in their villages and cities committed not only by the SS but also by young men aged 18, 19, 20 serving in the German army? Now we know the answer.

The answer is very simple - people like Colin Powell and our political, intellectual, religious, media elites who are supporting and by so doing giving respectability to one of the most evil ideologies ever created by man - Islam. They are bringing Islam to power throughout the West just as German political, intellectual; media elites brought Hitler to power. However, the answer is much more than these German elites who allowed the evil of Nazism to gain power by clothing Hitler and his evil ideology with the cloak of respectability but also the German people who stood idly by acquiescing and in the end fighting to the death by the millions protecting this evil. Just as the German people submitted to Nazism, the people of the West are submitting to Islam. People are turning a blind eye to the existence in their midst of an ideology of extermination and genocide - that like Nazism will be directed first at their neighbors – Jews, gays, Christians and then eventually at them. Cowardice is part of the answer but also supreme, immoral selfishness – the willingness to stand idly by while your neighbor's family is being led away to be brutality tortured and murdered in the faint hope that your family will not be led away to a similar fate. By acquiescing to evil, we all but guarantee our future surrender to evil or a dramatic life and death struggle against evil with the ensuring deaths of tens of millions. Let us not judge the Germans of the 1920's, 30's and 40's for we are no different.

On October 19th 2008, Colin Powell (former Secretary of State) endorsed Barack Obama for President but in so doing went out of his way to legitimatize Islam and not only give legitimacy to this very evil ideology but undermine the efforts of those fighting Islam by strongly implying that they were racist Americans - that those revealing the teachings of the Quran, quoting Islam in its own words/writings - questioning whether a Muslim could be President with the retort - "The really right answer is what if he is" were un-American.

What Colin Powell does not care to realize is that all democratic loving, free people are engaged in a life and death struggle against Islam. In order to answer Colin Powell's question and our question as to why a Muslim can never be allowed to be President let's do a short summary of the earlier chapters of this Islamic evil.

1400 years ago in Arabia there was born a barbarian who invented a being he called Allah, declared that he had received revelations from this Allah (who was the same God worshipped by Jews and Christians) that called for the murder, torture, terrorizing, raping, looting and pillaging, enslaving of all unbelievers in Allah's new religion - Islam. This Allah declared that all non-Muslims were sub-humans called kafirs and their murder was not a crime but a holy act to be rewarded by accession to a Paradise filled with virgin sluts whom these Muslim killers could sexually molest for all eternity.

These revelations from Allah calling for the conquering of the world for Islam ordered the extermination and genocide of all kafirs epically Jews and Christians who refused to convert to Islam or agree to pay a devastating jizya tax and accept dhimmi semi-slavery status.

It was Muhammad who put these teachings from Allah into action enacting the First, Final Solution of The Jewish and Christian Question of Saudi Arabia - the extermination and mass exile of the Jews and Christians of Arabia.

The extreme hatred of Allah, the Nazi-like God of Muslims, for unbelievers was manifested in the 4,000 Quranic teachings to His followers concerning the idolaters. Islam and Nazism are one and one and the same.

In order to understand the sheer horror of Hitler and Muhammad and the statement of Powell look again at a few important parallels between Islam and Nazism on pages 224/226 and ask the very important question - how any normal, moral person could be a Muslim?

Hitler enacted the Final Solution of the Jewish question and almost succeeded. Islam and its allies such as Western political, intellectual, religious, media elites who are supporting this evil are in the process of completing the job Muhammad started and Hitler almost completed - they are enacting the Final, Final Solution of The Jewish and Christian Question.

How could Colin Powell give aid and comfort to an ideology whose God and prophet had the pants of Jewish boys pulled down and genital area inspected for pubic hair? (Reread the Massacre of Banu Qurayzah on page 62) Can you imagine the terror in these boys? To be beheaded at the age of 13/14. Can Powell not hear the wailing of the women and the children as the prophet of God orders the Jewish men dragged out completely shackled, forced to bend down in front of a trench Muhammad had assisted in constructing to control the blood flow as the beheaded heads fell into the trenches by the hundreds: a stagnant river of blood flowing nowhere. Does Powell not picture the prophet's sword being raised - the bright Arabian sun flashing off the sharp blade and then the prophet smashing downward with all his might – the skin and tissues binding the Jewish head to the Jewish body violently severed spurting blood in all directions covering the prophet's face and clothing. The head of the still living Jew would slump over not yet fully chopped off requiring the prophet covered in blood to bring down his bloody sword a second time smashing through the remaining skin and tissue and the head finally falling to the ground then stacked in a pile like bloody cordwood with eyes.

What a fearsome sight Muhammad was that day.

What of these poor 13/14 year old Jewish boys dragged away naked and beheaded.

Employing your minds eye, go back to the market place all those many years ago; having being found to possess pubic hair and therefore knowing that beheading will be their fate, the Jewish boys will be frantically begging for mercy. It will take two Muslim men to control this frightened young child man and drag his naked bum across the hot desert ground. The poor Jew will be yelling and screaming frantically, his arms moving wildly in all directions. Upon arrival at the killing station, another Muslim man will grab the boy's head as he tries to avoid the downward thrust of the sword. Stretched out like a human airplane, with the eyes and bloody severed heads of his father, older brothers, uncles, friend's fathers, older brothers, uncles, staring up into the wild eyes of this helpless man child, the sword will make a clean thrust right thru the skin and neck bones severing the head in one great flourish. Blood will spurt all over these holy Muslims sanctifying their heroic deeds. Blood will pour from the empty cavity. The head will be tossed into the street joining the head pile. Laughter will ensue as these holy of holies congratulate each other on a job well done.

Is there no humanity for these poor, murdered, murdered?

What of Hitler who's SS had Jews (young and old, men, women and children, healthy and infirm) stand naked in front of mass graves as in Baby Yar, Ukraine and then shot in the head, so they would fall forward into the ditches. Blood would spurt from the blown off head onto the SS executioners.

At the massacre of Banu Qurayzah, Muhammad obeyed Allah's teaching Quran 8:6 to the letter:

"It is not fitting for an Apostle that he should have prisoners of war until He thoroughly subdued the land...." (Allah insisting Prophet to kill all the prisoners, and should not keep any surrendered prisoners alive until He (Prophet) occupied entire Arabia."

Colin Powell asked the question: "The really right answer is what if he is"

In answering Colin Powell (and our question), we must state that - the really right answer is how can a moral human being believe in a God who instructs the murder of all prisoners? These are CRIMES AGAINST HUMANITY. THESE ARE CRIMES AGAINST GOD. This law was an order from Allah (the AntiGod) to murder all prisoners until Arabia was conquered for Islam. Take no prisoners. Kill them all. "Make slaughter in the land." MASS MURDER. The word slaughter is so outrageous that only the insane can believe in Islam.

In answering Powell, we repeat here from "The Criminality of Muhammad" that with Muhammad as his prophet, Allah had found the perfect executioner of his grand plan for humanity - the perfect executioner for enforcing the will of God. "Here was a true apostle - a man devoid of all human feelings of love and mercy - a man who would show no mercy. Here was an apostle who would not allow the crying of kafir women and children to touch his heart. Here was an apostle who would stand as a moral example for all Muslim men to emanate through the ages - men like Osma bin Laden, suicide bombers, jihadists, beheaders, etc who would follow the example set by the apostle of God at Banu Quraiza and enforce God's laws as set out in the Quran without mercy."

The really right answer to Powell is how could any normal, rational, moral person be 'proud' to follow a heartless monster – a man who was a child abuser, slave trader. rapist, stoned women to death, mass murderer beheading captives, terrorist, ordered followers burned alive in their homes, the eyes burnt out of people's heads - unending horror?

The really right answer to Powell is how can, a rational, moral person believe that God would choose a demented, criminal as His prophet and then allow this evil person to declare that obeying the messenger was obeying Allah and vice versa?

Muhammad: A Mass Murderer

Tabari VII: 133 " When Muhammad saw Harnzah he said,' If Allah gives me victory over the Quraysh at any time, I shall mutilate thirty of their men!' When the Muslims saw the rage of the prophet they said, 'By Allah, if we are victorious over them, we shall mutilate them in a way no Arab has ever mutilated anybody."

The really right answer to Powell is how could any normal, rational, moral, person believe in a God who ordered extermination of all kafirs, raping of sex slaves, enslavement of women and children, looting and pillaging kafir property.

The really right answer to Powell is how could any normal, rational, moral, person believe in an evil God that rewards Muslims who murder kafirs with guaranteed accession to a Paradise filled with virgin sluts possessing voluptuous breasts and lustrous eyes. Again, this most evil of evilest verse:

VERSE 9:111 – MUSLIM'S PASSPORT TO PARADISE

"Allah hath purchased of the believers their persons and their goods; for theirs (in return) is the garden (of Paradise): they fight in His cause, and slay and are slain: a promise binding on Him in truth, through the Law, the Gospel, and the Qur'an: and who is more faithful to his covenant than Allah? then rejoice in the bargain which ye have concluded: that is the achievement supreme."

"As for the righteous (Muslims)... We (Allah) shall wed them to beautiful virgins with lustrous eyes" [Q 44:51-54]

We can never ask this question enough times: Can you imagine in the 21st century believing in a Paradise filled with virgins that re–generate as virgins after each sex act with Muslim killers who sport eternal erections? Again, this teaching is the greatest evil in human history. As stated, 270,000,000 kafirs have been murdered in the past 1400 years by Muslim men seeking guaranteed accession to this eternal brothel. This is in addition to the 2,976 kafirs murdered on 9/11.

The really right answer to Powell is how could any normal, rational, moral, person believe in a God that oppresses and subjugates women allowing their sexual and mental brutalization.

Lewd Women Imprisoned Until Death

4:15 "As for those of your women who are guilty of lewdness, call to witness four of you against them. And if they testify (to the truth of the allegation) then confine them to the houses until death take them or (until) Allah appoint for them a way (through new legislation)."

The really right answer to Powell is how could any normal, rational, moral, person believe in a God that murdered 120,000,000 blacks on their way to the slave markets and to ensure black males could not reproduce had them castrated. Many died from this bloody, brutal operation.

The really right answer to Powell is how could any normal, rational, moral, person believe in a God that tortured kafirs by having them crucified, their hands, feet or tongues cut off or eyes burnt out of their heads.

Muhammad: Torturer

Ishaq: 595 " The Apostle said,' Get him away from me and cut off his tongue.'"

Ishaq:312 "Umar said to the Apostle, 'Let me pull out Suhayl's two front teeth. That way his tongue will stick out and he will never be able to speak against you again.'"

Tabari VIII:96 "A raiding party led by Zayd set out against Umm in Ramadan. During it, Umm suffered a cruel death. Zyad tied her legs with rope and then tied her between two camels until they split her in two. She was a very old woman. Then they brought Umm's daughter and Abdallah to the Messenger. Umm's daughter belonged to Salamah who had captured her. Muhammad asked Salamah for her, and Salamah gave her to him."

    The really right answer to Powell is how could any normal, rational, moral person believe in a God and a prophet who were the mirror image of Adolf Hitler, Allah the Nazi God and Muhammad - Fuehrer of the Muslims with his SS killers, torturers – the companions.
    The really right answer to Colin Powell must be emphatically proclaimed - No such person who believes in Allah and his messenger - Muhammad and his ideology - Islam can ever be allowed to be President of The United States. How could you elect a person to be President who believes in a Paradise for Muslim killers filled with virgin sluts – that murdering, torture, is divine – plus all the other 1,500 teachings listed in this book which are 36% of the 4,000 evil teachings in the Quran? Repeating, if a Muslim questions just one word of the Quran he is no longer a Muslim but an apostate and must be killed. Therefore, since ALL Muslims must believe in Allah and his messenger and all the evil teachings of the Quran than no Muslim can ever be President. It would be like electing Adolf Hitler or a member of the German SS or Nazi Party or a believer in the fuehrer, SS and Nazism as President. **THERE IS NO DIFFERENCE.**
    Most Western political, religious, intellectual and media elites hate the West with a passion. They despise Western Civilization and everything it stands for. These elites have formed an alliance with the AntiGod Allah to totally destroy the foundations of our civilization.
    By not exposing the truth of Islam, these elites utilizing terms: Islam is a religion of peace, Muhammad is a prophet of peace etc. are perpetrating the myth of a hijacking and perversion of the teachings of Islam and by so doing are granting Islam – LEGITIMACY. They have renounced God and are worshipping the AntiGod.

By supporting Islam, Western elites are coating themselves in evil and become accomplices in the very great acts of Muslim terrorist carnage plaguing the world and in many respects just as evil if not more evil than the Muslims committing these acts of slaughter. Again - they are rejecting God and embracing the AntiGod – Allah.

When you are a President, Prime Minister, legislator, you are in a position of power to fight evil. If instead you acquiesce to the evil of Islam and indeed facilitate the spread of this evil by giving it legal protection from intellectual examination like the other categories of Western elites not only have you coated yourself in evil and become an accomplice in the very great acts of Muslim terrorist carnage and in many respects just as evil if not more evil than the Muslims committing these acts of slaughter but are creating a future whereby our children will be faced with the dire choice of surrendering to Islam or civil war in the streets with troops fighting for freedom and democracy right in our own cities.

To prevent this disaster, citizens of America, Canada, Europe must stand up and demand that their Congress/ Parliaments/ Legislatures declare Who We Are and What We Stand For as stated in the Defense of Democracy: Democratic and Freedom Act and Declaration of a God of Moral Perfection: free peoples living in free societies under the protection of democratic constitutions that embrace the equality of all races, peoples and sexes. (See Chapter 49.)

For teachings concerning this chapter go to:
http://www.islamreform.net/new-page-20.htm
http://www.islamreform.net/new-page-14.htm

MUHAMMAD: A HUMAN BEING OF PERFECTION

Muhammad's Dead Poets Society

The assassinations of satirical poets in early Islam

For a very important detailed analysis of Muhammad's assassinations go to:
http://www.islamreform.net/new-page-37.htm

CHAPTER THIRTY NINE

THE BANALITY OF ISLAM EVIL AND THE NORMALCY OF ISLAM EVIL

THE BANALITY OF SILENCE

The banality of evil is a phrase coined in 1963 by Hannah Arendt in her work "Eichmann in Jerusalem" describes the thesis that the great evils in history generally, and the Holocaust in particular, were not executed by fanatics or sociopaths but rather by ordinary people who accepted the premises of their state and therefore, participated with the view that their actions were normal.

During the Second World War, ordinary everyday Germans woke up in the morning, mothers readied their children for school, packed a lunch for her husband who after having a breakfast of wieners and bread with coffee would head out probably on a bicycle to his job at the local Concentration Camp. Once at the camp, when the trains arrived, he ordered the inhabitants out, went through the throngs separating the able bodied who could work from the infirm, husbands from their families, children from their mothers, any opposition, and he would order the offender shot on the spot, women that he judged good looking received special attention for raping and sexual molestation later.

The sickly and unwanted were marched directly into the gas chambers. During the day, our German family man circulated through the camp ensuring the efficient functioning of the facility. Any slave workers who were not pulling their weight were taken out on his orders and sent to the gas chamber. Once he was convinced that everything was in order, our good German returned to his office and raped his sex slaves. In the evening, he returned home exhausted. His children greeted him yelling daddy, daddy. His dog jumped up and licked his face. He hugged and kissed his wife, ate a hearty supper, then retired to read the newspaper or listen to the radio. The very real reality is that our German family man probably never met a Jew or hated Jews. He was just doing his job. In his mind, he was not committing evil whatsoever. He was just a normal every day German doing his normal every day duty.

This is the banality of evil. This is the normality of evil – German style.

As has already been described, after the Battle of Banu Quraiza - Muhammad had all the Jewish men assembled and beheaded. The young Jewish boys were beheaded after having their pants pulled down and genitals inspected for the slightest traces of pubic hair. The good looking Jewish women were separated out to be raped and gang raped after the beheading job was completed. The rest were sold into slavery. At the Massacre of Kaibyr, Muhammad ordered a fire set on the Jewish chieftain's chest torturing him to reveal the whereabouts of the cities treasure. When he refused after great unimaginable suffering, the chieftain was taken and beheaded. Muhammad raped this leader's 17 year old wife that night. On orders from Muhammad, the Muslim companions would assassinate his opponents. On orders from Muhammad, Muslim women were buried to their chests and stoned to death. On orders from Muhammad, Muslims who were judged by Muhammad to be deficient in their faith were burnt alive in their homes. Muhammad through his phony Allah created an immoral, frame work of depravity, whereby murder, rape, torture etc were divine acts of God. All this evil was sanctioned by Allah.

This is the Banality of Evil, the Normality of Evil - Islamic Style.

For Muslims, these teachings are normal. It is normal to kill and torture kafirs. What Muhammad did in his massacres was okay. The great acts of a great prophet of a great God. 100% of mosques in the US and Europe are teaching the Koran. When Muslim children go to school, they are taught these teachings, and it is all just normal. In the Muslim mind, what we regard as evil, they regard as good, divine, and normal. Pulling down the pants of young Jewish boys to determine death was a normal act by good, normal Muslims doing their duty just as our good, normal German did his duty. Blowing up the kafir London subway system was just a normal act fulfilling the teachings of God. Smashing jets into the twin towers was God's will to punish the kafir for not submitting to Islam. A Paradise filled with virgin sluts for kafir killers is a normal human depiction. Burning Muslims alive in their homes for missing prayer, stoning Muslim women to death for adultery, cutting off the hands of thiefs, killing apostates are all just normal behavior.

The Islamic banality of evil and the normality of evil reach its true climax when Muslims defend the Quran, Allah, Muhammad and Islam. It reaches its climax with the great wall of silence that greets each act of carnage – the Banality of Silence. Draw a mustache on an image of Muhammad and you get millions rampaging through the streets. Kill thousands of kafirs and millions pour into the streets screaming their cheers. Not millions protesting. The reason is because killing kafirs is not murder but holy acts of good, normal Muslims fulfilling the will of Allah.

The test of true goodness is when you confront evil head on and expunge it from your heart and soul. This sounds easy but it is not. It means reaching into the very core of your being and pulling out all your mental insides, everything you have ever been taught from childhood, washing it out with the soap of truth. This requires expunging from the Muslim mind - the Quran with its close to 4,000 teachings of evil, terror, murder, torture and subrogation of women.

WHY THESE TEACHINGS OF EVIL, TERROR, MURDER, VIOLENCE AND SUBROGATION OF WOMEN MUST BE REMOVED FROM THE QURAN AND ISLAM ABANDONED.

By leaving these violent and abhorrent teachings in the Quran, Muslims are in effect saying that these teachings are NORMAL. They are acquiescing to evil. Once you accommodate evil, you lose your moral center and become willingly or unwillingly an accomplice to evil. You cannot call yourself a Good Muslim - pray 5 times a day – and ignore the evil – the moral black hole that lies at very the heart of Islam. You cannot call yourself a good person and refuse to condemn the violence of the Quran and demand that evil be expunged from this very evil book. By not fighting against the evil in the Quran and abandoning Islam, Muslims become accomplices in these very great acts of terrorist carnage and in many respects just as evil if not more evil than the Muslim men committing these acts of slaughter. **THEY ALSO SERVE WHO ONLY STAND AND WATCH.**

We can no longer allow Muslims to declare Islam as a religion of peace and love etc. while leaving in the Quran and Islamic texts evil teachings calling for the destruction of kafirs. We can no longer allow these Muslims to live in a fantasy world of an Allah of all goodness and Muhammad – the prophet of peace while the Quran contains teachings of a hateful, murderous Allah (the AntiGod). By demanding that Muslims prove that they are truly peace loving – by renouncing these evil teachings, condemning their evil founder Muhammad and his fake Allah and leaving Islam will be **THEIR TRUE MOMENT OF CATHARSIS. THE MOMENT THEY SAVE THEIR IMMORAL SOULS.**

CHAPTER FORTY

AMERICA AND EUROPE'S FUTURE: DHIMMIHOOD

British Muslims are already calling for British kafirs to distinguish themselves from the Muslims by wearing identifiable clothing. In this way, the Muslim will know that they are kafirs and treat them as dhimmis as called for by Allah in Quran 9:29.

WHAT DHIMMIHOOD MEANS FOR THE KAFIR

Holy blood runs through the veins of the Muslim. They are the chosen ones of Allah. Muslim men are exalted by Allah over all other men. Dhimmis are sub-humans. On a scale of humanity from minus1 million to plus 1 million with zero being the dividing line between a sub-human creature and a human being: Muslim men are plus 1 million. Kafir men are minus 1 million. Since kafir women have value as sex slaves and breeding stock, they are minus 700,000. Muslim women are minus 500,000 so great is the distain and contempt that Allah and his messenger possess for them.

As previously stated, peoples of the book – Christians and Jews must either convert to Islam or agree to pay a jizya tax and accept dhimmihood or be murdered. Dhimmihood is a semi slave status for the book peoples to the Muslim.

The status and responsibilities of the Dhimmi are set down in the Pact of Umar an agreement made, according to Islamic tradition, between the caliph Umar, who ruled the Muslims from 634 to 644, and a Christian community. In return for "safety for ourselves, children, property and followers of our religion"

The Christians will not:

1. Build "a monastery, church, or a sanctuary for a monk";
2. "Restore any place of worship that needs restoration";
3. Use such places "for the purpose of enmity against Muslims";

4. "Allow a spy against Muslims into our churches and homes or hide deceit [or betrayal] against Muslims";
5. Imitate the Muslims' "clothing, caps, turbans, sandals, hairstyles, speech, nicknames and title names";
6. "Ride on saddles, hang swords on the shoulders, collect weapons of any kind or carry these weapons";
6. "Encrypt our stamps in Arabic"
7. "Sell liquor"
8. "Teach our children the Qur'an";
9. "Publicize practices of Shirk" – that is, associating partners with Allah, such as regarding Jesus as Son of God. In other words, Christian and other non-Muslim religious practice will be private, if not downright furtive;
10. Build "crosses on the outside of our churches and demonstrating them and our books in public in Muslim fairways and markets" – again, Christian worship must not be public, where Muslims can see it and become annoyed;
11. "Sound the bells in our churches, except discreetly, or raise our voices while reciting our holy books inside our churches in the presence of Muslims, nor raise our voices [with prayer] at our funerals, or light torches in funeral processions in the fairways of Muslims, or their markets";
12. "Bury our dead next to Muslim dead";
13. "Buy servants who were captured by Muslims";
14. "Invite anyone to Shirk" – that is, proselytize, although the Christians also agree not to:
15. "Prevent any of our fellows from embracing Islam, if they choose to do so." Thus the Christians can be the objects of proselytizing, but must not engage in it themselves;
16. "Beat any Muslim."

Meanwhile, the Christians will:

1. Allow Muslims to rest "in our churches whether they come by day or night";
2. "Open the doors [of our houses of worship] for the wayfarer and passerby";
3. Provide board and food for "those Muslims who come as guests" for three days;
4. "Respect Muslims, move from the places we sit in if they choose to sit in them"
5. "Have the front of our hair cut, wear our customary clothes wherever we are, wear belts around our waist" – these are so that a Muslim recognizes a non-Muslim as such and doesn't make the mistake of greeting him with

As-salaamu aleikum, "Peace be upon you," which is the Muslim greeting for a fellow Muslim;
6. "Be guides for Muslims and refrain from breaching their privacy in their homes."

The Christians swore: "If we break any of these promises that we set for your benefit against ourselves, then our Dhimmah (promise of protection) is broken and you are allowed to do with us what you are allowed of people of defiance and rebellion."

Muhammad declared that the dhimmi cannot walk on the same road as the Muslim.

"Do not initiate the Salam [greeting of peace] to the Jews and Christians, and if you meet any of them in a road, force them to its narrowest alley."

This will be the fate of Americans and Europeans kafirs if they fail to convert to Islam and submit to Allah. Kafirs must feel themselves subdued and face an existence of complete humiliation, degradation and disgrace.

This process of dhimmihood - acceptance by the kafir that the Muslim is special and more superior and therefore, must be accorded special status: whether by being allowed to live under Sharia Law, pray 5 times a day on the job, given foot baths built in schools or work place, public swimming pools with hours for Muslim women only with windows darkened to the outside, special foods in prison, prison toilets facing Jerusalem, hospital beds facing Jerusalem, all Christian symbols removed from hospitals and all other public venues, cab drivers allowed to refuse service to the blind (with their guide dogs) or people carrying a liquor bottle, no go zones where kafirs and their laws are not allowed, rape jihad of kafir women, honor killings of Muslim girls, is well underway in both America and Europe. It's just a matter of time before kafirs will dress as required by dhimmihood and walk on the other side of the street or be forced by the Muslim to its narrowest alley or meekly give up their seat if a Muslim demands it. Surrender or be beheaded. Your democratic choice.

BREAKING NEWS

I just received an E-mail from President Jose Manuel Barroso, EU Parliament in Brussels. Quoting, "WE SURRENDER. Please draw up the surrender documents." I will immediately send the Treaty of Brussels to President Barroso for signature. I'm just waiting for word from Washington. I expect surrender shortly so I'm preparing the Treaty of Washington for President Barack Obama's signature. For this Treaty go to: http://www.islamreform.net/new-page-39.htm

CHAPTER FORTY ONE

SHARIA LAW WILL BE THE RULE OF LAW

In order to understand the disastrous consequences of Sharia Law please read the following interview conducted by *FamilySecurityMatters.org* with Nonie Darwish author of Cruel and Usual Punishment: The Terrifying Global Implications of Islamic Law then purchase her book.
The Editors
In her latest book, *Cruel and Usual Punishment: The Terrifying Global Implications of Islamic Law,* author Nonie Darwish paints a chilling description of what lies ahead for Western civilizations that continue down the road of political correctness and appeasement as Islamic (Shariah) law creeps its way into free societies across the globe. Darwish, who was born in Cairo, and moved as a child to Gaza with her family, was raised Muslim – her father founding Palestinian fedayeen units which launched terrorist raids across Israel's southern border. When Nonie was only eight, her father was assassinated by the IDF, after which he was recognized as a shahid, or martyr for Islam. Darwish immigrated to the United States in 1978.
Islamic Law and the ensuing threats to Western civilization are subjects Darwish discusses with a passion and knowledge borne only of one who grew up within it can have. Having left Islam as an adult and having converted to Christianity, she has shared her experiences in Islam with her first book, *Now They Call Me Infidel.* Now with her second book, *Cruel and Usual Punishment: The Terrifying Global Implications of Islamic Law,* she explains in layman's terms the meaning of Shariah law and the implications that face those who embrace it. Nonie Darwish visited with *FamilySecurityMatters.org* to discuss the book:
Renee Taylor for FSM: What are some of the implications for Western civilizations of accepting Shariah law into their societies?

Nonie Darwish: Today, Muslims have moved to Europe, America, Australia and Canada. They argued for Shariah law and got it. In England now, they are practicing marriage and inheritance laws. It is important for the West to realize and understand that Islamic law does not give equal rights to all. It discriminates between men and women. There are laws for Muslims, laws for non-Muslims.

Women and non-Muslims have much more oppressive laws, giving Muslim men authority over them. If we allow such laws, we will find ourselves approving discrimination in our society between people. That is totally against Western democracy and values, especially the U.S. Constitution. I wrote this book because it is very important for the West to understand what they allow. Shariah law itself was not part of Islam when Mohammed died. It was created by the Muslim heads of state because Islam was moving very fast to conquer many countries. They needed Islamic law to rule over all these lands. It is inspired by the Quran and by the Hadith sayings of Mohammed. All areas of Islamic society are rooted in Islamic law, which is tyrannical law.

Slavery, for example, has never been abolished by Islam. If you read Muslim Shariah law, it is full of regulation of slaves. Sexual slavery of women captured in war is allowed, which was practiced by Mohammed. Even today, sexual slaves are accepted and all over the Middle East. Honor killings are rooted in Islamic law. For example, the murders for which a Muslim will never have punishment: to kill an apostate, to kill an adulterer – which is usually a woman, and honor killings. If you allow the killings of an apostate or an adulteress woman in the form of vigilante justice under Islamic law, you are endorsing honor killing. There are so many laws you cannot imagine that are brutal and unfair. A woman, for example, cannot divorce her husband, only a man can divorce her. I have an entire chapter in my book about the Muslim marriage contract. All of this is to open the eyes of the West to something totally against their own value system and democracy.

RT: With the world at risk, why do you think other countries are not taking the situation seriously? There seems to be a lot of appeasement.

ND: Unfortunately, there is no united policy across the West with regard to radical Islam. I believe the reason is there are so many Muslim countries around the world and many of them are oil rich and use oil as a weapon blackmailing Western countries. Appease them and assimilate them. Under Shariah, one of the major threats of a Muslim head of state is jihad. There is a law in Shariah law that says the head is to move Muslims to establish their religion. He must organize jihad against non-Muslim countries. They must be conquered. Why the West is in denial, I do not know. That is why I wrote the book, to inform the average Westerner what Shariah is. The book deals with all aspects of Shariah, what jihad is, and the obligations of Muslims to kill Jews and Christians and any non-Muslims in the jihad to who do not accept Islam.

That is why, unfortunately, when a Muslim leader stands up for Israel, he is labeled an apostate because he is doing something against his own Islamic law. A Muslim head of state must continue the Jihad against non-Muslim countries, especially those who neighbor a Muslim country. When President Sadat signed a peace treaty with Israel, he was assassinated. The reason was he violated Islamic law which demanded he be at permanent war with a non-Muslim adjacent state. This is happening everywhere. In India, Kosovo, Chechnya. If the West stays in denial, we will see the same in France.

RT: How can the average citizen get involved in understanding Islamic Law and how it is going to affect them and their way of life?

ND: It is very important that we separate the law of Islam from the religion of Islam. You see, a religion is private. When a minority comes to a country, they have a relationship with their god. The minute they begin to enforce a law on that country, that act goes into the realm of politics. It goes into the realm of the law of the land. That also violates our separation of church and state, the separation of mosque and state. The West doesn't understand that under Shariah law, there is no separation of mosque and state. The mosque is the state and the state is the mosque. The West which prides itself on freedom and democracy, freedom of speech, equal rights for women and minorities, they have to understand that this is not a religious right. Muslims will say you are depriving them of their religious rights. No, you are not. This is political Islam. It has nothing to do with a personal relationship with God. It is about trying to control the country which they have immigrated to. America has fought so hard for women's rights – are we going to start honor killings? There was an honor killing of two beautiful young girls in Texas by their father who was from Egypt, a taxi driver. He was not caught because he left the country. There are so many horrible laws. We must never think this is a religion because the duty of a religion is to protect you with rights. A religion doesn't discriminate and torture and that is a violation of your rights, a violation of church and state.

A majority of Muslims are much like everyone else. What I am talking about is not the people – the problem is the law which discriminates and oppresses. There are so many oppressed people in the Muslim world. Look at the eyes of the people in the West Bank of Gaza or in Iraq or Egypt. The bottom line in every society is the law. Under Islamic Shariah law, the testimony of a woman is half that of a man. If a man and a woman go to court, guess who wins? This is what I am talking about – I'm not talking about the people, I'm talking about the law. If people don't have justice under the law, they are living in a jungle. There are stocks and bonds sold from Islamic countries in American called Shariah finance. The profits from such financial deals go in the pockets of those Muslim countries. They use these profits to enforce Shariah law across Africa and other poor countries.

RT: Do most Muslims outside the political hierarchy understand and support Shariah law? Or would they like to see an end to it?

ND: There are some movements against Shariah, but they are calling them apostates and killing them. Unfortunately, under Islamic law, in all the books of Shariah, to deny Shariah is equal to denying Islam. The penalty is death. That is why there is no feminist movement in the Muslim world. I know two feminists in the Middle East, one in Egypt and one in Baharain. The one in Baharain was advocating divorce. She is now prevented from speaking or writing. The one in Egypt has a fatwah against her and had to leave the country because she could not protect herself.

RT: What do you think it would take to stop the encroachment of Islamic law into the West?

ND: The West must understand what Islamic law is without political correctness. The dictatorships in the Middle East are the creation of Shariah law. The only thing the West wants from the Middle East is an honest transaction of here is our dollars, give us your oil, but the Muslim world wants to blackmail the West to convert it to Islam. It is a very high price for oil.

RT: Why do you think non-Muslims, with all the information out there regarding Shariah law, are ignoring the warning signs?

ND: My book is the first book ever to explain Shariah. hariah books themselves are rarely translated into English and very few people want to go into the legal terminologies. I studied for one year to be able to explain Shariah in a way that it is understandable. I did a lot of quotations from Shariah and explained them. It is all documented. The West must wake up and start understanding because Shariah law says that for Muslims it is obligatory to lie if the purpose of the lie is the furtherance of Islam. Many Muslims don't even know what Shariah law is exactly. They have lived under it for so many years.

RT: Do you believe that, under any circumstance, Shariah law and Western law can co-exist?

ND: No It is totally opposite and if we allow it among Muslims it is not going to end there.

RT: We have had several instances in the United States where Muslims sued their employers for prayer times during work hours, cab drivers refusing to carry passengers with alcohol....
ND: That is how they operate. You have women who want to cover their faces to get a driver's license. You cannot bend the rules. The police must be able to look at your face and your license to identify you. So what do they want? They want to completely abolish our laws and put in their own laws. It doesn't work this way.

RT: How does the "peaceful Muslim", who says they don't advocate the violent teaching of the Quran, reconcile their beliefs?

ND: I don't understand. I personally cannot reconcile my beliefs, which is why I left Islam. It is very clear that Jews and Christians are infidels. The Quran has very derogatory words for them. Muslims are ordered not to talk to them, that they are filth. Some Muslims just do the five pillars of Islam – to pray and to fast… To them, that is their religion, which is very minimal and they are happy with those five pillars. They ignore 99% of their religion and only concentrate on the prayer. When something like 9/11 happens, they are silent because they know if they speak out against Jihad, they become apostates. That is why so many Americans are left wondering why are they silent. As much as they might be good people and citizens, they don't commit crimes, by being silent against the tyranny of radical Islam, they are really feeding the monster. They are not standing up against it.

RT: What are your thoughts on the situation in Israel and what do you think Israel must do to stop Hamas?

ND: It is rooted in Shariah. Why is it an eternal problem for Muslims? Why do they want to destroy Israel? Many Muslims don't want to tell you the truth. They don't want to tell you it is their intention to destroy Israel completely. Jews have rooted themselves under Islam. Islamic law does not want them to govern themselves in the Middle East. Muslims these days don't want to say it is their holy laws to totally eradicate Israel. They complain of occupation. Israel left Gaza. In response, Gaza took all their missiles to the border and started bombing Israel again. This is something the West doesn't understand. At the end of every Friday prayer, I used to always hear that the Jews and the Christians must be destroyed. This is something we grew up hearing every day. It is such a radical system.

RT: Is there anything we haven't touched on that you would add for our readers?

ND: The dynamic of the Muslim family, because of polygamy, is very different. Giving one man/one woman marriage has given them [women] respect and honor. If you start giving away the one man/one woman marriage in the West, we give away our future. The reason the Muslim world is so angry is because the Muslim marriage has no dignity and it humiliates women. A Muslim woman is so insecure in her marriage and there is no trust between the family members. That is why the Christian marriage and family unit is the most blessed thing America has.

RT: Thank you so much, Nonie, for your valuable insights into Shariah Law and how it threatens us right here in America, too. We are most grateful to you for your candor and courage. The book is titled *Cruel and Usual Punishment: The Terrifying Global Implications of Islamic Law*,

ND: Thank you.

For How Sharia Law Punishes Raped Muslim Women go to:
http://islamreform.net/new-page-112.htm

CHAPTER FORTY TWO

THE ABOMINATION OF SHARIA LAW: A DIRECT CHALLENGE TO DEMOCRATIC CONSTITUTIONS AND RULE OF LAW

11 REASONS WHY SHARIA LAW MUST BE BANNED BY ALL DEMOCRATIC SOCIETIES

Wherever Muslims live under Sharia law adulterers are publicly flogged or stoned to death, sometimes before thousands of spectators in public stadiums. There are no rights for women or children, with women genitally mutilated, and beaten in the streets for the slightest infraction. They care nothing for other beliefs, about being fair, have no juries, no free speech. Television and radio are forbidden, music and dance prohibited. It is their way or execution, the death penalty, with no appeal, no delay. You are simply shot in the head where you stand, and your children shot before you. And these practices of the Sharia, once largely confined to the Middle East, even though mostly finished in Afghanistan, are now spreading to other parts of the world.

Here are the top eleven reasons why Sharia or Islamic law is EVIL for all societies.

(In order to reduce book pages I posted the remaining 12 pages of Chapter 42 at http://islamreform.net/new-page-117.htm)

This Chapter lists the main teachings of Sharia that endanger the freedom and way of life for all Western democracies.

CHAPTER FORTY THREE

Sharia: Islam's Warden: THE BRUTAL BARBARISM OF THE TRUE ISLAM

By Jamie Glazov

Frontpage Interview's guest today is Abul Kasem, an ex-Muslim who is the author of hundreds of articles and several books on Islam including, Women in Islam. He was a contributor to the book Leaving Islam – Apostates Speak Out as well as to Beyond Jihad: Critical Views From Inside Islam.

FP: Abul Kasem, welcome back to Frontpage Interview.

Kasem: Thank you Jamie. It is my pleasure to be interviewed by Frontpage.

FP: I would like to discuss Islamic law with you today and how it dictates almost every single aspect of human life. I think the best way to begin is with how Sharia is the life-force of Islam.

Kasem: To be sure, we must understand why Sharia is the life-force of Islam, and why Islam must impose (by force, if needed) Sharia to the entire world. Once we grasp this tenet, then we can understand how and why myriad specific Sharia laws affect lives.

The basic tenets of Sharia emanate with the assumption that Allah has chosen the believers (i.e., the Muslims) to rule the world. It might sound fascistic, but make no mistake: the Qur'an is absolutely determined to hand over the rule of the world to the followers of Islam: more specifically, to the Bedouin Arabs. Because Islam = Arabism. In the Qur'an (3:104, 3:110) Allah says that Arabs are the best of people ever created.

In verse 2:143 Allah says He changed Qiblah to distinguish between Muslims and non-Muslims. Maulana Maududi, the ideological guru of the current Islamists explains this verse in this manner: This constitutes the proclamation appointing the religious community (ummah) consisting of the followers of Muhammad to religious guidance and leadership of the world.

For continuation of Chapter 43 go to: http://islamreform.net/new-page-118.htm This is a very important listing of ALL Sharia Law. Every aspect of your life will be controlled. Shaving your beard is an obscenity.

CHAPTER FORTY FOUR

DEFENSE OF AMERICA: DEMOCRACY AND FREEDOM ACT OF CONGRESS IT'S ALL ABOUT THE CONSTITUTION STUPID KAFIR

IT'S RONALD REAGAN TIME SHOW ISLAM NO RESPECT YOU ARE NOT US: WE ARE NOT YOU

Tonight, mankind stands on the verge of extinction not only from global warming but from weapons of mass destruction within reach of Muslim terrorists. Again, if nothing is done then it's just a matter of time before a nuclear weapon is exploded in the Name of Allah in a Western or Indian city killing and maiming millions. Civilization as we know it is at stake.

There needs to be a revolution in mankind's concept of God if the species Homo sapiens is to survive: **ONLY A GOD OF MORAL PERFECTION IS GOD**. We must declare without equivocation that ALL writings in ALL religious texts of God preaching hate, violence, war, murder, torture, brutality, terror, racism, revenge etc. are **NOT THE TEACHINGS OF GOD BUT THE TEACHINGS OF MAN** - that if God killed or ordered the killing of just one human being or any other creature then God will no longer be God.

We have proven that the Quran is not the word/teachings of God not just with one word or one teaching of immoral depravity but with thousands of words and four thousand teachings. Islam is totally and completely fraudulent.

Again, repeating from an earlier chapter, the Allah (of the Quran) is not God. Allah never existed except in the mind of Muhammad. There were never any revelations from any Allah to Muhammad. Muhammad never met the Angel Gabriel – never talked to Gabriel – never received any teachings from Allah. ALL THE WORDS /TEACHINGS OF THE QURAN were created by Muhammad. He invented Islam and the fake teachings, to give himself the moral authority of Allah (the AntiGod) to justify his very great crimes of murder, raping, slavery, looting etc. In this way, he established a perfect totalitarianism system that could never be questioned. How can mere humans defy the will of God? As the exponent of revealing God's will to humanity, Muhammad manufactured a total dictatorship controlling every aspect of his follower's lives. Muhammad was no prophet.

The Pope must call for a world religious conference bringing together all the top religious leaders and scholars from EVERY world religion to sign the DECLARATION OF UNIVERSAL RELIGIOUS RIGHTS AND FREEDOMS OF A GOD OF MORAL PERFECTION. This Universal Declaration to be read in every Church, Synagogue, and Mosque – and taught in every school.

All freedom loving peoples must join together and demand from their political leaders that the Defense of Democracy Act including THE CONSTITUTIONAL AMENDMENT: UNIVERSAL DECLARATION OF EQUALITY OF WOMEN and Declaration of A God of Moral Perfection be enacted by their legislatures/parliaments/congresses.

Congress needs to revitalize the Constitution and make it relevant to the modern world. Young American's have no understanding of this document. To them it is something from the Stone Age. The Constitution with all its amendments needs to be enshrined in the Defense of America: Democracy and Freedom Act. The Congress must declare WHO WE ARE and WHAT WE STAND FOR AS A PEOPLE. This Act of Congress will be a reaffirmation of American Democracy. Women's rights, equality of all peoples, freedom of speech, press, rule of law etc will be central parts of this Declaration. The Quran and Sharia Law are Islamic totalitarianism. They are the swords that will kill democracy.

The hard won rights of women are under assault throughout the Western world by Sharia Law. The Congress must protect the rights and freedoms of women and ensure that all schools teach the fundamental democratic rights of female equality to every student. Muslim women need to be granted full protection of the constitution, rule of law and taught that the Quranic teachings of the subjugation/ inequality of Muslim women and the raping /enslavement of kafir women are evil

In this struggle, women are key to winning and therefore in this Declaration, women's rights must be placed front and center. The total and complete equality of women to be recorded in the Constitutional Amendment: Universal Declaration of Total Equality of Women that would form an integral part of the Defense of America: Democracy and Freedom Act. All nations asked by the President to enact this historical Declaration into Constitutional Law and those nations that refused would no longer have any UN voting rights nor any right to speak, receive any UN assistance, belong to any UN bodies etc. etc. For a copy of this Woman's Declaration of Freedom reread page 1. and Plan of Action page xlix.

This Act must state in simple English and not legal, legalese that women have the full right to equal education, the right to leave their home unaccompanied by a family male escort, drive a vehicle, freely choose their own husbands, deny sex to their husbands etc. In short, ALL tenets of Sharia Law denying women their basic humanity need to be stated in this document – each one listed with the declaration that women have their democratic freedoms denied by Sharia as the Constitutional force of law. If these rights are violated, women can seek legal redress and enforce the law thru a legal remedy called a felony epically forced sex which is felony rape. All Muslim women and children are not second class citizens and MUST be guaranteed full protection of the law.

The brutality of Sharia Law is already enforced by some State governments against American citizens who are being deprived of their Constitutional rights. I bring your attention to the case of Rifqa Bary – a 16 year old woman who recently converted from Islam to Christianity and is being held in solitary confinement by the State of Ohio. The State is enforcing the law code of Sharia that an apostate of Islam must be held in solitary confinement until she repents. This is an outrage against all that the US stands for. Where is the outrage? Where is the constitutional protection for Rifqa? For Rifqa's story go to: http://www.jihadwatch.org/2009/12/wishful-thinking-biased-reporting-endanger-rifqa-bary.html and http://www.islamreform.net/new-page-85.htm

In Chapter 2, we learned that under Sharia law, all kafirs are second class citizens. Women can be beaten and slavery is allowed. And just as in political Islam, Sharia law as the divine Law of God can never be reformed. It is the long term goal of Islam to replace the US Constitution with Sharia, since it contradicts Islam. For that matter, democracy violates Sharia law. Democracy assumes equality of all peoples. Islam teaches that a Muslim is a better person than kafirs and that the kafirs should submit to Islam. But in voting, a Muslim's vote is equal to a kafir's vote. This violates Islamic law, since a Muslim and a kafir are never equal.

There is no separation between the religious and the political in Islam; rather Islam and Sharia constitute a comprehensive means of ordering society at every level. Any meaningful application of Sharia is going to look very different from anything resembling a free or open society in the Western sense. The stoning of adulterers, execution of apostates and blasphemers, slavery, repression of other religions, and a mandatory hostility toward non-Islamic nations punctuated by regular warfare will be the norm. It seems fair then to classify Islam and its Sharia code as a form of totalitarianism.

Central to the Defense of America Act, a declaration that the Constitution is the highest law authority in the country and Sharia law courts to be made illegal. This means banning totally and completely all Sharia Law courts without any exceptions. Slavery and oppression of women are central to Sharia. The Congress will be stating that We - The People stand for the dignity, equality and freedom of every human being, every race, and every woman - that the United States stands against slavery, stands against degradation of women, believes in the equality of all mankind, and for human rights. The banning of Sharia will stand as a beacon for freedom and will give leadership and support to the democracies of Europe which are being rapidly Islamized.

The Congress will then start a debate on the Quran by calling on all Muslims to declare that the Quran is not the word of God asking them to prove that Islam is a true religion of peace and they are good, true, peaceful Muslims by renouncing, denouncing and removing from the Quran the 4,000 verses of extermination, murder, hate, terror, torture, rape, slavery etc that are not Moral

Perfection. We ask Muslims to take the 4 pillars of Islam namely: establishment of the daily prayers; concern for and almsgiving to the needy; self-purification through fasting one month per year (Ramadan), pilgrimage to Mecca once in a lifetime (Hajj) for those who are able and adopt the Declaration and Teachings of a God of Moral Perfection (see chapter 1) - that Only a God of Moral Perfection is God. In this way, Islam will become a religion of Moral Perfection worshipping a God of Moral Perfection.

If Muslims refuse to make this declaration that the Quran is not from God, then the authorities will inform them that they must obey the law and Constitution and if they preach violence and hate in their mosques, or if they incite violence to cause bodily harm or death they will be arrested, sent to prison for 5 years and their mosques will be shut down

, An order declaring that the Defence of America Act be taught in every class, in every school, every year. Not only these declarations but young women taught their rights and freedoms as citizens and young men taught these same rights and freedoms so they understand that women are completely equal.

Congress needs to pass laws inoculating US businesses from lawsuits for refusing to acquiesce to Muslim demands such as praying 5 times a day while at work, establishing prayer rooms, wearing headscarfs, firing Muslims for refusing to transport via taxis blind people with seeing eye dogs, or people with alcoholic beverages. There can be no showing of any respect for Islam. No inviting Muslims to pray at political or any other events. No dinners celebrating Ramadan at the White House. As stated - how can the President celebrate prophet Muhammad - a psychotic who beheaded, raped, pillaged, terrorized, enslaved and had the pants of 14 year old Jewish boys pulled down SS style?

FREEDOM OF SPEECH: PROPOSAL TO BAN – BANNING OF SPEECH CONDEMNING ISLAM: LAW MAKING STEALTH CENSURESHIP ILLEGAL

Incredibility the US is co-sponsoring a resolution at the UN with Egypt making criticism of religion a hate speech crime. This is a direct threat to the First Amendment protecting free speech. It is directly designed to protect Islam/Quran. Throughout the United States, stealth censorship is shutting down speech condemning Islam. This denies the American people their right to hear the truth that Islam represents to their way of life. Congress must end this censorship. Congress must ban - the banning of speech critical of Islam. This includes websites exposing Islam forced to shut down. Books displaying the truth of Islam not allowed to be published or distributed. Universities refusing to allow speakers critical of Islam to exercise their First Amendment right of free speech by barring them entrance after being invited by conservative student groups. TV programs refusing to invite guests exposing the danger of Islam. Advertisers cancelling their sponsorships when a guest exposes the truth about Islam on either TV or radio and Muslim organizations like CAIR demand advertisers cancel. Without sponsorship these programs will be unable to function. Through these tactics, Islam has a dictatorial grip on all organs of communication. A perfect media dictatorship imposed without force. Congress must make these actions illegal

As a free person, I have the full right to examine and condemn any thought, ideology, religion, person, books etc. However my exercise of this great freedom ends with any call to violence or speech that denigrates any person. If a student group invites someone to give a speech at a university condemning Islam – the university must allow this speech. If a website condemns Islam it cannot be shut down. Letters to editors or blogs criticizing Islam cannot be erased. Publishing firms cannot refuse to print books exposing Islam that are of printable quality. Distribution firms including internet websites cannot refuse to post on their sites such books or distribute them. TV/radio must allow airtime to noted guest experts on Islam. Advertisers cannot cancel their sponsorship under threat of a boycott. Congress must pass an anti-stealth censorship law forcing individuals/corporations to respect free speech. By passing such a law, Stealth Censorship can be broken. All citizens have the full right under the constitution and indeed the democratic responsibility to intellectually attack Islam and save freedom and democracy.

One of our greatest freedoms guaranteed by the constitution is freedom of religion. However this great freedom of religious belief does not allow the establishment of a state religion, human sacrifice, honor killing, murdering apostates, dhimmitude for Christians and Jews, raping and then slavery of kafir women and children, subjugation and repression of women, extermination of unbelievers, killing those who condemn Islamic teachings, destroying the constitution and with it freedom and democracy by implementing Sharia Law. The Quran is nothing more then a book of ritualistic human sacrifice to please Allah and guarantee accession to Paradise. Beheading of unbelievers, flying planes into their cities, bombing their subways, gunning them down is ritualized murder - human sacrifice to the greater glory of God. Again, Osama and Hasan are good Muslims following the Quran and the divine example of Muhammad.

We need to reach out to Muslims with the pure love of Moral Perfection. However **AT NO TIME CAN VIOLENCE BE DIRECTED AT MUSLIMS.** We cannot attack Muslims or discriminate against them as these acts would violate the teachings of a God of Moral Perfection. We cannot preach Verse 5:33 "The only reward of Muslims who make war upon the United States and strive after corruption in the land of America will be that they will be killed or crucified, or have their hands and feet on alternate sides cut off."

The West is not at war with Muslims. They were the first victims of the AntiGod and Muhammad. The West will not land troops in Saudi Arabia and threaten the destruction by nuclear weapons of Mecca, Medina etc unless Muslims convert to Christianity or agree to pay a submission tax as per Verse 9:29 or be nuked. Don't oppose the head covering of Muslim women if they are wearing it of their own free will. This is a phony issue. Muslim women have every right to dress whatever way they want provided it is of their own free will.

We must launch an intellectual jihad against the Quran. This book is the inspiration and religious justification for Muslim men to kill. French President Sarkozy got it backwards when he stated that women wearing the burqa were the issue not Islam. Dear Mr. President, Islam is the issue. Dear Mr. President - the Quran is the issue. Again – **IT'S ALL ABOUT ISLAM STUPID**

KAFIR PRESIDENT SARKOZY. IT'S ALL ABOUT THE QURAN STUPID KAFIR PRESIDENT SARKOZY. As stated countless times in this work, the Quran is not the teachings of a God of Moral Perfection and therefore it is a fraudulent book of mass evil, of mass murder and Islam is fraudulent. We don't care if Muslims pray 5 times a day or 24 times a day, fast one month or 12 months a year, go on pilgrimage once in a lifetime or a dozen times. But this book and the evil ideology of Islam must be totally ostracized by the West. Ostracization of Islam from society not it's inclusion. You cannot accommodate, cater to, coexist with evil in a free society otherwise The Evil will overpower and conquer The Good.

The Declaration of a God of Moral Perfection and the Defense of America: Democracy and Freedom Act are historical documents and will be the beginning of the end for Islam. Intolerance can never be tolerated in a free and democratic society. Those who preach religion and refuse to accept democratic rights and freedoms, the teachings of a God of pure love, mercy, peace, and non violent perfection - A God Of Moral Perfection must be rejected and cased out into the darkness.

At the beginning of our journey, we started with Ronald Reagan - let us end by re-stating – it was Reagan by refusing to grant the Soviet Union and Communism - RESPECT when he stated -The Soviet Union was an evil empire and YOU ARE NOT US – that lead directly to the defeat and collapse of this very evil empire. We must follow Reagan's example and **SHOW ISLAM NO RESPECT** but treat it with the distain that this evil ideology of slavery, rape, brutality, extermination, terror, torture, looting and murder deserves. This means declaring that Islam is not a religion and we are no longer prepared to accept it as a religion. We must declare that we reject Islam, the Quran and Muhammad. **YOU ARE NOT US – WE ARE NOT YOU -** that there is absolutely no moral equivalency between Christianity/Judaism and Islam.

Tonight, Western Civilization is under assault not only from Islam but also from it's own political, religious, intellectual, media elites who are demonizing Jesus, Christianity, Judaism, in an attempt to expunge all vestiges of what made the West – the West from our free societies and allying themselves with this very great evil. They are coating themselves in this evil and driving the Islamization of the West. These elites are utilizing the Rule of Law to impose Sharia Law as the Rule of Law.

CHAPTER FORTY FIVE

OF MINARETS AND FREEDOM OF SPEECH: THE BATTLE FOR FUTURE OF EUROPE AND MANKIND

The recent ban on minarets in Switzerland which 57.5% voted in favour is another case of attacking a symptom of the disease of Islam while avoiding radical surgery necessary to cure the patient – Europe. Minarets are a political symbol of Islamic power. Although they were derived from Christian Church bell towers, they are meant to project the political power of Islam. We are superior to you. We dominate your cities. You must submit to Islam. The ear piercing call to prayer 5 times a day from atop the minaret is a call to all kafirs to submit to Islam. From atop the minaret as far as the Muslim man can see Sharia Law must be enforced. Minarets are the nuclear launching pads from which the nuclear missile of Sharia Law will be launched. The cold hard reality is that Muslims are migrating to Europe not to live in democracy and freedom, but as colonists to impose their version of civilization on their host countries.

The political elites of Europe are outraged at the Swiss calling them nativist, racist bigots for defending democracy and freedom. These elites are determined to tear down Western Civilization. Just as the Swiss stood against the might of Nazism, now they must stand against the might of Islam. Switzerland can send a powerful message that freedom has not died yet in Europe. As we have already explained - the Quran and Sharia Law are Islamic totalitarianism. They are the swords that will kill democracy.

The Swiss are in a very dangerous situation. Landlocked and totally dependent on the EU, they can be crippled by economic sanctions. What the Swiss need to do now is follow the example of their parents who during the darkest days of WW2 kept the forces of Hitler from invading and smashing their national freedom.

They must take the high road and not get distracted into attacking head scarf's, burqas which some of their politicians might be tempted to do. As proposed for Congress with the Defence of America Act so to the Swiss Parliament should immediately formulate the Defence of Switzerland: Democracy and Freedom Act, the Declaration of A God of Moral Perfection and pass a law of Parliament banning Sharia Law - this means banning totally and completely all Sharia Law courts without any exceptions and move the Constitutional Amendment: Declaration of The Equality of Women. This will send a tsunami tidal wave earth quake cascading across Europe and I believe other EU states will follow suit. In banning Sharia Law, the Swiss document all the teachings of slavery, oppression of women, and totalitarianism that are central to Sharia and present these barbaric teachings in the Equality of Women Constitutional Amendment granting them Constitutional legality. They must state unequivocally that we - the people of Switzerland stand for the equality and freedom of every human being, every race, and every woman. By these actions, the Swiss will be declaring to Brussels that they stand against slavery, against degradation of women and for human rights.

Mirroring the US proposal presented in previous Chapter, after banning Sharia Law, Switzerland commences a debate on the Quran by calling on all Muslims to declare that the Quran is not the word of God and asks them to prove that Islam is a true religion of peace and they are good, true, peaceful Muslims by renouncing, denouncing and removing from the Quran the 4,000 verses of extermination, murder, hate, terror, torture, rape, slavery etc that are not Moral Perfection.

If Muslims refuse to make this declaration that the Quran is not from God then the authorities will inform them that they must obey the laws of Switzerland and if they preach violence and hate in their mosques, those mosques will be shut down.

Lastly again following the US proposal - a lawful order issued that the Defence of Switzerland Act and Declaration of a God of Moral Perfection be taught in every class, in every school every year. Not only these declarations but young women taught their rights and freedoms as citizens and young men taught these same rights and freedoms so they understand that women are completely equal.

GEERT WILDERS: THE WINSTON CHURCHILL OF THE NETHERLANDS

Geert Wilders, a political leader in the Netherlands who created a short film attacking Islam called Fitna has been charged with multiple counts of insulting Muslims and inciting hated against them by quoting hateful teachings directly from the Quran. The gathering storm of civil war hangs over Europe. If civil war breaks out, it will start either in the Netherlands or Denmark. It is important to understand that my book is a criminal act in Europe – a felony that guarantees at least 5 years in prison.

I do not agree with everything Wilders espouses such as banning the Quran or taxing headscarf's a 1500 Euro yearly fine. No book should ever be banned and women have the right to dress or not dress however they see fit provided they do so of their own free will. However my freedom of speech does not give me any right to advocate violence against Muslims. At no time as far as I know has Geert ever called for the physical harming of any Muslim. For letter I wrote to Geert go to: http://www.islamreform.net/new-page-48.htm

For the document charging Wilders go to http://www.jihadwatch.org/2009/12/geert-wilders-receives-summons-a-sledgehammer-blow-to-the-freedom-of-speech.html

Following are the two Articles of the Netherlands Criminal Code that Wilders is charged with violating:

137c Dutch Penal Code o 1.

He who publicly, verbally or in writing or image, deliberately expresses himself in an way insulting of a group of people because of their race, their religion or belief, or their hetero- or homosexual nature or their physical, mental, or intellectual disabilities, will be punished with a prison sentence of at the most one year .o 2. If the offence is committed by a person who makes it his profession or habit, or by two or more people in association, a prison sentence of at the most two years or a fine of fourth category will be imposed.

Article 137 d Dutch Penal Code o 1.

He who publicly, verbally or in writing or in an image, incites hatred against or discrimination of people or violent behavior against person or property of people because of their race, their religion or belief, their gender or hetero- or homosexual nature or their physical, mental, or intellectual disabilities, will be punished with a prison sentence of at the most one year or a fine of third category. o 2. If the offence is committed by a person who makes it his profession or habit, or by two or more people in association, a prison sentence of at the most two years or a fine of fourth category will be imposed.

Isn't this incredible. You can be charged with insulting Muslims and inciting hatred by quoting the hateful teachings of Islam directly from the Quran. Under Article 137 d 01 Muslims should be arrested in their mosques for as we have already demonstrated throughout this book, the Quran incites "hatred against, discrimination of people, or violent behavior against person or property of people because of their race, their religion or belief, their gender or hetero- or homosexual nature." The Quran orders the mass murder of all kafirs denigrating them to the status of rats /apes and demands as orders from God - their physical torture, terrorizing and extermination. The Quran calls for their subjugation, enslavement, and debasement of Jews and Christians as dhimmi. The Quran preaches the rape and degradation of women. Homosexuals are to be tortured and murdered. Apostates of Islam are must be killed. What we have here is George Orwell's 1984 double speak. Article 137d is exactly how the elites of Europe are determined to end freedom of speech for these articles are Europe wide. Don't be surprised if a similar law is passed by the US Congress.

Quoting Geert Wilders "This Court is not interested in the truth. This Court doesn't want me to have a fair trial. I can't have any respect for this. This Court would not be out of place in a dictatorship."

Our journey has come to an end. As the last prophet of God, I have brought to mankind the teachings of a God of Moral Perfection and a new Ten Commandments. I have destroyed Islam with just one word. The choice before you is either submit to the AntiGod Allah and sacrifice your immoral soul and the very essence of your being or fight for freedom and democracy. Evil is a force like dark matter – you cannot see dark matter that comprises some 90% of the universe but scientists know that this matter exists. Evil exists and in order to survive like a hungry beast, evil needs evil to feed on. Islam is the hungry evil beast. If Islam conquers the West, a New Dark Age of barbarism will descent upon mankind from which humanity will never be able to emerge. Cranes will be brought into Western city centers to publicly hang adulterers. Murder, slaughter, torture will become the rule of law. Slavery will become a multi-national business. Women will be brutalized and lose their humanity. The light will be extinguished on the human race forever. Again, sitting on your bum is not an option.

WE MUST REJECT ISLAM WITHOUT EQUIVOCATION JUST AS OUR FATHERS REJECTED HITLER AND NAZISM WITHOUT EQUIVOCATION.

NOTHING LESS THAN THE SURVIVAL OF OUR FREE SOCIETY AND OUR SURVIVAL AS A SPECIES ARE AT STAKE.

For book notes go to http://islamreform.net/new-page-84.htm For VERY IMPORTANT ARTICLE CONCERNING ISLAM CONCEPT OF FITNA GO TO: http://islamreform.net/new-page-60.htm

For The Origins of Allah and Koran go to: http://islamreform.net/new-page-61.htm

For VERY IMPORTANT ARTICLE: Muhammad and People of The Lie go to: http://islamreform.net/new-page-71.htm

Thomas Jefferson: "When the people fear government, that is TYRANNY. When government fears the people, that is FREEDOM."

BlAISE PASCAL "Men never commit evil so fully and joyfully as when they do it for religious convictions."

Edmund Burke "All that is necessary for evil to triumph is for good men to do nothing.

www.ingramcontent.com/pod-product-compliance
Lightning Source LLC
Chambersburg PA
CBHW031611160426
43196CB00006B/88